SAMUEL BECKETT'S LIBRARY

Samuel Beckett's Library critically examines the reading notes and marginalia contained in the books of Samuel Beckett's surviving library in Paris. This is the first study to assess the importance of the previously inaccessible to scholars marginalia, inscriptions and other manuscript notes in the 700 volumes of the library. Setting the library into context with other manuscript material such as drafts and notebooks, *Samuel Beckett's Library* examines the way in which Beckett absorbed, 'translated' and transmitted his reading in his own work. This book thus illuminates Beckett's cultural and intellectual world, and shows the ways in which his reading often engendered writing.

DIRK VAN HULLE, professor of literature in English at the University of Antwerp, is the current president of the European Society for Textual Scholarship. He edited Beckett's *Company* (2009) and is the author of *Textual Awareness* (2004); *Manuscript Genetics, Joyce's Know-How, Beckett's Nohow* (2008) and the first volume (2011) of the Beckett Digital Manuscript Project.

MARK NIXON is reader in modern literature at the University of Reading, where he is also the director of the Beckett International Foundation. He has published widely on Samuel Beckett's work, and is an editor of *Samuel Beckett Today / Aujourd'hui*, a member of the editorial board of the *Journal of Beckett Studies* and co-director of the Beckett Digital Manuscript Project.

SAMUEL BECKETT'S LIBRARY

DIRK VAN HULLE
Universiteit Antwerpen, Belgium

MARK NIXON
University of Reading, UK

CAMBRIDGE
UNIVERSITY PRESS

University Printing House, Cambridge CB2 8BS, United Kingdom

Published in the United States of America by Cambridge University Press, New York

Cambridge University Press is part of the University of Cambridge.

It furthers the University's mission by disseminating knowledge in the pursuit of education, learning and research at the highest international levels of excellence.

www.cambridge.org
Information on this title: www.cambridge.org/9781107001268

© Dirk Van Hulle and Mark Nixon 2013

This publication is in copyright. Subject to statutory exception
and to the provisions of relevant collective licensing agreements,
no reproduction of any part may take place without the written
permission of Cambridge University Press.

First published 2013

A catalogue record for this publication is available from the British Library

Library of Congress Cataloguing in Publication data
Hulle, Dirk Van.
Samuel Beckett's Library / Dirk Van Hulle ; Mark Nixon.
p.   cm.
Includes bibliographical references.
ISBN 978-1-107-00126-8
1. Beckett, Samuel, 1906–1989 – Knowledge.   2. Authors, Irish – 20th century –
Books and reading.   3. Authors, French – 20th century – Books and reading.
I. Nixon, Mark.   II. Title.
PR6003.E282Z686   2013
848′.91409–dc23   2012034485

ISBN 978-1-107-00126-8 Hardback

Cambridge University Press has no responsibility for the persistence or accuracy of URLs for external or third-party internet websites referred to in this publication, and does not guarantee that any content on such websites is, or will remain, accurate or appropriate.

For
James Knowlson, Geert Lernout and John Pilling

I have been reading wildly all over the place.
        (Samuel Beckett, letter to Thomas MacGreevy, 25 March 1936)

Contents

Acknowledgements		*page* ix
Abbreviations / Editions Used		xi
Introduction		xiii
1	Reading Traces: Beckett as a Reader	1
2	Literature in English	20
3	Literature in French	43
4	Literature in German	82
5	Literature in Italian	103
6	Classics and Other Literatures	117
7	Philosophy	128
8	Religion	170
9	Dictionaries and Reference Works	192
10	Science	200
11	Music and Art	214
Concluding Marginalia		221
Notes		225
Appendix: A Catalogue of Books in Beckett's Library		261
Bibliography		289
Index		303

Acknowledgements

Our principal debt of gratitude is to Edward Beckett, without whom this book would simply not exist, and whose generosity is a further testament to his ongoing support of investigative scholarship. He allowed us to consult Samuel Beckett's library in Paris in 2006, and has since patiently put up with our many impositions on his time. We are also grateful to Anne Atik, who welcomed us to her home in order to consult the books Samuel Beckett had given to her and her late husband, the painter Avigdor Arikha. Their daughters Noga and Alba Arikha also kindly answered queries.

We would like to thank the Beckett International Foundation as well as the Special Collections Services at the University of Reading for giving us access to books once owned by Samuel Beckett now held in Reading. We have benefited from the help and expertise of a number of scholars and colleagues in preparing this book. In particular, we would like to thank Geert Lernout and John Pilling, who kindly read the manuscript and provided us with relevant material and suggestions. For their help small and large we are also grateful to: Iain Bailey, Martha Black, Mark Byron, Ronan Crowley, Wout Dillen, João Dionisio, Peter Fifield, Thomas Hunkeler, James Knowlson, the late Seán Lawlor, Vincent Neyt, Lois Overbeck, Sam Slote, Pim Verhulst, Shane Weller and Feargal Whelan. Needless to say, all errors are our own. Finally, we would like to thank Ray Ryan and the staff at Cambridge University Press for their support, patience and expert guidance in seeing this book through to publication.

Extracts from Samuel Beckett's notebooks, 'Notes on German Literature' (held at Trinity College Dublin), 'Whoroscope' Notebook; manuscripts of *Pas moi*, *Eh Joe*, *Fin de partie* (held at Beckett International Foundation, University of Reading); questionnaire by James Knowlson (held at Special Collections, University of Reading); and letters to Ruby Cohn, Jocelyn Herbert, James Knowlson, Stuart Maguinness and Pamela Mitchell (held at Beckett International Foundation, University of Reading), Harold Pinter (held at British Library London), Kay Boyle, Aidan Higgins, Mary Hutchinson, John Kobler, A. J. Leventhal, Mania Péron, George Reavey and Jake Schwartz (held at Harry Ransom Humanities Research Center, University of Texas at Austin) and Barbara Bray, Thomas MacGreevy, H. M. O. White and Nick Rawson (held at Trinity College Dublin; cited with permission of the Board of Trinity College Dublin) are reproduced by kind permission of the Estate of Samuel Beckett, c/o Rosica Colin Limited, London. We are grateful to the above institutions for kindly granting permission to cite from relevant unpublished material. For permissions to cite from Beckett's 'German Diaries', we are grateful to Suhrkamp Verlag, and from Beckett's 'Echo's Bones', to Faber & Faber.

Our greatest debt, not only in the writing of this book but throughout our scholarly endeavours, is reflected in the dedication. James Knowlson, Geert Lernout and John Pilling have over the past decade shown us the way, through their friendship, intellectual generosity and integrity, and their rigorous scholarship.

Abbreviations / Editions Used

Works by Beckett

ATF	*All That Fall and Other Plays for Radio and Screen*, preface and notes by Everett Frost (London: Faber & Faber, 2009).
BDMP1	*Stirrings Still / Soubresauts and Comment dire / what is the word*: an electronic genetic edition (Series 'The Beckett Digital Manuscript Project', module 1), ed. by Dirk Van Hulle and Vincent Neyt. Brussels: University Press Antwerp (ASP/UPA), 2011, <http://www.beckettarchive.org>.
CDW	*The Complete Dramatic Works* (London: Faber & Faber, 1986).
CIWS	*Company / Ill Seen Ill Said / Worstward Ho / Stirrings Still*, ed. by Dirk Van Hulle (London: Faber & Faber, 2009).
Dis	*Disjecta: Miscellaneous Writings and a Dramatic Fragment*, ed. by Ruby Cohn (London: John Calder, 1983).
DN	*Beckett's 'Dream' Notebook*, ed. by John Pilling (Reading: Beckett International Foundation, 1999). [citations from this book refer to item rather than page number.]
Dream	*Dream of Fair to Middling Women* (Dublin: Black Cat Press, 1992).
ECEF	*The Expelled / The Calmative / The End / First Love*, ed. by Christopher Ricks (London: Faber & Faber, 2009).
HII	*How It Is*, ed. by Magessa O'Reilly (London: Faber & Faber, 2009).
MC	*Mercier and Camier*, ed. by Seán Kennedy (London: Faber & Faber, 2010).
MD	*Malone Dies*, ed. by Peter Boxall (London: Faber & Faber, 2010).
Mo	*Molloy*, ed. by Shane Weller (London: Faber & Faber, 2009).
MPTK	*More Pricks than Kicks*, ed. by Cassandra Nelson (London: Faber & Faber, 2010).
Mu	*Murphy*, ed. by J. C. C. Mays (London: Faber & Faber, 2009).

PTD	*Proust and Three Dialogues with Georges Duthuit* (London: John Calder, 1965).
SP	*Selected Poems 1930–1989*, ed. by David Wheatley (London: Faber & Faber, 2009).
TFN	*Texts for Nothing and Other Shorter Prose 1950–1976*, ed. by Mark Nixon (London: Faber & Faber, 2010).
Un	*The Unnamable*, ed. by Steven Connor (London: Faber & Faber, 2010).
W	*Watt*, ed. by Chris Ackerley (London: Faber & Faber, 2009).

Samuel Beckett – Archival and Other Material

GD	'German Diaries' [six notebooks], Beckett International Foundation, The University of Reading.
LSB	*The Letters of Samuel Beckett, vol. I, 1929–1940*, ed. by Martha Dow Fehsenfeld and Lois More Overbeck (Cambridge: Cambridge University Press, 2009).
LSB II	*The Letters of Samuel Beckett, vol. II, 1941–1956*, ed. by George Craig, Martha Dow Fehsenfeld, Dan Gunn and Lois More Overbeck (Cambridge: Cambridge University Press, 2011).
WN	'Whoroscope' Notebook, Beckett International Foundation, The University of Reading, UoR MS3000.

Library Archives

HRC	Harry Ransom Humanities Research Center, The University of Texas at Austin.
JEK	James and Elizabeth Knowlson Collection, Special Collections, The University of Reading.
TCD	Trinity College Dublin Library, Department of Manuscripts.
UoR	Beckett International Foundation, The University of Reading.

Notes on the Text

Extracts from Samuel Beckett's letters, notebooks and manuscripts reproduced by kind permission of the Estate of Samuel Beckett, c/o Rosica Colin Limited, London. All translations from other languages are our own unless stated otherwise. Beckett's marginalia and notes are transcribed with as little diacritical signs as possible. Underlining is used to indicate passages or words underscored by Beckett.

Introduction

> The greatest part of a writer's time is spent in reading in order to write. A man will turn over half a library to make a book.
> (Samuel Johnson, qtd. in Boswell's *Life of Johnson*)

Libraries represent not only the material manifestation of knowledge, but also the labyrinthine world of creation. As Johnson's quotation suggests, the relationship between reading and writing is often seen to be at the core of the creative enterprise. And the library lies at the heart of this complex transmission of knowledge, whether it is the endless Borgesian Library of Babel, Umberto Eco's ideal library (with 3,335 rooms, at least one of which had 33,335 walls, at least one of which had 33,335 bookshelves, and at least one of which could hold 33,335 books) or simply the British Library. If, as Johnson states, a writer reads in order to write, then the books that feed this creative nexus are often viewed as keys that can unlock the mysteries of texts. This is even more the case if these writers' books contain reading traces, marginalia, discrete or clear signs of a dialogue between reader and writer. The library, whether real or virtual, is the postmodern symbol of intertextuality, of the fact that 'books always speak of other books', as Eco says in *The Name of the Rose*. As a result, the libraries of authors have often found their way into national collections and university archives, and many of the books once owned by the most important twentieth-century writers still survive today. Thus the libraries, complete or incomplete, of writers such as Auden, Pound, Woolf, Wilde and Joyce can now be consulted in public collections.

Samuel Beckett's library also survives. It is still where it was at the time of his death in 1989, in his apartment on the Boulevard St. Jacques in Paris. Only a relatively small amount of books had previously been taken out of the library. Shortly before his death, Beckett asked his friend and biographer James Knowlson to integrate volumes of scholarly interest in the Beckett International Foundation's Collection at the University of Reading. Beckett's copies of Proust's *À la recherche du temps perdu*, his volume of Hölderlin's works and some of his editions of Dante, amongst others, were thus made available for consultation. Even earlier, Beckett had given books from his library to friends, such as his collection of books on art and other volumes, which he gave to his friends, the painter Avigdor Arikha and Arikha's wife, Anne Atik. But the bulk of Beckett's books are still in his apartment in Paris. The library contains roughly 700 books, which includes those volumes that Beckett kept at his country retreat in Ussy and that were moved to Paris when he died.

Samuel Beckett's library has hitherto not been available for consultation, although the Estate of Samuel Beckett has in the past assisted scholarly enquiries by providing bibliographical details of the volumes with the help of a hand list, compiled by James Knowlson and Edith Fournier after the author's death. However, in the summer of 2006 Edward Beckett, the literary executor of the estate, allowed us access to the library, in order to study the volumes for reading traces. This book thus represents the first examination of Beckett's library and attempts to sketch a map of Beckett's intellectual world.

The lack of access to the library has so far been a missing link in terms of understanding Beckett's intellectual heritage as well as his cultural milieu. At the same time, it must be noted that the existent 'real' library only represents a very small part of all the books Beckett consulted and read during his life. Indeed, particularly during the 1930s, Beckett, out of financial necessity, frequently worked in libraries or borrowed books from friends. Moreover, Beckett gave many of his books away during his life. A letter to Barbara Bray of 9 June 1959 evidences this; having thanked her for sending the Yale edition of Johnson's *Diaries, Prayers, Annals*, he went on to state that 'it will not be among the vast numbers I intend soon to scrap' (TCD MS10948/1/35). There were further culls, as Beckett sorted out his books on moving from the Rue des Favorites to the Boulevard St. Jacques in 1960 (letter to Bray, 22 October 1960; TCD MS10948/1/117), and then told Jocelyn Herbert on 2 November 1977 that he was in Ussy 'enjoying throwing everything out, books and other rubbish, not absolutely indispensable'. As Beckett informed James Knowlson in 1973, 'Little remains of my paltry library but reference books and a few old chestnuts, unworthy of the meanest catalogue' (24 August 1973; JEK B/1/39). Nonetheless, the significance of the books that survive in Beckett's library in charting Beckett's intellectual landscape, and the way they were transmitted within the creative process, is considerable. Moreover, as these are the books that survived the successive purges, they must have been of significant value or interest to him.

The present book discusses Beckett's library along the lines of categories; as one would find in a library, the chapters are divided into the various fields of knowledge encountered in the existing volumes. One of the most important aims of this book is to assess the amount of knowledge Beckett had to acquire before he was able to develop a poetics of unknowing. The books in Beckett's library in Paris range from volumes that he acquired as a student at Trinity College Dublin to books presented to him in the last years of his life. One of the earliest surviving books is a copy of A. Hamilton Thompson's *A History of English Literature, and of the Chief English Writers*, which Beckett bought in 1923 at the age of sixteen. Several other books from Beckett's student days survive, many of them containing marginalia showing an assiduous and precocious reader. Beckett's library offers a unique opportunity to witness the witty young and critical student commenting on the masters of English, French and Italian literature. When he read Robert de la Vaissière's *Anthologie poétique du XXe siècle* (1923), he was particularly struck by Apollinaire's poetry. 'La chanson du mal-aimé' is still rather schoolishly marked in the margin as 'One of the really great modern French poems', but ten pages further on the excitement is much more spontaneous. This is evident from Beckett's marginal note next to Apollinaire's poem 'Réponse des Cosaques Zaporogues au Sultan de Constantinople', which is based on the defiant Cossacks' letter in reply to the Turkish Sultan's demands for their subjugation. The letter's bellowing Cossack guffaw ('goat-fucker of Alexandria, swineherd of Greater and Lesser Egypt, Armenian pig, Podolian villain, catamite of Tartary, hangman of Kamyanets, and fool of all the world and underworld, … pig's snout, mare's arse, slaughterhouse cur, unchristened brow, screw your own mother!') is perfectly captured in Apollinaire's poetic brawl:

> Bourreau de Podolie Amant
> Des plaies des ulcères des croûtes
> Groin de cochon cul de jument
> Tes richesses garde-les toutes
> Pour payer tes médicaments

And Beckett exclaims in the margin: 'Better than a Dublin jarvey!'

Similarly, in the middle of Molière's *Tartuffe*, Beckett interjects in the margins '!! Who's a hypocrite?' and calls the author 'Molière the lickspittle' (see Chapter 3). Many of the books which date from the 1930s contain marginalia, whilst the amount of reading traces tends to diminish after the Second World War. However, as the subsequent chapters show, the absence of reading traces can be as revealing as a heavily annotated book.

Beyond books acquired for his university syllabus, the library holds many volumes by authors that were important to Beckett. Thus one encounters books by authors that have frequently been connected with Beckett's work – Schopenhauer, Berkeley, Joyce and Dante, to name but these. But whilst Beckett's engagement with these authors has been previously discussed by way of evidence in the published work and manuscript material, the actual books in the library provide several answers to questions that have been taxing Beckett scholars for many decades. At the same time, the library also introduces new enigmas and does not offer the ultimate 'solution & salvation' to critical headaches. Thus for example an issue Beckett scholarship has been puzzling over for decades is Beckett's reading of Spinoza, who is mentioned several times in the 'German Diaries' and the letters. After Brian Coffey had 'talked attractively of Spinoza' in July 1936, he lent Beckett a few books that gave him 'a glimpse of Spinoza as a solution & a salvation' (*LSB* 361, 371). The crux of this matter, however, is still not fully clarified, despite the presence of a heavily marked copy of Spinoza's *Ethics, and 'De Intellectus Emendatione'* in Beckett's personal library.

While reading is of course an isolated activity, the books in the library embed Beckett in the cultural milieu of his time. The many presentation copies – from writers such as Pinter or Cioran, or thinkers such as Adorno and Derrida – cut through the image of the reclusive nature of Beckett, and reveal just how aware he was of his intellectual surroundings. Moreover, the library gives first substantial proof of Beckett's engagement with other writers and authors, such as Maurice Blanchot, Walter Benjamin and Ludwig Wittgenstein. Beyond the 'old chestnuts', as Beckett tended to call his favourite authors, one finds fascinating material in the library in areas one would not suspect, and on the whole the volumes attest to Beckett's wide-ranging interests, with dictionaries and bibles, as well as science books very much in evidence. Even in well-documented areas such as Beckett's interests in philosophy and psychology, there are some unexpected surprises. The library also reflects the fact that Beckett was a multilingual reader, and as a result our book will contain many non-English references and quotations.

Beckett was, throughout his life, an avid reader, although his reading habits and the way he made notes on his reading changed. At times, in particular in the 1930s, Beckett would annotate his books, at others using notebooks in order to record aspects of his reading that he wished to preserve. Describing himself as 'phrase-hunting' (letter to MacGreevy, 25 January 1931; *LSB* 62) or being 'soiled by the demon of notesnatching' (letter to MacGreevy, undated [early August 1931]; qtd. in Pilling 1999, xiii), Beckett filled several notebooks with notes taken from books he was reading. These notebooks, as well as references in manuscripts and his correspondence, have over the years given readers and scholars an insight into the books he had consulted or read.

Introduction

xvii

Moreover, Beckett's texts self-consciously refer, in intertextual allusions and direct references, to other texts; from the heavily allusive work of the 1930s, such as *Dream of Fair to Middling Women*, to the 'lost classics' in *Happy Days*, Beckett's texts are imbued with references to his reading.

However, Beckett himself was often dismissive of his own reading, telling Aidan Higgins, for example, that 'I never read much Yeats. Never read much anything' (29 October 1952). It appears as if Beckett's attitude to his own reading was not so much provoked by an anxiety of influence, although he was fond of the Latin dictum (ascribed to St Jerome) that 'pereant qui ante nos nostra dixerunt' [let them perish, those who have uttered our words before], which he used variously in his texts and letters.[1] The issue is rather connected to Beckett's poetics of unknowing, despite an awareness that any such creative fabric had to be established before it could be abolished. As he told Claude Raimbourg in a remarkable letter of 3 May 1954:

If you must write, you should do it in the face of all opposition. . . . Do not spend too much more time on culture & reading, these are traps. When everything conspires to make the thing impossible, when you are tired, worried, with no time, or money, it is then that things get done. (qtd. in Silverman 2010)[2]

Beckett did not take his own advice, as his library and the record of his reading clearly indicate.

A final note: mindful of Molloy's admission that 'if you set out to mention everything you would never be done' (*Mo* 39), we must point out that this book is not exhaustive in its presentation of the material evidence in Beckett's books. We have tried to address the most salient features of Beckett's library, but inevitably there are omissions. Moreover, it is impossible to give a full catalogue in such a volume, to provide details of all the marginalia, inscriptions and material circumstances of each and all of the books.[3] However, the reader may be interested to know that all the scans from Beckett's library will be made available in the electronic environment of the 'Beckett Digital Manuscript Project' in the near future (www.beckettarchive.org). By taking this step, we hope that other scholars will continue the exploration of Beckett's reading. For it is our belief that the perusal of Beckett's library is a pleasure that compares only to what Borges had in mind when he wrote: 'I have always imagined that Paradise will be a kind of library' (qtd. in Maiorino 2008, 196).

CHAPTER I

Reading Traces: Beckett as a Reader

USE VERSUS READING

Writing in books is a taboo to many modern readers. In *Used Books*, William H. Sherman refers to a warning on readers' tables at Cambridge University Library: 'MARKING OF BOOKS IS FORBIDDEN' (156). But as the graffiti on the warning sign itself indicate, the bibliophilic *Reinheitsgebot* has the same effect on readers as any zoological garden's prohibition sign 'Do not feed the animals'. In the nineteenth century, the idea that one is not supposed to write in the margins of books was so strong that archivists purged the margins of printed books from handwritten annotations by washing and bleaching the pages. But this ideal of purity is relatively recent. In the Renaissance, annotating was common practice precisely because of the effect it had on the perception of the text. The idea that a book should be 'a good read' was unfamiliar to the reading culture of the Renaissance. Students were explicitly instructed to 'use' rather than just 'read' books. Sherman quotes John Brinsley's influential handbook *Ludus Literarius; or, The Grammar Schoole* (1612), which explains why annotations were considered such an important aspect of education: 'To read and not to understand what we read, or not to know how to make use of it, is nothing else but a neglect of all good learning' (Brinsley in Sherman 2008, 4).

As a result, some of the most fascinating thoughts have been formulated for the first time in the margins of books. Fermat's last theorem is a case in point. In his 1621 edition of Diophantus' *Arithmetica*, Pierre de Fermat wrote a few Latin lines next to Problem II.8, about the way to split a given square number into two other squares. In 1637, Fermat noted in the margin opposite this problem: 'Cubum autem in duos cubos, aut quadratoquadratum in duos quadratoquadratos, et generaliter nullam in infinitum ultra quadratum potestatem in duos eiusdem nominis fas est dividere cuius rei demonstrationem mirabilem sane detexi. Hanc marginis exiguitas non caperet' [It is impossible to separate a cube into two cubes, or a fourth power into two fourth powers, or in general, any power higher than the second into two like powers. I have discovered a truly marvellous proof of this, which this margin is too narrow to contain]. Fermat's copy of the *Arithmetica* was lost, but under the subheading 'Observatio Domini Petri de Fermat', his son incorporated the lines into the text of a new edition of Diophantus' work that was published in 1670. What was originally presented in the margin as the promise of a solution made it into print as an augmented problem that was to puzzle mathematicians for more than three centuries, until it was finally solved, only recently. Thus the mother of all mathematical brainteasers was engendered by the material matrix of a marginal space.

With regard to more recent marginalia, Mats Dahlström has drawn attention to a project by the Swedish artist Kajsa Dahlberg, who made a compilation of marginal annotations in public library copies of Virginia Woolf's *A Room of One's Own*. The work of art consists of one copy of the 'central' text, surrounded by numerous layers of comments, exclamation marks and other responses by dozens of readers. The result shows how impressive the impact of a text can be and how much energy readers are willing to invest.

The irony of this art project, however, is that Virginia Woolf was an adamant opponent of marginalia. In her essay 'How Should One Read a Book?' she characterized the paradox of reading as a combination of immersion and the simultaneous realization that complete immersion is impossible:

> We may stress the value of sympathy; we may try to sink our own identity as we read. But we know that we cannot sympathize wholly or immerse ourselves wholly; there is always a demon who whispers, 'I hate, I love', and we cannot silence him. Indeed, it is precisely because we hate and we love that our relation with the poets and novelists is so intimate that we find the presence of another person intolerable. (Woolf 1972, 9)

This 'presence of another person' could be a presence in the same room as the reader, but Heather Jackson suggests that it could also be a previous reader, who makes his or her past presence felt by means of reading traces.

In an unpublished essay, catalogued under the title 'Writing in the Margin', Virginia Woolf employs stark images of assault to condemn marginal annotating – 'this anonymous commentator must scrawl his O, or his Pooh, or his Beautiful upon the unresisting sheet, as though the author received this mark upon his flesh' (Woolf in Jackson 2001, 239). Woolf presents these annotations as readings that are forced upon her. This is more than just an individual feeling. William W. E. Slights, studying 'The Cosmopolitics of Reading', suggests that 'marginal annotation, whether printed or handwritten, can radically alter a reader's perception of the centred text' (1997, 201).

But perhaps this altered perception might be an enrichment as well. In the case of Samuel Beckett's personal library, many Beckettians would wish he had left even more of 'his O, or his Pooh, or his Beautiful' in his books. Unlike Virginia Woolf, Beckett had no scruples about writing in the margins. Beckett and Woolf are exponents of the two different types of readers in Heather Jackson's playful dichotomy between 'As' and 'Bs': 'For most of the twentieth century, ... two groups – call them A for Annotator and B for Bibliophile – have existed in a state of mutual incomprehension. (A thinks that B might as well stand for Bore, and B that A is for Anarchist.)' (Jackson 2001, 237). Jackson respects Woolf's viewpoint, because it raises an interesting issue. Even a confirmed 'A' must admit that a majority of marginal reading traces are either quite trite and pedestrian, or so short and enigmatic that they fail to be of interest to subsequent readers.

In her unpublished essay on 'Writing in the Margin', Woolf wondered what might be the audience an Annotator tries to address, suggesting it might be the author, or else the next borrower of the book. But there is at least a third option: the Annotator may be addressing a later self. Edgar Allan Poe suggested a theory of reading notes in 'Marginalia', an introduction to a series of articles, and gave a fascinating account of such an encounter with one of his younger selves:

During a rainy afternoon, not long ago, being in a mood too listless for continuous study, I sought relief from *ennui* in dipping here and there, at random, among the volumes of my library – no very large one, certainly, but sufficiently miscellaneous; and, I flatter myself, not a little *recherché*. Perhaps it was what the Germans call the 'brain-scattering' humor of the moment; but, while the picturesqueness of the numerous pencil-scratches arrested my attention, their helter-skelter-iness of commentary amused me. I found myself at length forming a wish that it had been some other hand than my own which had so bedevilled the books (Poe 1965, 3).

Poe openly admits his secret thoughts at that moment: 'there might be something even in *my* scribbling which, for the mere sake of scribbling would have interest for others' (Poe 1965, 3). But if so, he wonders, how could one transfer those comments and separate the text from the context 'without detriment to that exceedingly frail fabric of intelligibility in which the context was imbedded' (3)? Preserving (or reconstituting) this 'frail fabric of intelligibility' is perhaps even harder if the 'marginalist' is no longer alive. That is the challenge in the present attempt to interpret Samuel Beckett's reading traces.

TYPES OF TRACES

The term 'marginalist' was coined by Daniel Ferrer to distinguish this type of 'A' (Annotator) from the so-called extractor, who prefers to write notes in a separate notebook. The 'extractor', however, is not necessarily a 'B' (Bibliophile). Moreover, some annotating readers are both 'marginalists' *and* 'extractors'. Samuel Beckett, for one, combines both these capacities, and apart from that, he also belongs to a third category of 'rereaders'. These three categories correspond to three types of reading traces.

1. Traces of the 'Marginalist'

(a) *Marginal comments*: Marking books is such a private activity that no typology of marginal comments is generalizable. Elaine Whitaker suggested the three categories of
- editing (including 'censorship' and 'affirmation');
- interaction (such as 'devotional use' and 'social critique'); and
- avoidance (expressed by means of 'doodling' and 'daydreaming').

This compact categorization contrasts sharply with Carl James Grindley's extremely elaborate typology in 'Reading *Piers Plowman* C-Text Annotations'. Apart from marks that are only loosely connected to the content of the text (such as ownership marks, doodles or pen trials), the marginal traces that clearly constitute a response to the body of the text are divided into five categories:
- narrative reading aids (including translation);
- ethical pointers (from perceptive points and exemplifications to disputative annotations);
- polemical responses (such as social, ecclesiastical or political comments);
- literary responses (from irony to language issues); and
- graphical responses.

But no matter how useful this typology may be to analyse the annotations to *Piers Plowman*, any typology entails the danger of overcategorization. With a view to studying Beckett's annotations, perhaps the most useful starting point is the basic distinction between 'intensive reading' and 'extensive reading'.

According to book historians such as Roger Chartier, 'intensive' reading was inspired by the Protestant practice of studying the Bible, whereas 'extensive' reading could only develop thanks to the expanding market of printed materials, especially from 1750 onwards (Chartier 2003, 92). But as Chapter 8 will show, Beckett turned this pattern upside down in that he applied an *ex*tensive reading method to *La Sacra Bibbia*.

The most striking example of intensive reading in Beckett's personal library is his copy of Olga Plümacher's *Der Pessimismus*. It clearly bears the marks of 'hard use', to employ the essayist Anne Fadiman's words (Fadiman 1999, 32). This kind of 'hard use' is not necessarily a sign of bibliographical disrespect. It can also be an expression of intimacy and interest. One cannot

Figure 1 Cover of Olga Plümacher's *Der Pessimismus*

exclude the possibility that the 'book's *words* were holy, but the paper, cloth, cardboard, glue, thread, and ink that contained it were a mere vessel, and it was no sacrilege to treat them as wantonly as desire and pragmatism dictated' (32). Fadiman's description is applicable to the way this volume has been read to pieces, to the extent that it had to be glued together again with adhesive tape (see *Figure 1*).

This is the only book in Beckett's extant library that is interleaved with white pages. The interleaves were used for summaries and translations, whereas the body of the text seems to have been read several times, because numerous passages are underlined in different colours. To what extent these traces of intensive reading are Beckett's is another matter, which will be discussed in Chapter 7.

As opposed to this kind of intensive reading, instances of extensive reading – marked by references to other books read by the same reader – are also present in Beckett's library. For instance, in his copy of George Berkeley's *A New Theory of Vision and Other Writings*, Beckett responded to Berkeley's treatise concerning the principles of human knowledge by writing with a blue-green pencil in the margin: 'against Geulincx (?)'. Notably the question mark indicates the frailty of the 'fabric of intelligibility', not just in Poe's terms (the relationship between the marginalia and the body of the text) but also in terms of the relationship between Beckett's marginalia and reading notes on separate sheets or in notebooks. In the 1930s Beckett committed himself to the study of philosophy, both by means of surveys or histories of philosophy, such as John Burnet's *Greek Philosophy* or Wilhelm Windelband's *A History of Philosophy*, and by means of intensive readings of particular philosophers. His notes on Geulincx's *Ethics* are a case in point. In search of the *Ethica* from *Arnoldi Geulincx Antverpiensis Opera Philosophica*, Beckett had to 'put [his] foot within the abhorred gates' of Trinity College Dublin in January 1936 and 'penetrate more deeply' in the next few months (*LSB* 299). But it is interesting that the intensity of his philosophical investigations is often marked precisely by traces of extensive reading. He tried to understand these philosophies by contrasting or comparing them with other philosophies, as the annotation 'against Geulincx (?)' indicates.

(b) *Non-verbal codes*: The most enigmatic marks in Beckett's books belong to what Heather Jackson categorizes as 'non-verbal codes' (Jackson 2001, 14). A good example is *Beiträge zu einer Kritik der Sprache* by Fritz Mauthner. 'In Beckett's library at his death', John Pilling writes, 'was a copy of the three-volume Felix Meiner 1923 *Beiträge*, printed in Leipzig and Munich. It was from this edition, and presumably from his own copy ... that Beckett took the handwritten notes for the entries in the 'Whoroscope' Notebook, and also for the four pages of typewritten notes now in the archives of Trinity College Dublin (TCD MS10971/5)' (Pilling 2006b, 164). After several studies on the relationship between Beckett and Mauthner (Ben-Zvi 1980, 1984, 2004; Feldman 2006a; Garforth 2005; Hesla 1971; Lernout 1994; Pilling 1976a, 1992, 2006b; Skerl 1974; Van Hulle 1999, 2002), Pilling's article is duly entitled 'Beckett and Mauthner Revisited', and it is not likely to be the last visit, for the edition in Beckett's library turns out to contain no less than 700 marked pages. With regard to the question of the volumes' provenance, John Pilling referred to the executor of the Beckett Estate, Edward Beckett, who was of the view 'that the three volumes were purchased in Germany, although there is no mention of them in the six German Diaries of 1936–37, which may or may not point to a purchase in Kassel on any one of half a dozen visits between 1929 and 1932' (Pilling 2006b, 164). Perhaps we should not even exclude the possibility that, although Beckett read Mauthner before the Second World War, he may have purchased or received the book later on. This matter will therefore be revisited (see Chapter 7) with the help of the reading traces.

Even though the number of marks in the three volumes is impressive, they seldom correspond to Beckett's extensive excerpts in the 'Whoroscope' Notebook and his typed notes on Mauthner. The marks in the *Beiträge* are consistently straight, vertical lines in the margins, all in grey pencil, suggesting a disciplined, diligent and remarkably even-tempered reading. None of the book's more than 2,000 pages shows any sign of either enthusiasm or depreciation; none of the marked pages contains any comment or annotation. The marginal codes are purely non-verbal, which makes it extremely hard to make any assumption as to the 'authorship' of these pencilled lines.

The question of agency is possibly even more of an enigma in the case of another kind of 'non-verbal code': 'dog-ears', or signs that corners of pages have been folded down at some point. Beckett's copy of Charles Darwin's *The Origin of Species*, for instance, contains only two passages marked in pencil, but also numerous traces of remarkably large dog-ears, which occur throughout the book and sometimes in close succession. It cannot be excluded that these dog-ears were not made by Beckett, but even this most enigmatic of reading traces is sometimes identifiable by means of a sort of signature. In this case the signature is the size of the dog-ears. The dog-ears in Beckett's copy of *The Origin of Species* are just as large as, for instance, the dog-ear marking the article on Manichaeism in the *Encyclopaedia Britannica*, which served as a source of inspiration for Beckett's *Krapp's Last Tape* (see *Figure 2*).

In 1969, Beckett was asked by the Schiller-Theater Werkstatt in Berlin to direct his own play. During the rehearsals he took notes in his so-called production notebook, which contains – among other things – three pages about the religion of Mani or 'Manichaeism' and the Gnostic dualism between good and evil, light and darkness. Beckett summed up the moments in the play that emphasize the dualism between light and darkness. On the second page, he made two lists of 'Light emblems' (the mild zephyr / cooling wind / bright light / quickening fire / clear water) and 'Darkness emblems' (Mist / heat / sirocco / darkness / vapour) (Beckett 1992, 135), corresponding to a passage in the article on 'Manichaeism' by Adolf Harnack and Frederic Cornwallis Conybeare in the eleventh edition of the *Encyclopaedia Britannica*: 'As the earth of light has five tokens (the mild zephyr, cooling wind, bright light, quickening fire, and clear water), so has the earth of darkness also five (mist, heat, the sirocco, darkness and vapour)' (573). The large dog-ear in Beckett's copy of the *Encyclopaedia Britannica* in his personal library not only serves as a material trace of Beckett's use of this source text for *Krapp's Last Tape*, but also (indirectly) as an indication that he did read the complete text of Darwin's book. In that sense at least, 'size matters', and dog-ears certainly deserve to be recognized as fully fledged marginalia.

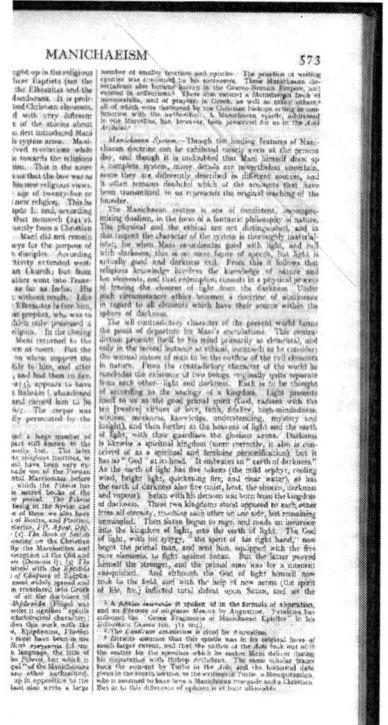

Figure 2 'Manichaeism' page from the *Encyclopaedia Britannica* with large dog-ear.

(c) *Non-marginalia*: Sometimes a book in the personal library is heavily marked, and yet the author eventually used an *un*marked passage for his own writing. To denote such passages that are *not* marked, Axel Gellhaus coined the term 'non-marginalia' (Gellhaus 2004, 218–19). This category applies to the caterpillar 'working away at his hammock', which is mentioned in Beckett's story 'Echo's Bones' and referred to in *Murphy* and *Watt* (Ackerley and Gontarski 2004, 125–6). The story that resonates in these references is one of the few direct allusions in Beckett's works to Darwin's *Origin of Species* (1902, 187; see Chapter 10). Although Beckett's copy of *The Origin of Species* shows reading traces in the form of both pencil marks and dog-ears, it was this *un*marked passage about the caterpillar that made it into Beckett's works, not just once, but repeatedly.

The insistence with which some *un*marked passages in Beckett's books are alluded to in his works, calls for special attention to 'non-marginalia'.

Beckett's copy of *The Works of William Shakespeare* is marked on merely half a dozen of its pages, and it even contains material that adds some *couleur locale* to Beckett's reading, such as a shopping list, mentioning 'Briquets / Foie / Whiskey' (see Chapter 2). But what Beckett has marked is not necessarily anything he has ever used for his writing, whereas what he *did* use is not marked. A good example is the 'vile jelly' in *Ill Seen Ill Said*: 'Suddenly enough and way for remembrance. Closed again to that end the vile jelly . . .' (paragraph 51) – an allusion to the last scene in Act III of Shakespeare's *King Lear*, when Cornwall pulls out Gloucester's eyes: 'Out, vile jelly!' One of the subsequent passages in *King Lear* (the blind Gloucester, led by his disguised son Edgar on the cliffs of Dover) recurs frequently in Beckett's works as an Ur-scene of someone who is on the verge of committing suicide and yet does not kill himself. For instance, the blind Gloucester and his son reappear as the 'Galls father and son' in *Watt*: 'They were two, and they stood, arm in arm, in this way, because the father was blind. . . . How very fortunate for Mr. Gall, said Watt, that he has his son at his command, whose manner is all devotion . . . when he might obviously be earning an honest penny elsewhere' (*W* 57–8). What is remarkable about the scene of the Galls is that it continues to unfold in Watt's head:

This was perhaps the principal incident of Watt's early days in Mr. Knott's house. In a sense it resembled all the incidents of note proposed to Watt during his stay in Mr. Knott's house. . . . It resembled them in the sense that it was not ended, when it was past, but continued to unfold, in Watt's head, from beginning to end, over and over again, the complex connexions of its lights and shadows . . . it continued to happen, in his mind . . . inexorably to unroll its phases . . . it revisited him in such a way that he was forced to submit to it all over again, to hear the same sounds, see the same lights, touch the same surfaces, and so on, as when they had first involved him in their unintelligible intricacies (*W* 59–63.)

Given the link with the scene in *King Lear*, this description of the incident's 'unfolding' in Watt's mind can be read as a precise description of the effect of reading in Beckett's own mind, especially with regard to what Anthony Uhlmann refers to as the 'occluded image' (Uhlmann 2007, 68–9) and the persistence of philosophical images and particular literary scenes throughout Beckett's oeuvre.

Sometimes this persistence of images is based on graphic images in Beckett's personal library. For instance, Beckett's bibles show numerous reading traces, several of which have not been used in his writings, whereas it is the *un*marked map of the Holy Land that made it into *Waiting for Godot*. When Gogo is asked whether he remembers the Gospels, he replies: 'I remember the maps of the Holy Land. Coloured they were. Very pretty. The Dead Sea was pale blue.

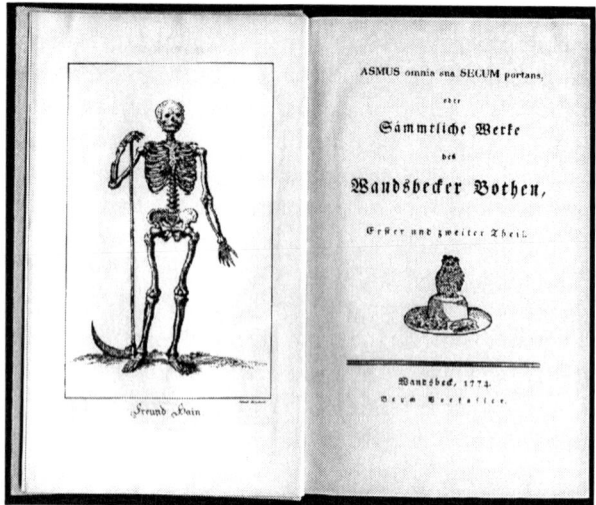

Figure 3 Unmarked illustration of 'Freund Hain' in Matthias Claudius' *Sämmtliche Werke*

The very look of it made me thirsty. That's where we'll go, I used to say, that's where we'll go for our honeymoon. We'll swim. We'll be happy' (*CDW* 13).

This kind of unmarked illustrations and 'non-marginalia' can be relevant with reference to Beckett's role as director of his own plays. When the protagonist in *Krapp's Last Tape* is said to '*look over his shoulder into the darkness backstage left*' (Beckett 1992, 4), he senses the presence of death, which in Beckett's production notes is called 'Hain' (220). Beckett explained to James Knowlson that he alluded to Matthias Claudius' poem 'Death and the Maiden' (set to music by Franz Schubert) and to the eighteenth-century German poet's use of the word 'Hain' to refer to the death figure. In Beckett's personal library, his copy of Matthias Claudius' *Sämmtliche Werke* contains a card, inserted between pages 884 and 885, quoting a letter from Claudius to Voss (21 August 1774) that includes 'Der Tod und das Mädchen' (see Chapter 4). But the image of Hain he had in mind is most probably the unmarked illustration next to the title page (see *Figure 3*).

2. Traces of the 'Extractor'

Monroe Beardsley once claimed that the first question of the 'objective critic' should not be 'What is this supposed to be?' but 'What have we got here?' (Beardsley, qtd. in Wimsatt 1968, 195). This soundbite was evidently directed

Reading Traces: Beckett as a Reader

against the so-called intentional fallacy and a plea for treating the literary text as a self-contained whole. But in the concrete case of Samuel Beckett, 'what we have got here' is also an abundance of reading traces and notebooks (often voluntarily donated by Beckett to university libraries, thus enabling his readers to study these documents). On the one hand 'what we have got here' is more than what Beardsley may have had in mind; on the other hand, 'what we have got here' is not more than what it is: no single private library of an author contains all the books he or she has ever read or used. The danger of a rigorous empirical methodology could be that it limits a text's exegesis to the extant materials. Genetic research, however, needs to take into account that the extant materials (from books and marginalia to manuscripts and proofs) are merely a fraction of what the author has ever read or written. So it may be just as important for a textual scholar or a genetic critic to show 'what we have got here' as it is to indicate 'what we haven't got here'.

Although this examination of Beckett's reading focuses on the material traces that can be verified in the extant books, it is good to be constantly aware of the lacunae in this personal library. Beckett's reading in the 1930s often took place in public libraries and could only become the object of study because Beckett was not just a 'marginalist' but also an 'extractor'. Sometimes, however, Beckett acted both as a marginalist and as an extractor. For instance, in his four-volume copy of *Le Journal de Jules Renard 1887–1910*, Beckett underlined the sentence: 'Si mignonne que si vous vouliez vous pendre, vous n'auriez pas le poids'. In the bottom margin Beckett translated this as: 'Not heavy enough to hang herself' (see *Figure 4*).

Thanks to the letters we know precisely when Beckett read Renard (see Chapter 3). On 24 February 1931 he wrote to Thomas MacGreevy: 'I am reading "Journal intime de Jules Renard"' (*LSB* 69). In this period Beckett's writing method was still influenced by James Joyce, who is famous for what he called 'notesnatching' in his more than fifty notebooks with short jottings. Beckett applied the same method to write his first novel, *Dream of Fair to Middling Women*, but as early as August 1931 he had already written to Thomas MacGreevy that he was 'soiled ... with the old demon of notesnatching' (*DN* xiii). From the four volumes of Renard's *Journal* he snatched about thirty passages and jotted them down in his 'Dream' Notebook, without any reference to their source, including the line 'She's not heavy enough to hang herself' (*DN* 230). Toward the end of the year he had gathered such a stock of words that he wrote: 'I have enough "butin verbal" to strangle anything I'm likely to want to say' (xiv).

Gradually, Beckett was to take his distance from Joyce's writing method by changing over to a different way of taking reading notes. His excerpts

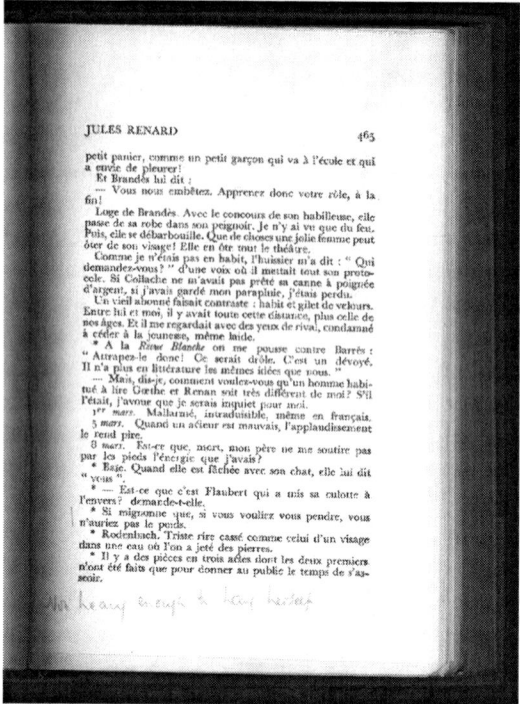

Figure 4 *Le Journal de Jules Renard 1887–1910*, vol. 2, p. 465.

and notes gradually became more extensive and – unlike Joyce's *Finnegans Wake* notes – often do not seem to have been made with the purpose of integrating them directly or indirectly in a work he was writing.

3. Traces of the 'Rereader'

Some of the traces of the 'extractor' are not just reading notes but the result of 'rereading'. On 14 February 1935, Beckett told Thomas MacGreevy that he was reading 'the divine Jane' (*LSB* 250) and that he 'like[d] Jane's manner' (252), admitting that Austen had much to teach him. His personal library contains four novels by Austen (*Northanger Abbey*, *Persuasion*, *Mansfield Park*, *Sense and Sensibility*; see Chapter 2) and even a volume of selected letters, but they were all published between 1953 and 1960, which seems to indicate a renewed interest in Austen after the Second World War. After *Godot*, Beckett may have invested in some familiar books with the money he did not have two decades earlier, when he only had time to spend on them.

How intensively Beckett reread these familiar books is hard to tell, because they seldom show reading traces, but the few extant traces are telling. Beckett's excerpts from the dog-eared article on 'Manichaeism' in the *Encyclopaedia Britannica* (in preparation of his 1969 direction of *Krapp's Last Tape* in Berlin) may be *re*reading notes. It is not implausible that Beckett had already consulted the article while he was writing *Krapp's Last Tape* in early March 1958. In the first half of that month, Beckett had received the eleventh edition of the *Encyclopaedia Britannica* as a present from Jake Schwartz after having admitted – according to Deirdre Bair – that he had an 'innate passion for knowledge, which demanded periodic satisfaction' (Bair 1978, 493–4). By that time he had already written a few pages of the 'Magee Monologue' in his so-called 'Eté 56' notebook (dated '20.2.58'), but it is not implausible that the subsequent versions were coloured by his reading of the 'Manichaeism' article in the *Encyclopaedia Britannica*, for which he thanked Jake Schwartz on 15 March 1958. Yet, less than a month later, Beckett's scepticism vis-à-vis enlightenment encyclopaedism again gained the upper hand, as a letter to Jacoba van Velde (12 April 1958) shows: 'On m'a donné l'édition 1911 de l'Encyclopédie Britannique. 28 volumes. Trop tard' (qtd. in Van Hulle 2007, 17). Perhaps it was too late for encyclopaedic projects, but that did not prevent him from reading in his encyclopaedia, using it for his writing, and rereading it in preparation for the staging of his play (Beckett 1992, 131–41). Moreover, Beckett's autodirections also involved a rereading of his own texts, which is an integral part of his method of writing and self-translating.

At the start of Beckett's career, while he was writing his essay on Proust, rereading was already a topic in his letters. On 25 August 1930, Beckett told Thomas MacGreevy that he intended to read Schopenhauer's *Aphorismen zur Lebensweisheit* because Proust admired it 'for its originality and guarantee of wide reading – transformed'. Beckett regarded reading what Proust read as an inherent part of his job as an essayist or 'crritic' (*CDW* 70). Consequently, he paid special attention to Schopenhauer's 'chapter in Will & Representation on music' because Proust 'certainly read it'. In his letter, Beckett then paraphrases the passage about 'rereading' in *Le Temps retrouvé*: '(It is alluded to incidentally in A. la R.) A noble bitch observes to the Duchesse de Guermantes: «Relisez ce que S. dit sur la Musique.» Duchesse snarls & sneers: "Relisez! Relisez! Ça alors, c'est trop fort!", because she had the snobbism of ignorance' (*LSB* 43).

Roland Barthes, who coined the word *savoir-lire* (Barthes 1984, 39), brings up the issue of rereading in *S/Z*:

> Rereading, an operation contrary to the commercial and ideological habits of our society, which would have us 'throw away' the story once it has been consumed ('devoured'), so that we can then move on to another story, buy another book, and which is tolerated only in certain marginal categories of readers (children, old people, and professors), rereading is here suggested at the outset, for it alone saves the text from repetition (those who fail to reread are obliged to read the same story everywhere), multiplies it in its variety and its plurality: rereading draws the text out of its internal chronology ('this happens *before* or after *that*') and recaptures a mythic time (without *before* or *after*); ... rereading is no longer consumption, but play (that play which is the return of the different). (Barthes 1993, 15–16)

A similar kind of 'play' takes place in Beckett's writings toward the end of his career. While he was writing his *mirlitonnades* and the late prose texts *Company, Mal vu mal dit* and *Worstward Ho*, he made notes in his so-called 'Sottisier' Notebook, based on a rereading of – among other authors – Schopenhauer and Shakespeare. The scene of the blind Gloucester and his son Edward, underlying such passages as 'the Galls father and son' in *Watt* or the scene of the blind Dan Rooney and the young boy Jerry in *All That Fall*, is the same source of the 'Sottisier' excerpt 'The worst is not, / So long as one can say, This is the worst' (UoR MS2901, 14v). This line, in its turn, became a thematic starting point for the composition of *Worstward Ho*. It illustrates what Roland Barthes described in his essay 'Sur la lecture', arguing that reading is actually a form of production in that the 'consumed' product is turned into the desire to produce: 'la lecture est véritablement une production: non plus d'images intérieures, de projections, de fantasmes, mais, à la lettre, de *travail*: le produit (consommé) est retourné en production, en promesse, en désir de *production*' (Barthes 1984, 45). As a consequence, studying an author's personal library is not just an examination of his reading habits, but inevitably also an exploration of the dynamics of writing as a process that is inextricably bound up with the mechanics of reading.

THE MECHANICS OF READING

'No work', Beckett reported to George Reavey on 27 September 1938. Instead of writing, he tried to read: 'I read an average of an hour a day, after an hour the illusion of comprehension ceases' (*LSB* 643). This is one of the few traces of Beckett's attempts to make the mechanics of reading explicit. In studies on the history of reading, two models are predominant.

(1) The 'conversation model' is probably the oldest. In the introduction to his translation of John Ruskin's *Sesame and Lilies* (*Sésame et les Lys*), Marcel Proust sums up Ruskin's thesis in the words of Descartes: 'the reading of all good books is like a conversation with the worthiest individuals of past centuries who were their authors' (Descartes, qtd. in Proust 2008, 65–6). This model is applicable to more modern authors as well, as Daniel Ferrer has shown with reference to Virginia Woolf's reading of Joyce's *Ulysses*. Ferrer refers to the opening line of Woolf's story 'Together and Apart' – 'The conversation began some minutes before anything was said' – to suggest that a similar procedure marks 'the dialogic qualities that we recognize in printed texts [which] are often but the faint traces of an intense conversational process that preceded them' (Ferrer 2004, 47). That Woolf's original title for the story was 'The Conversation' may indicate a link between this concept and the paradox of being 'Together and Apart' at the same time – which Ferrer translates into 'something that implies cooperation and antagonism' (47).

The antagonism is often more prominent than the cooperation. In his discussion of the term 'marginalia', William Sherman notes that the word only became the standard term for marginal annotations in the nineteenth century, thanks to Samuel Taylor Coleridge. Sherman's enumeration of terms that were more common in the Renaissance, such as 'adversaria' or 'animadversion' (22–3), indicate that – more often than not – the margin of a book was a conflict zone, marking the terms of engagement with the text. On the other hand, if a marginal engagement with the text is not antagonistic, it is not automatically cooperative either. The traces in the margin often do not even relate to the content of the body of the text and simply serve as a sort of graffiti, expressing not much more than the basic message 'I was here' (23). But even if that is their only significance, Edgar Allan Poe duly points out that '*marginalia* are deliberately pencilled, because the mind of the reader wishes to unburden itself of a *thought*' (Poe 1965, 2). In these terms of unburdening, marginalia are seen as little more than mental defecation. And if this form of relief is to be regarded in terms of a conversation, Poe argues, it is the equivalent of talking to oneself – which is not necessarily to be judged in negative terms: 'In the *marginalia*, too, we talk only to ourselves; we therefore talk freshly – boldly – originally – with *abandonnement* – without conceit' (Poe 1965, 2). In the context of this sentence, the notion of abandonment is probably meant to be understood in the sense of ease and informality, but the word's first meaning, in the literal sense of abandoning and distancing oneself from the body of the text, points in the direction of the second model of reading, which Heather Jackson refers to as the 'communication model' (Jackson 2001, 85).

(2) The 'communication model' was suggested by Proust, arguing that reading 'cannot be assimilated ... to a conversation, even with the wisest of men':

> the difference essentially between a book and a friend lies not in their greater or lesser wisdom, but in the manner in which we communicate with them, reading being the reverse of conversation, consisting as it does for each one of us in receiving the communication of another's thought while still being on our own, that is, continuing to enjoy the intellectual sway which we have in solitude and which conversation dispels instantly, and continuing to be open to inspiration, with our minds still at work hard and fruitfully on themselves. (Proust 2008, 67)

If reading is to be seen as a form of communication, its most important feature, according to Proust, is that it is 'effected in solitude' (67). Whereas the notion of conversation may imply cooperation and antagonism – as expressed in Woolf's decision to replace 'The Conversation' by 'Together and Apart' – Proust's view on the mechanics of reading is less bidirectional and emphasizes its inciting quality. What may be 'Conclusions' for the author are 'Incitements' for the reader, Proust argues: 'We feel very strongly that our own wisdom begins where that of the author leaves off' (70). As Barthes also indicated, Proust is of the opinion that authors do not so much provide us with answers, only with desires: 'we are unable to receive the truth from anyone else but must create it ourselves' (70). In this context, Proust speaks of 'mental optics' ('l'optique des esprits') – suggesting that the author of a book does not provide his readers with a truth, but with a sort of microscope to discover their own truth.

Proust insists that readers who are 'mired in a sort of impossibility of willing' (72) can 'recover the power of thinking for themselves and of creating' (73), but only in solitude. Employing his favourite trope, Proust suggests the metaphor of a mental space: 'reading is for us the instigator whose magic keys have opened the door to those dwelling-places deep within us that we would not have known how to enter' (75). The inciting or instigating role of reading was recently confirmed from a neurological perspective. 'Reading is a neuronally and intellectually circuitous act', Maryanne Wolf notes. The fact that readers tend to stray while reading is not a defect: 'Far from being negative, this associative dimension is part of the generative quality at the heart of reading' (Wolf 2008, 16). Precisely this generative quality makes the act of reading so interesting, because in this respect it mirrors the circuit wiring of the human brain. Both the tendency to stray while reading and the tendency to make associations and inferences incite us to form new thoughts, and thus go *beyond* the particular text or situation at hand: 'In this sense reading both reflects and re-enacts the brain's capacity for cognitive breakthroughs' (Wolf 2008, 17).

The paradox of reading, from a Proustian perspective, is that the thoughts developed in the text are presented in such a way that they incite their readers to develop independent thoughts rather than to simply accept the author's. This generative nature of reading is employed in a special way by readers who are, in their turn, writers – such as Samuel Beckett. Reading was a way to start writing. At the beginning of his career Beckett read – among many other things – *À la recherche du temps perdu* (see Chapter 3). Proust's ideas on reading as expressed in the introduction to his Ruskin translation recur in the first part of the *Recherche*, when the act of reading becomes thematic. In *Sur la Lecture* (the introduction to his Ruskin translation), Proust had suggested that books are 'impulses' and that reading is the ideal remedy for 'the lazy mind' (Proust 2008, 74), which he compared to a special kind of languor, characterized by 'a sort of impossibility of willing' ('impossibilité de vouloir', 72). One of the first things Beckett underlined in the first volume of the *Recherche* is the narrator's self-proclaimed 'manque de volonté' (1.24). According to Proust, the only activity that could incite these minds was not solitude, nor a conversation, but reading. Against this background, the first part of the *Recherche* reads as an illustration of his thesis. Urged by his grandmother to come outside, the narrator takes his book and continues reading in the garden. He describes reading as a way of facilitating a process of unfolding, a movement 'des aspirations les plus profondément cachées en moi-même jusqu'à la vision tout extérieure' (1.124; underlined). Next to this underlined passage Beckett noted in the margin about this 'emersive tendency' that it was 'to be replaced by an immersive necessity' and on subsequent pages (125; 129) he twice underlined the movement 'du dedans au dehors'. After hundreds of pages, Proust applied the same movement to writing. The task of the writer, according to Proust, was to 'translate' what was within – another movement 'du dedans au dehors' [from inside to outside], which did not escape Beckett's notice.[1] He marked it twice.

Nonetheless, when it came to the concrete and urgent task of writing the essay on Proust, writing turned out to be not quite that easy. On 25 August 1930 Beckett wrote to MacGreevy: 'I started writing this morning, worked like one inspired for 2½ hours, then tore everything up and made a present of it to the panier: '. . . I can't do the fucking thing. I don't know whether to start at the end or the beginning – in a word should the Proustian arse-hole be considered as entrée or sortie – libre in either case' (*LSB* 43). Not exactly Beckett's most inspired moment, but interesting nonetheless, precisely because of the frustration it expresses.

The circuitous nature of the act of reading is reflected in several passages, where Proust discusses indirect forms of apprehension. So after having read the whole novel, Beckett noted in the margin: 'indirect – & consequently in[tegral] – apprehension of reality – frequent motiv' (1.123). Sixteen volumes further, Beckett marked the famous metaphor of the book as a graveyard: 'Un livre est un grand cimetière où sur la plupart des tombes on ne peut plus lire les noms effacés' (16.59). But when Proust returned to his old metaphor of the 'mental optics', Beckett's reaction in the margin was quite vehement. The narrator argues that his readers won't be simply *his* readers, but readers of their own selves; his work will be like a magnifying glass: 'mon livre n'étant qu'une sorte de ces verres grossissants comme ceux que tendait à un acheteur l'opticien de Combray, mon livre grâce auquel je leur fournirais le moyen de lire en eux-mêmes' (16.240). Beckett's curt marginal comment is the fiercely monosyllabic: 'Balls' (see *Figure 5*).

In early August 1930, Beckett had voiced his impatience in even more explicitly phallic terms to Thomas MacGreevy: 'I am looking forward to

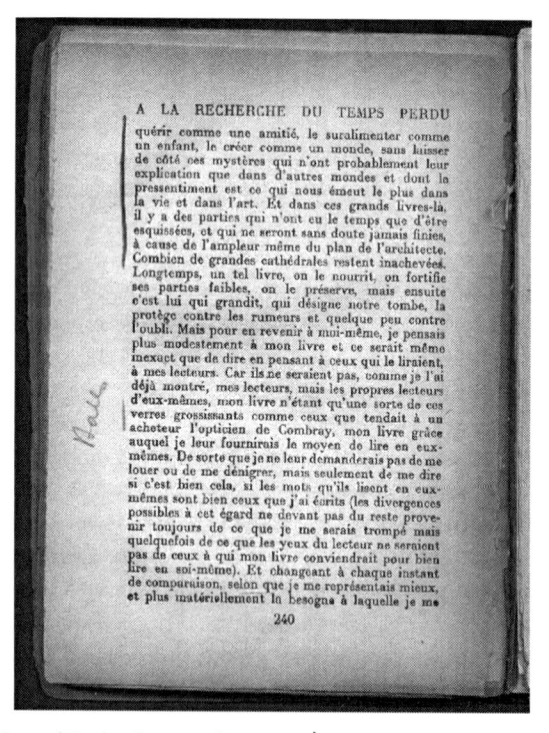

Figure 5 Samuel Beckett's copy of Proust's *À la recherche du temps perdu*, vol. 16 (*Le Temps retrouvé*), p. 240.

pulling the balls off the critical & poetical Proustian cock. He adored Ruskin & the Comtesse de Noailles and thought Amiel was a forerunner! I am going to write a poem about him too,[2] with Charlus' lavender trousers in a Gothic pissotière' (*LSB* 36). But no matter how antagonistic this reaction may be, Beckett's reading clearly had the 'inciting' effect Proust described in *Sur la Lecture*. In their protest, the fiercest marginalia actually illustrate the generative capacity of reading. They thus confirm the Proustian paradox of reading: a text can only be absorbed through the act of reading, but this very act does not limit itself to absorbing the text; its generative capacity incites the reader to go beyond and develop autonomous ideas. As Maryanne Wolf argues, 'the experience of reading is not so much an end in itself as it is our best vehicle to a transformed mind' (Wolf 2008, 18). It is impossible to look 'inside' a reader's or a writer's mind with hindsight, but its transformations are partially retraceable on the basis of reading notes. Such transformations, marked by Samuel Beckett's reading traces, are the object of investigation in the following chapters.

CHAPTER 2

Literature in English

Readers and critics have often commented on Beckett's reading in such diverse fields as philosophy, mathematics, medical text books, science and religious curiosities. In the letter cited as epigraph to this book, in which Beckett states that he had been 'reading wildly all over the place', he goes on to specify that he has been reading 'Goethe's Iphigenia & then Racine's to remove the taste, Chesterfield, Boccaccio, Ariosto & Pope'. This list illustrates Beckett's wide reading in European literature, and much has been said about Beckett's multilingual, polyglot cultural formation, so much so that it is often forgotten that his intellectual grounding lies in English and Irish literature. His library reflects this, in that most of the books that survive on its shelves consist of literature written in English.

LITERARY HISTORIES

Indeed, one of the earliest surviving books in the library is A. Hamilton Thompson's *A History of English Literature, and of the Chief English Writers*, which carries the inscription 'S. B. Beckett / Feb. 1923'. It is not unreasonable to presume that the sixteen-year-old Beckett bought this book in preparation for his university studies, as he enrolled at Trinity College Dublin in October 1923. Although an Honours student in French and Italian, with English as a subsidiary subject, Beckett over the next four years, until he graduated in November 1927, studied the 'pillars' of English Literature, with a focus on Chaucer, Milton and Shakespeare. In accordance with Irish and indeed British university syllabi of the time, he also studied the classical works of the sixteenth and seventeenth centuries, such as Spenser's *The Faerie Queene*, Sidney's *Apology for Poetry* and Dryden's *Absalom and Achitophel*. Most of these texts Beckett would have read in one of TCD's set texts, A. J. Wyatt and W. H. Low's *Intermediate Text Book of English Literature*, published in two volumes in 1920. Beckett's edition of the first volume indicates that this was required reading; having bought a second-hand copy at the beginning of his first term, Beckett inscribed the volume with the words 'Samuel B. Beckett / Trinity College / Dublin / Michaelmas Term – 1923'. He then proceeded to buy the second volume, as required, in 1925. Unlike his other student books, Beckett's editions of this set text contain few markings, the only marginalia consisting of numbers appended to the list of sources underlying the individual stories of Chaucer's *The Canterbury Tales*.[1] The other text book or anthology which Beckett bought for his English Literature course at TCD was Palgrave's *Golden Treasury*, selections from which were examined in May 1924. Beckett bought this book, as well as David Somervell's *Companion to Palgrave's Golden Treasury*, in the first two years of his university studies.

As part of his studies, Beckett naturally engaged with secondary criticism, and in particular with literary histories. As noted, there is a copy of A. Hamilton Thompson's *A History of English Literature, and of the Chief English Writers* (revised edition of 1914) in the library. The book contains three kinds of reading traces. Pencil marks at specific points in the book as well as 'dog-ears' indicate place holders. Further reading traces consist of red pencil marks set beside specific chapter titles. It is hard to date these marks with any precision, although Beckett tended to use coloured pencils mainly during his student days (and then again briefly in the mid-1930s). Indeed, most of the chapters indicated by marks deal with authors and periods he studied at university, such as Shakespeare, Milton, 'Butler, Dryden and Prose writers of the Restoration' and 'The Age of Anne. Pope, Swift and the Augustan Poets'. Finally, the book contains a rare, and the earliest, instance of dating, in that Beckett has inscribed the date '25/4/23' just before the chapter on Marlowe (Thompson 1914, 171).

Although Beckett's first creative works were largely influenced by foreign language authors and thinkers, he continued to read English literature. To be sure, the 'Dream' Notebook (kept between 1930 and 1932), and the novel it fed, *Dream of Fair to Middling Women*, contain few English literary references, with Beckett's attention in these years focusing on writers as diverse as Proust, Joyce, Schopenhauer or St. Augustine, even if Shakespeare, Dickens and Chaucer, to name just these, make fleeting appearances. Much of Beckett's reading of English literature coincided with the period during which he was based in London, from 1934 to 1936 when he underwent psychoanalytic treatment. Indeed, it is only during the composition of *Murphy* in these years that Beckett returns to a systematic engagement with English literature. As noted earlier, having turned his back on an academic career in 1931, Beckett in the 1930s continued to read, record and acquire knowledge in a scholarly manner. Indeed, as with other fields of knowledge, such as psychoanalysis, philosophy and German literature, Beckett relied at first on secondary sources to furnish him with examples and an overview, before reading the works of authors that had caught his interest. The corpus of reading notes kept today at Trinity College Dublin Library contains a set of notes (TCD MS10970) largely (but not entirely) deriving from the two-volume, first edition of *The History of English Literature*, written by Emile Legouis and Louis Cazamian and published in 1925–6. These extensive notes are similar to those treating other literary histories in that they are predominantly verbatim excerpts and summaries with few commentaries. Beckett on the whole copies out author names, dates and bibliographic details of important works. In the case of this history, Beckett's notes cover the entire period discussed in the two volumes. Some titles of books are marked with an 'x', while others are ticked, as if to indicate further reading and completed reading, respectively. Although impossible to date with any certainty, the nature of the notes and their similarity to other reading notebooks would suggest that Beckett read the book during his time in London (1934–6), when he frequently worked in the British Museum.[2] However, it is equally plausible that these notes were made somewhat earlier, in 1932 (during his visits to the British Museum in August) or in early 1933 when Beckett was in Dublin.

Whatever their precise date of composition, the TCD notes must be earlier than other, directly related manuscript material, in particular the 'For Interpolation' section at the back of the 'Whoroscope' Notebook. John Pilling, in his discussion and annotations of this section, has aptly remarked that 'nothing matches the "For Interpolation" section of the "*Whoroscope*" *Notebook* as an example of how much interest Beckett took in English literature' (Pilling 2006c, 232). As the title of these notes suggests, these literary extracts were explicitly taken with the composition of *Murphy* in mind, a book that, in Pilling's view, is largely 'governed by a concern with English models of excellence' (Pilling 1992, 10). The quotations in the 'Whoroscope' Notebook largely derive from the poetry written by Elizabethan and Jacobean dramatists, Greene, Nashe, Marston, Peele, Marlowe, Ford and Ben Jonson. It is likely that Beckett read these authors during his time in London, and in particular during the second half of 1935 and early 1936 when he was struggling to make progress with the writing of *Murphy*.[3] Crucially, the quotations in the 'Whoroscope' Notebook derive from books that are ticked as having been read in the TCD notes, which suggests that Beckett was using his notes to guide his reading. Somewhat complicating the picture is a further set of notes with the heading 'University Wits' (TCD MS10971/3), which contain biographical and bibliographical details on John Lyly, George Peele, Thomas Lodge and Robert Greene. Similar to Beckett's Philosophy notes, the material contained in these notes derives from more than one source. What can be said for certain is that Beckett initially used his copy of Thompson's *History of English Literature*, before expanding his notes with other material. Furthermore, these notes do not derive from Legouis and Cazamian, which suggests that at the time of their composition he did not own an edition of their literary history. In terms of dating, it would seem that this material was collated during, or shortly before, Beckett's engagement with these authors during the later stages of composition of *Murphy*. Beckett supplemented the notes from Thompson's *History* on the University Wits with material drawn from John W. Cousin's *A Short Biographical Dictionary of English Literature* (rev. ed. 1925). This book is most probably also the source for digressions from the Legouis and Cazamian notes at TCD. The book itself contains various reading traces, and once again illuminates Beckett's systematic and scholarly approach in his study of English literature. He must have consulted the book over a period of time, and definitely after 1930, as this date is inserted by hand in the entry on William John Locke to denote the novelist's death. Most of the marginalia represent ticks beside specific entries, and in the back inside cover Beckett must have begun a correlating list, possibly to indicate writers that he wished to pursue. Furthermore, Beckett updated the book by inserting, in the shorter biographical outlines of 'lesser' authors at the end of the volume, names of more recent authors or writers that he thought should be included. Thus at their appropriate alphabetical position, the names of writers such as W. S. Maugham, Edgar Wallace or P. G. Wodehouse are inserted.[4]

This rather long digression into those reading notes deriving from Beckett's study of English literature is necessary when we return to his library, for it contains a copy of Legouis and Cazamian's English literary history. It is, however, the single-volume French edition of 1929 entitled *Histoire de la littérature anglaise*. It contains an inscription of a previous owner, which means that Beckett acquired the book second-hand, and presumably did so in France. The presence of this book however poses many questions, not least with regard to its date and place of acquisition, but also in terms of the extensive yet varied kinds of marginalia it contains. The reading traces can roughly be divided into two categories: extensive underlining of passages in pencil and shorter underlining made with red and blue pencils. The former are very probably Beckett's marginalia, as they occur in passages dealing with authors we know he studied closely. In particular, the most extensive reading traces are found in the sections 'The Flowering of the Renascence' (covering Lyly, Sidney and Spenser), 'Drama until Shakespeare, from 1580–92' (especially Marlowe) and 'Shakespeare's Contemporaries and Immediate Successors' (Chapman, Jonson, Dekker, Marston, Heywood, Middleton and Fletcher). The marginalia in chapters dedicated to eighteenth-century novelists, including

Richardson, Sterne and Fielding, also correlate with Beckett's documented interest in these authors. The use of coloured pencils to annotate other parts of the book suggests that they were taken at a different time, and whilst Beckett did use different colours to annotate other volumes in his library in early 1936, the highlighted material is perhaps less readily mapped onto what we know of his interests. The coloured marginalia are thus to be found in the two sections on the 'Pre-Romantic Period' and the 'Romantic Period'.

These reading traces within the sections dealing with Jacobean and Elizabethan poets and dramatists correlate with other reading notes on these authors, and could indicate that the book was read during the same time frame in which they were made. However, the existence of the TCD notes from the English edition suggests that the book was acquired at a later date, which is to say after the mid-1930s. Yet following a brief visit to Paris in June 1934, Beckett was not in France again until he permanently settled in Paris in October 1937 (beyond a one day stop-over in Le Havre on his way to Germany in October 1936). Unfortunately, the marginalia do not give us any clue as to when Beckett may have consulted the book, as none of the marked material appears to have made its way into the compositional process during the 1930s. Beckett's correspondence also gives inconclusive clues. It is, however, interesting that two letters written in July 1937 (*before* the move to Paris) appear to contain material that could derive from Beckett's reading of the French edition of Legouis and Cazamian. In a letter to Joe Hone of 3 July 1937, Beckett in a discussion of Jack B. Yeats' own description of his voice 'as a sack of coal being delivered', goes on to state: 'The clack of a mill hopper occurs to me rather. It is Nash or Greene. Which alas is the difference, part of the difference' (*LSB* 508). And three weeks later, Beckett mentioned to MacGreevy the 'vulgarisation' in Shakespeare's *Othello*, and proceeded to argue that this 'would do as a starting point for the whole literary va et vient between England & France' (23 July 1937; TCD MS10402/127). This reference, perhaps tellingly made in French, relates to the long discussion in Legouis and Cazamian regarding the differing manner in which the theatre developed in the two countries, from which Beckett had however already in his English notes excerpted a long extract. Beckett's renewed interest in English literature after his return from Germany in April 1937 is further evidenced by a cluster of quotations from a variety of English authors entered in the 'Whoroscope' Notebook, in late 1938 or early 1939.

There is, in the correspondence, one direct reference to Beckett's copy of the *Histoire de la littérature anglaise*. In a letter to Mania Péron of 6 December 1952, having quoted a poetic fragment addressed by Swift to Sheridan, Beckett discusses a range of metrical schemes that would need to be taken into account when translating poetry. He goes on to ask, 'N'auriez-vous pas profité de ce que j'avais le dos tourné pour voler mon Legouis et Cazamian?' [Wouldn't you have taken advantage of my turned back to steal my Legouis and Cazamian?].

ELIZABETHAN AND JACOBEAN LITERATURE

As we have seen, Beckett read widely in Elizabethan and Jacobean literature when writing *Murphy* (1935–6). Beckett's novel *Watt*, written whilst on the run in France during the Second World War, contains further quotations from those writers that Beckett studied intensely in the 1930s. Once again, these quotations, from John Earle's *Microcosmographie* or John Marston's *The Malcontent*, to name but these, were drawn from Beckett's TCD notes on Legouis and Cazamian as well as the 'Whoroscope' Notebook. Considering the extensive notes Beckett took on these writers, it is perhaps not surprising to find them largely missing from his bookshelves. That is not to say that Beckett's interest in these writers would disappear after the war. His library thus contains a copy of Marlowe's *Plays and Poems* (1963), which had been given to him in June 1965 by Barbara Bray (TCD MS10948/1/339). In a June 1967 letter to Ruby Cohn he quotes 'What buzzeth in my ears I am a body?' from *Dr Faustus*. There was one passage from George Farquhar's *The Beaux Stratagem* in particular that Beckett liked to quote, having initially noted it in the 'Whoroscope' Notebook (72r): 'O Sister, Sister! if ever you marry, / beware of a sullen, silent sot, one / that's always musing but never thinks'. Having used the line in *Watt* (239), Beckett would refer to himself as a 'sullen silent sot, always dreaming and never thinking' (letter to Giorgio and Asta Joyce, 13 October 1955; *LSB II* 555).[5]

SHAKESPEARE

It is difficult to overestimate the importance of William Shakespeare on Beckett's work. Beckett had studied the great bard's writings as a student at Trinity College Dublin, and he continued to read Shakespeare throughout his life.

Most of his texts contain some kind of nod toward Shakespeare, ranging from allusions, to direct quotations to formal or thematic influences; tracing all of these references is clearly beyond the scope of this chapter. It is striking how Shakespeare furnished Beckett with more than just the nicely turned phrase, or the apt verbal confluence, but often chimed in a more direct way with Beckett's poetic enterprise. Thus for example Shakespeare's *A Midsummer Night's Dream* acts as an intertext to *Imagination morte imaginez*, written in the mid-1960 from the detritus of *All Strange Away*. The text attempts to project in an act of imagination, with mathematical precision, 'two white bodies' within a defined space. It is essentially a minimal, stark dramatization of a passage from Shakespeare's play which Beckett noted in his manuscript notebook:

> And as imagination bodies forth
> The forms of things unknown, the poet's pen
> Turns them to shapes & gives to airy nothing
> A local habitation & a name
>
> (TCD MS11223, 22)

Beckett's library contains a number of volumes by and on Shakespeare,[6] including two complete works: the 1954 Oxford *The Complete Works of Shakespeare* (in 1957 reprint) and *The Works of William Shakespeare* (published by Frederick Warne & Co.). The latter volume is the one that contains marginalia and annotations. This 'Universal Edition' was first published in 1890, although this copy presumably dates from the 1920s, and may well have been acquired by Beckett in that decade. Indeed, the first annotation in the book is made in blue pencil, the kind Beckett tended to use in the 1930s. Here Beckett sets lines beside Amiens' songs at the end of Act II, Scene 7 in *As You Like It*, which open:

> Blow, blow, thou winter wind,
> Thou art not so unkind
> As man's ingratitude.

Beckett had studied the play at Trinity College Michaelmas Term 1924, but the annotation in the book was probably made nearer the time of the writing of *Dream*, as the novel contains an explicit allusion to Shakespeare's lines. The off-rhyme on 'wind' and 'unkind' must have caught Beckett's eye, and in *Dream* he draws attention to it by writing 'under the east wind, weind please' (72). Beckett referred to the same issue nearly 25 years later in his play 'Rough for Theatre I', when the stage directions indicate that the character B's words 'There croaking to the winter wind' are to '*rime with unkind*' (*CDW* 233).[7]

Further annotations in Beckett's edition of Shakespeare's works appear in *King Lear*. This was the play that occupied Beckett most during his life, and he frequently spoke about the play in conversation and correspondence, and referenced it in his work. However, the annotations are somewhat mysterious, in that Beckett on three separate pages underlines (with red biro) the words 'shall', 'shalt' and then 'shall' again. The other reading trace in the play consists of Beckett's underlining of King Lear's words 'I shall endure', which chimes with Beckett's lifelong aesthetic and personal commitment to a quietist attitude. Beckett's annotation here may be related to a meeting he had with John Kobler in April 1965, as described in a letter to Barbara Bray: 'looking for him in Lear "I shall prevail" and finding he meant and wanted "I will endure"' (TCD MS10948/1/323).

Shakespeare's *King Lear* is at the core of Beckett's creative endeavours in the 1980s, as a cluster of quotations in the 'Sottisier' Notebook suggests (UoR MS2901, 14v; qtd. in Nixon 2007b, 116). These quotations, mainly playing on the distinction between 'worse'/'worst', informed Beckett's late texts *Ill Seen Ill Said* and *Worstward Ho*:

> 'The lamentable change is from the best,
> The worst returns to laughter –'
> (Ib. IV: Edgar)
>
> 'Who is't can say, I am the worst.'
> (Ib.)
>
> ' – The worst is not
> so long as one can say, This is the worst'

Beckett's library also contains two copies of Shakespeare's *Sonnets* (Penguin, 1986 and 'Everyman' Dent, 1988). Quotations from the *Sonnets* appear throughout Beckett's work, but they were placed at the centre of an aborted dramatic fragment contained in a notebook held toward the writing of *Stirrings Still*.

> Come & read to me.
> What?
> That ~~Shakespeare~~ sonnet we ~~once so~~ used to loved.
> You mean 'No longer weep . . .'
> What? (P.) No longer what?
> Weep. (P.) [']No longer weep . . .'
> No no.
>
> (UoR MS2934, 2r; qtd. in Van Hulle 2011, 42)

This passage is interesting for the way in which Beckett hesitates when trying to determine the right 'level' of intertextuality, moving from a clear identification to a fragmented reference to the opening of Sonnet 71 ('No longer mourn for me when I am dead'; Sonnet 116 is also mentioned in the fragment). Beckett discussed his idea of 'writing a play *about* reading a poem' with Avigdor Arikha and Anne Atik on 23 December 1984 (Atik 2001, 120).

Figure 6 Scrap of paper inserted between pages 946–7 of *The Works of William Shakespeare*

Yet Beckett's literary pursuit is wonderfully brought back to the domestic sphere with a scrap of a diary page (see *Figure 6*) inserted in the pages of *The Works of William Shakespeare*, which contains a shopping list:

'Briquets / foie / whiskey'

Beckett also harnessed particular lines from Shakespeare, as he did from other authors, to communicate his struggles with writing: 'I flounder on down the long devious straight. "Age with his stealing steps hath clawed me in his clutch." I try in vain to say as much' (from *Hamlet*, Act V, Scene 1; letter to Nick Rawson, 9 November 1983).

SEVENTEENTH CENTURY: DONNE AND MILTON

In a letter to Barbara Bray of 17 October 1959, Beckett confessed that he could 'never be a Donne fiend' but admits that there are 'blazes here and there' (TCD MS10948/1/53). The occasion of the letter was Bray's gift of Donne's poetry (*A Selection of his Poetry*; 1958 [1950]). Beckett had cited

Donne – the *Paradoxes* – in his early work *More Pricks than Kicks*, but does not seem to have had much interest in the seventeenth-century poet otherwise. In his own edition, the corner of the page on which the poem 'The Will' appears has been folded down, and it is possible that Beckett was marking the poem with its disillusioned and thus biting address to Love.

If Donne was not necessarily to Beckett's taste, one would think that the more classical poet John Milton would be. Beckett's reading of Milton is however rather difficult to evaluate; he was undoubtedly familiar with Milton's major works from his reading in the 1920s; *Paradise Lost* was a set text at TCD in 1925. The library contains three editions: *Paradise Lost* (1904), a modern edition of the *Poetical Works* (1969) and an antiquarian edition of *Milton's Paradise Regained and Samson Agonistes* dating from 1713. Beckett may have been troubled by Milton's doctrinal positions, and an undated [7 August 1934] letter to MacGreevy indicates: 'I think what you find cold in Milton I find final, for himself at least, conflagrations of conviction cooled down to a finality of literary emission' (*LSB* 217). Yet Beckett undoubtedly also admired the poet's linguistic craft: 'Can't get a verse of Milton out of my mind: "Insuperable height of loftiest shade"' (letter to MacGreevy, 6 November 1955, citing from Book IV of *Paradise Lost*; *LSB II* 565).

EIGHTEENTH CENTURY

By far the largest proportion of books in English relate to eighteenth-century literature. As Frederik N. Smith and others have shown, Beckett had a clear affinity with the writers of this century, in particular with those satirical voices, like Swift or Sterne, who tackled the 'age of reason'. Some of the books contained in Beckett's library date back from his student days at Trinity College, such as his copy of *The Poems of Thomas Gray, with a Selection of Letters and Essays* (1928). Another example is *The Vicar of Wakefield* by Oliver Goldsmith (n.d.), a writer whose description as 'the English Don Quixote' in Cazamian and Legouis provokes Beckett's comment 'Pfui' in his notes (TCD MS10970, 29v). Beckett purchased further books in early 1936, as he hunted deliberately around for material that would facilitate his increasingly desperate attempts to finish *Murphy* (completed in June). As noted above, it appears that for this 'English' novel, Beckett sought out books that would furnish him with a specific cultural atmosphere. The library thus contains a copy of Tobias Smollett's *The Expedition of Humphrey Clinker*, inscribed in green pencil 'Samuel Beckett' and carrying the bookseller's sticker of Greene & Co. in Dublin.

The nature of this inscription and the sticker suggests that Beckett bought the book in the first months of 1936, after his return to Dublin from London.[8] He also bought, in the same bookshop, Izaak Walton's *The Lives of Donne, Wotton, Hooker, Herbert, Sanderson* in April 1936. The 'Whoroscope' Notebook contains extracts from Walton's *Lives* (WN 82r) dating from 1938 (and thus too late for incorporation in *Murphy*), and a quotation on Hooker was used by Beckett in the Addenda to *Watt* (#5).

The library also contains several modern reprints of classic texts of the eighteenth century, many of which Beckett had read in the 1930s (such as Defoe's *The Life and Adventures of Robinson Crusoe*). There are, for example, four books by Jane Austen – *Northanger Abbey* and *Persuasion* (1953), *Selected Letters 1796–1827* (1956 [1955]), *Sense and Sensibility* (1959) and *Mansfield Park* (1960).[9] At the same time, it is rather surprising that there are no copies in the library of Fielding's work, which Beckett read extensively in the early 1930s.[10]

POPE

Unlike Beckett's French and Italian student books, few of the English texts contain any marginalia, undoubtedly because there was no need to annotate difficulties of vocabulary. However, one book dating from the 1920s does contain pen and pencil annotations, Beckett's 1909 edition of Alexander Pope's *Essays on Criticism*. Most probably marked in anticipation of the Michaelmas 1925 examination, Beckett in particular paid attention to the different uses of the word 'wit' in Pope's text. However, a precocious mind is also at work here, in that Beckett frequently disagrees with Pope, appending the word 'Nonsense' to the discussion of how 'Horace still charms with graceful Negligence' (Pope 1909, 27). And, at another point, he highlights a passage as a 'case of Pope's bad grammar' (2).

In March 1936, as the inscription indicates, Beckett bought a second-hand edition of *The Poetical Works of Alexander Pope, with Life*. He proceeded to dip around in the Pope volume, citing the 'Elegy on an Unfortunate Lady' in a letter to MacGreevy of 25 March 1936, and adjudged the line 'is there no bright reversion in the sky' to be 'lovely' (*LSB* 324). Roughly two years later, Beckett copied out various passages from Pope's *Dunciad* and the *Pastorals* from this book into his 'Whoroscope' Notebook (83r–83v). Beckett continued to read Pope into his old age, and the 'Sottisier' Notebook (UoR MS2901, 2r) contains a quotation from Pope's

Essay on Man. Furthermore, by quoting the line 'damned to fame' in an undated letter to Knowlson of 1981, Beckett inadvertently suggested the title of his own biography.

STERNE

The library contains a copy of Laurence Sterne's *The Life and Opinions of Tristram Shandy*, from *The Works of Laurence Sterne* (1910).[11] The book plate indicates that this book was given to Beckett by his friend A. J. Leventhal, and Beckett mentions reading it in a letter to MacGreevy of August 1938. Whilst Beckett was known to have been interested in the 'famous tear' at the end of volume 6, chapter 8 (see letter to John Fletcher, 18 August 1986), the only marginalia in this book are pencil marks beside the end of chapter 7 and beginning of chapter 8 of volume one, where Sterne is discussing the importance of hobby horses. It is unclear whether these marks were made by Leventhal or Beckett. The library also contains the fourth volume, which includes the *Sentimental Journey*, of Sterne's *Complete Works* published in 1780.

SWIFT

As John Pilling has recently argued, in 'A Note on Swift' (2011a, 237–9), Beckett's knowledge of Jonathan's Swift's work was extensive, and although his most intense scrutiny of the Dean's work took place in the early 1930s, he would continue to read and use Swift in his own writing. Beyond a 'World's Classics' edition of *Gulliver's Travels* (1963), Beckett possessed Swift's *The Drapier's Letters* (vol. 6 of the Temple Scott edition; 1922), which he acquired in April 1925 in preparation of the Michaelmas Term examinations later that year. The book contains two marginalia, although one, which appends the words 'Lord Dartmouth & Knox' to clarify the background of the patenting of coinage in Ireland, is purely factual. The other, however, shows Beckett's keen interest in matters Irish, and can be linked with his (ultimately abandoned) plans to write a text on Irish history entitled 'Trueborn Jackeen' in 1933 or 1934 (to echo Defoe's satirical 'The True-born Englishman'). Here Beckett commented on the famous passage of the Third Letter:

Were not the people of Ireland born as free as those of England? How have they forfeited their freedom? Is not their Parliament as fair a representative of the people as that of England? And hath not their Privy-council as great or a greater share in the administration of public affairs? Are they not subjects of the same King? Does not the same sun shine on them? And have they not the same God for their protector? Am I a freeman in England, and do I become a slave in six hours by crossing the Channel? No wonder then, if the boldest persons were cautious to interpose in a matter already determined by the whole voice of the nation, or to presume to represent the representatives of the kingdom, and were justly apprehensive of meeting such a treatment as they would deserve at the next session. (67)

Beckett's comment on this passage, written on the right-hand margin of the page, is that Swift pens 'Rather a poor reply to this clause of the report'.

JOHNSON

It comes perhaps as no surprise to find that the largest number of books in Beckett's library is dedicated to the work of Samuel Johnson. Throughout his life, Beckett read Johnson intensely, at times even obsessively, especially in the years 1937–40 when he filled three notebooks with material that was to enable the writing of the theatre piece *Human Wishes*. The play, predicated on Beckett's hypothesis that Johnson loved Mrs Thrale but was possibly impotent, remained unfinished, and was indeed barely begun, but his fascination with the man and his work stayed with him all his life. Beckett was introduced to Johnson's work during his student days at Trinity College Dublin. His library contains more than a dozen books by and on Johnson. It is difficult to ascertain which of these books he owned in the 1930s, in particular as existing evidence suggests that Beckett pursued his study of Johnson in the National and Trinity College Libraries.[12] Moreover, Beckett would presumably not have taken the effort to copy out extensive material in notebooks if he owned the books from which he was excerpting. It is, however, possible that his copy of C. E. Vulliamy's study *Mrs Thrale of Streatham: Her Place in the Life of Dr Samuel Johnson etc* (published by Cape in 1936) was acquired during this time of study, and the previous owner's book plate, which is dated 15 December 1938, just about makes this possible. One book that Beckett definitely bought in the 1930s is, although not by Dr Johnson, directly linked to him: Lord Chesterfield's *Letters, Sentences & Maxims* (6th ed., 1881). Beckett was fascinated by Johnson's letter to Lord Chesterfield, dismissing the possibility of patronage once he had found success on his own. Beckett bought the book in February 1936 in Greene & Co. bookshop on Clare Street in Dublin, as many other volumes around this time. Beckett, who cited the letter in correspondence and manuscripts throughout his life, proceeded to translate the letter into German on 12 August 1936 ('Clare Street' Notebook, UoR MS5003, 22r–25r) in anticipation of his six-month trip to Germany. A further book that Beckett may well have owned as a young man is a 1799 edition of Johnson's *Dictionary of the English Language* (2 vols, 8th corrected and revised edition).[13]

Beckett's use of this famous book is evident throughout his writing career, from the 'Dream' Notebook onward (see Chapter 9).

Most of Beckett's Johnson books date from after the Second World War, and many of them were gifts from friends and authors who were aware of his love for this writer. However, Beckett did also pursue the acquisition of books actively himself. In a letter to Barbara Bray, a close friend and controller at BBC radio, who sent him many books over the years, especially in the 1960s, Beckett wrote: 'if you happen to be near Foyles, they might have the 6 vol. Hill (1890?). But don't go to any further trouble. Unimportant' (3 February 1961; TCD MS10948/1/136). Referring to Boswell's *Life of Johnson, with Hebrides Journal and Johnson's Diary of Journey to North Wales*, edited by George Birkbeck Hill in six volumes (1887), the issue was clearly not 'unimportant' to Beckett. A month later Beckett could tell Leventhal that he had spent a day in Brighton with the manuscript dealer Jake Schwartz and had 'found Hill's edition of Boswell which I've been looking for in vain for years', and which is still in Beckett's library (27 March 1961; qtd. in Knowlson 1996, 482).[14]

This episode is a little mysterious, as Beckett must have had a copy of Boswell's biography in the early 1950s. In a letter of 8 August 1951 to Georges Belmont, Beckett quoted the tag 'vitam continent una dies' from Boswell's *Life of Johnson* (*LSB II* 278). Nine days later, he told Mania Péron: 'Je relis Boswell dans la belle édition de Birkbeck Hill. Effet calmant, comme toujours' [I re-read Boswell in the wonderful edition by Birkbeck Hill. Calming effect, as always] (17 August 1951; *LSB II* 281). In this same letter, Beckett told Péron that unpublished documents by Boswell had been found in Malahide Castle near Dublin, and that they were soon to be published by Heinemann as the *London Journal*. Aware of their scandalous nature, Beckett went on to presume that the edition would certainly be 'Edulcoré' [sugar-coated], that is to say edited. It is possible that this letter is misdated, as in fact the volume had by the time of his writing already been published (1950). A 1951 copy of Boswell's *London Journal* survives in Beckett's library and shows reading traces. A postcard is attached to page 49, which speaks of precisely one of the more 'scandalous' and frankly described episodes of Boswell's time in London, when his 'want of women' led him to pick up a prostitute. Beckett returned to reading Boswell's texts in the early 1970s when Ruby Cohn was writing her study of *Human Wishes*,[15] and sent Barbara Bray details on the 'learned divine and mathematician' Lydiat from the *Life* on 27 December 1971 (TCD MS10948/1/504). Moreover, Beckett's edition of Boswell's *Life* contains a scrap of paper dated 18 May 1973, inserted at precisely the point where Johnson's letter to Lord Chesterfield of 7 February 1755 is reproduced.

Beyond Boswell's *Life of Johnson*, Beckett's library also contains several other, more modern biographical studies, including Walter Jackson Bate's 1979 biography (presented by Ruby Cohn that same year) and studies by Robert Lynd (1946), James Clifford (1955) and Christopher Hibbert (1971). Furthermore, there are of course several primary texts by Johnson. The most important of these was undoubtedly the first volume of the Yale Edition of Johnson's work, which contains the *Diaries, Prayers, Annals* (1958). Beckett was familiar with Johnson's autobiographical texts in the 1930s (via Birkbeck Hill's two-volume *Johnsonian Miscellanies*, a 1966 reprint of which survives in the library), as they formed a central focus of his concern with Johnson's various psychological and physical ailments. It is unclear who gave this book to Beckett after its publication in 1958, and when he actually reread it. In a letter to Mary Manning Howe dated 2 January 1959, he stated that he had 'read the Johnson book', which had made it even clearer to him than it had already been that 'my Thrale theory was all haywire', before ruing the 'time I spent on that red herring!' (qtd. in Pilling 1997, 169). It is possible that Beckett was not referring to the Yale edition here, as two months later (26 March 1959; TCD MS10948/1/24) he told Barbara Bray that

> I accept with gratitude the Yale Johnson if it's not too expensive, I find it hard to resist anything to do with that old blusterer, especially his last years.

Indeed, having finally begun to read the book in April 1959 after distractions with 'the mud' (the composition of *How It Is*), and having got 'stuck in Johnson's Welsh journey' (27 May 1959, TCD MS10948/1/34), he could tell Bray on 9 June that he 'finished the Johnson with relish – when I got out of the Welsh hills and into the Aegri Ephemeris'. The reference here is to Johnson's list of ailments, which already in 1937 had fascinated Beckett, as many entries in his *Human Wishes* manuscript notebooks show. A year later, in 1960, Beckett proceeded to read another Johnson book that had been given to him by Bray, Raleigh's edition of *Johnson on Shakespeare*, which collects the various Proposals, Prefaces and Notes.[16] Beckett's continued reading and use of the Yale edition of the *Diaries, Prayers, Annals* is evident from an entry in the 'Super Conquérant' Notebook (UoR MS2934, 1r; qtd. in Van Hulle 2011, 43) – 'Nothing amuses more harmlessly than computation (Johnson, 1782, drying leaves)' – which combines Johnson's drying of leaves in a diary entry for 15 August 1783 with the editorial commentary linking this activity to Johnson's love of mathematics, as outlined in a letter to Sophia Thrale (Johnson 1958, 362).

ROMANTICS

Despite making an exception for its German incarnation, Beckett was rather dismissive of literary Romanticism, so that the lack of books by the great English Romantic writers in the library hardly surprises. Already in his essay *Proust* (1931), Beckett had inveighed against the 'gangrene of Romanticism' (*PTD* 80). In the 'German Diaries', he specified that the 'only kind of romantic still tolerable [was] the bémolisé' [the minor key] (GD, 14 February 1937; qtd. in Knowlson 1996, 254). This attraction to the quiet melancholy, most notably expressed in the German concept of *Schwermut*, explains his love of Keats's poetry, for example, as Keats 'doesn't beat his fists on the table' (letter to MacGreevy, undated [late April or early May 1930]; *LSB* 21). There are two books by Keats in the library, *Selected Letters* (1954) and the bilingual *Poèmes choisis / Selected Poems* (1968), neither of which contain marginalia. Further books from the Romantic period include a nineteenth-century edition (1861?) of Byron's *Poetical Works* and a two-volume edition of Coleridge's *Biographia Literaria* (1958), which he read in 1962 'without much pleasure' (letter to Mary Hutchinson, 11 June 1962) but may well have influenced, as John Pilling (2006a, 160) has suggested, the use of 'Fancy' in *All Strange Away* (begun in August 1964). Finally, there is a copy (probably dating from 1895) of the *Selected Essays of De Quincey*, which bears the inscription 'S.B. Beckett / Trinity College / Dublin / March 1927'. Beckett must have read the first essay in the book, 'On Murder Considered One of the Fine Arts', as he copied a line from it into the 'Dream' Notebook (718).

ENGLISH AUTOBIOGRAPHIES / BIOGRAPHIES

One of the more remarkable features of Beckett's library is the surprisingly large amount of auto-/biographical books in various languages. Leaving aside those life-writing texts discussed elsewhere in this and other chapters, it may be useful to mention here some of the other biographical tomes in the library. What one would call the 'standards' of diaries in English literary history, for example, are all present in the library, beginning with Pepys's diaries in a two-volume Dent edition (1920 [1906]) and Penguin's *The Shorter Pepys: Selection from the Diary of Samuel Pepys* (1987).[17] There are also editions of James Woodforde's *The Diary of a Country Parson 1758–1802* (1967), Kilvert's *Diary* (n.d.) and the diary of the seventeenth-century writer and gardener, John Evelyn (1965 [1963]). Beckett also (curiously) owned a copy of *The Life of Edward Lord Herbert of Cherbury, Written by Himself* (1809). The book contains numerous marginalia, but they do not appear to be in Beckett's hand.

EDWARD THOMAS

Beckett's library contains a copy of the *Selected Poems and Prose* (1981) of Edward Thomas, an Anglo-Welsh poet who was killed in 1917 during the Battle of Arras. The book is rather unusual in that it contains extensive reading notes in the form of ticks and crosses beside the titles of eighteen poems and some of the prose pieces, although it is unclear whether they were made by Beckett. In the extracts from Thomas' book *The South Country*, marginal pen lines are found beside various passages: 'A great writer so uses the words of every day that they become a code of his own which the world is bound to learn and in the end take unto itself. But words are no longer symbols' (68); 'Better a thousand errors so long as they are human than a thousand truths lying like broken snail-shells round the anvil of a thrush' (72); 'He was of middle height and build, the crookedest of men, yet upright, like a branch of oak which comes straight with all its twistings' (75).

IRISH WRITING

As a Protestant institution deriving its traditional outlook from England, Trinity College Dublin's syllabus markedly ignored books by Irish writers (apart from Swift). As a result, Beckett's reading in Irish literature was focused on contemporary writers, and judging by his comments in the 1934 essay 'Recent Irish Poetry', there was little to impress a young author dismissive of the local 'scene' having been introduced to the European tradition and the bohemian avant-garde. One author who Beckett does seem to have read extensively, both in the 1930s and after 1945, was the novelist George Moore. According to Ellmann, Moore influenced the work of James Joyce, and although he is a neglected literary figure today, he is often cited as standing on the threshold between the realism of the nineteenth century and the modernism of the twentieth century. Beckett mentions Moore as early as 1929, and a January 1936 letter to MacGreevy cites Moore's trilogy *Hail and Farewell* (Pilling 2006a, 55). Moreover, Beckett's friend Joe Hone worked on Moore, as did Nancy Cunard, whose biography of Moore Beckett read in 1956. Beckett owned six of Moore's books, although none of them have any marginalia. Beckett's library also contains a 1928 edition of Sean O'Casey's *The Silver Tassie*.

WILDE

The library includes several books on and by Oscar Wilde, mostly dating from the late 1980s. Several of these books were presented to Beckett by Katharine Worth, scholar and theatre practitioner. Beckett is reported to have been reading, amongst other things, Richard Ellmann's biography of Wilde (1987) in the nursing home shortly before his death. The book contains a shaky handwritten correction, as Beckett corrects 'river Erne' (page 4) with the word 'Lough', but then corrects himself.

YEATS

Beckett's response to William Butler Yeats's work was rather ambiguous. His library however contains several books by W. B. Yeats, although all of them came into his possession after 1945 and lack marginalia.[18] Beckett also possessed numerous studies of Yeats's work, predominantly by Richard Ellmann.[19] As a young man, Beckett saw several of Yeats's plays performed in Dublin, although when asked about his early exposure to these plays by James Knowlson, his response was 'Forget which of his plays I saw. More concerned with them as writing than as theatre' (JEK A/1/2/4, 4r). If Beckett kept his distance from Yeats' work as a young man, he was far more generous in his response in later decades. Indeed, he returned to reading Yeats at regular intervals, and quotations from the older writer's work abound in correspondence, manuscripts and texts. Some of this reading can be closely linked to specific books in the library.

Beyond individual volumes of collections, Beckett owned the *The Collected Poems* (1955) and *The Collected Plays* (1960), both published by Macmillan. It is unclear when Beckett acquired the two volumes, but it is telling that he told MacGreevy in January 1961 that he had been reading Yeats's *Collected Poems* as well as the plays with 'intense absorption' (Pilling 2006a, 153). The one play that Beckett clearly admired was *At the Hawk's Well*, in which he thought there was 'so much great poetry'; he suggested adding this play, or one by Ionesco, when George Devine was looking to flesh out an evening with Beckett's theatre (letter to George Devine, 15 December 1956; *LSB II* 683).

In the mid-1970s, Beckett's interest in Yeats' poetry was rekindled after he purchased or was given the bilingual edition *Choix de Poèmes*, published by Aubier-Montaigne in 1975. His rereading of Yeats provoked Beckett to start writing the TV play *. . . but the clouds . . .*, based on the closing lines of Yeats's poem 'The Tower', in October 1976 (Beckett attempted to translate these very lines into French in a letter to Knowlson, 17 April 1977).

SYNGE

As a young man in Dublin, Beckett also attended performances of several plays by J. M. Synge, but Synge's work did not have the same lasting effect on the younger writer as the work of Yeats did. Beckett deemed David H. Greene and Edward M. Stephens's study *J. M. Synge 1871–1909* (1959) to be 'rather dull' but it contained 'a lot of material one did not know about' (letter to Barbara Bray, 29 July 1959; TCD MS10948/1/40). Beckett would in later life frequently recite passages and lines from Synge's work (see for example Atik 2001, 118–19, on Beckett's notation of Synge's 'Epitaph' from memory).

JOYCE

A place of prominence in Beckett's library is, perhaps unsurprisingly, given over to the work of James Joyce. The large number of books by Joyce in the library not only attests to the importance of the older writer for Beckett, but also to the fact that critics and friends often thought of Beckett as being in some sense a successor to Joyce, however radically divergent their poetics. When surveying the range of books on and by Joyce in the library, what is perhaps most striking is the meagre number of first editions. One would expect Beckett to have acquired, or to have received directly from Joyce, copies of his work when the two men were friends in the 1930s. Beckett hints at a reason for this absence in a letter to Jake Schwartz, in which he thanks him for sending a first edition of Joyce's *Pomes Penyeach*, published by Shakespeare & Co. in 1927: 'Many thanks indeed for the beautiful copy of PPE ... My own copy of the original edition was pinched years ago' (23 June 1958). Whether 'pinched', lost or given away, the only first edition of Joyce's work in Beckett's library is a copy of the first UK edition of *Finnegans Wake* (Faber 1939), which carries Joyce's name plate.[20] The other first edition is a copy of Joyce's play *Exiles*, published in 1918. It carries the inscription 'S. B. Beckett' in blue pencil, which suggests that Beckett bought the book as an undergraduate student or at least shortly thereafter, before he dropped the use of his middle name 'Barclay'. The book contains fourteen pencil markings, where Beckett has faintly underlined stage directions that deal with characters' moods, as well as an array of active verbs. It is as if Beckett in particular highlighted the sense of discomfort in the characters, marking for example the fact that Beatrice speaks 'shyly' or reacts 'moodily'. This is also evident in the verbs underlined by Beckett, which range from 'jabbering' and 'stammering' to 'fretting', and the fact that the characters are more than once described as being 'plighted'. Usually seen as a lesser work in Joyce's canon, Beckett in fact thought it interesting, and was keen to discuss its staging when Harold Pinter proposed to do so in 1970. As he told Pinter in a letter dated 21 April 1969, '[y]ou're a brave man to take on Exiles. I understand your excitement. I often wondered how it could be done, that speech overcome and the deep wounding played'.[21] His thoughts on the play were probably inspired by his attendance of a staging of the play in a 'bad' French translation, which had nonetheless affected him (letter to Ruby Cohn, 28 September 1967; UoR MS5100).

Many of the other primary Joyce texts were given to Beckett by friends after the war, in some cases people who knew Joyce and Beckett personally in the 1920s and 1930s. The library thus contains a copy of *Epiphanies*, presented by Jimmy Stern,[22] and the 1960 Bodley Head edition of *Ulysses* (the only copy in the library) given to Beckett by John and Bettina Calder. Joyce's letters, edited by Stuart Gilbert and Richard Ellmann, are also present. Beckett read Stanislaus Joyce's volume *My Brother's Keeper*, which, as he told Leventhal, contained 'interesting material on the early days in Dublin' (letter of 29 February 1958).[23]

Arguably the most striking aspect of the Joyce volumes (apart from *Exiles*) in Beckett's library is the absence of marginalia. But then one could not imagine Beckett annotating Joyce's texts, as he did Pope's, with the word 'Nonsense'. It appears as if Beckett's respect for Joyce's work simply made the idea of annotation impossible. Indeed, the absence of marginalia is in itself of interest in this case, and could profitably be compared to the absence of marginalia in Beckett books once owned by the poet Paul Celan, who otherwise heavily annotated his books.

The range of primary Joyce texts is matched by the large number of critical studies on his work. There are in particular many books and offprints inscribed by Richard Ellmann, Joyce's biographer. Ellmann of course contacted Beckett in the early 1950s, and Beckett's reaction to the meeting and scholars generally is representative of his usual attitude: 'Saw Ellmann, likeable enough, in spite of incessant note-snatching. He sent me his Yeats [*Yeats: The Man and the Masks*], haven't read it, it looks competent and dull' (letter to A. J. Leventhal, 6 August 1953; *LSB II* 396). Beckett was however very interested in Ellmann's biography, which he read in November 1959 and thought a 'good job of work' despite '[m]istakes here and there' and 'needless things' (letter to Aidan Higgins, 7 February 1960). Unfortunately, Beckett's copy of the first edition of Ellmann's biography is no longer in his library, although there are two reprinted copies. The 1965 paperback edition was given to Beckett by Ellmann, presumably because he had lost the first copy. The first part of this paperback appears to be unread, but the spine is clearly broken on pages 624 and 690, both of which deal with Lucia Joyce (Beckett's partial love interest in the 1930s and with whom he stayed in touch until her death). Other critical studies beyond Ellmann include books by Frank Budgen and a copy of Jacques Derrida's *Ulysse gramophone: Deux mots pour Joyce*, inscribed 'pour Samuel Beckett' in February 1987. There are also several books by Hugh Kenner, who became a friend of Beckett's. On reading Kenner's *Dublin's Joyce*, his response to such critical exegesis was once again clear, declaring the book to be 'very brilliant and erudite but dementedly over-explicative ... though admittedly Joyce invites such herrdoktoring as much as any writer ever' (letter to Mary Manning Howe, 13 August 1958; qtd. in Knowlson 1996, 454).[24] In a further letter, to Niall Montgomery, Beckett referred to it all as 'Joyceology' (29 December 1950; *LSB II* 209).

A final note on Joyce: on page 195 of Beckett's edition of *Finnegans Wake*, an offprint containing a Portuguese excerpt of Joyce's novel, presented by Francis Warner in 1968, has been inserted.[25] The page in question is the last page of chapter 14, which ends with a reference to Anna Livia Plurabelle, 'babbling, bubbling, chattering to herself, deloothering the fields on their elbows leaning with the sloothering slide of her, giddygaddy, grannyma, gossipaceous Anna Livia'. This is followed by: 'He lifts the lifewand and the dumb speak. – Quoiquoiquoiquoiquoiquoiquoiq!'

It is possible that this is pure coincidence, but if Beckett consciously inserted this offprint between these pages, the passage suggests that this scene in *Finnegans Wake* is referred to in Lucky's long soliloquy in *Waiting for Godot*:

LUCKY: Given the existence as uttered forth in the public works of Puncher and Wattmann of a personal God quaquaquaqua with white beard quaquaquaqua outside time without extension who from the heights of divine apathia divine athambia divine aphasia loves us dearly with some exceptions for reasons unknown (*CDW* 42)[26]

MACGREEVY

Among the many books written and presented by friends of Beckett's, the most interesting and important are those written by Beckett's closest friend and confidant in the 1930s, Thomas MacGreevy. Copies of MacGreevy's studies for Chatto & Windus's Dolphin Series, on Richard Aldington and T. S. Eliot, survive in the library, the latter inscribed with the date 22 January 1931. But the most interesting item is the copy of MacGreevy's *Poems*, given to Beckett by the author in May 1934. The book contains a number of annotations and marginalia, undoubtedly made when Beckett was writing a review of the volume entitled 'Humanistic Quietism', published in the July–September 1934 issue of *The Dublin Magazine*. Those poems that Beckett mentions in this review are marked in red pen in the volume, as are most of the passages he quotes, such as the last line of the poem 'Nocturne of the Self-Evident Presence', 'In a dry, high silence'. Moreover, the parameters against which the poems are to be measured are noted in the book, with the word 'Eliot' appearing beside the poem 'Crón Tráth na nDéithe', no doubt as the poem is self-consciously influenced by *The Waste Land*. Beckett also marks the repeated instances in which the word 'light' is used, and states this quality as being the fundamental characteristic of MacGreevy's poetry, the 'self-absorption into light'.

MODERNIST WRITERS...

... are absent in the library; no T. S. Eliot or Ezra Pound, for example, although it is well known that Beckett was reserved in his evaluation of both these writers. From this literary period, only Henry James's *The Turn of the Screw; The Aspen Papers and Other Stories* (1961) and a bilingual edition of D. H. Lawrence's *Poèmes* (1976) are extant.

Beckett's library does contain several books by friends, such as a copy of Nancy Cunard's *Parallax*, inscribed and presented in 1930. As Beckett told MacGreevy that same year, he felt that the book had fine passages, in particular the image of 'grey gulls / Nailed to the wind above a distorted tide' (*LSB* 25). After the war, Beckett remembered the phrase (not marked in his copy) in a letter to Cunard, but could not find his copy:

I want to read your Parallax again and the Battersea or thereabouts gulls skewered to the wind, but can't find it on my shelves. If you have a spare copy send it along sometime. (7 November 1956; *LSB II* 670)

Surprisingly, the library contains no extant copies of work by other acquaintances or friends from the 1930s, although there are books presented after the war by Kay Boyle, Denis Devlin, Arland Ussher, A. J. Leventhal and Brian Coffey. And then there are books by many new friends and fellow writers, many of them Irish, such as Desmond Egan, Derek Mahon, John Montague and Aidan Higgins.

PINTER

The library also includes an extensive collection of books, typescripts and drafts of Harold Pinter, whose work shows signs of being influenced by Beckett. Contact between the two writers was established by Barbara Bray, an early champion of Pinter's work at the BBC. Responding to her descriptions of Pinter's work, Beckett told her on 4 February 1960 that 'I shd [should] like some time to read a play by Pinter' (TCD MS10948/1/69). Initially sending *The Caretaker*, Pinter would subsequently inscribe and present copies of his work to Beckett up until the older writer's death in 1989. As tends to be the case with books stemming from the post-1945 period, Beckett did not annotate copies of Pinter's work, but their presence in his library attests to a close friendship between the two writers.

AMERICAN LITERATURE

Beckett's knowledge of American literature in the 1930s was rather sketchy. He bought Melville's *Moby-Dick* on 4 August 1932 in Foyles' in London, and enjoyed reading the book; as he told MacGreevy the same day he bought the book, 'that's more like the real stuff. White whales & natural piety' (*LSB* III).[27]

Beckett was generally open to new writing and younger writers after the war, and in particular began, no doubt under the guidance of friends across the Atlantic, to read contemporary post-war American fiction. Already in 1953 he told Pamela Mitchell that he had read 'a very good novel by a young American J. D. Salinger, The Catcher in the Rye ... best thing I've read for years' (25 November 1953; *LSB II* 421).[28] He also thought Vonnegut's *Slaughterhouse 5* to be a 'remarkable book' (letter to Barbara Bray, 18 September 1972; TCD MS10948/1/523). While neither Salinger's book nor *Slaughterhouse 5* are in the library, it does contain other contemporary American novels such as Malcolm Lowry's *Under the Volcano* (1963), Saul Bellow's *Dangling Man* (1963) and Paul Auster's *Wall Writing* (1976).

CHAPTER 3

Literature in French

When Beckett taught French literature at Trinity College Dublin, he deliberately mixed periods, juxtaposing for instance Racine and Gide. Evidently he was only able to apply this unconventional non-chronological method because he had a clear idea of the history of French literature. One of his guidelines as a student had been C. H. M. Des Granges's *Histoire illustrée de littérature française* (1920 [1910]). His copy is still preserved in his library. This was only a first stepping stone for Beckett as a student, who would soon be perfectly capable of finding his own paths in French literature. To study the books on French literature in Beckett's library, it may be useful to follow Beckett's example: start with the canon as it was presented to students in the 1920s and leave it when necessary – for Des Granges' canon shows a few remarkable omissions: the Marquis de Sade, for instance, and Arthur Rimbaud.

VILLON

The earliest period of French literature represented in Beckett's library is the fifteenth century, with the *Poésies complètes* by François Villon (1431–80). Although Beckett may have been introduced to Villon at TCD, he seems to have discovered him on his own, in the 1930s. Only one poem in the 1931 edition is marked (with a cross pencilled next to the title): 'Ballade Villon', opening with the line 'Je meurs de seuf auprès de la fontaine'. The first line of the second stanza could serve as a motto of the playwright who later claimed that the key word in his plays was 'perhaps': 'Rien ne m'est seur que la chose incertaine' (149).

RABELAIS

Rabelais marked the early sixteenth century in French literature. Beckett owned a 1968 pocket edition of *La vie très honorifique du grand Gargantua*, but he had already read Rabelais quite intensively in the 1930s. On 25 July 1935 he wrote in a letter to Thomas MacGreevy (on stationery of the Glen Lyn Hotel in Lynmouth, Devon) that he had 'bought a complete Génie de France Rabelais before setting out' (TCD MS10402/76). A month later (31 August 1935), he mentioned to MacGreevy that a 'sign, by which [Pantagruel] knew he was getting old, was that he could not put up with inferior wine as well as he used' (TCD MS10402/78). And on 22 September he told his friend that he 'got stuck in the Rabelais again, on the voyage round the world to consult the oracle of the Bottle' (*LSB* 278). Beckett's notes on Rabelais (TCD MS10969) do not cover books IV and V (Frost and Maxwell 2006, 96–7, 102), but they do extend to Book III, in which Pantagruel and Panurge (chapter XLVII) consider consulting 'l'oracle de la Divine Bouteille'.

LABÉ

Beckett's copies of works by three important sixteenth-century French authors are still extant: Maurice Scève, Louise Labé and Michel de Montaigne. He also had a copy of Maurice Allem's *Anthologie poétique française du XVIe siècle* (second volume). The *Élégies et sonnets de Louize Labé, Lionnoize* (1958), bearing the inscription 'Pour Sam – 13 avril 1959', was a birthday present. Although Beckett parodied his teacher Rudmose-Brown's recommendation of Labé's 'imperishable verse' in *Dream of Fair to Middling Women* ('a great poet, a great poet, perhaps one of the greatest of all time, of physical passion, of passion purely and exclusively physical'; *Dream* 165), he – in his turn – recommended Labé to Anne Atik (Atik 2001, 49). The Labé is not marked, but Beckett quoted the last stanza of 'Sonnet III' at the bottom of his manuscript notes for his 'Film Vidéo-Cassette projet' (UoR MS2928, 14r):

> Car je suis tant navrée en toutes parts
> que plus en moi une nouvelle plaie
> pour m'empirer ne pourrait trouver place.
>
> (qtd. in Nixon 2009, 41)

MONTAIGNE

Beckett seems to have purchased his Pléiade edition of Montaigne's *Essais* (ed. Albert Thibaudet, 1958 [1950]) when he could afford it, several decades after he had first familiarized himself with Montaigne's work.[1] Although many of these acquisitions of the late 1950s and 1960s are not marked, they do often indicate a special affinity. One of the essays Beckett read without a doubt is 'De la tristesse' (the second essay in Book I), in which Montaigne quotes – among other things – a few lines from Petrarch and Seneca, jotted down by Beckett in the 'Whoroscope' and 'Super Conquérant' Notebooks (see Chapter 5).

SCÈVE

Beckett's copy of Maurice Scève's *DELIE, object de plus haulte vertu* (1916) is a different type of book. This edition of the collection of love poems modelled after Petrarch's *Canzoniere* dates from Beckett's student days at Trinity College, Dublin. He later gave the book to Avigdor Arikha and Anne Atik. It is a copy of the critical edition by Eugène Parturier, published by Hachette, including the fifty emblems that divide the 449 ten-line poems or '*dizains*' in groups of nine, preceded by a '*huitain*' dedicated to his mistress, 'A sa Délie'. The pencil marks and underlined passages in Parturier's introduction indicate not only Beckett's customary interest in an author's biography and other contextual information, but also a particular focus on references to Petrarch and Dante. Thomas Hunkeler notes that in the early reception of his poetry, Scève was often related to Dante (rather than Petrarch) because of his poems' complexity and sometimes obscure nature. Parturier was one of the notable editors who pointed out that this link with Dante is not a systematic characteristic (Hunkeler 2008).[2] Scève's poetry may be difficult, but this is part of a fashion in the sixteenth century to complicate the expression of one's ideas and feelings, as the introduction explains. The passage is underlined and marked with three vertical lines in the left margin (xxvi). The only other instance that is marked with a triple line emphasizes the same 'complication', a Petrarchism that is complicated by means of diverse poetic elements of varied provenance (xx).

The annotations in pencil often indicate motifs or intertextual references, such as the addition 'Délie as a huntress' (relating to *dizain* V, page 8) or the note 'Inspired by Lemaire de Belges' preceding *dizain* CCXLVII, referring to the beauty of 'les Papegaulx', 'PARROTS' (black ink). As the footnote by the editor suggests, this *dizain* is inspired by the first *Epistre de l'Amant verd*, Jean Lemaire's parody of the Ovidian farewell love letter. In this first of two rhymed letters, written when Lemaire resided at the court of Margaret of Austria, the poet's persona is a green parrot, the 'Amant Vert'.

Apart from the pencil marks, the introduction also contains an underlining in black ink ('alambiqué', xxi) and the translation 'SUBTLE' in the right margin. Several of the *dizains* are marked with 'N.B.', either in black ink or pencil, or both. For instance, *dizain* IX, marked with a black ink 'N.B.', is annotated in pencil: 'Example of his extreme preciosity'. In general, the pencil annotations express greater maturity than the notes in black ink, indicating translations of individual words or factual, contextual information such as 'RHONE & SAONE MEET AT LYONS [SIC] WHICH IS BUILT ON TWO HILLS' (*dizain* XVII, page 17). Dizain XXVI is also marked (in pencil) as a 'Good ex[ample] of preciosity'; its last line ('Las tousjours j'ars, & point ne me consume') is underscored and accompanied by a note in black ink: 'WHEN SCÈVE ACHIEVES A FINE LINE IT IS AN EXCEEDINGLY FINE ONE, AS HERE' (page 24).

Translation sometimes appears to have been a way for Beckett to fully appreciate an underscored passage, such as the lines 'Soucys, qui point ne sont a la mort telz, / Que ceulx, que tient ma pensée profonde' – which is partially translated (black ink) in the left margin as 'Cares, such that death has not any like those, which' (*dizain* CXI; page 82). In CXCVII, the line 'Mes yeulx pleurantz employment leur deffence' is translated (black ink) in the left margin as 'MY EYES DEFEND THEMSELVES BY WEEPING' (140). The analysis of the poems is often linguistic in nature, marking for instance the word 'hayantz' in *dizain* CCCXCI as a participle, 'p.p. of haïr' (267); or in *dizain* CXLVIII, where the word 'tous' is underlined in 'Aux champs tous nudz', with the marginal comment (black ink) that it was 'Always declined in 16th cent'. (page 110). The adjective 'seurs' in 'Te practiquant par seurs, & gandz batteaulx' (CCVIII) is marked (black ink) as an 'Adj. agreeing with 'batteaulx'' (146). The rhyme 'terrestres' / 'lettres' toward the end of CCLII is marked (black ink) because it 'PROVES THAT S WAS NOT PRO-NOUNCED BEFORE A CONSONANT' (175).

Some of the annotations in black ink are more scholarly. The last word of *dizain* CCCXVIII, 'Nice', is marked because it 'ENABLES US TO DATE IT'; it refers to the armistice of Nice in 1538, as the footnote indicates. The name 'Marguerite', referred to at the end of *dizain* CCLIV, is identified (in black ink) as 'M. de Navarre'. As Beckett notes, the sister of king François I and grandmother of Henri IV was 'Probably the most famous personage of 16th century. Whole Renaissance sprang from her – Author of Heptameron – many other poems' (176). In some cases, such as CCCXXXI, the complexity of the poem is such that it seems a hopeless task to annotate it, to the extent that the marginalia simply reads 'VERY COMPICATED [sic]' (226). The expression 'ma vie mourante' in CCCVII is marked (black ink) as the 'FIRST EXAMPLE OF THIS EXP. WHICH BECAME VERY POPULAR cp. Corneille's Cid' (210).

CORNEILLE

The reference to Corneille broaches a new chapter in French literary history: the seventeenth century. Beckett's attitude toward Corneille's *Cid* is captured in the change of one letter, the capital K of *Le Kid*. Beckett and Pelorson's 'parody' (Le Juez 2007, 93), which was mostly Pelorson's work (Knowlson 1996, 123), was presented at the Dublin Peacock Theatre in 1931. But as Linda Hutcheon notes, 'parody is doubly coded in political terms: it both legitimizes and subverts that which it parodies' (Hutcheon 1989, 101). Parody involves both ironizing and installing (93). Evidently, Beckett was only able to write this parody because he was intimately familiar with Corneille's work, as the traces in his books confirm. Beckett's books (see JEK A/1/4/3) include two works by Corneille: *Le Menteur* (Paris: Librairie Hachette, 1913) and *Nicomède* (Paris: Librairie Hachette, 1921). Beckett read them during the Michaelmas Term 1923, as the inscriptions indicate. The marginalia (especially in *Le Menteur*) are mainly vocabulary. For instance, the word 'badauds' (Act I, Scene 1, line 76, page 65) is translated as 'Ninnies' in the right margin. In *Nicomède*, Beckett's intellectual investment was clearly greater than that of a mere student. Next to the underscored line 219 (Act I, Scene 2: 'Sachez qu'il n'en est point que le ciel n'ait fait naître', page 76), Beckett noted: 'One of C's horribly involved lines'. While the English marginalia may indicate a certain critical distance, another set of marginalia in French suggests that Beckett's dislike of Corneille cannot be generalized. The artist as a young reader did like certain passages and was not afraid of showing his appreciation: 'Quels beaux vers!' (83).[3]

At the end of his life, Beckett told James Knowlson (interview 5 July 1989) that not only his deep love for Racine's plays, but also his antipathy to Corneille's work was inspired by Thomas B. Rudmose-Brown (Knowlson 1996, 49). Apart from being Beckett's professor of Romance Languages at TCD, Rudmose-Brown was an editor of Corneille. Beckett purchased Rudmose-Brown's edition of *La Galerie du palais* (1920) for the Michaelmas Term 1923. Some of the translations of vocabulary (e.g. page 8, 'collets d'ouvrage', 'HAND-WORKED') are in block letters (black ink), like most of the black ink annotations in the Scève. In Act III, Scene 12 (with Dorimant, Florice and Cléante), Beckett has underscored Florice's line 'Et tous autres devoirs lui donnent de l'ennui', and added in the bottom margin: 'And yet this remarkable lady addressed the darling of her heart thus: "Je pense mieux valoir que le refus d'un autre"; and thus: "Epargnez avec moi ces propos affétés." Is this typical feminine inconsistency or bad writing?' (page 52). In the fourth act (line 1140) he reiterates his dislike of a female character: 'What a thoroughly unpleasant young woman is Célidée!' (bottom margin of page 57). Yet, sixteen pages further, an interesting underscoring, marking Célidée's contradictory emotions,[4] does seem to indicate a certain appreciation of the character's complexity. Again, some of the annotations are remarkably scholarly for a 17-year-old student.⁵ Beckett's attention seems to have been attracted mainly by formal matters, such as the 'Rime Normande' in lines 1491–2 ('cher' / 'fâcher') – 'Corneille did not pronounce the r in either word' (75) – or the 'Rime [M]asconne or Périgourdine' in lines 1587–88 ('meur' / 'humeur'), which 'May be pronounced mur, humur, or as written' (79).

RACINE

In Beckett's course on French literature at Trinity College, Dublin (1930–1), Corneille mainly served as a counterexample, a contrastive background to highlight Racine's modernity. As Brigitte Le Juez has shown on the basis of the student notes, Beckett employed Corneille to talk about French drama in a similar way as he used Balzac with regard to prose: 'Corneille/Balzac abdicate as critics vs Racine', Rachel Burrows wrote in her notes on Beckett's course (48; Le Juez 2008, 55). In the notes of one of Beckett's other students, Leslie Daiken, the first parenthesis in Beckett's analysis of Racine's *Andromaque* opens with a bold statement: 'There are no authentic women characters in Corneille' (UoR Daiken notes, 5r). Against this backdrop, Andromaque's psychology appears all the more complex: 'Andromaque is faced with a multiplicity of conflicting demands' (8r). To shed light on all the facets of her consciousness, Racine employs confidants: 'The function of the confidants is to express a fragment in the mind of the protagonist' (8r). The other students in Beckett's class similarly noted that Racine's dialogues are actually monologues. The confidants merely serve as sounding boards to reveal the protagonists' divided consciousness (Burrows 65; Le Juez 2008, 59). Grace McKinley may not have clearly heard or fully understood what Beckett had to say about this internal conflict. 'Division' became 'the vision' in her notes: 'Pylade etc. are the fragments of the divided minds of Orestes etc. Their function is to express the vision in the minds of their protagonists' (qtd. in Knowlson and Knowlson 2006, 308).

One of the books Beckett must have used to prepare his classes is François Mauriac's *La Vie de Jean Racine* (1928). The book is still preserved in the library and contains several pencil marks, such as the marginal line alongside Mauriac's emphasis on Racine's Jansenism (198). Daiken's notes are not as extensive as Burrows', but he did note Beckett's criticism of Mauriac:

> Mauriac explains Racine as a dark Jansenist, tortured and "inquié" [sic]. Nothing of the kind! Racine was self-consciously an artist: terribly conscious of his being so: living amongst values which are, besides basic-values, also face values: not among mysteries. In such a society the artist can be self-conscious without being skeptical. (UoR Daiken notes, 8r)

Mauriac discusses Racine's Jansenism and he compares him to 'un autre grand janséniste', Pascal (Mauriac 1928, 198), but he also draws attention to a more complex attitude toward religion (in a passage that is marked with a pencil line in Beckett's copy).[6] The idea of Racine's modernity, which is so prominent in Beckett's lectures, may have been inspired to some extent by Mauriac, albeit indirectly. According to Mauriac, one would expect an artist's increasing Angst to enhance his creativity. That was not the case with Racine, who stopped writing in a period of crisis, when other writers would be eager to rid themselves of their psychological burden by means of literary work. Mauriac acknowledges that this is a 'modern' perspective (142). A small pencil cross marks the beginning of the paragraph in which Mauriac develops that 'modern' viewpoint. Although this is still a far cry from Beckett's treatment of Racine as a protomodernist, comparable to Gide, it is not inconceivable that Mauriac's introduction of the 'modern' in this Racinian context may have been a source of inspiration for the young lecturer.

Racine's modernity becomes evident in the explicit demonstration of complexity (Le Juez 2007, 104). Unlike Corneille, Racine does not focus on social and political matters, but on the mind (Le Juez 2007, 101). His characters try in vain to penetrate each other's minds. The resulting lack of communication (110) as a characteristic of modernity is thematized by Beckett in his essay *Proust*: 'There is no communication because there are no vehicles of communication' (Beckett 1965, 64). *Phèdre* is mentioned in Beckett's *Proust* (1965, 59). The example he gave his students in 1930–1 – the scene in *Phèdre* of Hermione's protest after Pyrrhus's suggestion that perhaps she did not really love him – found an echo in one of the early versions of *Come and Go*: two women (Viola and Rose) are listening to a third one (Poppy) reading a dime novel, whose female protagonist is called Hermione. Whether the scene is taken from an existing novel or an invention by Beckett, the name Hermione is used to illustrate a lack of communication by means of a kind of linguistic slapstick:

POPPY Chapter seven. "Her my own rose at last –"
ROSE (wearily). Hermione.
POPPY "Hermione rose at last from the steaming sweet-smelling foam and stood all pink and dripping before the great cheval-glass, inspecting her luscious forms." (UoR MS1227/7/16/5, 1r; qtd. in Laubach-Kiani 2004, 180)

The character of Hermione in *Phèdre* was part of Beckett's demonstration of how to write a paper, the topic being Orestes's complexity, the inaccessibility of the mind and Racine's psychological modernity (Le Juez 2007, 116).

In Beckett's copy of the *Théâtre complet de J. Racine* (Paris: Garnier, n.d.), preserved at the University of Reading, only two lines are marked. Next to Oenone's line 'Juste ciel ! tout mon sang dans mes veines se glace!' (*Phèdre*, Act I, scene 3, page 569), the marginalia 'Voir page 628' refers to Esther's identical line 'Juste ciel ! tout mon sang dans mes veines se glace!' (*Esther*, Act I, scene 3), where the marginalia refers back to *Phèdre*: 'Voir page 569'.

Beckett reread Racine in 1956. Vivian Mercier and James Knowlson suggest that this rereading may have 'focussed his mind on the theatrical possibilities of monologue and of what could be done with virtually immobile characters inhabiting a closed world in which little or nothing changes' (Knowlson 1996, 426). These possibilities were fully explored in *Happy Days*, notably the technique of the monologue in the guise of a dialogue:

WINNIE: [*Same voice.*] Fear no more the heat o' the sun. [*Pause.*] Did you hear that?
WILLIE: [*Irritated.*] Yes.
WINNIE: [*Same voice.*] What? [*Pause.*] What?
WILLIE: [More *irritated.*] Fear no more. [*Pause.*]
WINNIE: [*Same voice.*] No more what? [*Pause.*] Fear no more what?
WILLIE: [*Violently.*] Fear no more! (*CDW* 148)

In Beckett's French version *Oh les beaux jours*, the intertextual reference to Shakespeare's *Cymbeline* is replaced by an allusion to the choir's line in Racine's *Athalie*: 'Qu'ils pleurent, ô mon Dieu ! qu'ils frémissent de crainte' (*Athalie*, II, 9; see Beckett 2001, 32). The context is quite different from the dirge in *Cymbeline*. The choir in Athalie follows after a *carpe diem*-like intervention by 'Une autre', critically voicing the bon vivants' opinion that one should enjoy life as long as it lasts. To which the choir replies that they'd better start crying in fear and trembling.

As to the reason why Beckett chose *Athalie* to replace *Cymbeline*, perhaps a mark in François Mauriac's *La vie de Jean Racine* points in the direction of an answer. A little cross is pencilled in the margin next to: 'Mais à relire de près ce drame terrible [*Athalie*], il apparaît nettement que Racine a voulu que la vieille reine eût de la grandeur' (Mauriac 1928, 194). Athalie's 'grandeur' is as grand as Joad's, Mauriac continues, but the difference is that Joad sides with the Almighty, whereas Athalie is alone.[7] Winnie's situation, as commented on by Beckett during the rehearsal period of *Happy Days*, could be interpreted in similar terms of this particular kind of 'grandeur': after picturing 'the most dreadful thing that could happen to anybody', Beckett told Brenda Bruce: 'who would cope with that and go down singing, only a woman' (Knowlson 1996, 501).

MOLIÈRE

Racine soon became a benchmark against which Beckett measured other French writers, such as Molière. One of the first marginalia in the five-volume *Théâtre complet de Molière* (with the inscription 'S. B. Beckett / July 1926') is the reference 'cp. Racine's Phèdre' (black ink) next to an underscored line in *La Princesse d'Élide*,[8] the play to which Beckett later referred in 'La Peinture des van Velde ou le Monde et le Pantalon': 'La prose de la *Princess[e] d'Elide* serait-elle aussi belle, s'il n'y avait pas les vers?' (*Dis* 122). Beckett's spontaneous impression was one of admiration, as the exclamation on the next page suggests: 'What a line!'[9] In the same black ink as these marginalia, Beckett has added lexical information and underlined phrases for grammatical reasons, such as the words 'de qui' (234).[10] On a scrap of paper inserted in the fourth volume, Beckett elaborated on this grammatical question: 'When does one use / de qui + when dont / voir "La Princesse d'Elide" / Page 234'. On the same piece of paper he added: 'Meaning of / je suis au poil et à la plume / voir La C.d'E. Page 148', referring to an underscored line in *La Comtesse d'Escarbagnas* in the fifth volume.[11]

Apart from these marginalia and notes in black ink, other marks in pencil and in blue ink give evidence of other readings. The pencil note 'Don Garcie 1660' is added to the title of *Les Fourberies de Scapin* (volume 5) and the 'wit of Molière' is pencilled next to an underscored line in *La Princesse d'Élide*.[12] In *Tartuffe*, Corneille explicitly serves as contrastive background. Mariane tells the maid Dorine that she ardently loves Valère and refuses to marry Tartuffe, the match her father Orgon tries to push. Dorine asks her what she intends to do and Mariane replies that she'd rather kill herself than be forced into this marriage. Next to Dorine's subsequent reaction,[13] Beckett has written 'ANTI-CORNELIANISM' in the left margin (volume II, page 268). *Tartuffe* is annotated in blue ink, starting with six marked lines spoken by Cléante,[14] which are regarded as an 'ARTICLE OF FAITH FOR M.[olière]' (II.257). Cléante's subsequent claim that devotion is only human and treatable is seen as an indication that 'M. SYMPATHIZES WITH TRUE RELIGION' (II.258).[15] This remarkable identification of character and author is even more striking when 'L'exempt' starts singing the prince's praise,[16] which first evokes the double marginal exclamation '!! Who's a hypocrite?' (II.314), after which the character is again identified with the author: 'Molière the lickspittle' (II.315).

Beckett also had a copy of Georges Lafenestre's *Molière* (1909). This is one of the few instances in Beckett's books where the text is physically mutilated. On pages 34, 35 and 36, Lafenestre discusses the open-air summer performances of what he refers to as '*le Cocu*' [*Sganarelle ou le Cocu imaginaire*]. Each time '*le Cocu*' occurs,[17] the ink of '*Cocu*' is scraped away and 'Trompé' is pencilled in the margin or above the line, probably referring to the alternative title 'Sganarelle, ou le mari qui se croit trompé'.[18] The only other mark is the double underlining of the typo 'habilité', which is corrected into 'habileté' in pencil (100).

The three great seventeenth-century playwrights Corneille, Molière and Racine are taken as examples in a remarkable book by Ludovic Lalanne, *Curiosités littéraires* (1857). In Beckett's copy, a shopping list is inserted between pages 126 and 127. Whether the location of the insertion is significant or just a coincidence is hard to determine with certainty, but the first paragraphs on page 126 strike us as surprisingly 'Barthesian' *avant la lettre*. According to Lalanne great literary creations are like any other kind of invention: whoever is destined to attach his name to it cannot extricate himself from the powerful links that tie him not only to his own age, but also to preceding ages (Lalanne 1857, 126). Thus, Corneille is linked to Pierre de Laudun, Molière to Dorimon, and Racine to Matthieu, May and the jesuits of Clermont. But this does not reduce the value of the masterpieces by Corneille, Molière and Racine, according to Lalanne, who – in 1857 – foreshadowed Roland Barthes' famous definition of 'the text [as] a tissue of quotations drawn from the innumerable centres of culture' more than a hundred years before 'The Death of the Author' was published.

LA FONTAINE

Jean de la Fontaine's *Fables* (1921), inscribed by 'S. B. Beckett / Trinity College, Dublin / 1924', is heavily annotated (see UoR JEK A/1/4/3). The annotations mainly concern vocabulary, with rather basic translations added for instance to the title of fable IX in Book nine: 'IX. L'huitre [oyster] et les plaideurs [pleaders]' (288).[19] Apart from notes on vocabulary, some lines do seem to be marked for content[20] and the titles of several fables are marked with an X.[21] The students apparently had to memorize parts of some fables, as the marginalia 'Learn by heart' indicates (next to Book 10, fable I, 'Les deux rats, le renard et l'oeuf'; 305). Later, as a writer, Beckett alluded to La Fontaine early in *Dream of Fair to Middling Women* (9; see Pilling 2004, 33).

The absence of some authors that mark the transition from seventeenth- to eighteenth-century French literature, such as Bernard de Fontenelle, is appropriate and illustrative of the way Beckett's web of intertextuality functions. Molière's motto 'Je prends mon bien où je le trouve' ('I take what I need where I find it') was one of Beckett's favourite citations in his Kassel days

Literature in French 53

(Pilling 2004, 311) and one of the greatest illustrations of this motto in his writings is the reference to Fontenelle's *Entretiens sur la pluralité des mondes*. His note 'Fontenelles [sic] rose that said no gardener had died within the memory of roses' (*DN* 581) does not derive from Fontenelle but from Diderot's *Le Rêve de d'Alembert*.[22] Beckett used it in *Dream of Fair to Middling Women* (175)[23] and in the story 'Echo's Bones': 'He brought up duly the words of the rose to the rose: "No gardener has died, within rosaceous memory."'[24] He subsequently quoted himself in 'Draff', rewriting the borrowing and presenting it as a dictation with explicit emphasis on the punctuation: 'No gardener has died, comma, within rosaceous memory' (*MPTK* 181). Apart from *Le Rêve de d'Alembert* and *Jacques le fataliste*, Beckett also read *Le Neveu de Rameau* by the same author (*DN* 964). In 1962, he recommended the work to Barbara Bray: 'For no apparent reason took up Le Neveu de Rameau. "Mes pensées sont mes catins. [My thoughts are my whores.]" Luvvily work if you can get it' (TCD MS10948/1/176). But neither Fontenelle nor Diderot is present in Beckett's library, which indicates the relativity of the material traces of his reading: what is still present is evidently useful, as long as it does not blind us to the numerous intertexts that have left no trace.

VOLTAIRE, ROUSSEAU

The eighteenth century is relatively ill-represented in the surviving library. Voltaire is marginally present in – of all places – the Bible. In his Italian *Sacra Bibbia* Beckett has written several French translations of 'dirty' lines in the Old Testament, which correspond to the footnotes in one of Voltaire's *Lettres d'Amabed* (see Chapter 8). Apart from this indirect presence, the only trace in the 1969 dedication copy of *Voltaire* by Theodore Bestermann (inscribed 'for Samuel Beckett / Th. B.') is a piece of paper inserted at the beginning of the chapter on 'The Maiden of Orleans', Voltaire's satirical poem on Joan of Arc (374), published in 1755, the year of the Lisbon earthquake.

The physical quake also had serious spiritual aftershocks among the European intelligentsia. While Voltaire accused providence and mocked optimism, Jean-Jacques Rousseau objected to this attitude in a letter, quoted in M. A. Chuquet's *J.-J. Rousseau* (1893), preserved in Beckett's library.[25] In the wake of this disagreement, Voltaire eventually called Rousseau 'fou et archifou, coquin, fanatique, débitant d'orviétan, bâtard de Diogène, bâtard du chien de Diogène et de la chienne d'Erostrate' (Chuquet 1893, 54; pencil line, left margin) – a list worthy of prefiguring the flood of abuse in *Waiting for Godot*. The only other mark in Chuquet's book (apart from a list of

Rousseau's works, pencilled on the back cover) is the underlined adjective 'maussades' (sulky, grouchy; 129) in the chapter on Rousseau's *Émile, ou de l'éducation*. In a letter to Thomas MacGreevy (16 September 1934), Beckett spent a whole paragraph on Rousseau, suggesting that, although he had not read *Le Contrat social*, he thought *Émile* at least was 'an attempt to resolve the dichotomy' between the right to be alone and the condition of being denied enjoyment of this right, 'not only by a society that considered solitude as a vice ... but by the infantile aspect, afraid of the dark, of his own constitution' (*LSB* 228).

Rousseau's name is mentioned specifically in the story 'Fingal', where he seems to exemplify the 'démon d'analogie' by means of which the Romantics, according to Beckett, tried to turn the complexity of reality into a 'patient fabricated order' (Rachel Burrows lecture notes, TCD MIC60, 9). In 'Fingal', Belacqua replies to Winnie's 'What ails you?': 'I must be getting old and tired ... when I find the nature outside me compensating for the nature inside me, like Jean-Jacques sprawling in a bed of saxifrages' (*MPTK* 22).

BEAUMARCHAIS

A noteworthy sample of eighteenth-century French drama in Beckett's library is the *Théâtre choisi* by Beaumarchais in the series *Les Lettres et la vie française* (1941), with an introduction and annotations by Alfred Péron. Inscriptions do not need to be elaborate to be moving, as this one exemplifies: 'A Sam, / Paris 27 janvier 1942'; the barely legible signature is most likely Alfred Péron's. The book must have been one of the last presents Beckett received from his friend, before Péron was arrested by the Gestapo on 16 August 1942 and died tragically in May 1945 (Knowlson 1996, 314, 342). The introduction does not show any marginalia, but the endnotes relating to *Le Barbier de Séville* have apparently been read rather critically. Note 8 explains that a sentence in Act I, scene 2 ('Accueilli dans une ville, emprisonné dans l'autre') was added in 1775 in the five-act version and preserved in the 'texte définitif'. The word 'ajouté' (added) is marked in pencil and the note in the left margin expresses strong disagreement: 'Non!' (382). Two pages further, note 12 indicates that the reading text is the 'texte définitif' and that the portraits of Bartholo and Rosine were originally somewhat longer. They were shortened by Beaumarchais after the première. Péron then presents the text of the longer version, which he calls 'la version première'. The word 'première' is marked and a question mark is pencilled in the left margin, for the text of the première was not necessarily the first version; most probably it was preceded by several drafts. If we may assume that the question mark is

Beckett's, he appears to have been extremely well aware of, and sensitive to, textual matters pertaining to both the *avant-texte* and the *après-texte*.

CHAMFORT

The most explicit example of the way the library functioned as a hinge between eighteenth-century French literature and Beckett's works is the page of the 'faux titre' of Chamfort's *Maximes et anecdotes* (1950 [1944]), on which Beckett has written the page numbers of the maxims he was interested in (21, 25, 28, 31, 35, 39, 42). On the corresponding pages, the maxims are marked with a vertical marginal line in black ink. On page 35, two maxims are marked, only one of which was eventually selected for publication.[26]

The second marked passage on page 35 is the only maxim Beckett eventually decided not to include in his selection 'Long after Chamfort', adding a 'Pensée' by Pascal instead. He also rearranged the order of the maxims (25, 28, 39, 42, 21, 31, 35). This order was tried out in a letter Beckett sent to Barbara Bray on 2 November 1973 (TCD MS10948/1/547). By that time he had already been sending some of the maxims separately to other friends. As early as 12 [May] 1967, he told Ruby Cohn that he had 'Found a good thing in Chamfort: "L'espoir est un charlatan..."' (UoR 5100). On 17 June 1967, he sent the same maxim to John Kobler, and on 21 April 1969 he told him: 'In *Endgame* you will find the Chamfort doggerelised for your entertainment I hope', followed by a discussion of *Breath* and what could be regarded as a *mirlitonnade avant la lettre*:

> On entre, on crie
> Et c'est la vie.
> On crie, on sort,
> Et c'est la mort.
>
> (qtd. in Knowlson 1996, 565–6)

To George Reavey (9 August 1972) he said he had 'disimproved some hours' by doggerelizing one of Chamfort's maxims (the one marked on page 42): 'Live & clean forget from day to day, / Mop life up as fast as it dribbles away'. And in October 1973 he told Ruby Cohn that he 'Did a couple more Chamfort and one P.P. (Pensée Pascal)' (UoR MS5100). In Tanger, he had 'Found a 2nd hand Pascal (Pensées) annotated in Arab hand',[27] as he told Barbara Bray on 10 October 1973, immediately adding: 'Nothing doggerelisable so far' (TCD MS10948/1/546).

As late as 1988, Beckett received a dedication copy of *Chamfort: Biographie, suivie de soixante-six maximes, anecdotes, mots et dialogues inédits* (1988)[28] with an inscription by the author: 'Pour Samuel Beckett, / en témoignage de très / grande admiration, / Claude Arnaud'.

SADE

A conspicuous absence among the eighteenth-century authors in Des Granges' *Histoire illustrée de la littérature française* is the Marquis de Sade. Although the Marquis may not have been on the official programme, Beckett does seem to have mentioned Sade in his classes on French literature. Leslie Daiken's lecture notes (UoR Daiken notes, 7v) contain the jotting:

> Je ne sais, de tout temps, quelle injuste puissance
> Laisse la paix au crime et poursuit l'innocence.
>
> (Marquis de Sade)

The context is the lecture on Racine's *Andromaque*. The note is written on the back of the page on which Daiken has made a drawing of Beckett reading a book, and the lines are actually a quotation from *Andromaque* (Act III, scene 1).[29] Whether the quote prompted Beckett to make an appropriate reference to the Marquis de Sade, which Daiken misunderstood, or whether the student's own preoccupations prompted him to attribute the lines to the wrong author, Beckett did not limit himself to the prudish canon as it was presented to him in academic anthologies and literary histories. When he asked MacGreevy rhetorically on 8 September 1934 whether there was 'any irritation more mièvre than that of Sade at the impossibility d'outrager la nature' (*LSB* 223), he merely referred to a famous quote from *La Nouvelle Justine*, but four years later he did consider translating Sade's *120 Jours de Sodome* at Jack Kahane's request. In this context, he told MacGreevy on 11 February 1938 that he was 'interested in Sade & ha[d] been for a long time' (*LSB* 605), and the matter was on his mind during the next few weeks as his letters to George Reavey (20 February, 8 March 1938) indicate. On 12 May, he mentioned plans for an article on 'the divine marquise in Hermathena', which did not materialize. Eventually he did not translate the *120 Jours* either. Although he had accepted the job in early March, a remarkable aspect of the Sade episode is Beckett's concern about his reputation (*LSB* 604).

In 1972, George Reavey again mentioned Sade to Beckett, notably the 1909 edition annotated by Apollinaire. Beckett replied to Reavey on 24 August 1972, suggesting that Apollinaire must have been the initiator of the Sade boom: 'I think I know the Apollinaire Sade you mention, in a series entitled "Les Maîtres de l'amour" (Bibliothèque des Curieux). I once had it and find I still have, in the same collection, his Divine Aretino in 2 vols'. The library in Beckett's apartment still contains (unmarked) copies of *L'Œuvre du Divin Arétin* (2 vols, 1933) and *L'Œuvre du Marquis de Sade* (1909), both of them introduced by Guillaume Apollinaire.

LAMARTINE, VIGNY

Lamartine – as in 'bons vins et Lamartine, a champaign land for the sad and serious' ('Fingal', *MPTK* 18) – is among the earliest exponents of nineteenth-century French literature in Beckett's library, but he is merely represented by René Doumic's book *Lamartine* in the series 'Les grands écrivains français'. Alfred de Vigny is present with a selection from his own works, *Poésies choisies* (1935). The books are not annotated, but at least de Vigny's poem 'Moïse' seems to have left an impression, judging from the annotations in Beckett's first bible (see Chapter 8). On 4 August 1938, he wrote to Thomas MacGreevy: 'I seem to have read nothing for months but Vigny's Journal in the bowdlerized Larousse edition, which bored me' (*LSB* 637).

STENDHAL

In Beckett's lectures at TCD, Stendhal had been presented as one of the novelists on the Gide side – the side of 'integrity of incoherence' (Rachel Burrows lecture notes, TCD MIC60, 37; Nixon 2007a, 64). In Beckett's pedagogical dichotomy, this form of literature, dealing with 'authentic complexity' (5), was contrasted with notably Romantic and Naturalist works, lacking this quality.

As Beckett's inscription on the 'faux titre' page indicates, he purchased his copy of Stendhal's *Le Rouge et le Noir* (1925) in 'November 1926'. Five years later, he read it again. On 20 December 1931, less than two weeks after he was awarded his MA degree at TCD, Beckett wrote to Thomas MacGreevy that he had been rereading *Le Rouge et le Noir* and *La Chartreuse de Parme*. The underlined words are probably traces of his first reading and his efforts to enrich his vocabulary,[30] but they are also part of the 'verbal booty' that characterized his writing method in the early 1930s. For instance, Beckett had marked the expression '*chapelle ardente*' [mortuary chamber] (Stendhal 1925, 107). Not unlike Belacqua in 'Yellow', he 'had read the phrase somewhere and liked it and made it his own' (*MPTK* 152): 'The mind, dim and hushed like a sick-room, like a chapelle ardente' (*Dream* 44; see Pilling 2004, 86). In *Dream of Fair to Middling Women*, he thus applied what he had made explicit earlier on in the novel, referring to the charges of plagiarism that had been levied against Stendhal: 'Without going as far as Stendhal who said – or repeated after somebody . . .' (*Dream* 12; see Nixon 2011, 208).

Starting from page 125, Beckett's copy of *Le Rouge et le Noir* also shows traces of a more content-related interest, such as a long double vertical line spanning a complete paragraph (125); the underlining of a longer phrase such as 'sa vanité s'en était coiffée' (146), or a marginal characterization of a whole scene, such as the comment 'Pure 'roman de ~~chambre~~ ^{femme de chambre»} (224–5). Beckett also started marking what he called 'Beylismes' (referring to Stendhal's real name, Marie-Henri Beyle). The first 'Beylisme' (pencil marginalia) is underlined on page 213.[31] While reading this page, Beckett acted not only as a marginalist, but also as an extractor: he excerpted (a translation of) its last sentence in his 'Dream' Notebook: 'If he wasn't the goods he'd be in pace already / (Stendhal)' (*DN* 902).[32] As John Pilling notes, the line is taken from a conversation between the Abbé Pirard and the Marquis de la Mole concerning the protagonist, Julien Sorel (Chapter 30). This is the first of a cluster of excerpts (*DN* 127–36), many of which are also marked in Beckett's copy of *Le Rouge et le Noir*.

Again, Beckett identified the physical author with passages in his works. He thus underlined what is 'BEYLE'S TROUBLE'[33] (358), pointed out 'Beyle's "Folie pour rien"..isme'[34] and noted that 'B's road was a Hedonist, Jacobite & Republican' next to the famous oneliner 'Eh, monsieur, un roman est un miroir qui se promène sur une grande route' (359). This line is referred to in 'Les Deux Besoins' (written in 1938): 'Il y a des jours, surtout en Europe, où la route reflète mieux que le miroir' (*Dis* 55). As John Pilling points out in 'Beckett's Stendhal', this reference shows how Beckett was 'distancing himself from Stendhal' (Pilling 1996, 313).

This distancing was a gradual process.[35] In the 'Dream' Notebook, Beckett jotted down a few excerpts that focus on 'l'inconnu'[36] and 'l'imprévu'.[37] This focus on the unknown and the unexpected accords with Beckett's appreciation – at least in his lectures at TCD – of Stendhal's complexity, as opposed to Balzac's 'vegetable inertia': 'Stendhal expressed particular at expense of general' whereas 'Balzac never stated a "cas particulier", expressed general at expense of particular', according to Rachel Burrows' notes (see also Pilling 1996, 315).

Shortly before Beckett resigned his lectureship at TCD, when he wrote to MacGreevy on 20 December 1931 that he had just reread *Le Rouge et le Noir*, his comment was: 'Such an obsession with heights & ladders & gothic pillars & terraces and grottos in the Juras & the dungeon up in the air at the end. And the same thing again all through the Chartreuse' (*LSB* 100). Beckett related this obsession with heights to the building of the highest biblical construction and concluded his critical assessment by calling Stendhal the 'Nimrod of novelists', referring to the architect of the Tower of Babel, who is also mentioned in the 'Whoroscope' Notebook (WN 61r; see Chapter 5).

When in April 1935 Beckett tried to make a start on *Murphy*, he reread Stendhal and even suggested to Thomas MacGreevy (26 April) that the autobiographical *Vie de Henri Brulard* 'might be an idea for a translation' (qtd. in Nixon 2011, 114).

FLAUBERT, NERVAL, LAUTRÉAMONT

Given the opposition between Stendhal and Honoré de Balzac, as presented in Rachel Burrows' lecture notes, it does not come as a surprise that the library shows no traces of Balzac, not even a copy of *Louis Lambert* to possibly elucidate Beckett's choice of names for the Louis and the Lamberts in the French and English versions of *Malone meurt / Malone Dies*. Beckett did read André Billy's two-volume *La Vie de Balzac* and Octave Mirbeau's 'La Mort de Balzac' in April 1951.[38] He also told Barbara Bray on 16 March 1973 (TCD MS10948/1/530) that he was 'Dipping into Les Illusions perdues',[39] but Balzac is conspicuously missing from what is left of Beckett's library. So are the Naturalists Émile Zola and Guy de Maupassant, who, according to Beckett's lectures, equally lacked the 'complexity' he so appreciated in pre-Naturalists such as Stendhal and post-Naturalists such as André Gide. Still, the absence of an author in the extant library does not necessarily imply a lack of interest. Gide, for instance, is not represented either. And as regards the Naturalists, even though they are no longer preserved in the library, Beckett did read a Naturalist novel once in a while, for instance in May 1955, when he mentioned to Pamela Mitchell that he 'lied down with Zola's *Assommoir* which is not what I want to lie down with' (UoR MS5060). Another missing monument of nineteenth-century French literature is Victor Hugo. He is only present in the form of a marked anecdote about him in Jules Renard's *Journal* (see below).

Gustave Flaubert is represented by means of an inscribed copy of Maurice Nadeau's *Gustave Flaubert écrivain* (1969) and Hugh Kenner's *Flaubert, Joyce and Beckett*, illustrated by Guy Davenport (1962), dated 'January 4, 1963' and dedicated 'To the sole living Stoic Comedian, / Samuel Beckett, / in homage to his achievement, / and in commemoration of that / of his gallant predecessors. / Hugh Kenner / Guy Davenport'. Beckett's *Mercier et Camier* owes a debt to (especially the opening of) Flaubert's *Bouvard et Pécuchet* (Knowlson 1996, 361) and the text of 'Les Deux Besoins' is preceded by an epigraph from *L'Éducation sentimentale* (*Dis* 55). On 29 June 1965, Beckett mentioned to Barbara Bray that he was 'Reading *Bouvard & P.*': 'The meeting beautifully done. Bad foreword by Queneau' (TCD MS10948/1/338). The next day he read the opening 'with relish' and thought it was a 'Pity one can't want any more in that direction' (339); a week later (7 July) he 'abandoned' the Flaubertian pseudo-couple.

Beckett did have an interest in nineteenth-century French literature, as is shown by his (unmarked) copy of Pascal Pia's *Romanciers, poètes, essayistes du XIXème Siècle* (1971), of *Sylvie* and *Aurélia* by Gérard de Nerval or the *Oeuvres complètes d'Isidore Ducasse* [Lautréamont] (ed. Maurice Saillet, 1963). 'Isidore' is mentioned in *Dream of Fair to Middling Women* (137) in close proximity of the 'Vieil Océan', an invocation borrowed from Lautréamont's *Les Chants de Maldoror* (Pilling 2004, 238), which is most probably also the source of Beckett's frequent use of the word 'infundibuliforme', for instance in *L'Innommable*.[40] Apart from these nineteenth-century authors, the poets Charles Baudelaire, Arthur Rimbaud, Paul Verlaine and Stéphane Mallarmé are more markedly present.

BAUDELAIRE

In Pierre Oster's *Nouveau dictionnaire de citations françaises* (1970), the only reading trace (apart from the book ribbon at page 358, marking Racine) is a piece of paper, inserted at page 1004 to indicate the quotations from Baudelaire. The library contains two editions of Baudelaire's *Les Fleurs du mal*: a *livre de poche* ('présenté par Jean-Paul Sartre')[41] and a 1928 edition introduced by Paul Valéry (1928). Later in life, Beckett kept purchasing or receiving editions of Baudelaire's works, such as the *Œuvres complètes* (ed. Y.-G. Le Dantec, 1951) or *Le Spleen de Paris* (ed. Yves Florenne, 1976). The former was given to Beckett by Pamela Mitchell. On 7 February 1955 he told her: 'I've been reading in your grand Baudelaire and in the Holy Bible the story of the Flood and wishing the Almighty had never had a soft spot for Noah' (qtd. in Knowlson 1996, 406). As James Knowlson shows, both these readings had an impact on the writing of *Fin de partie*. Although the sonnet 'Recueillement' is not marked, the line 'Tu réclamais le soir; il descend: le voici' (Beckett 1957, 111) is quoted by Hamm and freely translated by Beckett in *Endgame*: 'You cried for night; it falls; now cry in darkness' (*CDW* 133).

VERLAINE

While Pamela Mitchell gave Beckett the 'grand Baudelaire' as a leaving present in 1955, Beckett's 'goodbye present' to her was Verlaine's *Œuvres poétiques complètes* (Knowlson 1996, 404). Beckett's library features a later edition of the same *Œuvres poétiques complètes* (Paris: Gallimard Pléiade, 1968). One of Beckett's memories linked to these poetical works was Joyce's reciting of Verlaine in 1930.[42] The Pléiade volume does not feature any marginalia, but it does contain an inserted piece of paper with five opening lines of Verlaine's poems, followed by the initials of the collection in which they originally appeared (*Fêtes galantes, Sagesse, Poèmes saturniens*) and the page number (or blanks to be filled in with the relevant page number):

<u>Dans le vieux parc</u> – (F.G. 121)
<u>Un gd. sommeil noir</u> – (S.)
<u>Le ciel est par-dessus le toit</u> – (S.)
<u>Je fais souvent ce rêve</u> – (P.S.)
<u>Le Pal</u>

The list does not feature 'Colloque sentimental', the closing poem of the collection *Fêtes galantes*, from which Beckett derived the title of the play *Oh les beaux jours*. At the top of the inserted piece of paper, he has written: '"écrit sous lui" comme disait / Corbière de Verlaine / Hopitaux', referring most probably to Verlaine's *Mes Hôpitaux*. The expression 'écrit sous lui' is modeled on the scatological phrase 'faire sous lui' and goes back to Tristan Corbière's poem 'Rapsodie du sourd' ('Rien – Je parle sous moi ... Des mots qu'à l'air je jette'). Beckett's tendency to present his production of poetry as an act of excretion had a long tradition – a tradition he was clearly well aware of.

Another 'non-marginalia' is the famous poem 'Art poétique', with its opening stanza on music and 'the odd' ('l'Impair'):

De la musique avant toute chose,
Et pour cela préfère l'Impair
Plus vague et plus soluble dans l'air,
Sans rien en lui qui pèse ou qui pose.

He may not have needed to consult his Verlaine to remember this stanza, with the phrase 'plus vague' as a precursor of the 'vaguening' principle,[43] characterizing his own working method. Several years later, Beckett wrote the fragment '(V.) une âme en allée vers d'autres cieux' in the top margin of the first typescript of *Solo*, his French translation of *A Piece of Monologue*. He was looking for a French equivalent to translate the phrase 'All gone so long'. 'Gone' had been the provisional title of the play and it remained its final word. To translate this crucial word, he not only wrote Verlaine's words in the top margin, but also: '(G.) je me souviens des heures en allées. Depuis le temps. Oubliés. Plus trace. En allés'. Analogous to the '(V.)' of Verlaine, the

'(G.)' refers to one of his favourite authors: Gide. The line 'je me souviens des heures en allées' derives from *Les Nourritures terrestres* (1897).[44]

RIMBAUD

Verlaine's career is inextricably bound up with another *enfant terrible* of French literature, Arthur Rimbaud. In the early 1930s, Beckett had translated Rimbaud's 'Le Bateau ivre' (Knowlson 1996, 160) – to which he alluded in *Dream of Fair to Middling Women* (137) – and fifty years later, toward the end of his career, he still referred to Rimbaud when, in a letter to André Bernold, he associated Bam, Bem, Bim and Bom in *What Where / Quoi où / Was Wo* with the colours in the poem 'Voyelles'.[45] Throughout Beckett's career, Rimbaud was present in the background as a literary authority he could either appeal to, or compare himself with. In a letter to MacGreevy (8 November 1931), Beckett mentioned that Rimbaud 'used to compose poems walking' and immediately related this to his own writing practice: 'But for me, walking, the mind has a most pleasant & melancholy limpness, is a carrefour of memories, memories of childhood mostly, moulin à larmes' (*LSB* 93). After the war, Beckett still referred to Rimbaud in concrete working situations, such as discussions about lexical matters with Mania Péron.[46]

In Beckett's copy of the *Œuvres de Arthur Rimbaud* with a preface by Paul Claudel (1929), several lines and words in the poem 'Bateau ivre' are marked, pointing out for instance the double occurrence of the word 'éveil' (awakening).[47] Judging from the nature of these marks they may have been made by Beckett in his capacity of translator.[48] This focus on 'éveil' may suggest Beckett's familiarity with Rimbaud's so-called 'lettre du voyant' (see Nixon 2011, 173; Pilling 2000, 20),[49] containing the famous line 'Je est un autre', but the library does not contain any explicit clues in this respect. If Beckett was interested in any 'awakening' with regard to Rimbaud, it seems to have been a metaphorical 'éveil', implying a way of 'seeing' with one's eyes closed rather than opened. When he tried to 'explain the mystery' to the final-year students at TCD, he told them about Rimbaud's 'eye suicide' as practised by children pressing their fingers onto their eyeballs, thus inducing starry 'visions', described in the poem 'Les Poètes de Sept Ans'.[50] On 11 March 1931, Beckett told Thomas MacGreevy about the students' giggling reactions, and his conclusion was: 'I can't talk about Rimbaud' (*LSB* 73). When, on 18 October 1932, Rimbaud came up again in a letter to MacGreevy, the emphasis was once more upon closed eyes in another image, characterizing the integrity of some of Rimbaud's poems ('the integrity of the eyelids'; *LSB* 135).

MALLARMÉ

This kind of integrity was what Beckett missed in the poetry of Stéphane Mallarmé, whose 'De même' (from *Divagations*) Beckett translated for Georges Duthuit (*LSB II* 120, 122, 125). In the letter to MacGreevy (18 October 1932, quoted above) he wrote: 'I was trying to like Mallarmé again the other day, & couldn't, because it's Jesuitical poetry, even the Swan & Hérodiade. I suppose I'm a dirty low-church P[rotestant]. Even in poetry, concerned with integrity in a surplice. I'm in mourning for the integrity of a pendu's emission of semen, what I find in Homer & Dante & Racine & sometimes Rimbaud' (*LSB* 134–5). Nonetheless, Beckett continued 'trying to like Mallarmé'. The library contains a 1961 Pléiade edition of the poet's *Œuvres complètes*.

In the meantime, Beckett had received David Hayman's study *Joyce et Mallarmé*, on which he commented at length in a letter of 22 July 1955. Beckett did appreciate the difficulty of dealing with 'texts into which almost anything may be read', but he also pointed out how, according to him, 'in Joyce the form of judgement more and more devoured its gist ... in a way more consistent with Bruno's identification of contraries than with the intellectualism of Mallarmé' (*LSB II* 537). This 'intellectualism' can be read as a euphemism for the 'Jesuitical poetry' that 'disgust[ed Beckett] so much' according to his letter to MacGreevy of 18 October 1932 (*LSB* 134).

Nonetheless, some of Mallarmé's poems did make a lasting impression on Beckett. In *Dream of Fair to Middling Women*, the 'supreme adieu' or the 'Mallarmean farewell' (from the poem 'Brise marine') is alluded to (*Dream* 3, 12; Pilling 2004, 22, 39). After the war, in early November 1960, he quoted a line from Mallarmé's poem 'Le tombeau d'Edgar Poe', which he told Barbara Bray he had 'recuperated' in what was still a question mark at the time (probably *Comment c'est*): 'Recuperated in my ? the long forgotten Mallarmé line – / Calme bloc ici-bas chu d'un désastre obscur' (TCD MS10948/1/119). And on 14 May 1964, he quoted a 'Line from Mallarmé's Prisoner Poem, written young in London' ['Les fenêtres'].[51] The final entry in the 'Sottisier' Notebook, for instance, is a passage from 'Brise Marine':

> .. la clarté déserte de ma lampe
> sur le vide papier que la blancheur défend
> (UoR MS2910, 16v)

It is not impossible that Beckett had 'Brise marine' in mind when he told Barbara Bray on 12 February 1978 that he was 'Embroiled in a marine'. Four days later, however, he had to inform her that the 'Marine' was 'stillborn' (TCD 10948/1/626–7).

MAETERLINCK

In contrast with Mallarmé's 'intellectualism', Beckett developed his poetics of 'ignorance'. A book that elucidates some aspects of what Beckett may have meant by this concept is volume 1 of the *Théâtre* (Paris: Charpentier, n.d. [1939]) by Maurice Maeterlinck (1862–1949). The volume contains *La Princesse Maleine*, *L'Intruse* and *Les Aveugles*, but also a preface, in which a passage is underlined that stresses an interesting and complex assessment of 'ignorance' and 'the unknown that surrounds us' ('l'inconnu qui nous entoure'). Maeterlinck encourages his readers to discover in this unknown 'a new reason to live and persevere' ('une nouvelle raison de vivre et de persévérer'), for the 'supreme truth' of death and of the futility of our existence is, according to Maeterlinck, merely 'the extreme limit of our present knowledge' ('le point extreme de nos connaissances actuelles'), the point where our intelligence ends and where nothing is certain but our ignorance. Precisely because we do not know anything beyond this point, 'perseverance' – or going 'on', in Beckett's vocabulary – gets the benefit of the doubt. Toward the end of his career, in works such as *Worstward Ho*, *Stirrings Still* and *Comment dire*, Beckett consistently kept exploring this extreme border zone. As a writer, he never formulated the situation in equally positive terms as Maeterlinck did, but as a reader he did underline the idea that, in the state we are in, it is just as legitimate to hope that our efforts are not useless ('que nos efforts ne sont pas inutiles') as to think they are futile.[52]

RENARD

A French author Beckett had a special affinity with is Jules Renard. The passages marked in the four-volume *Journal de Jules Renard 1887–1910* constitute a fascinating portrait of the artist as a young reader. Both as a marginalist and as an extractor, Beckett was still 'phrase-hunting'[53] or looking for 'odd things'[54] in late February and early March 1931. As John Pilling notes in his edition of the 'Dream' Notebook, many of these odd nouns and verbs, such as 'dumaficeler' or 'amertumer', found their way into *Dream of Fair to Middling Women* ('Ne t'amertume pas', *Dream* 22), 'Echo's Bones',[55] and shorter pieces such as the review on Ezra Pound's *Make It New* ('Ex Cathezra', *Dis* 78).

On 11 March 1931, Beckett told Thomas MacGreevy[56] that he was 'tired out by Renard', but that he would 'come back to him' (*LSB* 73). He did indeed come back to Renard in a letter he sent to MacGreevy from London (Gertrude Street, 20 February 1935), referring cursorily to 'Renard's hedgehog'. The allusion is to the last marked entry in volume 3 of Renard's *Journal*, regarding the 'hérisson tourneur', a hedgehog that was believed to have been taught the trick of turning around, until it was discovered that it constantly turned around in order to try and scratch one of its ears, which was full of worms. In March 1936, he mentioned Renard among many other authors he was reading (Knowlson 1996, 295) and according to the German diaries he read Renard's *Journal* again, together with Voltaire's *Candide*, on 7 February 1937 (Nixon 2011, 24). Almost three decades later, Beckett wrote to Barbara Bray: 'Been browsing in Renard again. Not what he was, but marvellous things, like the pigeon helping with its wing the too frail branch on which it lights' (TCD MS10948/1/297; 1 September 1964).[57] Beckett's comment in his correspondence shows that the absence of pencil marks in the fourth volume of Renard's *Journal* does not necessarily indicate a diminished interest. Deirdre Bair even claims that the impact kept increasing until the very end and that

> it was the last entry which has had the most sustained and moving effect upon Beckett. Renard had been ill and confined to his bed for some time. In the entry of April 7, 1910, he wrote: 'Last night I wanted to get up. Dead Weight. A leg hangs outside. Then a trickle runs down my leg. I allow it to reach my heel before I make up my mind. It will dry in the sheets.' It was this cold, hard, exacting look at oneself which struck Beckett, so that the first time he read this passage he spent hours repeating it over and over as he sat in his armchair sipping whiskey in front of the fire. (Bair 1978, 118)

Leaving aside the clichéd evocation of the author in front of the fire, it is worthwhile taking Bair's remark into account regarding the correspondence between Renard's unvarnished self-analysis and Beckett's style. Also with respect to content, some of his post-war writings show remarkable echoes, such as the description of the hyacinth in *First Love*:

> One day I asked her to bring me a hyacinth, live, in a pot. She brought it and put it on the mantelpiece, now the only place in my room to put things, unless you put them on the floor. Not a day passed without my looking at it. At first all went well, it even put forth a bloom or two, then it gave up and was soon no more than a limp stem hung with limp leaves. The bulb, half clear of the clay as though in search of oxygen, smelt foul. She wanted to remove it, but I told her to leave it. (*ECEF* 77)

As to the question why Beckett chose a hyacinth to put in the otherwise empty room,[58] an initial impetus may have been Renard's admiration for this plant that does not need any love, marked in Beckett's copy of the journal (1 March 1894).⁵⁹ Some of the marked and excerpted entries served as a basis for short scenes in Beckett's most famous plays. The marginalia 'Not heavy enough to hang herself'⁶⁰ is echoed – with a twist – in the first act of *Waiting for Godot*, when Didi and Gogo consider the possibility of hanging themselves:

> Vladimir: Go ahead.
> Estragon: After you.
> Vladimir: No no, you first.
> Estragon: Why me?
> Vladimir: You're lighter than I am.
> Estragon: Just so!
> Vladimir: Use you intelligence, can't you?

Didi 'uses his intelligence', according to one of the wittiest stage directions in twentieth-century drama, but he remains in the dark. Gogo subsequently enlightens him 'with effort': 'Gogo light – bough not break – Gogo dead. Didi heavy – bough break – Didi alone' (*CDW* 19).

Another Renard entry that echoes in Beckett's work is the anecdote about the old Victor Hugo, complaining that he has not been given his 'biscuit' ('On ne m'a pas donné de biscuit!'; 1.114, *janvier 1892*). The scene reverberates in *Endgame*, when Nagg exclaims 'I want me pap!' and Hamm reacts: 'Give him a biscuit' (*CDW* 96).

Beckett's reading of Renard certainly helped him to find his own voice and it is no surprise that even as an established author he kept rereading Renard's journal until the end of his life. The quotations from the journal to which he referred in his correspondence in the 1980s⁶¹ are not marked.

Beckett's copy of the *Journal* is a paradigmatic example of his changing reading and writing habits in the course of his career:

1. Both the marked and the extracted passages still show traces of the Joycean method of looking for usable material (odd words, remarkable phrasings).
2. Some of the other marked passages, however, proved to be useful to Beckett in a less direct way. They seem to have worked in much the same way as what Anthony Uhlmann has termed 'the philosophical image' (Uhlmann 2007). Thus, a short entry on a hyacinth or a line on being too light to hang oneself could serve as a core image, which Beckett developed into a short fictional or dramatic scene several years later.
3. Moreover, Beckett's correspondence shows that the unmarked passages in the *Journal* contain entries that are just as important as the marked ones.

No matter how much Beckett's reading habits changed over the years, the traces of these readings at the same time indicate how remarkably *constant* some of his reading preferences were. Even though Beckett admitted in his September 1964 letter to Barbara Bray that Renard no longer left the same impression as he used to ('Not what he was'), Beckett kept finding 'marvellous things' in the *Journal*. These reading preferences (such as Renard, Schopenhauer, Dante, Shakespeare) indicate a thread in his career that marks much of what characterizes his work in terms of tone and style. In some cases, a passage marked early on in Beckett's career reads like a piece of advice taken to heart for the rest of his life, such as the entry of 3 August 1892: 'Si l'inspiration existait, il faudrait ne pas l'attendre; si elle venait, la chasser comme un chien' [If inspiration existed, one shouldn't wait for it; if it came, chase it like a dog] (Renard 1927, 1.133).

Apart from Renard's *Journal*, the library also contains the *Correspondance de Jules Renard 1864–1910* (1928), *Le Vigneron dans sa Vigne* (n.d.) and Pierre Schneider's *Jules Renard par lui-même* (1956), with an inscription by the author: 'à Sam Beckett / bien amicalement / Pierre Schneider'. And this is only part of the works by and on Renard which Beckett must have read. For instance, he certainly read *Poil de Carotte*, whose eponymous protagonist, after having soiled his bed, has to eat a soup which he is made to believe is prepared on the basis of his own excretion. Beckett cursorily identified himself with the child in this situation after *Murphy* was turned down by the London publisher Dent: 'Je m'en doutais, comme disait Poil de Carotte, quand on lui donna à boire du déjà bu' [I thought as much, as Poil de Carotte used to say when what he was given to drink had already been drunk] (*LSB* 442).

SAINTE-BEUVE

Before the history of French literature almost unnoticeably slips into the twentieth century, a notable nineteenth-century presence in the library deserves to be mentioned: the literary critic and writer Charles Augustin Sainte-Beuve (1804–69). A critical essay of his precedes Lord Chesterfield's *Letters, Sentences & Maxims* (1881). Apart from that, it is only appropriate that he is represented by means of a biography: Gustave Michaut's *Sainte-Beuve* (1921). Beckett told Thomas MacGreevy on 5 December 1932 that he had 'great admiration for Sainte-Beuve' as a novelist: 'if you have not read his novel Volupté I have it' (*LSB* 145). By the end of his life he did not have it any more; it is no longer part of his extant library. Beckett appreciated Sainte-Beuve's 'most interesting mind', but he could not help 'regretting that it was applied to criticism' (*LSB* 145). Sainte-Beuve's criticism is sometimes referred to as 'biographism'. In order to understand an author, it was necessary to know his biography, according to the critic. Although Beckett regretted that Sainte-Beuve's mind was wasted on criticism, his own approach to literature does bear the stamp of Sainte-Beuve's biographical criticism, as the numerous volumes of literary lives in his library suggest. Sainte-Beuve's biographism was famously taken issue with by Marcel Proust, whose *Contre Sainte-Beuve* is also present in the library.

PROUST

In order to write his essay *Proust* (1931), Beckett had made an inquiry into the life as well as the works of Marcel Proust. The library still contains Léon Pierre-Quint's (unmarked) *Marcel Proust, sa vie, son œuvre* (rev. ed. 1928). Although his edition of Ernst Robert Curtius' *Marcel Proust* (1952) could not have been consulted in the early 1930s, Beckett does seem to have read Curtius' essay in preparation of his own essay on Proust, either in the original or in the French translation by Armand Pierhal (1928). As this secondary literature shows, Beckett was not the first to point out that Proust employed numerous botanical metaphors. One of the chapters in Curtius' study bears the title 'Die menschliche Flora' / 'La Flore humaine', and the link with Schopenhauer is not far away in his chapter on 'Wille' (Curtius 1952, 70). As to how Beckett eventually felt about his own achievement as a critic of Proust, Deirdre Bair mentions a remarkable bibliophile discovery, a copy of the essay which according to its owner, Thomas Wall, contains a telling comment in Beckett's hand: 'I have written my book in a cheap flashy philosophical jargon'.[62]

Proust remained a presence in the library after the war, from the 1954 Pléiade three-volume edition of *À la recherche du temps perdu* to *The Proust Screenplay* by Harold Pinter, in collaboration with Joseph Losey and Barbara Bray (1977). On 23 February 1955, Beckett wrote to Pamela Mitchell: 'The thing I always felt most, best, in Proust was his anxiety in the cab (Last volume) on his way home from the party. Often feel like that now, in all due humility, no, unhumbly. And sometimes I think I shall dribble on to 80' (qtd. in Knowlson 1996, 405). But these were merely aftereffects, following the intensive reading of Proust's *Recherche* in 1929 and 1930.

The biographical background of this reading experience is illustrated by the only date mentioned in Beckett's marginalia in his copy of *À la recherche du temps perdu*. In volume 4, page 99, Proust describes the narrator's complex feelings of separation, presented as a form of death, when the old I ('l'ancien moi') is replaced by 'un moi différent'.[63] Beckett's corresponding marginalia is

Literature in French

another example of direct identification: 'Mail Boat – Aug 1928' (see Knowlson 1996, 82). In August 1928, Beckett had taken the mail boat from Dublin to the continent, leaving his family to go and visit his niece Peggy Sinclair in Kassel, Germany.

The chronology of Beckett's reading of Proust is well documented (Brun 1984; Knowlson 1996; McQueeny 1977; Pilling 1976b, 2006a; Rosen 1976). In the summer of 1929, he started reading the first volume of Proust's *À la recherche du temps perdu*. A year later, in June 1930, Beckett was recommended by Richard Aldington to the publisher Chatto and Windus as an excellent candidate to write an essay on Proust. While he was reading the *Recherche* in July, he also read Arthur Schopenhauer's *Die Welt als Wille und Vorstellung*. In August 1930, Beckett mentioned to Thomas MacGreevy that he had been rereading Proust's *Recherche* (Pilling 2006a, 26) and on the twenty-fifth of that month he started writing his essay. Three weeks later (17 September) it was finished and Beckett delivered the essay to Chatto and Windus in London.

In order to be able to write this essay, Beckett had bought the sixteen-volume edition of *À la recherche du temps perdu*, 'achevé d'imprimer' in 1927–8. Fifteen of the sixteen volumes are still extant (preserved at the University of Reading):

Volume
1 *Du Côté de chez Swann* *
2 *Du Côté de chez Swann* * *
3 [missing]
4 *A l'ombre des jeunes filles en fleurs* * *
5 *A l'ombre des jeunes filles en fleurs* * * *
6 *Le Côté de Guermantes I*
7 *Le Côté de Guermantes II (Sodome et Gomorrhe I)*
8 *Sodome et Gomorrhe II* *
9 *Sodome et Gomorrhe II* * *
10 *Sodome et Gomorrhe II* * * *
11 *La prisonnière (Sodome et Gomorrhe III)* *
12 *La prisonnière (Sodome et Gomorrhe III)* * *
13 *Albertine disparue* *
14 *Albertine disparue* * *
15 *Le Temps retrouvé* *
16 *Le Temps retrouvé* * *

In the first half of the first volume Beckett did not write any snappy comments in the margins, he only marked textual errors, such as a 'd' replacing the typo 'p' in 'que pe [sic] s'ennuyer' (Proust 1928, 1.51). Sometimes he even questioned Proust's choice of words, for instance on page 99, where he suggested in the margin that 'Même à Paris ... je sais une fenêtre' should be 'je connais une fenêtre'. He also introduced mistakes, as on pages 78 and 79 he thought 'un pétale de rose' should be 'une pétale'. Although he did note a few remarkable mistakes later on, these pedantic marginalia soon disappeared, but he was clearly not satisfied with the edition, to put it mildly. In his essay he called his version of the book 'an edition that cannot be said to have transmitted the writings of Proust, but to have betrayed a tendency in that direction' (Beckett 1965, 87). Beckett used different writing tools during his successive readings. Although it is difficult to reconstruct the chronology of the reading traces with absolute certainty, our working hypothesis is that most of the pencil marks seem to be the traces of a first reading, while the comments in ink mark a subsequent reading.

In volume one, Beckett marked several passages that thematize the act of reading (see also Chapter 1). When the narrator is urged by his grandmother to come outside, he takes his book and continues reading in the garden. Then he starts describing his reading experience, starting with the image of an evaporation zone as a metaphor for the way in which his consciousness prevented the contact between subject and object:

> When I saw an external object, my consciousness that I was seeing it would remain between me and it, surrounding it with a thin spiritual border that prevented me from ever touching its substance directly; for it would somehow evaporate before I could make contact with it, just as an incandescent body that is brought into proximity with something wet never actually touches its moisture, since it is always preceded by a zone of evaporation.[64]

Beckett did not only comment upon the subsequent description of this 'screen' unfolded by his consciousness[65] (see Chapter 1), he also 'stole' the image of the zone of evaporation[66] and applied it in *Dream of Fair to Middling Women* to Belacqua and the Alba, more precisely to the 'expression of themselves at odds' – 'the profound antagonism latent in the neutral space that between victims of real needs is as irreducible as the zone of evaporation between damp and incandescence' (*Dream* 191–2). But not without marking it explicitly as a theft: '(We stole that one. Guess where.)'

In the first volume of the *Recherche*, Beckett continued to underscore the movement 'du dedans au dehors' on subsequent pages (125, 129), but he also noted its naiveté. On page 128 he wrote in the margin: 'same naive movement' next to the passage in which the narrator talks about the possibility of visiting the region described in a novel (1.128).

While Beckett was reading volume 1, he continued marking passages relating to reading: ten pages further on he marked a passage on the narrator's explanation of how he recognizes some characteristics of Bergotte's writing, which add density to certain expressions, so that the particulars become universals; or 'un morceau particulier' becomes a 'morceau idéal' (1.139). On the next page, Beckett underlined the crucial words 'image' and 'métaphore':

> Chaque fois qu'il [Bergotte] parlait de quelque chose dont la beauté m'était restée jusque-là cachée … il faisait dans une <u>image</u> **exploser** cette beauté jusqu'à moi. … j'aurais voulu posséder une opinion de lui, une <u>métaphore</u> de lui, sur toutes choses (1.140)

> [Whenever he spoke of something whose beauty had until then remained hidden from me …, by some piece of imagery he would make their beauty explode into my consciousness. … I longed to have some opinion, some metaphor of his, upon everything in the world] (trans. Scott Moncrieff and Kilmartin, 1.102–3)

Apart from the underlined words, the verb 'exploser' seems to have struck Beckett as well. He wrote to Thomas MacGreevy about his ambivalent feelings with regard to the *Recherche*, but even while he expressed his doubts about what he was reading, he did absorb and assimilate a Proustian vocabulary, which he then applied to the *Recherche*. While Proust explained how Bergotte's images cause an 'explosion' of beauty, Beckett pointed out that some of Proust's metaphors had the same explosive effect:

> There are incomparable things … and then passages that are offensively fastidious, artificial and almost dishonest. It is hard to know what to think about him. He is so absolutely the master of his own form that he becomes its slave as often as not. Some of his metaphors light up a whole page like a bright **explosion**, and others seem ground out in the dullest desperation. (*LSB* 11)

An example of these metaphors ground out in the dullest desperation is the narrator's view of his work as a magnifying glass with which he would give his readers the tool to 'read themselves' – the passage next to which Beckett impatiently wrote 'Balls' (Proust 1928, 16.240; see Chapter 1). But although Beckett clearly did not appreciate all of Proust's metaphors, the last volume also contains reading traces of yet another writing tool (a blue crayon) with which he marked other metaphors and passages that indicate that he *did* appreciate many aspects of the narrator's developing *poetics*, presented as the intellectual development of photographic negatives of experience (16.48).[67] As a writer *in spe*, Beckett was clearly interested in Proust's reflections on talent.[68] With regard to Beckett's later development as a bilingual author, it is interesting to note that he twice marked the passage on the task of the writer, who should act as a translator.[69]

Whether or not Beckett was aware that Proust wrote the first and the last parts first, and then gradually filled the *entre-deux*,[70] he did manage to make a bridge between these two 'bookends' of the *Recherche*. In the last volume, Beckett pencilled the words 'Indirect perception' next to the important passage about the Proustian poetics of metaphors.[71] In volume 1, he noted in ink: 'indirect – & consequently in[tegral] – apprehension of reality – frequent motiv' (1.123; see Chapter 1) – next to the description of the narrator's room, more specifically the 'obscure fraîcheur de ma chambre' (1.123), which is in itself an indirect way of presenting the room as a darkroom in which the intelligence can develop the negatives of experience.

Beckett systematically counted the moments of *mémoire involontaire*, which he marked in ink as 'revelations', starting with 'Rev. 1', the Madeleine, on page 69 of volume 1. In his essay on Proust, he sums them up in what he calls 'the list of fetishes' (Beckett 1965, 36–7). After 'Rev. 6' in volume 8 (8.166, when the narrator stoops to unbutton his boots on the occasion of his second visit to the Grand Hotel at Balbec in the *Intermittences du cœur* section), it takes several volumes before the last, rapid sequence of *mémoires involontaires* sets in: 'Rev. 7' (16.7, the uneven cobbles in the courtyard of the Guermantes Hotel), 'Rev. 8' (16.9, the noise of the spoon against a plate), 'Rev. 9' (16.10, the narrator wipes his mouth with a napkin), '10' (16.18, the noise of water in the pipes). Beckett called this rapid sequence a 'bombardment' (16.18) of *mémoires involontaires*, and then he marked revelation '11' (16.30, George Sand's *François le Champi*).

Regarding George Sand's book, Beckett marked the passage about the link between a particular book and the corresponding 'version' of the individual at the time he first read it.[72] Judging from the marginalia, the passage reminded Beckett of the 'union of / sub[ject]. & ob[ject]. / (Baud[elaire].)' (16.34) – or as he wrote in full in his essay *Proust*: 'he understands the meaning of Baudelaire's definition of reality as "the adequate union of subject and object", and more clearly than ever the grotesque fallacy of a realistic art' (Beckett 1965, 76).

On the same page in the last volume (16.34), Beckett's eye was caught by a textual error. Proust mentions the kind of literature that calls itself 'realist' but is in fact the furthest removed from reality. Beckett was surprised to see that this was called 'la littérature qui se contente de "décimer les choses"'. In the margin he wrote the correction 'décrire!?' (followed by an exclamation mark and a question mark). Reality as it is treated by the realists is nothing but a 'déchet de l'expérience' (16.40), according to Proust. Here, the margin served as a transition zone between reading and writing: Beckett colourlessly translated the 'déchet' as 'waste product' (16.40), but then he transformed it into a virtuoso passage in his essay, where he refers to Proust's

contempt for the literature that 'describes', for the realists and naturalists worshipping the offal of experience, prostrate before the epidermis and the swift epilepsy, and content to transcribe the surface, the façade, behind which the Idea is prisoner. Whereas the Proustian procedure is that of Apollo flaying Marsyas and capturing without sentiment the essence, the Phrygian waters. (Beckett 1965, 78–9)

At that point in the text, Beckett quotes from a book that he had bought when he was still studying Italian in Dublin: *Storia della Letteratura Italiana*, in which Francesco de Sanctis notes, with regard to Dante's *Divina Commedia*: 'Chi non ha la forza di uccidere la realtà non ha la forza di crearla' [Who does not have the strength to kill reality, does not have the strength to create it] (de Sanctis 1925, 1.159).[73]

In *Le Temps retrouvé*, on the same page as the 'déchets', in the important metaphor passage, the sentence on realist literature recurs almost literally, but this time correctly with the verb 'décrire' instead of 'décimer': 'La littérature qui se contente de "décrire les choses", de donner un misérable relevé de leurs lignes et de leur surface est malgré sa prétention réaliste la plus éloignée de la réalité' (16.40).

This repetition creates an echoing effect that is thematized in the letter to MacGreevy quoted above:

He [Proust] has every kind of subtle equilibrium, charming trembling equilibrium and then suddenly a stasis, the arms of the balance wedged in a perfect horizontal line, more heavily symmetrical than Macaulay at his worst, with primos and secundos echoing to each complacently and reechoing ... And to think that I have to contemplate him at stool for 16 volumes. ([?summer 1929], *LSB* 11–12)

An example of these duplications is the 'Névralgie' lexia in Carnet 2, to which Nathalie Mauriac has drawn attention.[74] Proust used this idea both in the evocation of *Tristan und Isolde* and in the Septet. In the Tristan scene the narrator is reminded of certain themes in Wagner's music, which are 'si internes, si organiques, si viscéraux qu'on dirait la reprise moins d'un motif que d'une névralgie' (11.217); in the Septet, the narrator is fascinated by a musical phrase, 'presque si organique et viscérale qu'on ne savait pas, à chacune de ses reprises, si c'était d'un thème ou d'une névralgie' (12.78). Beckett underlined the word 'névralgie' in both passages, thus marking the 'primo' and the 'secundo', as he called them in his letter; and at the beginning of the Septet scene he indicated the page numbers of the correlating musical scenes in the bottom margin: '62–85 / cf. Prisonnière I.215–221' (12.62). This is a concrete instance Beckett may have had in mind when he wrote deprecatingly of the 'theory of *Correspondances*, that trusty standby of all the Romantics from Hoffmann to Proust' in the review 'Schwabenstreich' (published in the *Spectator* of 23 March 1934; *Dis* 62). Yet, in the next review he wrote for the *Spectator* one month later, he defended Proust against Albert

Feuillerat's attempt to stress the uniformity and cohesion, the 'stock-in-trade exactly of the naturalism that Proust abominated' (*Dis* 64), pointing out instead the 'uncontrollable agency of unconscious memory', the 'full complexity' of the book's 'clues and blind alleys', and the way Proust communicated his material 'in dribs and drabs' (65).[75]

In his essay *Proust*, Beckett coins the phrase 'the plagiarism of oneself' (33) in relation to Habit. To a certain extent this also applies to these almost identical phrases, which at first sight may seem to be a form of autoplagiarism. But Beckett understood that, in terms of narrative technique, this textual repetition created a similar effect as Habit does in real life, under Proust's motto 'les vrais paradis sont les paradis qu'on a perdus' [the real paradises are the ones one has lost] (16.103). Applied to Proust's text, it is thanks to the autoplagiarist repetition of the word 'névralgie' that Beckett experienced the textual equivalent of a *mémoire involontaire*. And he acknowledged his recognition by adopting the word in his own essay in connection with the almost religious experience of 'salvation':

This accidental and fugitive salvation in the midst of life may supervene when the action of involuntary memory is stimulated by the negligence or agony of Habit, and under no other circumstances, nor necessarily then. Proust has adopted this mystic experience as the Leitmotiv of his composition. It recurs, like the red phrase of the Vinteuil Septuor, a neuralgia rather than a theme (Beckett 1965, 35)

'Thus,' Beckett concludes, 'the germ of the Proustian solution is contained in the statement of the problem itself. The source and point of departure of this "sacred action", the elements of communion, are provided by the physical world, by some immediate and fortuitous act of perception' (36). The formulation of this insight, with the aptly chosen adjective fortuitous, is prepared in an exceptionally long note in the margin of page 300 in volume one:

Purely musical impression, independent of memory. Compare with the experiences of 'un peu de temps à l'état pur', released [for] P[roust]. / by fortuitous encounter with certain objects, at [times] when conscious memory is entirely obliterated. (1.300)

Beckett was critical of Proustian involuntary memories, Joycean epiphanies and Woolfian 'moments of being'. Nonetheless, he did appreciate Proust's accomplishment as a writer. When he reread the two volumes of *Le Temps retrouvé* in December 1932, he disliked its first volume to the point that he called it 'pure Balzac', but its second volume (volume 16, in particular the first 100 pages) was 'as great a piece of sustained writing as anything to be found anywhere' (5 December 1932; *LSB* 145)

In his introduction to *Sésame et les Lys* (see Chapter 1), Proust argued that a text can only offer an impulse, and reading becomes dangerous (Proust 2008, 75) when it does not incite, but serves as a substitute for the reader's spiritual life, 'when the truth no longer appears to us as an ideal which we can realize only by the intimate progress of our own thought and the efforts of our own heart, but as something material, deposited between the leaves of books' (75). Consequently, Proust distinguished between two kinds of readers, the scholar ('l'érudit') and the 'literary man' ('le lettré'). The former does not so much look for 'the truth itself' (77) in a text, but rather for its index or its proof. Instead of a 'motionless idol' (77), the text thus appears as a kind of hypertext *avant la lettre*, an always expandable network of references, which satisfy but at the same time whet the reader's appetite for knowledge. The attitude of the 'lettré', on the other hand, is characterized by a 'fetishistic reverence for books' (78). It is quite clear that Beckett did not belong to this latter category, as even the material aspect of some of his books shows, such as his copy of Thierry Maulnier's *Introduction à la poésie française*. Beckett's effort to 'bind up' the book's wounds by means of adhesive tape (see *Figure 7*) may be regarded as a form of reverence, but certainly not a fetishistic reverence.

Figure 7 Thierry Maulnier, *Introduction à la poésie française*

TWENTIETH-CENTURY LITERATURE

Another intensively used volume on French poetry is Robert de la Vaissière's *Anthologie Poétique du XXe Siècle* (vol. 1, 1923). Beckett has marked the poems that struck him, typically with a vertical line in black ink:

Roger Allard: 'Le Guerrier masochiste ou l'amour du danger' (4–5)
Guillaume Apollinaire: 'Salomé'(10), 'La Chanson du mal-aimé' (11, 13), 'Aubade chantée à Laetare un an passé' (14), 'Réponse des cosaques zaporogues au sultan de constantinople' (15), 'Les sept épées' (20–1) and 'L'Adieu' (21)
René Arcos: 'Le Printemps' (27) and 'A une Victime' (28)
Paul-Alexander Arnoux: 'Flammes dansantes' (29, 31, 33, 35–7)
Pierre Benoit: 'Trois Poèmes pour Bérénice' (42) and 'Le Retour' (44–5)
Jean-Marc Bernard: 'Durus Amor' (50) and 'Rosae Sacrum' (51–2)
René Bizet: 'Hotels où j'ai vécu' (58)
Pierre Camo: 'À la mort et à la mer' (66)
Paul Claudel: 'Fragments de tête d'or' (83)
Guy-Charles Cros: 'Au Luxembourg' (106)
Georges Delaquys: 'Envoi' (110)
Tristan Derême: 'Pélops, par l'épaule d'ivoire' (113)
Charles Derennes: 'Réminiscence' (122)
Lucien Dubech: 'Toi qui cachas ton cœur farouche' (144)
Georges Duhamel: 'Ode a quelques hommes' (149–52) and 'Ballade de Florentin Prunier' (152–4)
Luc Durtain: 'Un Port' (159)
Jacques Dyssord: 'Dancing' (162)
Francis Eon: 'Le Bois' (168)
Léon-Paul Fargue: 'Aeternae Memoriae Patris' (177)
Edouard Gazanion: 'Complainte des Chalands' (226)

Four names in the table of contents are marked in pencil: Guillaume Apollinaire, Paul Claudel, Georges Duhamel and Léon-Paul Fargue.

APOLLINAIRE

Beckett's interest in Guillaume Apollinaire is already indicated by the sheer quantity of marked poems. 'La Chanson du mal-aimé', which Beckett mentions in his review of Ezra Pound's *Make It New* as being 'worth the whole of the best of Merril, Moréas, Vielé-Griffin, Spire, Régnier, Jammes ... put together' (*Dis* 78),[76] deserves special mention. Next to its title, Beckett has written in the right margin (black ink): 'One of the really great modern French poems' (Vaissière 1923, 11). Beckett memorized at least one stanza[77] (if not the whole poem) and liked to recite it many years later, as Anne Atik notes (40). On 11 September 1981 he wrote to Barbara Bray from Tangier that he 'Tried to remember Apollinaire's Comment lentement passe l'heure. Can't get it right. Marvellous poem' (TCD MS10948/1/665). And two years later, he recited Apollinaire's 'Que lentement passent les heures' again (24 August 1983; Atik 2001, 119). Earlier that year, he had quoted this line and the rest of the poem 'A la santé, V' (from *Alcools*) in his correspondence with Kay Boyle.[78]

Beckett's interest in Apollinaire extended to the poet's life.[79] Apollinaire had been arrested on 7 September 1911 on suspicion of stealing the Mona Lisa. He was jailed for a week in the Santé prison, which Beckett could see every day from the window of the library in his apartment at the Boulevard Saint-Jacques. But long before Beckett had the apartment, he was struck by this fifth section in the poem 'A la Santé'. One of his first poems in French[80] (opening with the lines 'les joues rouges') features a few lines[81] that echo the line 'Que lentement passent les heures', as Anne Atik points out (Atik 2001, 7).

Beckett's continuing interest in Apollinaire is confirmed by several editions of his writings in the library and two works with an introduction by Apollinaire.[82] Apart from *Le Poète assassiné* (1927), Beckett had a 1967 Pléiade edition of the *Œuvres poétiques* and a 1975 Gallimard edition of *Le Flâneur des deux rives, suivi de Contemporains pittoresques*. The library also contains a special edition[83] of the poem 'Zone', originally published in *Transition Fifty* no 6, which Beckett had translated in March 1949 (Pilling 2006a, 106).[84]

ÉLUARD

Another poet for whom Beckett acted as a translator was Paul Éluard. His translations of Éluard poems appeared in the surrealist number of *This Quarter* (5.1) in September 1932. On 18 October, he quoted two lines of Éluard in a letter to MacGreevy (*LSB* 134). The only edition of Éluard's work in Beckett's library is a bilingual 'édition de haut luxe sous coffret' of the *Poèmes d'amour / Love Poems*, with an English version by Brian Coffey.

CONTEMPORARY NOVELISTS

Beckett was 'the greatest' among post-war novelists writing in French, according to Maurice Nadeau's handwritten inscription in Beckett's copy of *Le Roman français depuis la guerre* (1963).[85] Beckett also had a copy of Gerda Zeltner-Neukomm's *Das Wagnis des französischen Gegenwartromans: Die neue Welterfahrung in der Literatur* (1960), discussing Butor, Robbe-Grillet, Sarraute, Beckett, Queneau, Camus, Malraux and Sartre. Several of these authors, such as Camus and Malraux, are not present in the library, but that does not necessarily imply Beckett's indifference to their works. For instance, on 19 August 1954, he wrote to Pamela Mitchell: 'Here are a few books you could read, if you have not already:

Sartre:	La Nausée
Malraux	La Condition humaine
Julien Green	Léviathan
Céline	Voyage au Bout de la Nuit
Jules Renard	Journal
Camus	L'Etranger (*LSB II* 493)

He tried to read the work of Louis Aragon in 1947, but on 4 July of that year he wrote to Ernest O'Malley that he was 'sending back the Aragon': 'Forgive me. I can't read it let alone review it. And if I had been able to read it I wouldn't have been able to review it. This is a reflexion on me, not on Aragon' (*LSB II* 57).

SARTRE

La Nausée, which Beckett found 'extraordinarily good' in 1938,[86] is no longer part of the library, but Sartre is present nevertheless. The library contains not only *L'Imagination* (see Chapter 7), but also the autobiographical *Les Mots* (1964), showing traces of dog-ears, notably on page 87, with the anecdote about the young Jean-Paul asking his mother permission to read *Madame Bovary*. If he had already started reading this kind of novel at his age, his mother wondered, what would he do when he was older. To which her 'petit chéri' replied that he would 'live' them ('Je les vivrai!'; 87). All the marks of folded corners[87] occur in the first part, 'Lire', none in the second part, 'Écrire'.

CÉLINE

One of the other authors listed in Beckett's letter to Pamela Mitchell, Louis-Ferdinand Céline deserves special mention. On 15 June 1937, he thanked George Reavey for sending Céline's *Mea Culpa* and, as John Pilling has shown, he read the *Bagatelles pour un massacre* in 1938.[88] Beckett took a few notes from the *Bagatelles* in his 'Whoroscope' Notebook, just before the notes from Plümacher (45v) and Mauthner (46r; see Chapter 7). The character of Yubelblat, modelled after the Jewish doctor Ludwig Rajchman, director of the League of Nations and one of the founders of the United Nations International Children's Emergency Fund, is presented as a secretary who explains his function during meetings as that of an organizer of 'ecstasy'. After hours of talking, when the discussion has reached an impasse, he takes a piece of paper out of his pocket with the 'Resolution' – prepared beforehand. The effect is presented as an 'ejaculation'.[89] Beckett noted in his 'Whoroscope' Notebook: 'boîte à sperme' (WN 45v), followed by 'Cephalo Bill' and 'Toutvabienovich' (qtd. in Pilling 2005, 44–5).[90] The *Bagatelles* are not (or are no longer) part of Beckett's library,[91] but two other (unmarked) books by Céline are: *D'un château l'autre* (1957) and *Rigodon* (1969). The former was purchased in El Jadida, from where he wrote to Barbara Bray on 5 March 1972: 'I bought here a very dirty 2ⁿᵈ hand copy of D'un château l'autre which I had not read and do now with enjoyment. "pas plaire et vioquir et des rentes !... le vrai bonheur !"' (TCD MS10948/1/515).

BLANCHOT

Shortly after the war Beckett was impressed by Maurice Blanchot's work. In December 1950, he told Georges Duthuit that he had read 'le Sade de Blanchot' – most probably the essay 'À la Rencontre de Sade' (whose title was changed into 'La Raison de Sade' when it was published in *Lautréamont et Sade*). The essay contained a few tremendous quotations ('quelques citations formidables') according to Beckett (*LSB II* 210). He selected a passage, started translating it, read Maurice Heine (notably the essay 'Sade et le roman noir' and *Le Marquis de Sade*) and suggested spicing up the dossier with extracts from Klossowski's *Sade mon prochain*. As Shane Weller has shown, Beckett held Blanchot in high esteem, as is indirectly evidenced by a letter from Suzanne Deschevaux-Dumesnil to Jérôme Lindon (25 May 1951), written after Blanchot had sought to have Beckett awarded the Prix des Critiques for *Molloy*: 'Avoir été défendu par un homme comme Blanchot, cela aura été le principal pour Beckett quoi qu'il advienne' [To have been supported by a man such as Blanchot, that will have been the main thing for Beckett, however it may turn out] *LSB II* 253; qtd. in Weller 2007, 27). Toward the end of the 1950s, Beckett told Barbara Bray that he would send her Blanchot's *Le livre à venir*, adding: 'I think he's on to something very important which he probably over[systematizes]. I won't read it now, it would only get in my way' (7 August 1959, TCD MS10948/1/41). In the library, the only traces of Beckett's interest in Blanchot's work are unmarked copies of *L'Entretien infini* (1969) and *Après coup* (1983), and Blanchot's preface to Karl Jaspers' *Strindberg et Van Gogh, Hoelderlin et Swedenborg* (1953).[92]

BATAILLE

In a fascinating article on the affinities between *Fin de partie* and Georges Bataille's writings, Peter Fifield notes that 'the single extant record of Beckett having read any of Bataille's work' is a note from Bataille's introduction to *Justine* (1950), 'Le Soleil noir', jotted down by Beckett on the last page of the first *Textes pour rien* notebook (HRC; Fifield 2010, 113), shortly after the publication of Georges Bataille's review 'Le Silence de Molloy' in *Critique* No. 48 (May 1951) and after the meeting in Paris in the middle of May 1951 (Fifield 2010, 116). The only book by Bataille in the library is a 1979 edition of *Madame Edwarda*, originally published in 1941 under the pseudonym, Pierre Angélique. The third edition (1956) was published with a preface in Bataille's name. On the first four pages (9–12) of this *Préface* an unusually large number of individual words and phrases are underlined in pencil,[93] suggesting that this may be another record of Beckett reading Bataille.

DURAS, JANVIER, MICHAUX, PINGET, ROBBE-GRILLET, TOUSSAINT

Most of the books by Beckett's literary contemporaries in the library are unmarked, such as Henri Michaux's account of his experiences with mescalin, *Connaissance par les gouffres* (1961); the copy of *The Sea Wall* (1986), the English translation of Marguerite Duras' *Un Barrage contre le Pacifique*; or *La Salle de bain* (1985) and *Monsieur* (1986) by the Belgian author Jean-Philippe Toussaint.

The library contains seven books by Ludovic Janvier, from *Une Parole exigeante: le nouveau roman* (1964)[94] to *Monstre, va* (1988)[95] – all of them inscribed with a dedication, but none marked. Alain Robbe-Grillet expressed his admiration 'pour Sam' in an inscription in his copy *Le Miroir qui revient* (1984).[96]

Also Robert Pinget gave several inscribed copies of his books, at first only to Suzanne: the copies of *Le Renard et la boussole* (1953) and *Quelqu'un* (1965) were 'Pour Suzanne', inscribed on 22 June 1961. Apart from the copy of *Autour de Mortin* (1965), which is not inscribed, all the other books by Pinget in the library show a handwritten dedication 'Pour Sam & Suzanne': *Le harnais* (1984), *L'apocryphe* (1980), *Charrue* (1985), *Un testament Bizarre* (1986), *L'ennemi* (1987). Pinget even named two streets after his friends in *L'Inquisitoire*, where the 'Rue Sam and then the Rue Suzanne' come after the 'Rue des Irlandais'.[97] In June 1966, Pinget expressed his concern about the 'value' of his work, even though he had won the Prix des Critiques for

L'Inquisitoire (1962) and the Prix Fémina for *Quelqu'un* (1965). Martin Mégevand notes that Beckett 'replied vehemently' that they should not focus on that question of value and that he loved Pinget's work (Mégevand 2010, 12). Still, Beckett did not love all of Pinget's works to the same degree. He arranged for Pinget's play *Lettre morte* to be sent to Barbara Bray on 12 February 1959 because he thought she would like it (TCD MS10948/1/18) and on 8 April 1962, following the publication of *L'Inquisitoire*, he wrote to Pinget that his book had enormously impressed and moved him; but in October 1965 he told Barbara Bray: 'Reading [Pinget's] Quelqu'un. Prefer L'Inquisitoire' (TCD MS10948/1/345).

CONTEMPORARY DRAMA

In terms of drama, the library does not contain many surprises. Beckett was clearly aware of Antonin Artaud's work, as his unmarked copy of *The Theatre and its Double* (1958) suggests. He also had a copy of Gottfried Büttner's *Absurdes Theater und Bewusstseinswandel* (1968). Although Beckett read the chapter on his plays in Martin Esslin's *Theatre of the Absurd*,[98] no copy of Esslin's book is preserved in the library. Of the other playwrights discussed by Esslin, only Pinter's work is prominently present in Beckett's library. Ionesco is not represented by a single play, only by the novel *Le Solitaire* (1973). The six dedication copies sent to Beckett by Fernando Arrabal feature two volumes of his *Théâtre*: volumes XV (1984) and XVI (1986). The former is also signed (by means of a drawing) by Arrabal's son, Samuel, apparently named after Beckett, whom Arrabal regarded as 'Mon maître idolatré'.[99]

CHAPTER 4

Literature in German

In a letter written in French to Morris Sinclair in January 1934, Beckett remarked that he had 'very imperfect understanding ... of the German language' (*LSB* 180) and invited his young cousin to write to him in German so that he could redress the situation. Beckett had visited the Sinclairs in Kassel six times between 1928 and 1932, and he will surely have picked up some German during this time. However, in Spring 1934 Beckett began to study the German language in a more sustained manner, and two notebooks (UoR MS5002 and MS5006), kept at Paulton's Square in London, show Beckett assiduously improving his vocabulary and writing skills. Indeed, there is evidence that Beckett was being tutored at this time. Beckett's trip to Germany in 1936–7 was undoubtedly undertaken in part with an eye on improving his language skills. Early on during his stay in Hamburg, Beckett bought (for 5.50 Reichsmark, 'bitterly grudged'; GD, 27 October 1936) Emil Otto's *German Conversation-Grammar, Methode Gaspey-Otto-Sauer* (1930), and his copy is still in the library. Having bought the book, it appears as if Beckett made an immediate correction based on an experience he had had the day before (as recorded in his 'German Diaries'); having been mistaken for an 'Isländer' (Icelandic) instead of an Irländer (Irish), he completed the list of national appellations in Otto's book by adding in hand 'der Ire' (Otto, 79). In any case, by the time of Beckett's trip to Germany, his command of the German language (although never formally educated) easily rivalled that of Italian.

GERMAN LITERARY HISTORIES

In early 1934, as Beckett intensified his engagement with the language, he also began to study the literary history of Germany more carefully. As he did when acquiring knowledge in other fields, Beckett turned in the first instance to a history, in this case J. G. Robertson's *A History of German Literature*, published in 1902 (and the standard introductory work on the

TCD syllabus). Beckett took 71 pages of hand-written notes (TCD MS10971/1) on the book, replicating Robertson's historical survey by copying its table of contents, subdivision headings and keywords. Summarizing the main developments, Beckett's notes meticulously record the life dates, salient biographical features and major works (at times with bibliographic reference) of a large portion of authors mentioned in Robertson's book. This was Beckett's preferred method of note-taking from such books, and the same approach is visible in his notes on English Literary History and on Philosophy (see chapters 2 and 7). Beckett's procedure gives a good indication of the kind of literary history he thought best: it was to be factual rather than interpretative. This is obvious when Beckett tried to purchase a literary history while in Germany in 1936; having rejected Wilhelm Scherer's comprehensive *Geschichte der deutschen Literatur* because it was 'alas deficient in dates' (GD, 25 October 1936), he clarified his position when discussing Friedrich Stieve's *Abriss der deutschen Geschichte von 1792–1935* in a conversation with Axel Kaun:

What I want is the straws, flotsam, etc., names, dates, births and deaths, because that is all I can know. . . . So I want the old fashioned history book of reference, not the fashionable monde romancé that explains copious[ly] why e.g. Luther was inevitable without telling me anything about Luther, where he went next, what he lived on, what he died of, etc. (GD, 15 January 1937; qtd. in Knowlson 1996, 244)

Beckett had found one such literary history while in Germany, Karl Heinemann's *Die Deutsche Dichtung; Grundriss der deutschen Literaturgeschichte* (1930 [1910]), which he bought in Hamburg: 'Finally buy a short History of Literature by Karl Heinemann. Written before the Machtübernahme' (GD, 22 October 1936; qtd. in Quadflieg 2006, 66).[1] This copy survives and bears the inscription 'Samuel Beckett / Hamburg Oct 1936'. On Christmas Day, Beckett reluctantly admitted in his diary that he had nothing to read but Heinemann's *History*, and proceeded to read the section on Frank Wedekind (GD, 25 December 1936). It appears that the book failed to stimulate him, and that he instead subsequently relied on his notes from Robertson. As such this chapter will follow Robertson's historical survey in order to chart Beckett's wide-ranging, in-depth engagement with literature written in German.

MIDDLE HIGH GERMAN LITERATURE

Beckett's notes from *A History of German Literature* skip the first part on the 'Old High German Period', and begin with the 'Middle High German

Period', which Robertson dates as being 1050–1350. Beckett was clearly very interested in this period, and his notes on this section of the book are only outdone in length by the notes taken on the classical period around Goethe and Schiller. In particular, Beckett pursued his interest in the French troubadour tradition by focusing on the German 'Minnesang', noting that 'With growth of chivalry lyricism passed into hands of Minnesingers, aristocratic class after the manner of Provençal Troubadours'. Indeed, the link is obvious in Beckett's cross-reference between Dietmar von Aist's 'Tagelied' with his poem 'Alba' (TCD 10971/1, 1v). Beckett proceeded to take notes on the generic form of the 'Tagelied', noting for example that Heinrich von Morungen wrote a 'famous Tagelied with each verse closing: da tagte es' (TCD MS10971/1, 7v; qtd. in Nixon 2011, 63).

The notes on the 'Minnesinger' help us date Beckett's reading of Robertson's book to Spring 1934, as in May Beckett wrote the poem 'Da tagte es' (letter to A. J. Leventhal, 7 May 1934).[2] Beckett's writings and letters are littered with references to German literature around this time; his letter to Arland Ussher of 14 March 1934, for example, contains no less than 14 German words, quotations and references.

When Beckett later in life annotated a copy of *Echo's Bones*, he marked 'Da tagte es' with the words 'Walther von der Vogelweide?' instead of Heinrich von Morungen. Beckett's mistake is understandable, as his most extensive notes from the Middle High German Period are concerned with Walther von der Vogelweide, the most famous German *Minnesänger*. He thus transcribed, for example, the famous opening of Vogelweide's poem 'Ich saz ûf eime Steine', which would later variously resurface in his texts:

> Ich saz ûf eime Steine
> und dahte bein mit beine;
> dar ûf sast' ich den ellenbogen;
> ich hete in mîne hant gesmogen
> daz kinne und ein mîn Wange
>
> (TCD MS10971/1, 8r)[3]

Beckett also quoted the poem in his letter to Leventhal of 14 March 1934 ('Sitzen auf einem Steine, Und decken Bein mit Beine..').

Two books in Beckett's library reveal that his interest in medieval German poetry did not cease after his reading of Robertson's *History*. Both books were bought, as their inscriptions indicate, in Hamburg in November 1936, and both are included in the list of 'Books sent home' on 3 December 1936 in the 'Whoroscope' Notebook (WN 17v).[4] The first of these books is a selection of Walther von der Vogelweide's poetry published in 1930, which gives both the medieval German and contemporary renditions. Although the book bears no annotations, Beckett would refer to Vogelweide's poetry throughout his writing. References to his poetry can, for example, be found in *The Calmative* (*ECEF* 29) and *Stirrings Still* (*CIWS* 112).

The second book is the anthology *Älteste deutsche Dichtung* (Urtext und Übertragung), edited and translated by Karl Wolfskehl and Friedrich von der Leyen (1932 [1909]). Rather curiously, Beckett has annotated six poems in this collection, all light-hearted love poems, such as this one:

> Dû bist mîn ich bin dîn.
> des solt dû gewis sîn.
> dû bist beslozzen
> in mînem herzen.
> verlorn ist das sluzzelîn.
> dû muost immêr darinne sîn!
>
> (Wolfskehl 1932, 37)[5]

Beckett's interest in such verse can be set aside his own fondness of the doggerel, but also, as we shall see, of the German *Lied*.

GRIMMELSHAUSEN

Beckett's notes from Robertson tend to deal with the period between 1350 and the eighteenth century in a more cursory manner, and the only book in the library from this period is a copy of arguably the most famous German novel of the seventeenth century, Hans Jakob Christoffel von Grimmelshausen's *Der abenteuerliche Simplicissimus*. The book was most probably bought in Germany 1936, as Beckett notes his intention to purchase it in a diary entry (GD, 28 December 1936). *Simplicissimus* is a picaresque novel published in 1669, and in its playfulness and earthiness can be brought into relation with Rabelais and Fielding, both authors Beckett admired. Yet it was the rich literary outpourings of the eighteenth and nineteenth centuries that engaged him in a more sustained manner.

EIGHTEENTH CENTURY

It is difficult to discern a pattern in Beckett's response to the various movements in German literature of the eighteenth century. He was dismissive of the sentimental overflow of romanticism, as his attack on the 'Victorian Gael' in the essay 'Recent Irish Poetry' (1934) reveals. Harnessing his recent reading of Robertson's *History of German Literature*, Beckett dismisses the writers Samuel Ferguson and Standish O'Grady as an 'Irish Romantic Arnim-Brentano combination', and the romantic epic *Des Knaben Wunderhorn* (1806–8) is cited to mock the 'Ossianic' trend (*Dis* 70 and 77). At the same time, and as we shall see, Beckett was attracted to the melancholy strand within German writing of the eighteenth century, and he read particular poems and passages obsessively all his life. A good example is the work of Matthias Claudius.

CLAUDIUS

The poet Matthias Claudius gets short thrift in Robertson's survey, and his work is characterized as bearing 'the stamp of the homely provincialism of the German eighteenth century' (Robertson 1935, 306). Although not an 'inspired poet', Robertson does state that he is significant for writing important popular songs ('Volkslieder'). Beckett famously referred to Claudius's figure of Death, 'Freund Hain', with reference to Krapp's 'long look' 'over his shoulder into the darkness backstage left' in *Krapp's Last Tape* (see Chapter 1). There is an illustration of 'Hain' in the front of Beckett's edition of Claudius's complete works (*Sämtliche Werke*), published the same year (1958) as Beckett penned the play. However, it seems as if Beckett did not connect Claudius with the darkness surrounding Krapp until he directed the play in Germany, as his reading of the book is more likely to have occurred in March 1960. At the end of this month, he told correspondents that he was learning Claudius 'by heart' (letters to Avigdor Arikha, 30 March 1960; Atik 2001, 65, and Barbara Bray, 31 March 1960; TCD MS10948/1/78).[6] Beckett also inserted a card at pages 884–5, which contain Claudius's letter to Voss and the text of the poem 'Der Tod und das Mädchen'. However, when Beckett used this poem in *All That Fall* (1956), he was surely inspired by Schubert's setting rather than the text itself. Beckett's mediation of German poetry via their setting in song (*Lieder*) is evident from his copy of Walter and Paula Rehberg's *Franz Schubert, sein Leben und Werk* (1947[1946]). In the index of poems set to music by Schubert, Beckett put a pen line beside Claudius's name. Furthermore, he proceeded to write out the title and first line of various poems set to music by Schubert (see Chapter 11). At the top of this list, Beckett noted four poems by Claudius: 'Abendlied', 'An die Nachtigall', 'Der Tod und das Mädchen' and 'Wiegenlied'. Beckett appears to have acquired the 1958 edition to replace another copy of Claudius's works (in three volumes) which he had given to Avigdor Arikha, and which, according to Anne Atik (66), he had bought in Germany.[7]

CLASSICAL PERIOD – LESSING

Taking his cue from Robertson, Beckett reminded himself in his notebook to 'take 1740 as starting-point of German classical literature' (TCD MS10971/1, 17v), before proceeding to take extensive notes on the work of Gotthold Ephraim Lessing. Most famous for his philosophical writings, Lessing is also often seen as the founder of modern German dramaturgy. During his journey through Germany, Beckett visited Wolfenbüttel, where Lessing lived as a librarian from 1770 onward. He spent a few hours at the Herzog-August-Bibliothek studying the so-called *Wolfenbütteler Fragmente* (published as *Fragmente eines Ungenannten*), noting their 'plea for a reasonable religion' and then proceeded to buy a 'complete Lessing (!) ... 6 vols. bound together in 3 with very small print' and arranged to have them sent back home to Dublin (GD, 8 December 1936). The books are mentioned in the 'Books sent home' list in the 'Whoroscope' Notebook (18v), but remain unticked, which may suggest that they never arrived. Yet Beckett does refer to Lessing again in his essay 'La peinture des van Velde ou le monde et le pantalon' (1945–6): 'Ou alors on fait de l'esthétique générale, comme Lessing. C'est un jeu charmant' [Or we just deal with general aesthetics, like Lessing. It's a charming game] (*Dis* 118).

The most extensive notes Beckett took from Robertson are concerned with the literary period spanning the classical period of the eighteenth century, the 'Geniezeit' (Sturm und Drang), and then Romanticism, which all centre on arguably the most important German writer, Johann Wolfgang von Goethe.

GOETHE

The hand-written excerpts from Johann Wolfgang von Goethe's work, compiled in the space of 18 months, suggest that Beckett did not own any books by the German writer in the 1930s. Beckett was an intensive and extensive reader of Goethe in that decade. At first borrowing references and lines from Goethe's work via Schubert,[8] Beckett then turned to studying the poetry and also read (in part or in entirety) the major works: *Die Leiden des jungen Werther, Die Wahlverwandtschaften, Wilhelm Meister, Dichtung und Wahrheit* (forty pages of notes; TCD MS10971/1, 51r–71r), *Faust* (seventy pages of excerpts, UoR MSS5004 and 5005) and the two plays *Torquato*

Tasso (two pages of notes; TCD MS10971/1, 73r–73v) and *Iphigenia in Taurus*.

Beckett's library contains three of the four volumes published as *Goethes Werke; Auswahl in sechzehn Bänden* (volumes I, III and IV) by the Verlagsgesellschaft für Literatur und Kunst in Berlin (all unmarked). The volumes, in the 1909 edition, are second-hand copies, and it is unclear whether Beckett lost the second volume or was unable to purchase a full set; the missing volume contains, among other things, *Faust, Iphigenia, Torquato Tasso* and *Die Wahlverwandtschaften*. It is unlikely that Beckett possessed the volumes before his trip to Germany in 1936, seeing as he borrowed Hester Dowden's copy of *Dichtung und Wahrheit* when he read it in 1935. However, given that the volume containing *Die Wahlverwandtschaften* is missing, and the extracts from the book in the 'Whoroscope' Notebook are in French (probably dating from 1938–9), it is not unreasonable to suspect that he picked them up in Germany in 1936–7. It would however be surprising had Beckett settled for an incomplete set, and it is more likely that if the volumes were bought in Germany, the second volume went missing between then and now.

Whereas Beckett engaged with Goethe's work thematically and formally in the 1930s, this no longer appears to have been the case after the Second World War. Indeed, his interest in the German writer had steadily declined throughout the decade, moving from an early dislike of Goethe's sentimental writing, to an impatience with the Faustian insistence on ideas of 'progress' and 'onwardness' (see Van Hulle 2006), which finally culminated in the words 'Blast Goethe' in his 'German Diaries' (27 January 1937). However, after the war, and leaving aside work done for UNESCO on essays on Goethe in April 1949 (Pilling 2006a, 106), Beckett continued to admire some of the poems he had first encountered in the 1930s. Indeed, in his copy of Walter and Paula Rehberg's *Franz Schubert, sein Leben und Werk*, Beckett marked four poems in the index – 'Gesang des Harfners II' ('Wer nie sein Brot . . .'), 'Mignon', 'Prometheus' and 'Wandrers Nachtlied' ('Über allen Gipfeln ist Ruh') – and proceeded to copy out, as he did with Claudius, the titles and the first line of each on a loose piece of paper. It is unclear why Beckett focused on these particular poems as he does not mark, for example, other poems he had cited in his work, such as 'Der Erlkönig' or 'Gretchen am Spinrade'. All four poems however were cited by Beckett throughout his life in both his private correspondence as well as his work. Indeed, the importance here is surely the connection between music and text, as Beckett's use of Mignon's song – which begins 'Kennst du das Land, wo die Zitronen blühn' – in the short prose piece *First Love* illustrates. As

Lulu (or Anna) sings the song, the narrator remarks: 'I did not know the song, I had never heard it before and shall never hear it again. It had something to do with lemon trees, or orange trees, I forget' (*ECEF* 72).

Two of the other poems by Goethe that Beckett marked in the Rehbergs' book (which he read in 1969) look back to the 1930s, although Anne Atik reveals that he was fond of citing both in the 1960s and 1970s. The poem 'Prometheus' – with its revolt against the gods – had already struck a chord with Beckett, and he had typed the poem out in the notes on German Literature (TCD MS10971/1, 72r–72v) as a young man. Goethe's 'Wanderers Nachtlied II' was already familiar to Beckett since the very early 1930s, and he recast the line 'Die Vögelein schweigen im Walde' [The birds in the forest have finished their song] within various texts. In a rather unusual move, Beckett ignored the poem's melancholy anticipation of rest in sleep or death, and instead adapted the line as 'Die Bitchlein sweifen niemals im Wald' in the 'Dream' Notebook (1091). This was subsequently employed in *Dream* to bolster the misogynistic tone of the narrative: 'the Bitchlein . . . schweigen niemals im Wald' [the little bitches . . . are never silent in the forest] (*Dream* 80). Beckett then used the same line in his 1937 letter to Axel Kaun, in this case to dovetail with the criticism of language: 'Denn im Walde der Symbole, die keine sind, schweigen die Vöglein der Deutung, die keine ist, nie' [For in the forest of symbols, which aren't any, the little birds of interpretation, which isn't any, are never silent] (*Dis* 53; trans. 172).

Yet the four poems marked by Beckett don't merely look backwards. As Marion Fries-Dieckmann has recently argued,[9] Beckett would often embed quotations from German literature in his original French and English writing, but would then insist on textual accuracy when advising Elmar Tophoven on the German translation. Beckett's use of Goethe's second 'Gesang des Harfenspielers', with the opening lines 'Wer nie sein Brot isst', is a good example of this.[10] He thus annotated a passage in Rick Cluchey's bilingual copy of *Eh Joe* (UoR MS3626, 59; qtd. in Van Hulle and Nixon 2009, 68) with the words 'W[ilhelm] M[eister] Harfenspieler' in order to specify that two lines in the TV play were derived from Goethe's poem. He amended (in Stuttgart in 1979) the German translation of the two lines in question, changing intertextual allusions into quotations. In the English version, the female figure is 'sitting on the edge of her bed in her lavender slip. . .', which is rendered in the German version as 'Sitzt auf ihrer Bettkante in ihrem lila Unterrock. . .'. In his marginal note, Beckett replaces the edge of the bed with the words 'ihrem Bette', and noted Goethe's line at the top of the page: 'Auf seinem Bette weinend sass'. Similarly, the German

90   *Samuel Beckett's Library*

translation of the English 'heavenly powers', 'himmlische Mächte', is corrected with the hand-written addition of 'ihr' and an 'n' in order to replicate Goethe's 'ihr himmlischen Mächte'.[11]

As the above episode illustrates, Beckett continued to read and refer to Goethe's work, in particular the poetry. In March 1960, for example, he cited the lines 'Die Welt geht auseinander / Wie ein fauler Fisch, / Wir wollen sie nicht / balsamieren' in letters to Avigdor Arikha and Barbara Bray on 31 March 1960, and he also sent the latter a typescript of the poem 'Ginkgo Biloba' in September 1977 from Berlin. Moreover, he continued to approach Goethe's work through its musical settings by Schubert, as a quotation from *Wilhelm Meister* of late spring 1981 in the 'Sottisier' Notebook testifies: 'Nur wer die Sehnsucht kennt, weiss was ich leide (W.M. Mignon. Schubert. Wolf.)' (UoR MS2901, 15r; qtd. in Nixon 2011, 202).

SCHILLER

The fact that Beckett tended to admire German poetry through its settings in *Lieder* may account for the comparative absence of Friedrich Schiller's work in Beckett's reading. Although he read and saw a performance of Schiller's *Maria Stuart* while he was in Germany, the only book in the library is a copy of Charles Simond's study *Schiller 1759–1805* (n.d. [1907]).

Beckett's final verdict on reading Schiller's *Maria Stuart* was the question 'Why must one always find something to say' (GD, 6 January 1937; qtd. in Nixon 2011, 72). Beckett had, in his reading of Goethe's *Faust*, similarly thought that there was a 'surprising amount of irrelevance' in the book, partly because Goethe 'couldn't bear to shorten anything' (letter to MacGreevy, 7 August 1936; *LSB* 366). By July 1937, as noted in his letter to Kaun, Beckett had come to the conclusion that Goethe was the kind of writer who thought 'Lieber NICHTS zu schreiben, als nicht zu schreiben' [better to write NOTHING than not write at all] (*Dis* 52; trans. 170). This stands in marked contrast with the poet to whom Beckett turned in late 1937, Friedrich Hölderlin. As Beckett told Patrick Bowles in 1955, Hölderlin's poems

> ended in something of this kind of failure. His only successes are the points where his poems go on, falter, stammer, and then admit failure, and are abandoned. At such points he was most successful. When he tried to abandon the spurious magnificence. (Bowles 1994, 31)

HÖLDERLIN

Beckett's copy of Friedrich Hölderlin's *Sämtliche Werke* (no date, late 1920s) bears the inscription 'SB 24/12/37', and his most intensive reading of the volume can be dated to 1938 and 1939. However, Beckett was already aware of the German poet's work from the early 1930s. He had noted two and half lines from the third version of 'Mnemosyne' in his 'Dream' Notebook (1087), incorporating them (in part) in *Dream* (138). In his notes from Robertson's *History of German Literature*, Beckett wrote that Hölderlin was not 'romantic like Richter, but combination of Sturm u. Drang & Hellenism. Insane from 1802 till his death', and that his work was imbued with the 'melancholy of late 19th century' (TCD MS10971/1, 31v).

Beckett's copy of Hölderlin's complete works contains marginalia and other reading traces. The marked passages are usually expressions of nostalgia and melancholy, such as the line 'Wohin könnt ich mir entfliehen, hätt ich nicht die lieben Tage meiner Jugend?' [How could I escape from myself, if I had not the sweet days of my youth?] from *Hyperion* (Hölderlin n.d., 441; 1990, 11). Beckett's annotations also show that he is alert to intertextual dialogues, detecting for example echoes to Goethe's 'Wandrers Nachtlied' in two passages from *Hyperion*: 'da ich wandelt unter herrlichen Entwürfen, wie in weiter Wäldernacht' [when I roved among beautiful projects as through the night of a vast forest] (Hölderlin n.d., 442; 1965, 31), and Hyperion's answer to Alabanda's question why he had become so monosyllabic: 'In den heissen Zonen, . . . näher der Sonne, singen ja auch die Vögel nicht' [In the tropical regions, nearer the sun, . . . the birds do not sing either] (Hölderlin n.d., 454; 1965, 43).

Most of Beckett's marginalia are found in Hölderlin's novel *Hyperion oder Der Eremit in Griechenland* (1797–9). Many of the marked passages focus on Hyperion's feelings of self-doubt and self-alienation, which border on self-destructive impulses, as in the line 'Je glücklicher du bist, um so weniger kostet es, dich zugrunde zu richten' [The happier one is, the less it takes to destroy one] (Hölderlin n.d., 454; 1990, 22). At the same time, Beckett was attentive to Hyperion's existential anxieties over human striving generally, and the human being's position in the universe. At the top of the following passage (Hyperion writing to Bellarmin), Beckett marked an 'X' and an exclamation mark:

At times some energy would even yet waken in my spirit. But only for destruction!
    What is man? – so I might begin; how does it happen that the world contains such a thing, which ferments like a chaos or moulders like a rotten tree, and never

grows to ripeness? How can Nature tolerate this sour grape among her sweet clusters? (Hölderlin 1990, 35).[12]

Toward the end of the first book, Hyperion reaches a moment of existential calm in a scene that stages a Schopenhauerian renunciation of the will, a quietist refusal of the self. Beckett marked this long passage and appended the words 'Nox animae':

There is a hush, a forgetting of all existence, in which we feel as if we had lost everything, a night of our soul, in which no glimmer of any star nor even the fire from a rotting log gives us light. I had become quiet. No longer did anything drive me from bed at midnight. No longer did I singe myself in my own flame (Hölderlin 1990, 32).[13]

Whereas the first book of *Hyperion* kept Beckett's attention,[14] he appears to have abandoned his reading at the beginning of the second book, and the last marginal note is the remark 'Que de frohlockend's!' (Hölderlin n.d., 472).

As is the case with other books in the library, it is the non-marginalia in Beckett's copy of Hölderlin that throws the longest creative shadow. Or has an immediate effect: the first fruits of Beckett's reading of Hölderlin can be found in his 1938 writing: the late poem 'Der Spaziergang' is quoted in the critical review 'Intercessions by Denis Devlin', published April–May 1938 in *transition* (Dis 94):

> Ihr lieblichen Bilder im Tale,
> Zum Beispiel Garten und Baum,
> Und dann der Steg, der schmale,
> Der Bach zu sehen kaum
>
> (Hölderlin 1967, 576–7)[15]

The same piece also inspired Beckett's own poem 'Dieppe'; he would later make the identification in a letter to John Fletcher, 21 November 1964:

> encore le dernier reflux
> le galet mort
> le demi-tour puis les pas
> vers les
> vieilles lumières

However, in a letter to Barbara Bray (17 February 1959; TCD MS10948/1/19) he copied out the poem and pointed specifically to the word 'puis' as deriving from Hölderlin. That Beckett took note whenever he encountered the poem is further evidenced by his copy of Hölderlin's *Dichtungen und*

Briefe (1952), in which the corner of the page with 'Der Spaziergang' has been folded down at some point.[16]

Another instance where Beckett drew on his reading of Hölderlin's poetry without leaving reading traces in the relevant passages relates to the poem 'Hyperions Schicksalslied' (1789), which appears in the second book of *Hyperion*. Beckett had originally copied this stanza from Robertson into his notebook, undoubtedly struck by the poem's theme of human helplessness in the face of an unsympathetic universe, a topic which had previously attracted him to Goethe's 'Prometheus'. Beckett used the closing stanza, albeit in an extremely fractured manner, toward the end of *Watt* (207), and exasperated the mortal torment by replacing Hölderlin's 'Jahrelang' with the endless 'endlos'.

Over thirty years later, Hölderlin remained in Beckett's mind, as evidenced by a note in his production notebook of *That Time* (*Damals*) for the Schiller Theater in Berlin, dating from August 1976. Here Beckett made the following note, under the heading 'B': 'Alles war nun Stille. Wir sprachen kein Wort, wir berührten uns nicht, wir sahen uns nicht an ... Hölderlin Hyperion-Fragment' (UoR MS1976, 6r; qtd. in Ackerley and Gontarski 2004, 254). The quotation is, as identified by Beckett, from the *Hyperion-Fragment* (rather than the novel *Hyperion*), and is refracted across the first two utterances made by the figure B:

'vowing every now and then you loved each other just a murmur *not touching* or anything of that nature you one end of the stone she the other long low stone like millstone no looks just there on the stone in the sun with the little wood behind gazing at the wheat or *eyes closed all still* no sign of life not a soul abroad no sound'

...

'*all still* just the leaves and ears and you too still on the stone in a daze no sound *not a word* only every now and then to vow you loved each other' (*CDW* 388–89; our emphasis)

There is more than a textual echo at work here, but the integration of a textual mood. The same occurs when Beckett returned to a poem he had marked up in his copy in 1938. Within the material pertaining to Beckett's last prose piece *Stirrings Still* held at the 'Fonds John Calder' at IMEC[17] are photocopies of pages 88–9 and 90–1 from Beckett's edition of Hölderlin, with poems collected in the 'Antike Strophen' (see Van Hulle 2011, 63). In particular, the quatrain 'Ehemals und Jetzt' ('Then and Now') is marked by a vertical line:

94   *Samuel Beckett's Library*

>   In jüngren Tagen war ich des Morgens froh,
>   Des Abends weint ich; jetzt, da ich älter bin,
>   Beginn ich zweifelnd meinen Tag, doch
>   Heilig und heiter ist mir sein Ende.
>
>   (Hölderlin n.d., 88)[18]

While writing *Stirrings Still*, which deals with the impossibility of putting one's 'end' into words ('No words for his end'; UoR MS 2935/1/1 f. 1r; BDMP1), Beckett must have been reminded of Hölderlin's poem.

Over time Beckett's initial attraction to *Hyperion* and the poems written before the German writer retired to his tower at Tübingen gradually shifted to the 'terrific fragments of the Spätzeit [late period]' (letter to Arland Ussher 14 June [1939]; *LSB* 664–5). As such, Beckett's increasing emphasis on notions of speechlessness, incompetence and fragmentation found a correlative within the late works of the German poet. Beckett had, remarkably, already harnessed this aspect of Hölderlin's work before he had properly engaged with it in his reading. As noted above, Beckett quoted a line from the poem 'Mnemosyne' by 'poor Hölderlin' in *Dream* ('alles hineingeht Schlangen gleich'; 138). The context of the passage in which this quotation is placed concerns the idea of dehiscence, the idea of disunity, and Hölderlin's poem furnished Beckett – in the form of the word 'Ungebundene' from line 13 of 'Mnemosyne' – with a further term for this idea: 'a disfaction, a désuni, an Ungebund, a flottement, a tremblement, a tremor, a tremolo, a disaggregating, a disintegrating, an efflorescence, a breaking down and multiplication of tissue, the corrosive ground-swell of art' (*Dream* 138).[19]

HEINE

As J. G. Robertson aptly pointed out, it is remarkable how Goethe not only defined German literature in the eighteenth century, leading it through the 'storm days of "Sturm und Drang" to the calm age of classical perfection', but also influenced, 'as no other man of his generation, the new time' (451). Belonging essentially to two fundamentally different epochs, Goethe was thus present in what Robertson terms the 'Young Germany' movement that embraced the romantic age sweeping Europe at the turn of the century. One of the most important writers of the new age was Heinrich Heine, a writer who became increasingly important to Beckett after the Second World War.

Beckett was aware of Heine's work through his reading of Robertson's *History* and, earlier still, of Mario Praz's *The Romantic Agony* (which furnished an early reference to Heine, the 'Marientotenkind' noted in the 'Dream' Notebook; 326). Beckett may have read Heine's essay 'Die Romantische Schule', as he cites the words 'verkörperter Mondschein' in the review of Moerike (1934; *Dis* 61).[20] It is, however, difficult to ascertain the date of Beckett's introduction to Heine's work with any certainty, but it could, once again, have been via Schubert's *Lieder*. Indeed, most references to Heine's work in Beckett's published and unpublished work derive from musical settings; already in 1956 Beckett told MacGreevy that he and Suzanne had been listening to Schumann's *Dichterliebe*, based on poems by Heine (30 July 1956). He did, however, own a copy of Heine's *Buch der Lieder*, published by the Insel Verlag in Leipzig (no date, but the imprint is c. 1930).[21] Beckett most probably acquired the book second-hand, as it contains two kinds of reading traces. There are crosses in purple pencil set against various poems, none of which demonstrably correlate with any other material evidence in Beckett's work, published or unpublished. There are however also two marginalia made in black ink, which can most certainly be attributed to Beckett.

The first marginal note is a crossed-out word, probably reading 'Nacht', beside the poem opening 'Still ist die Nacht, es ruhen die Gassen' of the section 'Die Heimkehr' in *Buch der Lieder* (146). Better known under the title 'Der Doppelgänger', the poem is one of six that were included in Schubert's cycle *Schwanengesang* (published posthumously). In his copy of Walter and Paula Rehberg's *Franz Schubert, sein Leben und Werk*, Beckett had noted, beside the titles of the six relevant poems, the word 'Schwanengesang'. As Rosemary Pountney first pointed out (42), Beckett had invoked Heine's poem in the first manuscript draft toward *Film* in April 1963: 'If music unavoidable, Schubert's *Doppelgänger* – with perhaps Ich bin nicht wild, komme nicht zu strafen?' (Beckett is here confusing Heine's poem with a line from Claudius's poem 'Der Tod und das Mädchen'; UoR MS1227/7/6/1, 6v). It is difficult to know whether Beckett is interested in an allusion to Schubert's music or to Heine's text in such an instance, yet the confluence of the tone and theme of loss that runs throughout this piece would have been enough to ensure his interest.

The other reading mark in Beckett's copy of Heine's *Buch der Lieder* is a line beside the first two lines of a further poem in the section 'Die Heimkehr': 'Teurer Freund! Was soll es nützen, / Stets das alte Lied zu leiern?' (162). Either at a different time, or concurrently, Beckett noted the same lines into his 'Sottisier' Notebook, together with the entry relating Dante's *Inferno* to a line in Heine: '"Singende Flammen" / (D[ante])'s Inf. Heine: Deutschland: Ein Wintermärchen)' (UoR MS2901, 10v; qtd. in

Nixon 2007b, 115). Beckett noted these entries into his notebook between 18 January and 8 February 1978, at a time when he was writing *Company* (begun May 1977).²² Indeed, as Elmar Tophoven pointed out, during their work on the German translation Beckett had alerted him to an intertextual reference to Heine in this prose text. Once again, Beckett insisted on textual accuracy in translating the mind's inquiry 'What does this mean?' (*CIWS* 14) into 'was soll es bedeuten?', to echo the first line of Heine's 'Die Loreley' from 'Die Heimkehr' – 'Ich weiss nicht, was soll es bedeuten' (Tophoven 1984, 289).

Despite such engagement with Heine's poems as texts, Beckett's interest was always in their settings as musical *Lieder*. As he told Anne Atik on 19 April 1981, 'Heine is a great poet', but the context of the statement was made after they had listened to *Winterreise* and *Schwanengesang*, including 'Der Doppelgänger'. Around this same time, in April or May 1981, Beckett also noted down a further line from Heine's 'Die Heimkehr' cycle in his 'Sottisier' Notebook, noting its setting by Schumann: 'Ich grolle nicht u. wenn das Herz auch bricht. (Heine. Schumann. Dichterliebe)' (UoR MS2901, 15r; qtd. in Nixon 2007b, 116).

JACOB AND WILHELM GRIMM

Beckett's attraction to the more 'popular' dimension of German literature, such as *Lieder* or *Proverbs*, can be extended to his interest in German fairy tales, in particular in the brothers Grimm's *Märchen*. Beckett owned a two-volume edition of *Die Märchen der Brüder Grimm* (1918), and a letter headed 'Foxrock Cooldrinagh' inserted in the pages of 'Dornröschen' suggests that it came into his possession in the early 1930s. Beckett first referenced the 'Grimm brothers' in *Dream* (215), and appears to have read or reread their fairy tales in early 1934, as references in letters to Morris Sinclair (27 January 1934) and Arland Ussher (14 March 1934) indicate. Beckett was particularly fond of the last line in the story 'The Cat and the Mouse', which evinces a textual and existential acceptance of the way the universe operates: 'So it goes in the world'. He used the line to conclude the story 'Echo's Bones', and after it was rejected for *More Pricks than Kicks*, to conclude the last story 'Draff' (*MPTK* 181). Beckett also used it in numerous letters, in each instance to give voice to a weary acceptance of the trials encountered in life.²³

KLEIST

Another author that ghosts through Beckett's production notebooks, manuscripts and correspondence is Heinrich von Kleist, and in particular his text *Über das Marionettentheater* (1810). Beckett's copy of the book (1968 reprint) is still in the library, and was presented to him by the German actress Nancy Illig, with whom he had worked in *Spiel* and *He, Joe*.[24] As Beckett told Barbara Bray from Berlin: 'Got the Kleist Marionettentheater (extraordinary) and other essays' (3 October 1969; TCD MS10948/1/440).[25] Ten days later, writing from Nabeul this time, Beckett again referred to Kleist's 'marvellous essay on Marionetten theatre with unforgettable anecdote of duel with bear' (letter to Barbara Bray, 13 October 1969; TCD MS10948/1/443). Kleist's essay clearly struck a chord with Beckett; it argues that a puppet has more harmony and grace than any human actor or dancer because it has no self-consciousness, and this is also the motto of the story of the bear that defeats a master fencer because it is not burdened by an awareness of self. In his copy, Beckett marked one of Kleist's core arguments in his essay:

Und der Vorteil, den diese Puppe vor lebendigen Tänzern voraus haben würde?
   Der Vorteil? Zuvörderst ein negativer, mein vortrefflicher Freund, nämlich dieser, daß sie sich niemals *zierte*. – Denn Ziererei erscheint, wie Sie wissen, wenn sich die Seele (vis motrix) in irgend einem andern Punkte befindet, als in dem Schwerpunkt der Bewegung. (Kleist 1968, 8)[26]

The notion of movement is linked with the idea of a divine grace by Kleist in the subsequent pages, and Beckett summarizes the argument by appending the words 'göttliche anmut des gliedermanns' (10). Beckett used this text in his dealings with actors, referring to it for example in 1971 when producing *Happy Days* in Germany with Eva-Katharina Schultz, or during the BBC production of *Ghost Trio* in 1975 (Knowlson 1996, 584, 632–3).

In terms of theatre or poetry, there are no other writers of the nineteenth century represented in the library; given Beckett's interest in these writers in the 1930s, for example, one misses volumes by Grillparzer or by Friedrich Hebbel. However, there are several books by one of Germany's most important novelists of the century, Theodor Fontane.[27]

FONTANE

It is, somewhat surprisingly, the work of Theodor Fontane which Beckett mentions most in the post-war period. Born in 1819, Fontane was mostly known for his poetry, ballads and travel writings until he turned his hand to novels in the 1880s. He was one of the first novelists to absorb the influence of French realist writers, in particular Flaubert and Zola.

Beckett's first biographer, Deirdre Bair, argued that Beckett read *Effi Briest* (1895), Fontane's masterpiece, together with (a tearful) Peggy Sinclair in Kassel in the late 1920s (1990, 91), using a reference to the book in *Krapp's Last Tape* to form a retrospective biographical identification:

> Scalded the eyes out of me reading *Effie* again, a page a day, with tears again. Effie . . . . [*Pause*.] Could have been happy with her, up there on the Baltic, and the pines, and the dunes. (*CDW* 222)

Yet as Knowlson has argued (1996, 443), the biographical sources of the play are surely to be found in Beckett's relationship with Ethna MacCarthy, who was critically ill at the time of its writing. Indeed, just as Fontane's novel deals with adultery and past love, *Krapp's Last Tape* harnesses the book to evoke a more general sense of loss. It is similarly referenced in *All That Fall*, as Mr Rooney looks forward to hearing Maddy read from the book in the evening: 'I think Effie is going to commit adultery with the Major' (*CDW* 189).

The copy of Fontane's *Effi Briest* in Beckett's library bears no date, but the particular edition (Leipzig: Insel Verlag) was first printed in 1936. As such it is very likely that this is the copy sent to Beckett by the young German bookseller Günter Albrecht in 1937; in a letter of 30 March 1937, Beckett thanked him and stated that he neither possessed nor had read the book (*LSB* 477). One may be surprised by the fact that Beckett admired a book which in its realism was so keenly influenced by Flaubert and Zola, but he returned to the book, somewhat obsessively, on several occasions during his life. Beckett called it 'formidable' when listing it along with other books dealing with the misfortunes caused by love in a letter to Jacoba van Velde in 1952 (*LSB II* 342). Four years later he advised Rosset to publish 'that most moving and beautiful novel', *Effi Briest*, if he had a 'first-rate translator up [his] sleeve' (Letter to Barney Rosset, 26 May 1956; *LSB II* 621).[28] As he went on to say, he had 'read it for the fourth time the other day with the same old tears in the same old places'.[29] The reference to tears in this letter anticipates the scene in *Krapp's Last Tape*, begun two years later. Closer in time is of course the other play that openly alludes to *Effi Briest*, *All That Fall*, the genesis of which begins in July 1956 and which was sent to the BBC in September of that year.

Beckett's use of Fontane suggests that the two-volume edition of the German writer's works in the library is the one printed in either 1955 or

1958 (neither was published with a date). The latter may be a little more plausible, as *Krapp's Last Tape* not only references *Effi Briest*, but also Fontane's novel *Unwiederbringlich*.[30] As the play closes, the 39-year-old Krapp fends off the sense of loss and nostalgia by claiming 'Perhaps my best years are gone. When there was a chance of happiness. But I wouldn't want them back. Not with the fire in me now. No, I wouldn't want them back' (*CDW* 223). The sentiment and particular terminology (happiness, fire and a time lost) of this passage draws on Elisabeth's song in chapter 33 of Fontane's *Unwiederbringlich*, and translates the final line:

> 'Denkst du verschwundener Tage, Marie,
> Wenn du starrst ins Feuer bei Nacht?
> Wünschst du die Stunden und Tage zurück,
> Wo du froh und glücklich gelacht?'
>
> 'Ich denke verschwundener Tage, John,
> Und sie sind allezeit mein Glück,
> Doch die mir die liebsten gewesen sind,
> Ich wünsche sie *nicht* zurück ...'
>
> (Fontane 1958, 1046)[31]

Beckett's letters and reported conversations reveal that he also read other texts by Fontane, in particular 'Unter dem Birnbaum' and, surprisingly, the rather conservative art letters in 'Briefe aus London'. As Michael Haerdter's entry for 9 September 1967 in the 'Proben-Notate zum Endspiel' (Schiller Theater Berlin) reveals, the other novel that Beckett admired was *Irrungen Wirrungen* (Voelker 96). The novel is also in the two-volume edition of Fontane's *Werke* which Beckett possessed, and having read it in 1960, he thought that it contained 'marvellous things', although it was 'not as good as Effie' (letter to Barbara Bray, 1 October 1960; TCD MS10948/1/113).[32] When he reread the novel in Berlin 1978, he playfully invoked the title to describe the rehearsals of *Spiel* (letter to A. J. Leventhal, 24 September 1978).

HOFMANNSTHAL, RILKE

Robertson's *History of German Literature* ends with the close of the nineteenth century, and the last writer to be mentioned in Beckett's notes is Hugo von Hofmannsthal. Beckett had read Hofmannsthal's *Der Tor und der Tod* in Germany (with mixed feelings) and it is included in the list of books sent home in the 'Whoroscope' Notebook (WN 17v); it does not survive in the library however. The library does contain a small, two-page pamphlet entitled *Das dichterische Element in unserer Zeit*, inserted in

Beckett's copy of Olga Plümacher's *Der Pessimismus*. The pamphlet, which gives an excerpt of a lecture by the German writer, was printed in 20 copies in 1937 by Axel Kaun, who must have sent it to Beckett (Kaun's name still appears in a Routledge list of people who are to receive complimentary copies of *Murphy* in 1938). Hofmannsthal's contemporary, the poet Rainer Maria Rilke, is similarly absent from Beckett's library; it only contains a Hebrew edition of *Die Weise von Liebe und Tod des Cornets Christoph Rilke*, illustrated by Avigdor Arikha. From his earliest review of Rilke's poetry in 1934, Beckett's response to the writer was unenthusiastic.[33]

TWENTIETH-CENTURY GERMAN LITERATURE

It may not be surprising to note that there are not many German literary books from the twentieth century in Beckett's library. This is not simply an issue of an anxiety of influence; Beckett did not go out of his way to engage with contemporary writers. Those books that are in the library, and most of them do not have marginalia but signs of having been read, were sent to Beckett by authors, friends or publishers. There are thus inscribed copies from Heinrich Böll (*Entfernung von der Truppe*, 1964; *Geschichten aus zwölf Jahren*, 1969, not inscribed), Nelly Sachs (*Späte Gedichte*, 1965[34]; *Die Suchende*, 1966) and Franz Wurm (*In diesem Fall*, 1989), and copies of books by Peter Weiss, Erich Fried and Günther Eich.

Beckett's library is, as has been noted repeatedly in this book, not complete, and there is clear evidence of books that found their way out of the library. David Gulette, for example, records seeing works by Brecht in the library, whereas none were extant at the time of Beckett's death in 1989. Furthermore, Beckett's correspondence shows that he was more alert to contemporary German literature than the library suggests. He thus read Gottfried Benn's essays in 1960[35] and then his letters in 1977, Hans Magnus Enzensberger's *Einzelheiten* ('which might well be entitled Kleinigkeiten' according to Beckett; letter to Barbara Bray, 13 August 1962; TCD MS10948/1/189).

The way in which Beckett's library is a chance survival can be shown by his reading of Max Frisch (see Nixon 2010). At the time of his death in 1989, Beckett's library contained four books by the Swiss writer: *Die chinesische Mauer*, *Biographie: Ein Spiel*, *Ausgewählte Prosa* and *Erzählungen des Anatol Ludwig Stiller*. However, archival evidence and letters reveal that Beckett also possessed and read copies of Frisch's *Tagebuch 1966–1971*, *Andorra*, *Biedermann und die Brandstifter* and *Homo Faber* (which Beckett read twice; letter to Barbara Bray, 2 February 1960).

KAFKA

Beckett's reading of Kafka, or to be more precise, the dating of his reading of Kafka has troubled scholars for some time now. It is possible that Beckett would have first encountered Kafka's work in the pages of *transition*, especially in those issues that carried work by both authors. Between 1928 and 1932, its editor Eugene Jolas, who was an admirer of Kafka, published 'Das Urteil', three stories from *Beim Bau der chinesischen Mauer* and, in three instalments, *Metamorphosis*. It also appears as if Beckett was familiar with the two novels *Das Schloss* and *Der Prozess*, as both are mentioned in a letter Beckett wrote to Morris Sinclair advising him on potential academic research topics (21 October 1945; *LSB II* 22). The most telling statement of Beckett's response to Kafka's work is found in a letter he wrote to the translator Hans Naumann:

All I've read of his, apart from a few short texts, is about three-quarters of *The Castle*, and then in German, that is, losing a great deal. I felt at home, too much so – perhaps that is what stopped me from reading on. Case closed there and then. . . . I remember feeling disturbed by the imperturbable aspect of his [Kafka's] approach. I am wary of disasters that let themselves be recorded like a statement of accounts. (17 February 1954; *LSB II* 464–5)

Beckett would, in subsequent years, repeat his criticism of the way in which content and form contradicted each other in Kafka's work. As he told Ruby Cohn, 'What struck me as strange in Kafka was that the form is not shaken by the experience it conveys' (letter to Ruby Cohn, 17 January 1962; qtd. in Nixon 2011, 49).

The 'anxiety of influence' detailed in the Naumann letter may possibly explain the absence of literary works by Kafka in Beckett's library – the only edition that survives is that of *Er* (edited by Martin Walser in 1963), which collects shorter prose. A copy of Kafka's diaries, for example, which Beckett read in the early 1980s (see letter to Shainberg, 8 January 1983), is not extant. There is, however, a number of books about Kafka in the library, all of which attest to Beckett's interest in the writer.[36]

Beckett's engagement with German literature, throughout his life, was profound. More often than not, his appreciation of German culture was emotional rather than formal, or literary, which explains the way in which his most intense *Auseinandersetzung* with German texts occurred via music. Among the many chestnut phrases Beckett used to navigate his emotional states and events in his life, German quotations loom large. This is exemplified by his insistent use of the line 'Es wandelt niemand ungestraft unter

Palmen' [Nobody walks unpunished under palm trees], from Goethe's *Die Wahlverwandtschaften*. First cited in his 1934 essay 'Recent Irish Poetry' (*Dis* 76), Beckett would adapt and use it in the next 40 years in his correspondence:

C'est la misérable envie de ne pas être toujours seul. Ou d'être seul impunément, d'errer sous les palmiers sans que les vautours vous chient dessus [It is the wretched longing not to be always alone. Or to be alone with impunity, to wander beneath the palm-trees without being shat upon by the vultures]. (Letter to Georges Duthuit, 27 May 1948; *LSB II* 78–9)

I feel more and more that I shall perhaps never be able to write anything else. Niemand wandelt ungestraft on the road that leads to L'Innommable. I can't go on and I can't get back. (Letter to Thomas MacGreevy, 14 December 1953; *LSB II* 434)

struggling with French translation of Watt, in whose grim groves I feel I won't have wandered again unpunished. (Letter to Mary Manning Howe, 14 January 1968; qtd. in Nixon 2011, 120)

Wander in the groves ... – unbestraft so far. (Letter to A. J. Leventhal, 8 February 1972)

CHAPTER 5

Literature in Italian

Beckett's main guidebooks to the history of Italian literature were Raffaello Fornaciari's *Disegno Storico della Letterature Italiana* (1901)[1] and Francesco de Sanctis's *Storia della Letteratura Italiana* (1925). The two-volume copy of De Sanctis's *Storia* is inscribed ('S.B. Beckett / Florence / May 1927'). All the underlined passages in the first volume relate to Dante. Beckett attentively read both the chapter on 'La Lirica di Dante' (underlining, among other things, an interesting variation on the theme of the 'wombtomb'[2]) and the chapter on 'La "Commedia"'. It is typical of his free-spirited, cross-generic and multilingual notion of literary history that he saw connections between, say, thirteenth-century Italian poetry and twentieth-century French fiction. For instance, the underlined passage 'Chi non ha la forza di uccidere la realtà non ha la forza di crearla' [Who does not have the strength to kill reality, does not have the strength to create it] (1.159) is quoted literally in Beckett's essay *Proust* (see Chapter 3; Caselli 2005, 26).

The first marginalia in the second volume of De Sanctis's *Storia* is a question mark (blue ink) next to an underlined comment regarding Ludovico Ariosto's *Orlando Furioso*.[3] The adjective 'ariostesco' on the same page, and more particularly 'l'ironia ariostesca' [ariostesque irony] and 'risolino' [snigger], mentioned in the same chapter XIII on 'L'Orlando Furioso', are applied by Beckett in his review of Jack B. Yeats's *The Amaranthers* (*Dis* 89). Again, Beckett effortlessly makes connections between divergent literatures, different languages and authors that are separated by several centuries.

Another section that was read with pen at the ready is the passage on Giovanni Battista Guarini's *Il Pastor Fido* (1590),[4] one of the texts for examination.[5] Beckett underlined Guarini's interplay between sensuality and spirituality in his description of a kiss in terms of an exchange of 'souls'[6] (quoted extensively by De Sanctis); the annotation in the left margin,[7] linking the passage to Marcel Schwob, exemplifies Beckett's method of 'extensive' reading.[8]

Between pages 222 and 223, two undated National Library of Ireland slips are inserted, both for books on 'Aubanel', one by 'Welter', the other by 'Legré', referring to Ludovic Legré, *Le Poète Théodore Aubanel: récit d'un témoin de sa vie* (1894) and Nikolaus Welter, *Théodore Aubanel, un chanteur provençal de la beauté* (1904). Beckett used these two books for the notes on Frédéric Mistral and the Félibrige Poets (TCD MS10971/4), which he prepared in January 1936 for Ethna MacCarthy.[9] The slips are inserted in the section on Giordano Bruno, which also contains marked passages regarding Bruno's reputation as an 'academic without academy', his nickname 'il Fastidito' [the annoyed one][10] and his comedy *Il Candelaio* (*The Candlebearer*, 1582), traces of which are found in Joyce's *Finnegans Wake* (Moliterno 1993).

Beckett seems to have been particularly interested in the chapter on *La nuova scienza*,[11] starting with the tortured Galileo who was made to confess that '*terra stat et in aeternum stabit*' (underlined in pencil) and culminating in a four-page passage, completely marked with long pencil lines in the margins, proclaiming Galileo, Bacon and Descartes 'the true fathers of the modern world'.[12]

In the chapter on *La nuova letteratura* the section on Alberto Gozzi (1720–1806) and Carlo Goldoni (1707–93) contains several underlined passages, although this does not necessarily express a genuine interest on Beckett's part, rather the interest of one his professors, possibly Walter Starkie. As James Knowlson notes, Beckett was taught Italian literature at TCD by both Rudmose-Brown and Starkie, but if one was a favourite of the former, one was unlikely to be an admirer of the latter (1996, 52). In 1925, Walter Starkie published a book on *Carlo Goldoni and the 'commedia dell'arte'*. On the TCD syllabus for 'Italian Language and Literature', the subjects for examination included Dante's *Divina Commedia* and the *Vita Nuova*, Machiavelli's *Il Principe*, Ariosto's *Orlando Furioso*, Tasso's *L'Aminta*, Guarini's *Il Pastor Fido* and several works by Goldoni. Beckett read up on Gozzi and Goldoni in de Sanctis (353–7), who notes that Gozzi started writing comedies with masks (354), which are now almost forgotten ('oggi sono quasi dimenticate'). Beckett tellingly underlined this clause and pencilled in the left margin: 'Unfortunately not by a certain professor in Dublin University' (2.354).

Beckett found someone else to nurture his enthusiasm for Italian literature: Bianca Esposito. He later even spoke of a 'Dante revelation', in which his professors at Trinity College Dublin were not involved, as he told James Knowlson: 'This I seem to have managed on my own, with the help of my Italian teacher, Bianca Esposito' (Knowlson 1996, 715n.35). A postcard,

Literature in Italian

preserved at the University of Reading, characterizes her as a considerate, caring teacher. When she heard that Beckett was ill, just before his twentieth birthday, she sent him a few comforting words. Judging from his voice the other day she had sensed that he must have felt worse than he said he was, and urging him not to get up before he was fully recovered, she told him that his mind would benefit from the forced rest.[13] The concern about his mind ('mente') is interesting in the context of Dante's works, which Beckett studied with Esposito. According to de Sanctis (1.56), Beatrice is a dream rather than a reality – a 'celestial ideal' ('ideale celeste') and a perfect model for *Murphy*'s Celia. She is located in the imagination rather than in the heart ('piú nell' immaginatione che nel cuore'). Next to this underscored line (in pencil), Beckett noted in the left margin (dark sepia ink): 'cp. "la gloriosa donna della mia mente"' (1.56), referring to the opening line of the section on Dante's first meeting with Beatrice in *La Vita Nuova*. The underlined 'mente' and de Sanctis's insistence on the fact that Beatrice exists inside rather than outside of Dante's mind ('esiste piú nella mente di Dante che fuori di quella') prefigure the special chapter 6 in *Murphy*, devoted to the protagonist's mind.

Beckett was also familiar with the *Convivio*. On 26 May 1949, he asked Georges Duthuit if he knew Dante's definition of poetry as a 'bella menzogna'[14]; a few days later, he explained the reference.[15] According to Dante (*Convivio*, Book II, chapter 1), poetic allegory was a truth hidden behind a beautiful lie. Beckett applied this explicitly in 'Draff' with reference to the Smeraldina's 'least clandestine aspect', or 'What a competent poet once called the *bella menzogna*', as the footnote 'clarifies' (*MPTK* 177).

With the guidance of Bianca Esposito (the model for Professoressa Ottolenghi in 'Dante and the Lobster') Beckett started studying *Inferno*. He gradually acquired numerous copies of the *Divina Commedia*, many of which are still preserved:

- *La Divine Comédie*, transl. Artaud de Montor (n.d.); page 395 has been folded down in the past;
- *La Vita Nuova, Il Convito, Il Canzoniere*; only the title page – with the inscription 'S.B. Beckett' – is preserved, inserted into the 1965 *Concordance* (see below);
- *La Divina Commedia*, ed. C.T. Dragone (1959);
- *Operum Latinorum Concordantia* (1912);
- *The Vision of Hell, Purgatory and Paradise by Dante Alighieri*, transl. Henry Francis Cary (1869);
- *The Divine Comedy*, transl. Henry Cary, introd. Edmund Gardner (1967).

The French translation by Artaud de Montor shows a few marginalia,[16] the first of which ('<u>premier amour</u>') deserves special mention in view of the title of Beckett's novella *Premier amour / First Love*. The underlined words are part of the inscription above the gate of Hell (the opening lines of Canto 3):

> I am the way into the doleful city,
> I am the way into eternal grief,
> I am the way to a forsaken race.
>
> Justice it was that moved my great creator;
> Divine omnipotence created me,
> And highest wisdom joined with primal love.
>
> Before me nothing but eternal things
> Were made, and I shall last eternally.
> Abandon every hope, all you who enter.
>
> (Dante 1995, trans. Musa 14)[17]

Beckett also possessed several books *about* Dante:
- *A Concordance to the Divine Comedy of Dante Alighieri*, ed. Ernest Hatch Wilkins and Thomas Goddard Bergin (1965), given to Beckett by Barbara Bray (with the inscription 'For Sam from Barbara with love. / December 1965 / O luce . . .');
- Henri Dauphin, *Vie du Dante: Analyse de la Divine Comédie* (1869);[18]
- Alan George Ferrers Howell, *Dante, His Life and Works* (1920), with the inscription 'S.B. Beckett / Dublin – September '27' and a bookseller's plate from Greene's Library, Dublin); the corners of pages 57, 71, 73, 87 and 107 have been folded down in the past;
- G.L. Passerini (ed.), *Le Vite di Dante*, Scritte da Villani, Boccaccio, Aretino, Manetti (1917), with the inscription 'Samuel Beckett 1936';
- Giorgio Siebzehner-Vivanti, *Dizionario della Divina Commedia* (1965 [1954]).

While the Ferrers Howell may have been put to use in Beckett's review of *Dante Vivo* by Giovanni Papini, published in *The Bookman* in 1934 (*Dis* 80–1), the provenance of Passerini's *Vite di Dante* is documented in a letter to Thomas MacGreevy (25 March 1936): 'He [Maurice Sinclair] has dug out some more Italian books for me, including the <u>Storie Fiorentine</u>, which pleases me greatly; and I found some for myself at <u>Webb</u>'s, left in by some little Jez called Boyle or Doyle, lepping fresh from Florence, including the accounts of Dante by the Villani, Boccaccio, Aretino & Manetti brought together in one volume' (*LSB* 324). The cover is indeed marked with the inscription 'M. J. Doyle / Florence / 1920', crossed out by Beckett with the green pencil that recurs in many of the books he read and marked in 1936.

However, the large number of books by and about Dante cannot make up for what is arguably the darkest lacuna in Beckett's library: his beloved Salani edition of the *Divina Commedia*, edited with comments by Enrico Bianchi, which he carried with him all his life, is no longer in his apartment, but in a private collection. In *Dream of Fair to Middling Women*, 'the Florentia edition in the ignoble Salani collection' is described, on the one hand, as 'horrid, beslubbered with grotesque notes, looking like a bankbook in white cardboard and a pale gold title, very distasteful', and on the other hand as a 'treasure': 'the book itself was nice, bound well ..., printed well on paper that was choice, with notes that knew their place, keeping themselves to themselves' (*Dream* 51). Beckett's copy of the Salani edition contained the traces of his lifelong engagement with the *Divina Commedia*, from the first lessons by Bianca Esposito in 1926 to the late 1980s. James Knowlson describes it as follows: 'He had a constant and apt reminder of his debt to Signorina Esposito. When, following a serious fall in his eighties, he had to live in an old people's home in the rue Rémy-Dumoncel, he took with him the little edition of Dante's *Divina Commedia* that he had underlined and annotated in classes with her' (Knowlson 1996, 53).

DANTE: INFERNO

More than fifty years after the lessons with Esposito, on 11 September 1981, Beckett was still 'Using [his] old student edition' to reread *Inferno*, as he told Barbara Bray (TCD MS10948/1/665). A month later, he was preoccupied by the 'Suicides in hell. Remember it well. His pity. For 3rd or 4th time. Despite V's "qui vive la pietà quando è ben morta". But later he kicks in the face a head embedded in ice and goes back on a promise' (TCD MS10948/1/668). The Italian quotation that is so central in the early story 'Dante and the Lobster' shows that Beckett was not only fascinated by 'pietà' in formal terms (the untranslatability of the 'superb pun', as 'pietà' is made to mean both 'piety' and 'pity'), but also in terms of content.[19] The question why one should not feel pity even for the 'justly' condemned – 'Why not piety and pity both, even down below?' (*MPTK* 13) – accords with Beckett's interest in Schopenhauer's preoccupation with 'Mitleid' (see Chapter 7) and in the notion of 'compassione' in his Italian Bible and its traces in the lines 'Lo-Ruhama Lo-Ruhama / pity is quick with death' in 'Text' (see Chapter 8).

Based on the Salani edition and the notes by Enrico Bianchi, Beckett had made an analysis of the 'Allegory of Canto I', in which Virgil stands for 'Reason' (TCD MS10963, 3r). Daniela Caselli suggests that 'Virgil's role as an *auctoritas* within Dante's text fashions Dante as an *auctoritas* within

Beckett's text' (Caselli 113, n.14), notably the novel *Mercier et Camier / Mercier and Camier* – in which the line 'lo bello stile che m'ha fatto onore' as Dante's recognition of his 'master' is present in the French text (Beckett 1970, 100) but omitted in the English version. The subtleties of Beckett's view on authorship and authority are further complicated by his marking of the following passage in Jules Renard's *Journal* (volume I, page 59, '*22 février 1890*') regarding 'tradition': 'Insupportable comme un homme qui vous parle du "divin Virgile". . . . Honore ton père, et ta mère, et Virgile' [Insufferable like someone who talks about the "divine Virgil" . . . Honour your father and your mother and Virgil] (see Chapter 3). In the story 'Echo's Bones', Virgil is replaced by Goethe: 'honour your father, your mother and Göthe'.[20]

Another Dantean link with French literature was Stendhal, whom Beckett – in a letter to MacGreevy – called the 'Nimrod of novelists' because of his 'obsession of heights' (see Chapter 3).[21] Nimrod, traditionally regarded as the main architect of the Tower of Babel, occurs in Canto 31 of Dante's *Inferno*. According to Virgil, it is due to him that the world no longer speaks a single, common language (Canto 31.77–8). In the context of the letter, the comparison certainly does not sound like a compliment, but whether that necessarily implies that it is a reproach, is not so equivocal. Especially given Beckett's interest in Mauthner's work on linguistic scepticism, there is an element of self-recognition in the epithet 'Nimrod of novelists'. Beckett quoted six lines from Dante's Nimrod passage (Canto 31, lines 66–7; 77–81) in his 'Whoroscope' Notebook (61r): 'Nimrod's words: / "Rapèl maí amèch zabí almì"' and: "questi è Nembrotto, per lo cui mal coto / pur un linguaggio nel mondo non s'usa. / Lasciànlo stare e non parliamo a vòto; / ché così è a lui ciascun linguaggio / come 'l suo ad altrui, ch'a nullo è noto."' [He is Nimrod, through whose infamous device / the world no longer speaks a common language. / But let's leave him alone and not waste breath, / for he can no more understand our words / than anyone can understand his language] (trans. Musa 1995, 171). Beckett's excerpts in the 'Whoroscope' Notebook are followed by the parenthesis: '(what possible application!)'.

A preoccupation with the notion of 'depth' could be regarded as a sort of leitmotiv in this notebook.[22] While, in 1931, Beckett took notes on the depth (*profondeur*) and the 'unknown' of Julien Sorel's character and he condemned Stendhal's obsession with heights, he wrote in *L'Innommable*, twenty years later: 'Stupide hantise de la profondeur' (Beckett 1953, 11). In the English version, the Unnamable asks himself whether there are 'other pits, deeper down? To which one accedes by mine?', and then concludes: 'Stupid obsession with depth' (*Un* 3; see also Chapter 10). The mirroring of

Stendhal's 'obsession of heights' with this 'obsession with depth' is realized in *Inferno*, where Nimrod, architect of the Tower of Babel, is banished to the Giants' pit. The pun on 'mine' remains a crucial theme, also in Text 4 of the *Textes pour rien / Texts for Nothing*, where the pit recurs: 'who says this, saying it's me? Answer simply, someone answer simply. It's the same old stranger as ever, for whom alone accusative I exist, in the pit of my inexistence, of his, of ours, there's a simple answer' (*TFN* 17). Even the line 'for whom alone accusative I exist' may be an oblique reference to Nimrod, who is not just introduced by Virgil as 'This is Nimrod', but as 'Elli stessi s'accusa' ('He is his own accuser' or in Mark Musa's translation: 'His words accuse him'; *Inferno*, Canto 31, 76).

Beckett reread the *Divina Commedia* at several instances in the course of his life. For instance, on 15 April 1959, he told Barbara Bray that he was looking forward to what he called 'another Dante season' (TCD MS10948/1/27). More than fifteen years later, on 13 June 1975, Beckett started 'Reading Dante' again when he was in Tangier: 'Like 50 years ago & unlike' (TCD MS10948/1/578). He took his time to savour each Canto and reported with regular intervals to Barbara Bray. This unique record of his reading experience makes it possible to follow him on his journey through *Inferno*. After four days, he referred to the opening of Canto 2, which he described to Bray as the 'start of what can no longer be started' (579). In Mark Musa's translation, Canto 2 opens as follows: 'The day was fading and the darkening air / was releasing all the creatures on our earth / from their daily tasks, and I, one man alone, / was making ready to endure the battle / of the journey, and of the pity it involved, / which my memory, unerring, shall now retrace' (Dante 1995, 9). After having made his translation of *Mercier et Camier*, Beckett also told Bray that he 'Should have used it for M. & C'. On subsequent days, Beckett reported where he was in the *Commedia*, as if it were his own journey, for instance on 19 June: 'Have come to blizzard'. On the same day, he also read 'Paolo & Francesca' (*Inferno*, Canto 5), a passage on which he had made some notes in the 'Whoroscope' Notebook in the late 1930s, commenting that 'Francesca da Rimini [was] the first spirit in *Inferno* to speak with Dante' and that 'Dante may have known Paolo in Florence' (WN 61r; qtd. in Caselli 2006, 247).

During that later 'Dante season' in 1975, the journey through *Inferno* was 'Slow going',[23] but on 23 June, Beckett arrived at the 'Stygean Marsh with the angry', notably Filippo Argenti (Canto 8): 'Silver Phil bites himself so furious is he'. On 26 June – when Beckett remembered 'This afternoon, 42 years ago, my father died' and immediately added 'Why bring that up again' – he reported to Bray that Dante was 'now among the heresiarchs, about to kick one in the face'. Beckett continued to 'saunter down Inferno', reaching 'Disland' on the first of July. In the eighth circle, 'halfway through Inferno, i.e. starting through Malebolge' (Canto 18), 'Thaïs & her ilk are up to their eyes in human shit' (10 July). Then, 'Halfway through 10 fold 8th V. takes him in his arms and slides supine down steep bank to hypocrites'. That same Bastille Day, 'quatorze juillet', Beckett himself was lying 'supine trough and crest looking at sea through haze of sand murmuring canto I'. He told Bray he hoped to finish his reading of *Inferno* before leaving Tangier. Whenever he was in Tangier again, he 'Brought Dante', first in February 1977; another year later, 'Rereading Purgatory' (16 February 1978); and on 27 September 1979, when he had time 'to reread Purgatory' again.

DANTE: PURGATORIO

In *Purgatory*, Beckett had found his earliest protagonist, Belacqua, whom he described as 'a friend of Dante and notorious for his indolence and apathy': 'There are a good many degrees between him and l'Innommable, but it's the same engeance', he wrote in a letter to Con Leventhal (21 April 1958; qtd. in Nixon 2011, 223). Some of the traces of Beckett's reading of *Purgatorio* can be found on three cards with Dante notes, preserved at the University of Reading (UoR MS4123). The verso of the first card shows the excerpt: 'Amor che ne la mente mi ragiona' (*Purgatorio*, Canto 2, line 112). Beckett quotes the same line on a postcard he sent to Barbara Bray on 16 February 1978 from Tangier: 'Rereading Purgatory. Yesterday it was Casella singing Amor che ne la mente mi ragiona on the shore' (TCD MS10948/1/627). On the card with the line from Canto 2, quoted above (UoR MS4123), Beckett also summarized *Purgatory*, Canto 3: 'Dante's shadow, Virgil transparent. Seeing only one on ground D. thinks V. gone'. One of the lines Beckett excerpted from this third Canto, is '37 State contenti, umana gente, al quia' (UoR MS4123,01v; qtd. in Caselli 2005, 107).

The line reappears unexpectedly in the margins of a modernist work in another language: Proust's *À la recherche du temps perdu*. The scene is the soirée at the Verdurins. Proust describes doctor Cottard, who is said to be 'insatiable de renseignements' regarding idioms.[24] One of these idioms is 'être réduit à quia' (1.289). Beckett's comment (in ink) in the top margin reads: 'state contenti, umana gente, al quia' (1.289). The line from Dante's *Purgatorio*, Canto 3 (line 37) relates to the medieval notion of the *quia*, which was understood as the observable manifestation of things, in contrast with the *propter quid*, regarded as their 'essence', the reason why things were the way they were. In the third Canto of *Purgatorio*, Dante looks up to see the enormous mountain that stretches up to Heaven; then he looks down again, sees his own shadow but does not see the shadow of his guide and is worried, thinking Virgil has abandoned him. But Virgil is still with him, he simply does not have a shadow, as he explains to Dante: the shades of the dead do not cast a shadow, yet they are sensitive to pain, heat and cold, for such is the will of the Creator, who also prefers not to reveal its secrets. So Virgil urges Dante and all his fellow human beings to 'state contenti, umana gente, al quia', that is, to 'Be satisfied with *quia* unexplained, / O human race! If you knew everything, / no need for Mary to have borne a son' (Dante 1995, trans. Mark Musa, 208).

This seems an equally cunning trick as the notion of the 'felix culpa' in Catholicism: one can regret the Fall or the original sin, but the trick is to see it as a happy sin or a fortunate fall. Following this reasoning, it is only 'thanks to' the sin of Adam and Eve that Christ was incarnated as the Saviour and Redeemer. Beckett was familiar with the 'felix culpa' as a major motif in *Finnegans Wake*. In his essay *Proust*, Beckett seems to be interpreting Proust's moments of *mémoire involontaire* in a similar fashion: the essence or *propter quid* is *in* the *quia*; 'the germ of the Proustian solution is contained *in* the statement of the problem itself' (Beckett 1965, 36), the source of the essence is provided by the physical world, the 'essence des choses' is provided by the 'choses' themselves. Linking Proust's involuntary memories to the *quia* comment is a critique in itself, which Beckett did not need to make explicit. Sixteen volumes further, he simply underlined each occurrence of the recurring phrase 'l'essence des choses' with the same insistence with which Proust repeated it in *Le Temps retrouvé* (16.14; 16.16; 16.21).

To Georges Duthuit, Beckett pointed out another purgatorial peculiarity: 'Connaissez-vous le cri commun aux purgatoriaux? Io fui' [Do you know the cry common to those in purgatory? Io fui] (2 August 1948, *LSB II* 90). 'I was', Beckett wrote in Text 6 of the *Texts for Nothing*, mixing Dante with Wordsworth's emotions recollected in tranquility:

> I was, I was, they say in Purgatory, in Hell too, admirable singulars, admirable assurance. Plunged in ice up to the nostrils, the eyelids caked with frozen tears, to fight all your battles o'er again, what tranquillity, and know there are no more emotions in store, no, I can't have heard aright (*TFN* 27).

And after having asked 'Have you read the Purgatory, miss, of the divine Florentine' in *Rough for Radio II*, Animator characterizes it as the place where 'all sigh, I was, I was', whereas he would have expected them to say 'I shall be', since the souls in *Purgatorio* do have a future to contemplate, as opposed to the ones in *Inferno* (see Bryden 1998a, 153).

DANTE: PARADISO

The passage from *Paradiso* that plays a role in 'Dante and the Lobster' kept fascinating Beckett. On 9 April 1958 he told Mary Hutchinson that he was 'reading Il Paradiso and trying again to understand Beatrice's explanation of the spots on the moon where the spirits appear to Dante as shadowy as "a pearl or a white forehead"'. Three days later, however, he had to admit to Kay Boyle that he had 'been in the moon canto again with no better success than 30 (odd) years ago'. In an exercise book bought in Tours, Beckett had made notes on Dante's *Paradiso* in September 1926, in preparation of the Michaelmas Junior Sophister examinations in October. This period of intensive reading in Dante's *Commedia* is evoked in 'Dante and the Lobster'. The story takes place on Wednesday 8 December 1926, the day before the hanging of the 'Malahide murderer', Henry McCabe. The composition of this story, however, may have started much later. Beckett told Ruby Cohn[25] that he forgot the order in which he wrote the stories of *More Pricks than Kicks*, but that he believed 'Dante and the Lobster' was written first. The first-recorded version of any of these stories is 'Walking Out', as John Pilling notes (August 1931; Pilling 2006a, 32). 'Dante and the Lobster' was first published in December 1932 in *This Quarter*, but in August of that year he was already waiting for an answer from *This Quarter*'s editor Edward W. Titus, to whom he had offered 'Dante and the Lobster' for publication. Whether he was still working on the story in the summer of 1932 remains inconclusive, but the suggestion that boiling alive is 'a quick death' shows a remarkable correspondence with the closing lines of the third chapter ('Struggle for Existence') of Charles Darwin's *On the Origin of Species*, which Beckett was reading in early August 1932 (see Chapter 10). The chapter ends with the 'consoling' thought 'that the vigorous, the healthy, and the happy survive and multiply': 'When we reflect on this struggle, we may console ourselves with the full belief, that the war of nature is not incessant, that no fear is felt, that death is generally prompt' (Darwin 1860, 79).

'It is not' (*MPTK* 14).

PETRARCH

For the January 1926 Hilary Term Junior Sophister Examinations, Petrarch's poems and Dante's *Inferno* were among the set texts (Pilling 2006a, 11) and Beckett's library still contains several of the 'Prescribed Books'. The two-volume set of *Le Rime di Messer Francesco Petrarca* (from the Classica Biblioteca Italiana series, Milan: Nicolò Bettoni, 1824), which Beckett later gave to Avigdor Arikha and Anne Atik, was probably purchased in preparation for this examination.[26] The first volume bears no reading traces, whereas the second is heavily annotated. The closing sextets of Sonnets VIII (Petrarch 2.23) and XX (2.35) are marked with the marginalia '1926'. Next to Sonnet XXI (2.36), opening with 'L'alma mia fiamma', the word 'Merde' is pencilled in the left margin, and three pages further 'Macchè!' next to the underlined, penultimate line of Sonnet XXIV: 'Secca è la vena dell'usato ingegno' [dry is the vein of my old genius] (2.39; see also Ferrini 2006, 59–60).

Anne Atik remarked a peculiarity that accords with the importance of 'non-marginalia' (see also Chapters 1, 8 and 10): the line 'chi può dir com'egli arde, è 'n picciol foco' – which Beckett translated as 'He who knows he is burning is burning in a small fire' and which he liked to quote on several occasions – 'was in the *un*annotated volume' (Atik 2001, 83). Anne Atik concludes that the sonnet had 'burned into his memory' (83). This apt metaphor relates to Mercier's description of the line from Dante's *Inferno* that is burning his lips and rustling in his head (Beckett 1970, 100; cf. supra). But unlike Atik's description ('burned into his memory'), Mercier relates (1) the burning to the lips and (2) the way the line occupies the mind to the rustling sound of leaves – the same rustling sound Gogo associates with the 'dead voices' in *Waiting for Godot*. This 'rustling' metaphor, implying a multitude of leaves, may suggest an explanation for the observation that Beckett's favourite Petrarchan line is unmarked in his copy of Petrarch's works. Possibly he encountered it among the leaves of a completely different book: the line is quoted in isolation in one of Montaigne's essays. Beckett would not even have needed to read all of Montaigne's essays to encounter it, because it already features in the second essay of Book I: 'De la tristesse'. Circumstantial evidence for this hypothesis can be found in the 'Sam Francis' Notebook (UoR MS2926, 17v), where the same line is quoted in isolation, followed by a French reference to the name of the author ('Pétrarque') and the first words of the sonnet in question ('Più volte già dal bel sembiante umano', usually referred to as sonnet CXXXVII). In the 1777 translation by John Nott, the last line ('chi può dir com'egli arde, è 'n picciol foco', in a literal translation: 'who can say how he burns is in little fire') reads as follows: 'Faint is the flame that language can express'.[27] Montaigne quotes this line as the expression of ardent lovers' unbearable passion,[28] but Beckett clearly interpreted the line in a more general sense, closer to his favourite line from *King Lear*, 'The worst is not, So long as one can say, This is the worst' jotted down in his 'Sottisier' Notebook (UoR

MS2901, 14v). In another notebook from the late period, the 'Super Conquérant' Notebook (UoR MS2934, 1r; BDMP1), Beckett noted Seneca's line 'Curae leves loquuntur, ingentes stupent' (from Hyppolytus Act II, scene 3, line 607), which is quoted by Montaigne in the same essay 'De la tristesse' (61).

On 21 April 1958, Beckett came back to Petrarch's 'picciol foco' in a letter to A. J. Leventhal, who had asked him about the affinities between his work and Italian literature: 'Can't conceive by what stretch of ingenuity my work could be placed under sign of italiania', he said, but after a discussion of the character of Belacqua, he did suggest:

> Perhaps more interesting approach, from the technical view, is a line from Petrarch –
> "Chi può dir com' egli arde è in picciol foco" –
> arde being understood more generally, and less gallantly, than in the Canzoniere. As thus solicited it can link up with the 3rd proposition (coup de grâce) of Gorgias in his Nonent:
> 1. Nothing is
> 2. If anything is, it cannot be known.
> 3. If anything is, and can be known, it cannot be expressed in speech. (qtd. in Feldman 2006a, 76; Nixon 2011, 181)

The 'arde' has the same root as the old French expression 'j'ars' [I'm burning] in the line Beckett marked in Scève's *Délie*, noting that when Scève achieves a fine line, it is exceedingly fine (see Chapter 3). But as Scève still managed to say that he was burning without going out ('Las tousjours j'ars, & point ne me consume'), it must have been a small fire, according to Petrarch.

BOCCACCIO, MACHIAVELLI, ARIOSTO, ARETINO

Boccaccio's *Novelle scelte* was on the TCD list for the senior freshmen's Michaelmas examination. The library features an 1812 edition of the *Decamerone*, but only volume 3 is preserved, starting with 'Giornata Sesta'. It shows pencil underlinings, side markings and marginal notes on numerous pages[29] and the stamp on the inside of the cover reads: 'French Library, T.C.D'. In August 1931 Beckett had already made up his mind with regard to Boccaccio in relation to his own writing, as he told MacGreevy: 'I can't write like Boccaccio and I don't want to write like Boccaccio' (*LSB* 83).

Machiavelli's *Le Istorie Fiorentine* (1888), mentioned by John Pilling in 'Beckett and Italian Literature (after Dante)' (2009, 10), shows numerous marks, underlinings and marginal comments in fine pencil, but it is uncertain whether these marks are made by Beckett. The previous owner's name, 'Joynt', is inscribed, which suggests that this book was among the ones Beckett describes in a letter to MacGreevy (29 January 1936): 'Cissie pushed up some Italian books that had been left behind by outgoing tenant, Machiavelli's plays including the Mandragora, nice editions of Manzoni and that old bum-sucking pedant Varchi (cinquecento) and the Gerusalemme [Tasso]. Also Giusti's poetry. All bought at Florence by Maud Joynt, at the end of last century. She might have been nice to know' (*LSB* 306). The other book by Machiavelli in the library is a translation: an unmarked copy of *Le Prince* (1949).

There are no traces of Ariosto,[30] but Ludovico Aretino is present with a volume in the so-called 'Bibliothèque des Curieux': *L'Œuvre du Divin Arétin* (2 vols, 1933), with an introduction and notes by Guillaume Apollinaire, who also introduced the Marquis de Sade in the same series (see Chapter 3).

TASSO

Beckett's study of Italian in Dublin was clearly marked by a fascination for the Renaissance. After the First Class Honours in Italian, he prepared for the Michaelmas senior freshman examinations in 1925 by purchasing Torquato Tasso's *Gerusalemme Liberata* (1923). The book is inscribed ('Samuel B. Beckett / May 1925') and heavily annotated, with marginalia that shed some light on Beckett's learning method as a student. The text is framed by numerous marginal translations of individual words, by means of which Beckett extended his vocabulary. Here and there he expresses his doubt with regard to a particular passage, possibly in view of the next Italian lesson in which he would be able to discuss it with his professors or his 'Professoressa'. Two modes of annotating are discernible (similar to other TCD books): ink (black and blue pen) as well as pencil underlinings. Annotations tend to be translations of specific words or lines. They continue to the end of Canto X, but stop abruptly after that. Beckett refers to 'Pio Goffredo' from Tasso's *Gerusalemme Liberata* in *Dream of Fair to Middling Women* (125; see Pilling 2004, 225). On 5 March 1936, he wrote to MacGreevy that he was reading 'Tasso again also, with boredom, & Ariosto, feeling him to be the greatest literary artist (as distinct from poet) of them all perhaps & Goethe's Tasso, than which, except for some good rhetoric, anything more disgusting would be hard to devise' (*LSB* 319).

LEOPARDI

Apart from the Renaissance, the only other period in the history of Italian literature that is represented in the library is the nineteenth century, with a few books by Leopardi and Giacosa.[31] Leopardi's poem 'A se stesso' (see Ferrini 2006, 62), in particular the lines 'Non che la speme, il desiderio è spento' [Not only hope, desire is dead] and 'e fango è il mondo' [the world is dirt], recurs in *Dream*, in *Molloy*, in several letters (*LSB II* 509, 537) and twice in Beckett's *Proust* (1965, 18, 63). Beckett defined himself as 'one who is interested in Leopardi & Proust rather than in Carducci & Barrès' (*LSB* 33). Giosuè Carducci and Gabriele d'Annunzio, on whose work Beckett made notes as an 'extractor' (TCD MS10965 and 10965a), are not represented in the library. In the letter to Leventhal quoted above (21 April 1958), Beckett also wrote: 'Leopardi was a strong influence when I was young (his pessimism, not his patriotism!) and his "fango è il mondo" serves you may remember as epigraph to the Proust essay (1931). I remember it pleasing Joyce because of consonance between "il mondo" [the world] and "immonde" [impure, unclean]. The same anecdote is mentioned in a letter to David Hayman (*LSB II* 537), which also indicates how important Beckett's 'Dante revelation' must have been to him, and how much modern literature owed to the thirteenth-century Italian poet:

> I think perhaps you derive Joyce's use of the technique of suggestion too directly and exclusively from the Symbolists and Mallarmé. The device after all is as old as writing itself. The Divine Comedy is full of it. And one can well imagine the effect on Joyce, when he read it in Dublin as a very young man (537).

One can equally well imagine the effect on Beckett, when he read it in Dublin as a very young man.

CHAPTER 6

Classics and Other Literatures

In the 'Whoroscope' Notebook, Beckett entered the following note: 'Dante, knowing no Greek (*Convivio* II 5) never read Homer, then untranslated' (WN 61r; qtd. in Caselli 2006, 245). It must have come as a relief to Beckett when he realized that however rudimentary his Greek, it was still better than Dante's. Indeed, it was seemingly better than Joyce's, and Beckett on at least one occasion helped the older writer with Greek passages during the writing of *Finnegans Wake*.[1] As Beckett told Anne Atik in 1982, he did not study the language whilst at Trinity College Dublin (115), although there is evidence that Beckett sought to rectify this perceived linguistic deficiency. At the back of the 'Whoroscope' Notebook, Beckett in the mid-1930s made a list of Greek language primers, including W. Gunion Rutherford's *First Greek Grammar* and *First Greek Accidence*, W. H. D. Rouse's *First Greek Course* and *Greek Reader*, as well as Ulrich von Wilamowitz-Moellendorff's *Griechisches Lesebuch* (WN, page 24 from back). There is no evidence that Beckett ever expanded on this first step toward acquiring Greek, but it testifies to his awareness that he had little Greek. In contrast, Beckett's knowledge of Latin was excellent. He had studied it as a schoolboy at Portora and his library still contains a second-hand copy of E. H. Blakeney's standard *A Smaller Classical Dictionary* (1923) and two further Latin dictionaries (one from French, the other from German)[2] at the time of his death (but, tellingly, no Greek dictionary). Indeed, Beckett's Latin must have been very good, seeing as he read Geulincx's *Ethica* in Latin in 1936. As his library shows, unlike Winnie in *Happy Days*, Beckett never lost his classics.

LEMPRIÈRE'S CLASSICAL DICTIONARY

As John Pilling, in the only substantial essay on Beckett's relationship with classical literature, points out, 'Beckett's access to Greek culture was necessarily a matter of transmission by way of intermediate filters and standard authorities, and uppermost among these, apparently, was *Lemprière's Classical Dictionary*' (Pilling 1995, 6). Beckett bought an 1831 edition of the famous dictionary at Greene's bookshop in Dublin in February 1936, as the inscription (written with a purple pencil) shows.

His use of Lemprière's *Dictionary* once again shows a preference for reference works over primary material. Rather surprisingly, Beckett's copy does not contain any marginalia, but he clearly used this book extensively during the 1930s. In particular, he jotted down various passages from entries into his 'Whoroscope' Notebook. The first of these, on the Thebans, is identified as coming from 'Lemprière's Classical Dict.' (WN 59r) and must have been copied in 1938 judging by its location after the notes on Mauthner. There are several entries dealing with Greek matters which could conceivably come from Lemprière's *Classical Dictionary*, such as the last words of Aristotle (38r), cited in Latin and used in the Addenda to *Watt* (#32), notes on Erostrate and Eratostrate (70r), or the note on Endymion, who had been granted eternal youth and sleep: 'Endymionis somnium dormire' (73v).

At some point in the late 1930s Beckett embarked on a more systematic study of Ancient Greek literature, as six pages in the 'Whoroscope' Notebook reveal (74r–76v). The source of Beckett's structure for these notes is uncertain, although it is very probably Harold N. Fowler's *A History of Ancient Greek Literature* (1902). The notes begin with Hesiod, then move through the Gnomics, Choral poetry and prose, the Attic period, Tragedy and Comedy, then History to finally 'Eloquence', of which there is only the heading. Beckett left several pages blank in his notebook before resuming entries, which suggests he may have wanted to complete his overview. If the source of the overall headings and life dates of the writers is obscure, the actual text given under these headings clearly derives from Lemprière's *Classical Dictionary*, although supplemented here and there by other texts. Indeed, there are several other entries on Greek literature and culture in the 'Whoroscope' Notebook that come from unidentified sources, such as the two entries on Hippasos and Pythagoras, which appear to stem from a French dictionary, even as the first entry is in French and the second in English. Other entries complement Beckett's notes on Greek philosophy from Windelband. At times Beckett also turned to dictionaries other than Lemprière's in order to note the background to Greek figures and terms, such as the *OED* or the *Encyclopaedia Britannica*. From the latter, for example, he noted biographical details pertaining to Thespius, Ixion, Sisyphus and Tantalus (WN 31r–33r).

BURTON

Beckett's main source for Greek and Latin phrases and sayings was Robert Burton's *The Anatomy of Melancholy*, ostensibly a seventeenth-century medical treatise on melancholy but in reality a compendium of human knowledge. It is the kind of book that Beckett loved – encyclopaedic in range, learned yet flippant about scholarly accuracy, and utterly eccentric. Beckett possessed the three-volume edition of the *Anatomy*, edited by A. R. Shilleto, published in 1893, which he gave to Anne Atik in May 1977 (as the dedication in the first volume reveals). Burton furnished Beckett with literally hundreds of phrases and quotations, many in Latin, and more in English. He first read the book in the early 1930s, extracting more than 200 lines and expressions in his 'Dream' Notebook (items 720 to 998, but with other material interspersed). Many of these expressions were used in the novel *Dream*, then *More Pricks than Kicks* and subsequently also in *Murphy* (and then, more sparsely, in post-war texts). Beckett returned to reading the *Anatomy* in the late 1930s, as a further set of notes in the 'Whoroscope' Notebook (86r–87v) indicates. Whereas the earlier notes derive from all three parts ('Partitions') of the book, the notes in the 'Whoroscope' Notebook largely derive from the introductory section, 'Democritus to the Reader' and the first partition, ending with page 323 of the latter. It is tempting to think that Beckett did not own his copy of Burton's *Anatomy* when he took the notes in the two notebooks, but page references in the 'Whoroscope' Notebook show that he was using the same edition. The fact that the three volumes in Beckett's library also contain annotations further complicates the issue. Yet none of the annotated passages correlate with Beckett's work or manuscripts, even if some of them do speak to issues that we know interested him. Several of the annotations refer to instances in which Burton addresses the idea of the degeneration of the 'spirit':

- 'I may not deny but that there is some folly approved, a divine fury, a holy madness, even a spiritual drunkenness, in the Saints of God themselves' (I. 85);
- idleness as something that 'crucifies their souls' (I. 279);
- 'But giving way to these violent passions of fear, grief, shame, revenge, hatred, malice, &c., they are torn in pieces, as *Actaeon* was with his dogs, and crucify their own souls' (I. 298);
- 'the saws of the soul' (I. 308).

Furthermore, each of the three volumes contains a list of those pages that are annotated, and while the handwriting could or could not be Beckett's, such a systematic 'indexing' of annotated pages is not discernible in any of the other books in Beckett's library.³

Nevertheless, the fact that there is no overlap between the annotated pages in the edition and the entries in the 'Dream' and 'Whoroscope' notebooks only heightens the possibility that the markings were made by Beckett. Indeed, in the opening sections the notebook entries alternate with the annotations in Beckett's edition:

'Whoroscope' Notebook:	pages 1–78, first volume
Beckett's copy:	pages 85–214, first volume
'Whoroscope' Notebook:	pages 229–323, first volume
Beckett's copy:	pages 279, first volume, to 282, third volume

The edition was clearly bought in an English language country, as the bookseller's mark reads '3 vols.', which could also suggest that the copy had previous owners. At the same time, the only information regarding its dating derives from a piece of paper inserted in the first volume, which contains names of people Beckett was predominantly friendly with in the late 1940s and 1950s, such as Roger Blin, Mania Péron and Bram van Velde.

HOMER

Beckett did not only derive his information on Greek and Latin literature from secondary sources, but also read primary texts, although usually in English translation. He will undoubtedly have been aware of the pervasive use of classical references in literary modernism, by authors such as T. S. Eliot or Ezra Pound. And then there was of course Joyce's use of Homer's *Odyssey* as a structural subtext to *Ulysses*. Beckett read the *Odyssey* in Victor Bérard's translation in September 1931 with much enjoyment, and his 1925 edition, comprising three volumes, is still in his library. As Beckett told MacGreevy in a letter of late September (undated [?22 September 1931]; *LSB* 90–1), Bérard's rendering 'makes it easy to read', although he did go on to state that he disliked 'very much his Alexandrine diction' despite finding some 'wonderful glittering phrases'. Beckett's edition contains no annotations, but he did proceed to excerpt eight passages into his 'Dream' Notebook (710–17), all of which made their way into *Dream of Fair to Middling Women* and other early works. One line in particular, 'The hour when darkness fills the streets' (715) struck a chord with Beckett, and he employed it in *Dream* with, unusually, the source acknowledged: 'the long hour, when darkness fills the streets, it was Homer' (*Dream* 28).

It appears as if Beckett did not read Homer's epic poem in its entirety, as the last pages of the third and final volume, the section 'Chant XXIV', are uncut. At the same time, his engagement with the book stretched into 1932, as a postcard inserted on page 61 of volume 2 indicates. The postcard is of Albrecht Dürer's painting of the two praying hands, and there are holes in the top centre suggesting that it has been hung on a wall by a nail. It was sent by Cissie Sinclair on 16 February 1932, just after Beckett had returned from his last visit to Kassel.[4]

HORACE, OVID, VIRGIL

If Beckett's edition of Homer survives, books by other Greek and Roman authors he admired do not. Even though citations from Ovid, Virgil and Horace re-occur throughout Beckett's work, he must have either known the texts sufficiently to quote them from memory, or given away or lost the editions he used. We know, for example, that Beckett was given a 'beautiful polyglot edition of Horace' (1834) in November 1931 (letter to MacGreevy, 8 November 1931; *LSB* 94), from which the many quotes in Beckett's early work undoubtedly derive. Beckett thus cited Horace's *Ars Poetica* in *More Pricks than Kicks* and the poem 'Serena I', and copied several entries into the 'Whoroscope' Notebook, such as the opening of Horace's *Epistola ad Pisones* (*Epistle to the Pisones*) (WN 64r) or the admonition 'praesectum deciens ad unguem !!' (line 294 from the *Ars Poetica*) with the poem 'Cascando' in mind (WN 34r). Beckett was particularly fond of quoting Horace's 'Solvitur acris hiems grata vice' [severe winter is melted away] from the fourth ode, using it in *Dream* (138) and in conversation with friends (see Bernold 26, for example). Although most citations from Horace (as well as Ovid and Virgil) are to be found in the early work, the ninth ode of Book 3 of the *Carmine* is cited in both French and Latin in the manuscripts of *Textes pour rien* (Pilling 1995, 10), and as late as 1980 he quoted from the first poem in Book 2 of the *Epistles* in the production notebook for the staging of *Endgame* at the Riverside Studios in London (cited again in a letter to Knowlson, 6 March 1983).

Although primary texts by the great Latin poets are absent from the library, it does contain *The Penguin Book of Latin Verse* (1962), which Barbara Bray sent to Beckett in April 1962. Furthermore, there are several publications by the Classical scholar Stuart Maguinness, whom Beckett knew since his student days at Trinity College Dublin. Maguinness would send Beckett offprints and copies of his books, and it appears as if Beckett read them with enjoyment and interest; four of them are still in the library today. Indeed, it appears as if Maguinness reawakened Beckett's scholarly leanings: 'I am sadly far now from scholarship myself, but the touch of it brings me something of the old warmth and peace I ran away from so long ago, and often regret' (letter to Stuart Maguinness, 13 August 1957; UoR MS4199/1). In his letters, Beckett admired four pieces in particular, all of which he kept: Maguinness's essays 'Bimillennial Reflections on Ovid' (1958), 'Virgil and Milton' (1961), 'The Language of Lucretius' (n.d.) and the 'Petit Plaidoyer pour la poésie trochaique' (1963), of which he wrote to Barbara Bray: 'very good burst from MacGuinness on dactyls and trochees – things I could never have dreamt (of?)' (letter to Barbara Bray, 10 December 1962; TCD MS10948/1/213). With regard to Maguinness's piece on Lucretius, Beckett wrote 'I find it simply admirable and bemoan my wretched Latin that prevents me from getting it all' (letter to Maguinness, 19 May 1965).

ROMAN (AND OTHER) HISTORIES

In October 1963, Stuart Maguinness also sent Beckett Pierre Grimal's *La Civilisation Romaine* (1960), which is still in Beckett's library. Beckett's library contains two further books on Roman history, William Smith's *A Smaller History of Rome* (1868) and J. C. Stobart's *The Grandeur That Was Rome* (1912), the fourth edition edited and revised by Stuart Maguiness and H. H. Scullard (1961).[5]

Although Beckett would emphasize in a letter to MacGreevy that he had 'no sense of history' (4 September 1937; qtd. in Kennedy 2004, 65), his library shows – beyond the above-mentioned books on Rome – an engagement with historical narratives. The library for example contains a copy of John Richard Green's *A Short History of the English People* (1920 [1916]), which must have belonged to his brother Frank (the inscription is 'F. E. Beckett / July 1920'), and which he was reading in January 1933 (letter to MacGreevy, 5 January 1933; *LSB* 150).[6] The 'ancient Plutarch' which Beckett 'got hold of' in January 1933, but did not read because he was 'afraid for my eyes' (letter to MacGreevy, undated), is unfortunately no longer in the library.

PLAUTUS

Beckett's profound knowledge of the history of the theatre was, unsurprisingly, not restricted to the period reaching back to Shakespeare. Indeed, Beckett's response to a query in a questionnaire sent by James Knowlson – 'What particular plays from Greek classical theatre have you found most rewarding?' – is rather typically unhelpful and misleading: 'All completely gone from mind' (JEK A/1/2/4, 5v). Gone from mind, and also gone from the library, as beyond a German translation of Sophocles's *Oedipus Rex* (1955), which shows reading traces, the only edition of classical theatre in the library is the first volume of a four-volume edition of the Roman playwright Plautus's works. The book, published in 1916, is heavily marked with coloured pencil marks, which suggests that Beckett read it as a student at Trinity College Dublin. More often than not, the markings are in the Latin text rather than the English, and are guided by concerns of vocabulary. The one volume that Beckett owned contains the plays *Amphytrion*, *The Comedy of Asses*, *The Pot of Gold*, *Bacchides or The Two Bacchises* and *The Captives*; annotations break off halfway through the final play. Beckett inserted citations from these plays in his early work; the very first entry in the 'Dream' Notebook reads 'Mercury to Night Optumo optume optumam operam'; deriving from line 278 of Plautus's play *Amphitryon*, it was used in *Dream* (86). From *The Comedy of Asses* (I, i), Beckett took the line, amended, 'vivas puellas mortui incurrrrrsant boves', for the poem 'Sanies II'.

OTHER LITERATURES

As the previous chapters suggest, Beckett's reading in the early 1930s was mainly concerned with literary traditions he had studied at Trinity College Dublin – Italian, French and English – complemented by his engagement with German literature. Over the course of his life this changed, and his reading of literature written in languages in which he was not conversant becomes more widespread.

DOSTOEVSKY

An early exception to the above trend is his reading of the Russian writer Fyodor Dostoevsky. It is not clear when Beckett first read the Russian writer's works, although it must have occurred predominantly in 1930 and 1931. Dostoevsky's name first appears in Beckett's study of *Proust* (1931), in which he refers to the 'fine Dostoevskian contempt for the vulgarity of a plausible concatenation' and the fact that Proust, like Dostoevsky, 'states his characters without explaining them' (*Proust* 81–2, 87). It is a connection that Beckett thought of expanding after he had delivered the manuscript of the book to Chatto & Windus in September 1930, as a letter to Charles Prentice of 14 October 1930 indicates. It is unclear which of Dostoevsky's works

Beckett was basing his opinions on, although it may well have been *Le Crime et le Châtiment* (*Crime and Punishment*), a copy of which survives in Beckett's library but which bears no annotations. A more likely source is Gide's 1923 study of Dostoevsky, which Beckett cited in his lectures at Trinity College Dublin on Gide and the modern novel in the 1930 Michaelmas Term. The lecture notes taken by Rachel Burrows reveal that Beckett discussed Gide's debt to Dostoevsky, focusing in particular on characterization, and the fact that both writers (together with Stendhal) refuse to simplify incoherence. As such Beckett cited Gide's opinion that Dostoevsky's characters are 'irraisonné, irrésolu, et souvent presque irresponsable' (TCD MIC60, 20).

Dostoevsky remained on Beckett's mind throughout 1931. He read *Les Possédés* in May 1931, admiring 'the movement & the transitions' of the characters and the narrative, and the fact that no other author had 'ever caught the insanity of dialogue' as Dostoevsky (letter to MacGreevy, 29 May 1931; *LSB* 79).[7] He subsequently proposed, albeit half-heartedly, writing a study of Dostoevsky on meeting Charles Prentice in July 1931 (letter to MacGreevy, undated [early August 1931]). It is likely that Beckett had, by the time he made this suggestion, acquired and read the other two volumes of Dostoevsky that survive in his library (both lack any kind of annotation). The first is *La Confession de Stavroguine*, complétée par une partie inédite du *Journal d'un écrivain*, translated by Halpérine-Kaminsky (1922), which contained a chapter – describing Stavrogin's meeting with the Bishop Tikhon – omitted from the original edition due to Russian censorship. The other surviving book is *Souvenirs de la maison des morts* [*The House of the Dead*] in a 1930 edition.[8]

PASTERNAK

While Dostoevsky disappears from view in his later reading, Beckett continued to engage with Russian literature. In this he was partially guided by his friend George Reavey, who had been born in Russia and published both studies and translations of Russian works from the mid-1930s onward. Most of the surviving books of Russian literature in Beckett's library were either written or translated into English by Reavey, and thus presentation copies. The first such book is Reavey's study *Soviet Literature Today* (1947), which he wrote during the war working for the foreign office in Russia.[9]

Beyond sending his translations of Gogol's *Dead Souls* and Maxim Gorky's *A Sky-Blue Life and Selected Stories* in 1964, Reavey also appears to have repeatedly spoken to Beckett about Boris Pasternak's work.[10]

In particular, Reavey must have solicited Beckett's support during the political fiasco occasioned by Pasternak's award of the Nobel Prize in 1958, mainly on the strength of the novel *Doctor Zhivago*. Denied publication in the Soviet Union, Pasternak had the book smuggled out of the country by Isaiah Berlin in 1957, and it became an immediate bestseller upon publication in the West (the first English translation appeared in August 1958). In October 1958, Pasternak was announced as the winner of the Nobel Prize for Literature (rather oddly, the book had been submitted by UK and US intelligence services), which led to various threats of sanctions to be levied on the writer by Soviet authorities. Faced with the risk of being expelled, Pasternak turned down the award. It is in this rather volatile context that Reavey wrote to Beckett in November 1958, who responded as follows:

> I am horribly sorry to disappoint you, but I can't provide anything on Pasternak. I don't know his work well enough to speak of it and I can feel little sympathy for him in his present 'trouble'. Is it because of the mighty word 'nobel' that we are suddenly to cry out against that ancient ignomity? And be sorry for the 'artist' who condones it all with his stipend. You know more about it all than I do and I may be quite wrong. But I simply can't work up a squeak of indignation. (Letter to George Reavey, 15 November 1958)

Whether orchestrated by Pasternak or not, Beckett could not escape the hype surrounding *Doctor Zhivago*, as Barbara Bray sent him a copy of the book in early 1959. Thanking her for the book, he told her that he had only just started reading it as 'the name got me down, among other things', but finished it a fortnight later 'with mixed feelings' (23 January and 4 February 1959; TCD MS10948/1/16–17).[11] That same year, as his inscribed copy indicates (28 October 1959), Beckett received a volume of Pasternak's poetry, edited and translated by George Reavey, but it is unclear whether he read it.[12]

BIELY

However, Beckett continued to read Russian literature in 1959, in particular Andrei Biely's *St. Petersburg*, a proto-modernist novel which had only been translated into English that year.[13] Beckett had already encountered Biely's work while in Germany in 1936 and 1937, attending a lecture by Fyodor Stepun on the Russian writer (GD, 18 February 1937). He subsequently wrote to Reavey suggesting he translate Biely's *The Silver Dove*. It would take Reavey 37 years before he responded to that suggestion, and his (first ever) English translation was published by Grove Press in 1974.[14] Beckett read the book (inscribed by Reavey '11 April 1975') with 'much appreciation of translation' (letter to Reavey, 4 May 1975). There are other letters which similarly attest to Beckett's awareness of the quality of translations, as when he adjudged Victor Derély's French rendering of Dostoevsky's *The Possessed* to be 'foul'. Beckett must have been sufficiently interested in Russian literature to take some steps in acquiring the language, and he told Alan Schneider in 1962 that he was 'studying Russian on my own, a useful tongue and an impossible one' (letter to Alan Schneider, 15 January 1962; qtd. in Harmon, 117).

CHEKHOV

An ever-present yet shadowy figure in Beckett's theatrical reading is Anton Chekhov. When James Knowlson asked Beckett (in a questionnaire) how deep the influence of Chekhov's theatre had been on his work, Beckett responded 'Nothing deeply' (JEK A/1/2/4, 5r). Beckett was undoubtedly very familiar with Chekhov's work, particularly as his drama was very much part of the literary environment within which Beckett moved. Alan Schneider for example staged various plays by the Russian author, but it is unclear how many productions Beckett – beyond *Uncle Vanya* in January 1964 – actually saw. Beckett's library contains three books, two of which show reading traces. His edition of Chekhov's *Plays*, which includes all the major drama and was published by Penguin in 1959, contains a scrap of paper inserted at the passage in *The Seagull* where Trepliov and Arkadina hurl insults at each other, in a passage that Beckett may have connected to a similar exchange in his *Waiting for Godot*:

> MADAME ARKADIN. Decadent!
> ...
> TREPLEV. You miser!
> MADAME ARKADIN. You ragged beggar!
>   (TREPLEV *sits down and weeps quietly*.)
> MADAME ARKADIN. Nonentity! (159)

If Beckett never commented on Chekhov's plays, he did profess an admiration for some of the short stories. In the mid-1960s he read the volume *Tchekhov, l'essentiel* (1963), and told Barbara Bray that he particularly enjoyed 'A Boring Story' (8 August 1965; TCD MS10948/1/343).[15]

STRINDBERG AND IBSEN

One of the more surprising omissions in Beckett's surviving library is books by the most important European dramatists. There are for example no books by Henrik Ibsen, and the pages of all eight volumes of the complete edition of August Strindberg's *Théâtre* (1958–62) are uncut.[16] We know that Beckett knew the work of these two important dramatists, but it appears as if his exposure was in the theatre rather than on the page. He saw several plays by Ibsen in Dublin as a young man, and he was impressed by Blin's production of Strindberg's *Ghost Sonata*. He was thus familiar enough with Ibsen's work to declare (to David Gullette in 1972) that *An Enemy of the People* was a great play (he remembered seeing this play in Dublin as a young man; letter to James Knowlson, 17 December 1970), and that in his opinion *Peer Gynt* was not Ibsen's masterpiece (GD, 22 November 1936).[17] That Beckett saw his own theatrical work as being very distinct from Ibsen's is clear from his famous remark to Alan Schneider that all he knew is in the text of *Not I* and 'The rest is Ibsen' (16 October 1972, qtd. in Harmon, 283).

SPANISH AND PORTUGUESE LITERATURE

Unfortunately, Beckett's library does not give an adequate account of his engagement with Spanish and Portuguese literature. As his earliest notes on Cervantes in the 'Whoroscope' Notebook to his translations collected in the *Anthology of Mexican Poetry* indicate, Beckett was aware of literature written in the Spanish and the Portuguese languages. There is evidence that he tried to teach himself Spanish in the 1930s, and he did master rudimentary Portuguese in the 1970s (see Chapter 9). He did read the work of Fernando Pessoa in late 1960s; as he told Barbara Bray on 1 February 1969 (from Portugal), he was grateful to her for 'going to all that trouble for Pessoa who has the odd whisper of non-being that terrifies among the weeds' (TCD MS10948/1/424), finding it 'very moving' (8 February 1969; TCD MS10948/1/425). The library does contain six books by the Spanish dramatist Fernando Arrabal, all of them inscribed by the author in the 1980s (see also Chapter 3). On 28 September 1967, Beckett's letter in support of Arrabal, who was in difficulties with Spanish authorities, was cited in *Le monde* (Pilling 2006a, 176).

CHAPTER 7

Philosophy

'I never read philosophers', Beckett famously told Gabriel D'Aubarède on 16 February 1961. To the subsequent question 'Why not?' he replied: 'I never understand anything they write'.[1] Despite this alleged lack of philosophical understanding and in contrast to his provocative claim, Beckett of course never stopped reading philosophers. His books on philosophy not only confirm some of his well-known interests, but also include some surprising discoveries. The usual suspects – the Presocratics, Descartes, Berkeley, Spinoza, Schopenhauer, Mauthner, Sartre – are all present, but also for instance Nietzsche, Plümacher and Wittgenstein. Beckett undertook a systematic study of the history of philosophy (TCD MS10967; Frost and Maxwell 2006; Feldman 2006a), notably by means of *A History of Philosophy* by Wilhelm Windelband, whose chronology may serve as the basic structure of this chapter on Beckett's philosophy books.

FROM THE PRESOCRATICS TO THE NATURAL SCIENCE PERIOD

PRESOCRATICS

As one of Beckett's favourite Presocratics, Democritus is represented in Beckett's library with a French version of his *Doctrines philosophiques et réflexions morales* (transl. and introd. Maurice Solovine, 1928), unfortunately without marginalia. Even after the Second World War, new acquisitions in Beckett's library keep showing traces of this interest in the Presocratics, up until the year before the author's death (for instance, Yves Batistini (ed.), *Trois contemporains: Héraclite, Parménide, Empédocle* [1961] and the Pléiade edition of *Les Présocratiques* [1988]). Although there are no marginalia that illustrate this interest, Beckett's consultation of his reference works on this topic did leave a trace among the philosophy notes (April 1933; Pilling 2006a, 42). Apart from the works by Wilhelm Windelband (*A History of*

Philosophy), Archibald Alexander (*A Short History of Philosophy*), John Burnet (*Greek Philosophy: Part I: Thales to Plato*) and Friedrich Ueberweg (*History of Philosophy: From Thales to the Present Time*, 1871),[2] Beckett also consulted French works once in a while to complete his philosophy notes. For instance, the first two (French) entries under the heading Diogenes of Sinope (TCD MS10967, 68r) referring to the two most famous anecdotes about the cynic, derive from the *Nouveau Petit Larousse Illustré* (ed. Claude and Paul Augé, 1925, 1323–4). In particular the detailed, almost literal excerpt on the graphic representations of the second anecdote (with references to Poussin, Rosa and Dujardin)[3] indicates Beckett's often visual, rather than purely abstract, interests in the philosophers.

AVICENNA, ABÉLARD

With regard to Medieval philosophy, the library contains a work on Avicenna (980–1037) by A. M. Goichon (*La Philosophie d'Avicenne et son influence en Europe Médiévale*, 1951) and a study of the conflict between Abélard and Saint Bernard by Pierre Lasserre (*Un Conflit religieux au XIème siècle: Abélard contre Saint Bernard*, 1930). For a long time, the scholastic logician Abélard was famous only for his relationship with Héloïse and his subsequent castration, until Victor Cousin edited his works in the mid-nineteenth century. Windelband calls him 'the most impressive and energetic personality among the thinkers of this period' (I.174), with Bernard of Clairvaux as 'his unwearied prosecutor' (I.174). According to Windelband, Abélard had been 'the vigorous centre in the controversy over universals' (I.298). Universals cannot be things, but they are not merely words either, according to Abélard: 'Not as numerical or substantial identity, but as a multiplicity with like qualities, does the universal exist in Nature, and it becomes a unitary concept which makes predication possible, only when it has been apprehended and conceived by human thought' (I.299). Windelband therefore sees Abélard as the philosopher who united the different lines of thought in this medieval debate. His rationalist tendency naturally conflicted with the doctrine of the Church and his controversy with Bernard of Clairvaux is characterized as 'the conflict of knowledge with faith, of reason with authority, of science with the Church' (I.301). Abélard's ethics are called *Scito te ipsum* (Know yourself), and his last words are said to have been: 'I don't know' – which, to Beckett the reader, made him a man after his own heart.

The note 'stultologie – applied by St Bernard at [Council] of Sens to theologie [sic] of Abelard' in the 'Whoroscope' Notebook (WN 61v) most probably derives from *Un conflit religieux au XIème siècle: Abélard contre*

Saint Bernard by Pierre Lasserre, who devotes a chapter to 'Le concile de Sens' (chapitre V). The preceding chapter (chapitre IV: 'L'humanisme d'Abélard') opens with a long quotation from Bernard's *Traité de quelques erreurs d'Abélard*, addressed to Innocentius II, in which he coins the word 'stultologie' (Lasserre 1930, 98).

MONTAIGNE, BACON

Regarding the philosophy of the Renaissance, Beckett was especially interested in what Windelband termed 'The Natural Science Period', including such thinkers as Francis Bacon (1561–1626), René Descartes (1596–1650), Blaise Pascal (1623–62), Arnold Geulincx (1624–69), Baruch Spinoza (1632–77) and Gottfried Wilhelm Leibniz (1646–1716).

Beckett seems to have taken an interest in the genre of the 'essay', as initiated by authors such as Michel de Montaigne and Francis Bacon. The library contains the 1958 Pléiade edition of Montaigne's *Essais* and the *Essays and Apophthegms of Francis Lord Bacon*, neither of which is annotated. Beckett purchased the copy of Bacon's essays as early as 1924, judging from the inscription on the flyleaf. One of the distinctive features of the inscriptions in Beckett's books purchased in the 1920s is the inclusion of the initial of his second name Barclay ('Samuel B. Beckett' or 'S. B. Beckett'; see Chapter 2).

PASCAL

In the 1930s, he usually left out the middle name, as in the inscription in his copy of the *Pensées de B. Pascal (Edition de 1670)*, first published by Ernest Flammarion in 1913. The inscription 'Samuel Beckett' in green pencil is very similar to the inscriptions (also in green pencil) in other books purchased in 1936, such as Chesterfield's *Letters* and Passerini's *Le Vite di Dante* (both purchased in February 1936; Pilling 2006a, 56). The 1670 edition of the *Pensées*, mentioned between brackets on the title page, is the so-called Port-Royal version. In the 'Whoroscope' Notebook, Beckett extracted mainly passages from the following chapters: 'Des Juifs' (WN 70r; Pascal [1913], 120); 'De Jésus-Christ' (WN 70v; 138); 'Preuves de Jésus-Christ par les prophéties' (WN 70v; 150); 'Diverses preuves de Jésus-Christ' (WN 70v–71r; 157); 'Grandeur de l'homme' (WN 71r; 195); 'Réflexions sur la géométrie'.[4] The latter reflection on geometry, however, does not seem to feature in the Flammarion edition, which suggests that the excerpts in the 'Whoroscope' Notebook are based on another edition and that Beckett may not yet have possessed the Flammarion edition when he made them – which would explain why he felt the need to copy them in extenso.

Much later, on 12 September 1973, Beckett wrote from Marrakesh to Barbara Bray: 'Wondered about Pascal's Pensées doggerelised' (TCD MS10948/1/540). His plan to treat the *Pensées* in a similar way to Chamfort's *Maximes* was on his mind during the following month, and on 10 October 1973 he wrote to Bray from Tangiers that he had 'Found a 2nd hand Pascal (Pensées) annotated in Arabic hand. Nothing doggerelisable so far' (TCD MS10948/1/546). The copy annotated in Arab is not preserved in Beckett's personal library, but he did doggerelize one of the *Pensées* and was still 'stuck' in it six months later, as he wrote to Bray on 31 March 1974:

> Still stuck in poem. Found from last year in Pascal's Pensées:
>   How empty heart and full
>   of muck thou art.
>
> (TCD MS10948/1/554)

DESCARTES

Another exponent of the 'Natural Science Period', René Descartes, is also present in the library. Beckett had been reading Descartes in February 1930 with some help from Jean Beaufret (Pilling 2006a, 23). The name of Jean Beaufret is inscribed on the flyleaf of the copy in Beckett's library of the *Choix de textes* from René Descartes's works, edited by L. Debricon in the series 'Les grands philosophes français et étrangers' (Paris: Louis-Michaud Editions, n.d. [1909]).[5] A folded copybook page with notes, most probably by Beaufret, is inserted between pages 200 (featuring Descartes's visualization of 'La sensation' and his explanation of the 'Conditions cérébrales de la mémoire') and 201 ('Conditions cérébrales de l'imagination').

Debricon's preface consists of two parts: I. Descartes, sa vie et ses écrits (7–18) and II. Sa philosophie (18–50). The 'Extraits des œuvres de Descartes' (starting on page 53) contain the followings texts:

Discours de la méthode 53
Extraits complémentaires de la méthode 106
Les principes de la philosophie, Livre I 113
Métaphysique (extraits complémentaires) .. 152
La Science 178
La Morale 212

The preface is marked with a dozen short pencil lines, all within the second part (focusing on 'Sa philosophie').[6] A few basic ideas in this preface are underlined.[7] Which of these marks, if any, are Beckett's remains inconclusive. The content of some of the eight marked passages in the 'Discours de la méthode', such as the expressed aim to be master of nature,[8] does not exactly accord with Beckett's later interest in 'ignorance'. But it is remarkable that, in the run-up to the famous line *'je pense, donc je suis'* (75) in the 'Quatrième partie', the only marked sentence is about false reasonings.[9]

The section on 'Les principes de la philosophie' again shows a special interest in the line *'Je pense, donc je suis'* (116). The section explaining *'Ce que c'est que penser'* (116–17) is marked in its entirety with a pencil line in the margin. Gradually, an increasing number of marked passages is accompanied by short marginalia, also in pencil, in what is probably Beaufret's hand.[10] This imperfection, as well as the self-knowledge regarding this imperfection, is also noted by Windelband in *A History of Philosophy*: 'the individual self-consciousness knows itself to be finite, and therefore imperfect' (II.393). This self-consciousness, in its turn, plays an important role in Descartes' maxim 'Everything must be true which is as clear and distinct as self-consciousness' (II.392), excerpted by Beckett in his philosophy notes (TCD MS10967).

Books on philosophy could also serve the most day-to-day purposes, as a calculation of travel expenses on the back flyleaf in the *Choix de texts* illustrates:

> 20 miles per 5 l
> 32 kilom. " "
> 1 l = 3 fr. 15
> 32 km = 15.75 fr
> 1 [km] = ½ fr.

The presence of Descartes' disciple Arnold Geulincx in Beckett's library is literally marginal: his name occurs in the margin of his copy of George Berkeley's *A New Theory of Vision, and Other Writings*, which will be discussed in the next section.

SPINOZA

After reading Geulincx in the spring of 1936, Beckett studied Spinoza in the summer. In July, after Brian Coffey had 'talked attractively of Spinoza' (26 July [1936]; *LSB* 361), he lent Beckett a French translation of Spinoza's *Ethics* with Latin in parallel (after Beckett had tried in vain to read it in English, as he wrote in a letter to Thomas MacGreevy, 19 September 1936): 'I do not know if Brian is back. I want to see him before I leave. He lent me Brunchwiff's Spinoza et ses Contemporains, the Ethica in the Classiques Garnier with Latin en regard, of which I have had time only for enough to give me a glimpse of Spinoza as a solution & a salvation' (*LSB* 370–1).

Spinoza's 'solution', frequently referred to in the German Diaries (Nixon 2011; Tonning 2007), continued to preoccupy Beckett in subsequent years. A copy of Léon Brunschvicg's *Spinoza et ses contemporains* (1923) is part of the extant library. Its title is also mentioned among the 'Books sent home' listed in the 'Whoroscope' Notebook (WN 17v; see Chapter 4) and further on in the notebook (71r–72r), Beckett made several excerpts, suggesting that he (re)read the book after January 1939, the publication date of Spencer Jones's article 'Is there Life in Other Worlds?' from which Beckett took notes on pages 62r–63r (see also Chapter 10).[11]

Apart from *Spinoza et ses contemporains*, Beckett's library also contains Spinoza's *Ethics, and 'De Intellectus Emendatione'*, which once belonged to Con Leventhal: the inside of the front cover shows an ex libris bookplate that reads 'This Premium was adjudged to A. J. Leventhal for Latin at the Examination held in Wesley College Dublin Xmas-Easter 1911–12'. As the numerous enthusiastic underlinings and some marginalia in black pencil are quite different from the marks in Beckett's other books, they were most probably made by Con Leventhal.

Another important exponent of the 'Natural Science Period' is Leibniz, whose ideas surface regularly in Beckett's works. The library, however, does not contain any traces of Beckett's reading of Leibniz, whom he had called 'a great cod, but full of splendid little pictures' (December 1933; *LSB* 172).

THE PHILOSOPHY OF THE ENLIGHTENMENT

BERKELEY

Beckett started reading the philosophical writings of George Berkeley at the instigation of Joseph Maunsel Hone, whose *Bishop Berkeley: His Life, Writings, and Philosophy* had been published in 1932. On 23 December 1932,[12] Beckett mentioned in a letter to MacGreevy that he was reading 'Berkeley's Commonplace Book, which Hone recommended as a beginning, and which is full of profound things, and at the same time of a foul (& false) intellectual canaillerie, enough to put you against reading anything more' (*LSB* 154). *Berkeley's Commonplace Book* (1930) is still extant in Beckett's library and contains a few annotations in green pencil:

Page 4 [green pencil mark in left margin]: M. 36 W^n we imagine 2 bowls v. g. moving in vacuo, 'tis only conceiving a person affect with those sensations.

Page 6 [green pencil mark in left margin]: 49 ... One made to see that had not yet seen his own limbs, or any thing he touched, upon sight of a foot length would know it to be a foot length, if tangible foot & visible foot were the same idea – sed falsum id, ergo et hoc.

Page 9 [green pencil mark and marginalia in right margin: 'esse est percipere']: 84. Men die, or are in [a] state of annihilation, oft in a day.

Page 10 [green pencil mark in left margin]: T.94. *Qu.* whether if succession of ideas in the Eternal Mind, a day does not seem to God a 1000 years, rather than a 1000 years a day?

The same green pencil was used for some of the annotations in Beckett's copy of Berkeley's *A New Theory of Vision and Other Select Philosophical Writings*, ed. A. D. Lindsay (1926 [1910]), which contains the following:

CONTENTS
An Essay towards a New Theory of Vision 1
A Treatise Concerning the Principles of Human Knowledge........ 87
Three Dialogues between Hylas and Philonous
in Opposition to Sceptics and Atheists 197

If this reading of Berkeley can be linked to the letter of 23 December 1932, it almost coincided with his reading of Windelband (Pilling 2006a, 42).[13] The green pencil marks occur in the second section, *A Treatise Concerning the Principles of Human Knowledge*. The book shows two kinds of marginal marks, in green and grey pencil:

Marginal lines in grey pencil next to propositions XXXII (128); XXXIV (129); XXXV (129–30); XLIX (137); LI (138); LII (138); LVII (141); XCVIII (162); CI (164); CXXVII (180).

Marginal lines in green pencil next to propositions LXV (145); LXVI ['against Geulincx (?)'] (146); LXVII (146–7); LXVIII (147); LXIX (147–8); LXX (148); LXXI (148); LXXII (149); LXXIV (150); LXXV (150–1); LXXXI (153); LXXXVI (156); LXXXIX (157–8); XC (158); CXXXV (184); CXXXVI (184); CXXXVII (185); CXXXVIII (185); CXLI (186–7); CXLII (187); CXLII (187); CXLVII ['proof for existence of man'] (189); CLII (193).

The passages marked with green pencil start with a proposition concerning 'cause and effect' and alongside the subsequent two propositions Beckett has written 'against Geulincx (?)' in the left margin. As this is written in the same (or at least similar) green pencil as the marginal marks in Beckett's copy of Berkeley's *Commonplace Book*, it is not implausible that Beckett was reading the passages marked with green pencil around the time he was reading about Geulincx in Windelband. Starting from Cartesian philosophy, Windelband explains Descartes' interest in causality, or 'the principle by which the two elements of the causal relation, cause and effect, which do not in themselves belong together, are connected with each other':

> Where this principle was to be sought could not be a matter of doubt for the disciples of Descartes: God, who produced the union of the two substances in man's nature, has also so arranged them that the functions of the one substance are followed by the corresponding functions of the other. But on this account these functions in their causal relation to one another are not properly, and in their own nature, efficient causes, but only *occasions* in connection with which the consequences determined *by divine contrivance* appear in the other substance, – not *causae efficientes*, but *causae occasionales*. The true 'cause' for the causal connection between stimuli and sensations, and between purposes and bodily movements, is *God*. (Windelband 1958, 415; cf. Beckett's 'Philosophy notes' TCD MS10967, 189r)

The full development of this occasionalism, according to Windelband, is attained in the *Ethics*, where 'Geulincx expresses himself most clearly in the illustration of the clocks' (415), which Beckett already noted in the 'Belgo-Latin' quoted by Windelband (TCD MS10967, 189r) before he was to study Geulincx's *Ethics* more systematically. Windelband analyses this occasionalist explanation in terms of an 'anthropologism': 'This *anthropological* rationale of *Occasionalism* fits from the beginning into a more general metaphysical course of thought' (Windelband 1958, 416). Beckett not only picked up this observation, exclaiming 'What anthropologism!' in his notes; he also took the trouble of studying and excerpting Windelband's footnotes, which trace the intertextuality of the clock metaphor:

> If, therefore, Leibniz, when he later claimed for his 'pre-established harmony' (*Éclairc.* 2 and 3) this same analogy in frequent use at that time, characterized the Cartesian conception by an immediate dependence of the two clocks upon one another, and the Occasionalistic by a constantly renewed regulation of the clocks on the part of the clock-maker, this was applicable at most to some passages in the first edition of the *Ethics* of Geulincx. (Windelband 1958, 416; cf. Beckett's 'Philosophy notes' TCD MS10967, 189r)

This interest in intertextual relations marks his reading of Berkeley's *Principles of Human Knowledge* as well. As soon as Berkeley touches upon the issue of causality, Beckett's green pencil starts undulating in the margin, next to Berkeley's example of the fire:

> The *fire* which I see is not the cause of the pain I suffer upon my approaching it, but the mark that forewarns me of it. In like manner the noise that I hear is not the effect of this or that motion or collision of the ambient bodies, but the sign thereof. (Berkeley 1926, 145; proposition LXV)

The marginalia 'against Geulincx (?)' is triggered by Berkeley's proposition LXVI:

Proper employment of the natural philosopher. – Hence it is evident that those things which, *under the notion of a cause co-operating* or concurring *to the production of effects, are altogether inexplicable*, and run us into great absurdities, may be very naturally explained, and have a proper and obvious use assigned to them, when they are considered only as marks or signs for our information.

Berkeley argues that the job of the natural philosopher is to understand the 'language' of these signs, rather than to explain causality by attributing it to an external occasion. This implicit reference to occasionalism becomes more explicit in the next proposition ('the occasion of our ideas' 147: LXVII). In the subsequent propositions, Berkeley analyses the notions of matter (LXVIII) and occasion (LXIX) in more detail:

Let us examine a little the description that is here given us of *matter*. It neither acts, nor perceives, nor is perceived ... But, say you, it is the *unknown occasion, at the presence of which* ideas are excited in us by the will of God. [Now, I would fain know how any thing can be *present* to us, which is neither perceivable by sense nor reflection, nor capable of producing any idea in our minds, nor is at all extended, nor hath any form, nor exists in any place.] The words *to be present*, when thus applied, must needs be taken in some abstract and strange meaning, and which I am not able to comprehend. (LXVIII; italics and square brackets in original)

In the next proposition, Berkeley examines what is meant by 'occasion', 'as when the burning my finger is said to be the occasion of the pain that attends it', concluding that the term, used in this sense must be very distant from its received signification (LXIX). Berkeley creates a hypothetical dialogue in which 'you' come up with counterarguments and insist on the use of the word 'occasion',[14] after which Berkeley refutes 'your' suggestions. The use of the green pencil suggests that Beckett may also have read (or reread) Berkeley after his reading of Geulincx' *Ethics* in TCD in 1936. When he wrote to Thomas MacGreevy on 5 March of that year to try and explain (partly to himself) why he was reading Geulincx, he explicitly mentioned 'the terrified Berkeley' and his manner of repudiating Geulincx's 'sub specie aeternitatis vision' (*LSB* 319).

The only other marginalia in Beckett's copy of Berkeley's *A New Theory of Vision and Other Select Philosophical Writings* is written in the right margin alongside proposition CXLVII ('*The existence of God more evident than that of man*'), on page 189: 'proof for existence of man'. The marginal lines in grey pencil generally tend to span an argument in its entirety. Some of them zoom in on statements about human ignorance. In the following passage from proposition XCVIII (one of three grey pencil marks between the marks in green pencil), only the latter part ('I am lost and embrangled in inextricable difficulties') is marked:

XCVIII. '*Dilemma*.– (For my own part,) whenever I attempt to frame a simple idea of *time*, abstracted from the succession of ideas in my mind, which flows uniformly, and is participated by all beings, I am lost and embrangled in inextricable difficulties. (162)

Two pages further on, another line in grey pencil marks an epistemological issue, when Berkeley notes that 'we are influenced by false principles to that degree as to mistrust our senses, and think we know nothing of those things which we perfectly comprehend' (CI; page 164).

The marked passages (grey pencil) in the *Three Dialogues* (between 'Hylas' and 'Philonous')[15] probably date from late 1935. On 31 December 1935 Beckett wrote from Cooldrinagh to MacGreevy: 'I read Philonous'. The only marginalia is a question mark in pencil on page 275:

274–5: [Third Dialogue]

HYL. What say you to this? Since, according to you, men judge of the reality of things by their senses, how can a man be mistaken in thinking the moon a plain lucid surface, about a foot in diameter; or a square tower, seen at a distance, round; or an oar, with one end in the water, crooked?

PHIL. He is not mistaken with regard to the ideas he actually perceives; but in the inferences he makes from his present perceptions. . . . if he should conclude from what he perceives in one station, that in case he advances toward the moon or tower, he should still be affected with the like ideas, he is mistaken. [grey pencil question mark next to previous sentence in right margin] . . . The case is the same with regard to the Copernican system. We do not here perceive any motion of the earth; but it were erroneous thence to conclude, that in case we were placed at as great a distance from that, as we are now from the other planets, we should not then perceive its motion.

The marginal question mark next to Philonous' explanation contrasts sharply with Hylas's subsequent reply: 'I understand you'.

'THE GERMAN PHILOSOPHY'

KANT, CASSIRER

After 'the philosophy of the Enlightenment', Windelband reserves a separate chapter for 'The German Philosophy', with Immanuel Kant as the central figure. On 5 January 1938, Beckett told Thomas MacGreevy that the 'entire works of Kant arrived from Munich', the eleven volumes of *Immanuel Kants Werke* (ed. Ernst Cassirer, Berlin: Bruno Cassirer, 1921–2) packed in two immense parcels, which Beckett could hardly carry from customs to a taxi (*LSB* 581). Less than two decades later, he carried the eleven volumes out of his apartment again to give them to Avigdor Arikha. As Anne Atik writes in *How*

It Was, Beckett sent a note to Arikha on 20 December 1956 to change the location of their rendezvous from a café to Arikha's flat, 'vu le poids et volume d'Emmanuel' (Atik 2001, 9). This physical description of Kant's works appropriately reflects its heavy-weight content. Inserted at the back of the last volume of Kant's works is a four-page carbon copy of a typed list with all the titles of works included in the eleven volumes (with their original date of publication). Anne Atik also mentions another insert: the manuscript of the poem 'les joues rouges' (Atik 2001, 7, 10). The only volume that shows traces of a sustained effort to read from cover to cover is the last one. This eleventh volume is not Kant's own work, but the introduction to 'Kants Leben und Lehre' by Ernst Cassirer. Beckett made a few reading notes in his 'Whoroscope' Notebook. In his analysis of these notes, John Pilling draws attention the opposition between Beckett's own life and Kant's ordered life-style: 'So *antinomial* was this encounter between very unkindred spirits that it is difficult to reconstruct what Beckett thought he might achieve by it' (Pilling 2005, 43–4).

On 12 May 1938, Beckett told Arland Ussher: 'I read nothing and write nothing, unless it is Kant (de nobis ipsis silemus)' (*LSB* 622). The Latin phrase between brackets is the first passage Beckett marked in volume XI.[16] It also corresponds with a note in Beckett's 'Whoroscope' Notebook: 'Bacon's "De nobis ipsis silemus" taken by Kant as epigraph to KRITIK der R.V'. (WN 44r). He kept referring to this motto, for instance in *The Unnamable* (*Un* 42), and also applied it to himself, for instance in the 1980s, toward the end of a letter to Anne Atik (Ussy, 4 November 1983): 'As for me, as Bacon advised, silemus' (Atik 2001, 56).

On page 49r of the 'Whoroscope' Notebook (after the first excerpt from Fritz Mauthner's *Beiträge zu einer Kritik der Sprache*, III. 615–16; WN 46r; 47r–48r), Beckett continued taking notes from Cassirer:

Kant's exact description of Westminster Bridge (having never set foot outside Prussia).[17] – Vol. XI, p. 45

'Gebt mir Materie, ich will eine Welt daraus bauen' (WN 49r; qtd. in Pilling 2005, 45)

Beckett's reference to page 45 in volume XI of Kant's *Werke* indicates the changed notetaking strategy in the 'Whoroscope' Notebook in comparison with the 'Dream' Notebook (Pilling 2005, 42–3; Van Hulle 2004a, 329–30). The next entry is a quotation, marked in the left margin with a short vertical line in grey pencil: 'Gebt mir Materie, ich will eine Welt daraus bauen' (XI.46).

The traces of Beckett's reading, both as a marginalist and as an extractor, are not the only relics of his reading. One of the 'non-marginalia' that seems to have found its way directly to his own writing is a passage on the 1755 earthquake in Lisbon. Cassirer explains that it was a personal reaction, rather than a systematic logical investigation that led Kant to his rejection of popular philosophical, optimistic teleology. His original conviction was that the goal of the universe was a slowly but steadily approaching form of perfection, but the Lisbon earthquake forced him to question this belief (XI.59–60).[18] As John Pilling notes, this is most probably the passage to which the line 'sur Lisbonne fumante Kant froidement penché' refers in Beckett's poem 'ainsi a-t-on beau' (probably written after Ascension Day, 26 May 1938; Pilling 2006b, 163).

The next pencil mark in Cassirer's text is a short horizontal line before the opening of the second paragraph on page 68, possibly indicating a pause in the reading, during which Beckett switched to Fritz Mauthner. Alternating with the first excerpts from the second volume of Mauthner's *Beiträge* (II.309, cf. WN 49v–51v; II.506, cf. WN 52r), Beckett continued making notes on Cassirer: the next marked passage in Cassirer (on page 97, with the underlined words 'Bathos der Erfahrung') corresponds to Beckett's excerpt at the bottom of page 51v in the 'Whoroscope' Notebook:

> das fruchtbare Bathos der Erfahrung (Kant)
>
> Bathos = deep (Gr.)!
>
> (WN 51v; qtd. in Pilling 2005, 45)

The thirty-first of the Addenda to *Watt* ('das fruchtbare Bathos der Erfahrung') probably did not derive directly from Kant's *Prolegomena zu einer jeden künftigen Metaphysik die als Wissenschaft wird auftreten können* (Ackerley 2005, 215), but entered the text through the mediation of Ernst Cassirer, who makes the meaning of 'Bathos' in the sense of 'depth' explicit ('diese Tiefe der Erfahrung', 97).

This mediation characterizes much of Beckett's engagement with philosophy. There are relatively few reading traces in Kant's *own* texts and it is possible that the five marked pages in volume 3 ('Kritik der reinen Vernunft') and the three marked pages in volume 5 ('Kritik der praktischen Vernunft') merely represent 'digressions' from his reading of Cassirer's text. For instance, on page 140 of Cassirer's analysis, Beckett wrote in the left margin: 'The what of object [&] the how of judgment', corresponding to a passage[19] that introduces a quotation from the 'Kritik der reinen Vernunft': 'Ich nenne alle Erkenntnis transzendental, die sich nicht sowohl mit Gegenständen, sondern mit unserer Erkenntnisart von Gegenständen, sofern diese a priori möglich sein soll, überhaupt beschäftigt' [I call all knowledge transcendental that is occupied, not with objects, but with the way that we can possibly know objects even before we experience them]; XI.140). The corresponding footnote refers to volume III, page 49, where the same passage is again marked in the margin (and underlined). Moreover, Beckett excerpted this passage twice in his 'Whoroscope' Notebook: on pages 65r (with references to the 'Einleitung VII' and to volume 'III, 49') and 133v.

The notes surrounding the former excerpt (65r) derive from Heinrich Heimsoeth's additional chapter in Wilhelm Windelband's *Lehrbuch der Geschichte der Philosophie* (1935),[20] which Beckett had sent home from Germany; the notes surrounding the latter excerpt correspond to the other marked passages in the *Kritik der reinen Vernunft* (volume III). In a similar way to Beckett's Mauthner notes, the Kant excerpts are fully cited. The first excerpt, under the heading 'Synthetic & analytical judgments' (WN 134v)[21] corresponds to the fourth section of the introduction, '(Einleitung IV, p. 40)', marked with a grey pencil line in volume III.[22] Kant explains the difference between analytic and synthetic judgments by means of the relation of a subject to the predicate, which is possible in two different ways: either the predicate B belongs to the subject A as something that is contained in this concept A; or B lies outside the concept A, although it is connected to it. In the first case the judgment is analytic, in the second synthetic. Beckett also noted in his 'Whoroscope' Notebook that Kant's examples are the judgments 'All bodies are extended' (analytic) and 'All bodies are heavy' (synthetic). The way in which Beckett carefully excerpted this passage on the relations between A and B, not so much as an abstract description but as a visual scene in a bare landscape, prefigures his description of 'A' and 'B' in the French version of *Molloy*: 'Il passe des gens aussi, dont il n'est pas facile de se distinguer avec netteté. ... C'est ainsi que je vis A et B aller lentement l'un vers l'autre, sans se rendre compte de ce qu'ils faisaient. C'était sur une route d'une nudité remarquable' (Beckett 1996, 9–10).

Beckett's reading of Kant coincides with the period of renewed contact with Joyce. The eleven volumes arrived the day before he was stabbed by a pimp (6/7 January 1938), after which Joyce visited Beckett daily in hospital. In the next few months Beckett lived in hotels and had to do without his books (letter to MacGreevy, 11 February 1938; qtd. in Pilling 2006b, 162).

In this period, Beckett was helping Joyce and during his reading of Cassirer he encountered a German equivalent of the expression 'Work in Progress' (Cassirer 1921, 144), noting in the left margin: 'WIP / unter Händen habende Arbeit'. On the opening page of Cassirer's third chapter ('Der Aufbau und die Grundprobleme der Kritik der reinen Vernunft'), Beckett marked Goethe's claim that reading a page of Kant was like entering a well-lit room (XI.149).

Some of the marginalia – such as the question 'Any limit to categories?' (XI.163), the distinction 'Vernunft / Verstand' (XI.218) or the question mark next to the opening paragraph of chapter 5 ('Der Aufbau der kritischen Ethik'; XI.247) – indicate a genuine intellectual engagement with the content of Kant's philosophy, through the mediation of Cassirer. Beckett also marked Kant's famous definition of Enlightenment (XI.242). On rare occasions, when a passage is underlined, Beckett's interest seems to be mainly stylistic and reminiscent of his notetaking strategies of the 'Dream' Notebook ('Entwurf der Vernunft' [XI.179]; 'Rhapsodie der Wahrnehmungen' [XI.181]; 'Technik der Natur' [XI.316]).

On page 208, Beckett's regular vertical line in pencil is accompanied by a rare exclamation mark alongside Cassirer's remark concerning Kant's suggestion 'dass die Bedingungen der Möglichkeit der Erfahrung zugleich Bedingungen der Möglichkeit der Gegenstände der Erfahrung sind' (XI.208). When Beckett translated this passage in his 'Whoroscope' Notebook, the number of exclamation marks tripled:

Kant's [proof] that the conditions of the possibility of experience are also the conditions of the possibility of the objects of experience!!! (WN 59r)

This excerpt is quoted by P. J. Murphy to illustrate Beckett's 'neo-Kantian' reading of Kant, following his 'post-Kantian' reading (Murphy 2011, 203).[23] On the same page of the 'Whoroscope' Notebook, Beckett wrote:

Omnis determinatio est negatio

Ens originarium, ens summum, ens entium

His rare imperatives were hypothetical.
(cf. Kant: XI.161; qtd. in Pilling 2005, 45)

Whereas the two Latin entries are not marked in Beckett's copy of Cassirer's text (225–6), the latter note does correspond with a marked passage, albeit on page 261 rather than 161, as Beckett's erroneous page reference indicates.[24] On the next page of the 'Whoroscope' Notebook, Beckett noted down two Greek expressions, relating to Socrates and Aristotle's respective attitudes toward the particular and the universal. The passage to which these lines correspond (295) is not marked; only one word on page 295 is underlined, with a question mark in the right margin: the word 'Fortschritt' (progress). The context is the development of a concept ('Begriff') by means of the distinction between the general and the particular. Although Aristotle was not an 'empiricist', the difference with Socrates and Plato is that Aristotle's notion of the 'concept' is related to a more concrete ontological question (Cassirer 1921, 295). Cassirer is interested in the history of ideas, but he calls it 'mental progress' ('gedanklicher Fortschritt'; 295). After reading the editor's introduction to Goethe's *Faust*, Beckett had become hypersensitive to expressions of 'progress' and 'onwardness', including the so-called 'Vorwärtsstreben' (Van Hulle 2006, 294). On 19 August 1936, Beckett wrote to MacGreevy that he had 'been working at German & reading Faust', and was clearly irritated by Goethe's 'onwardness': 'All the <u>on & up</u> is so tiresome also, the determined optimism à la Beethoven, the unconscionable time a-coming. The vinegar & nitre of Kant & Heraclitus. It takes a German to apotheose the busybody. I can understand the "keep on keeping on" as a social prophylactic, but not at all as a light in the autological darkness, or the theological' (*LSB* 368). As the editors of the letters indicate, the vinegar and nitre are a biblical reference to Proverbs 25:20 ('as vinegar upon nitre, so is he that singeth songs to an heavy heart') – one of the proverbs excerpted in the 'Dream' Notebook (*DN* 567). The reference to the Proverb suggests that Beckett saw Kant as the singer of songs, as opposed to 'heavy heart' Heraclitus, whom he had described in his philosophy notes as 'the dark, the obscure, the weeping philosopher' (TCD MS10967, 24; qtd. in Feldman 2006a, 70).

Two years after he wrote this letter, when he did make a serious effort to comprehend Kant's writings, he simultaneously read several other works: 'No work', he wrote to George Reavey on 27 September 1938, 'I read an average of an hour a day, after an hour the illusion of comprehension ceases, Kant, Descartes, Johnson, Renard and a kindergarten manual of science: "L'air est partout", "Le plomb est un métal lourd et tendre"' (*LSB* 643). Although Beckett refers to Kant, chances are that he actually means Cassirer's introduction. On page 284 of Cassirer's essay, Beckett marked the passage 'Der "bestirnte Himmel über mir und das moralische Gesetz in mir"' and wrote in the left margin (grey pencil): 'The stars are undoubtedly superb . . .' – a reference to Freud (see Chapter 10).

Toward the end of Cassirer's text, some of the marks show an increasing enthusiasm with reference to Kant's aesthetic reflections, with two big exclamation marks on page 339,[25] an underlining ('<u>subjektiven Allgemeinheit</u>') on the next, a few marks alongside passages on the notion of '<u>genius</u>' (XI.343, 344) and an exclamation mark next to the underlined '<u>Wieland</u>' (XI.347). Beckett has marked Kant's description of aesthetics in terms of 'Zweckmässigkeit ohne Zweck' (XI.334), which he refers to in his 'Whoroscope' Notebook:

Art: 'Zweckmässigkeit ohne Zweck' / (Kant)
Quatsch: 'Zweck ohne Zweckmässigkeit' / (?) (WN 60r)

The movement 'From the sublime to the ridiculous' (Murphy 2011, 208) was seldom so abrupt as in these lines. Earlier in the 'Whoroscope' Notebook, Beckett had already jotted down the title of a fictitious or prospective 'Kritik des reinen Quatsches' (22r) and, while he was in Germany,[26] he noted 'der Krit[z]el der reinen Vernunft [etc]' (35r). Those Kantian 'scribbles' were probably written before the arrival of the eleven volumes of Kant's works. Beckett's initial playful attitude toward Kant does not seem to have radically changed after reading Cassirer, but he did not have a clear purpose for the 'Quatsch' either. Toward the end of volume XI, Beckett saw a connection with Schopenhauer, once on page 333[27] and again on page 334: as soon as the 'Will' is mentioned, Beckett immediately made the link with 'Arthur' – as he calls him in the left margin.

SCHOPENHAUER

Arthur Schopenhauer is without a doubt one of the philosophers with whom Beckett had most affinity. The literary qualities of his writings and their consequent appeal to artists such as Jorge Luis Borges, Hermann Broch, André Gide, D. H. Lawrence, Thomas Mann, Robert Musil, Marcel Proust and Rainer Maria Rilke have led to what Ulrich Pothast has called an 'asymmetric' reception (Pothast 2008, 8) – with fewer admirers among philosophers than among writers. Beckett's appreciation started in July 1930, when he read Schopenhauer in spite of the sneers from Beaufret, Péron and the other friends and colleagues at the Ecole Normale Supérieure (ENS). In his letters to MacGreevy, he emphasized that he was 'not reading philosophy' but studying Schopenhauer's 'intellectual justification of unhappiness – the greatest that has ever been attempted'. Seven years later, he told MacGreevy that the only thing he could read when he was ill was Schopenhauer: 'I always knew he was one of the ones that mattered most to me' (*LSB* 550). He also appreciated Schopenhauer as 'a philosopher that can be read as a poet' (550).[28]

Ulrich Pothast has analysed Beckett's interest in Schopenhauer, notably in the notion of the Will – with a 'capital W so as to distinguish the Will as thing-in-itself from the individual will we attribute to empirical persons' (Pothast 2008, 29). The Will objectifies itself in the empirical world and to every grade of the Will's objectification there is a corresponding, timeless Idea, according to Schopenhauer. What made his philosophy attractive to many artists was the question how the artist can gain access to, and knowledge of, these so-called Ideas. Schopenhauer suggested that this requires a special awareness that is not dominated by the Will, a state in which the artist's self-awareness as an individual has vanished. This way the artist or 'Genius' can 'reduplicate in worldly material *the Idea* which originally was experienced in will-less contemplation', as Pothast formulates it (37). Of all the arts, music provides the richest metaphysical knowledge, according to Schopenhauer. By giving access to this 'deeper' reality beyond the phenomenal world, music can momentarily tear the veil of Maya apart. In the 'Clare Street' Notebook, Beckett changed Schopenhauer's (borrowed) notion of the 'veil of Maya' into the 'veil' or 'membrane of hope' ('Hoffnungsschleier'), which can be torn apart, but only briefly, because the eyes can only bear such pitiless light for a short while (UoR MS5003, 33; qtd. in Nixon 2011, 170).

The first item on Beckett's list of 'Books sent home' from Germany is 'Schopenhauer: Werke' (WN 17v). These 'Werke' are the six volumes of the *Sämmtliche Werke*, edited by Julius Frauenstädt (Leipzig: F.A. Brockhaus, 2nd ed., 1923), which are still among the books in the library.

Beckett studied the first volume quite intensively, especially the first 200 pages, comprising the 'Editor's Introduction' and the biographical sketch (also by the editor, Julius Frauenstädt). Given the importance of Schopenhauer in Beckett's poetics, it is worthwhile examining his reading traces in detail, following the sometimes capricious pattern of interest set out by the marginalia.

Against the backdrop of Beckett's interest in linguistic scepticism it is remarkable that one of the first passages he marked in the editor's introduction (with a marginal cross in grey pencil) is Schopenhauer's view on philosophy as a continuous abuse of universals or general concepts (Frauenstädt in Schopenhauer 1923, 11).[29] On 9 July 1937, Beckett wrote a letter in German to Axel Kaun in which he revealed his plans for a 'literature of the unword' marked by 'nominalist irony'. This intriguing concept has puzzled Beckett scholars for several decades. In particular the line 'der mir noch nicht bekannte Versuch den Nominalismus (im Sinne der Scholastiker) mit dem Realismus zu vergleichen' (*Dis* 53) shows remarkable affinities with Fritz Mauthner's emphasis on nominalism and the ironic use of 'words as mere words'.[30] But the dating of Beckett's Mauthner notes ('late spring and early summer of 1938', Pilling 2006b, 164) conflicts with the date of the letter to Kaun (9 July 1937). Around this time, Beckett also sent a letter to Arland Ussher (11 July 1937) with a copy of part of the Kaun letter enclosed and with the following request: 'Your thoughts on Logoclasm, will you please put them in order and bestow them on me' (*LSB* 516). The same day, he wrote to Mary Manning Howe: 'I am starting a Logoclasts League' (521). He described his idea of logoclasm as 'ruptured writing, so that the void may protrude, like a hernia' (521). That the letter to Kaun is written in German is a comment in itself, since Beckett claimed that it became increasingly difficult for him to write an official English ('Es wird mir tatsächlich immer schwieriger, ja sinnloser, ein offizielles Englisch zu schreiben'; *Dis* 52). In this period, shortly after his stay in Germany, Beckett immersed himself in the German language through his reading. Six days before he wrote the letter to Kaun, he told Thomas MacGreevy that he was reading 'Schopenhauer on women' (*LSB* 509). In the *Sämmtliche Werke*, the essay 'Über die Weiber' is part of volume VI (*Parerga und Paralipomena: kleine philosophische Schriften*, zweiter Band, Kapitel XXVII, 649–62). The text is surrounded by essays on language and writing, books and reading, noise and silence.[31] In particular chapter 25 ('Ueber Sprache und Worte', only two chapters before the essay on women) is almost certain to have drawn the attention of a young writer[32] on the verge of writing a German letter with a poetical statement on logoclasm. Combined with Frauenstädt's introduction and Beckett's familiarity with nominalism through his reading of Windelband, his reading of Schopenhauer in the week preceding his writing of the letter to Kaun on Friday, 9 July 1937 suggests the possibility that he may not have needed to read Mauthner first to come up with the idea of comparing Gertrude Stein and James Joyce's diverging writing methods to Nominalism and Realism (*Dis* 53). Beckett characterizes Gertrude Stein as a lady who is in love with her vehicle in the way in which a mathematician is in love with his figures ('wie ein Mathematiker in seine Ziffern'), a mathematician for whom the solution of the problem is of entirely secondary interest (*Dis* 53). Mathematics is also employed by Schopenhauer. Frauenstädt notes that Schopenhauer did not spin concepts from other concepts in the style of the 'Fichte-Schelling-Hegelian speculation' (I.11), but that he drew his concepts from the physical (outer and inner) world of experience. One of Schopenhauer's examples, mentioned by Frauenstädt, is algebra and the way it can lead one astray with concepts, uncontrolled by observation.[33] Observation is to the intellect what solid ground is to the body, according to Schopenhauer. As soon as this firm ground is abandoned, everything becomes like Ovid's description of primal chaos: '*instabilis tellus, innabilis unda*'.[34] The Latin phrase, underlined and marked in the right margin, is employed by Kant in this *Kritik der reinen Vernunft* and by Schopenhauer in his 'Epiphilosophie' (§50) toward the end of *Die Welt als Wille und Vorstellung*.

A dozen pages further in Frauenstädt's introduction, Beckett marked a long passage on physics and metaphysics (I.23), noting that according to Schopenhauer the advances in physics are merely an accumulation of our knowledge of phenomena, not of that which is manifested in them (I.24). Frauenstädt quotes a passage from *Parerga und Paralipomena*, in which Schopenhauer suggests that one could regard history as a continuation of zoology ('eine Fortsetzung der Zoologie'; Frauenstädt 1923, I.26) – which Beckett translated in the left margin (grey pencil) as 'History a higher zoology' (I.39). Frauenstädt notes that a form of anthropomorphism could be held against Schopenhauer, because he develops his philosophy by projecting the microcosm of human self-awareness onto the macrocosm (I.40). At the core of Schopenhauer's philosophy is his generalization of the Will (I.48; marked with a grey pencil line), which Frauenstädt presents as an incontrovertible given (I.54; grey pencil).

Beckett sometimes also underlined individual concepts, such as 'Aseität' (I.56), existence originating from (that is, having no source other than) itself. The relativity of the notion of 'freedom' is a philosophical topic Beckett had a special interest in, notably since his reading of 'old Geulincx, dead young, who left me free, on the black boat of Ulysses, to crawl toward the East, along the deck' (*Mo* 50). Regarding this 'great measure of freedom, for him who has not the pioneering spirit' (50), Frauenstädt makes a link with Schopenhauer, through Kant.[35]

On page 94 Beckett marked Frauenstädt's ultra-condensed summary of Schopenhauer's philosophy and focused on the causes of his 'Pessimismus': the basis of the Will is want, and therefore suffering; and if there are no objects to be wanted, the result is a feeling of emptiness (I.96). Beckett marked Schopenhauer's image for the extreme internal paradox of the Will: Thyestes, greedily devouring his own flesh (I.100); and he pencilled two big exclamation marks alongside Frauenstädt's expression 'die pesthauchende Sumpfpflanze des Pessimismus' (I.106). Schopenhauer's pessimism is not so much based on existential suffering, Frauenstädt argues, but on what he regards as its source, that is, the antimoral capacity of the will to live (I.112; marked with grey pencil). What turned Schopenhauer into a pessimist, according to Frauenstädt, was the 'sinfulness of the natural will' (I.112; marked with grey pencil) and compassion with all living creatures, not just his own suffering (I.114). Struck by the subsequent discussion of pity, Beckett marked a long quotation from Jürgen Bona Meyer,[36] relating pity to Buddhism and the notion of 'tat twam asi' (which Beckett also encountered in Heinrich Zimmer's *Maya: Der indische Mythos*, a book he read for Joyce around October 1938; cf. Van Hulle 1999). Meyer's point is that if one considers all living creatures as part of one being, as Schopenhauer does, pity is not noble at all, but simply a form of narcissistic self-pity.[37] This preoccupation with 'pity' is also noticeable in other marginalia relating to Dante and to Beckett's Italian Bible (see Chapters 5 and 8).

Frauenstädt defends Schopenhauer by referring to his ethics and arguing that he did not approve of misanthropy. Nonetheless, Beckett left the argumentation unmarked. Instead, he drew a pencil line next to the 'cabinet of caricatures', Schopenhauer's eloquent description of what the world looks like from a misanthropic point of view, especially in a hypochondriac mood, which Frauenstädt quotes from *Die beiden Grundprobleme der Ethik*.[38]

Ethics – in the general sense of Walther von der Vogelweide's famous poem about the poet sitting on a stone and wondering how one should live on this earth – was one of Beckett's major interests whenever he engaged in reading philosophy. It should come as no surprise, then, that he was also interested in the way Schopenhauer applied, or rather failed to apply, his own philosophy of the denial of the Will in his own life.

Against this background, Beckett read Frauenstädt's biographical sketch ('Lebensbild') with his pencil at the ready. The first note he pencilled in the margin is a much wittier explanation of Schopenhauer's pessimism than Frauenstädt's. The editor mentions that Schopenhauer's father used to read an English and a French newspaper every day, urging his son at an early age to read the *Times*, from which he believed everything could be learned; Schopenhauer followed his father's advice for the rest of his life. Alongside this passage, Beckett pencilled in the left margin: 'Schopenhauer's pessimism explained: he read the Times all his life' (I.142).

Schopenhauer's father wanted his first son to be born in England, so that he would have all the rights of an Englishman, but eventually Johanna Schopenhauer gave birth to Arthur in Danzig (Gdansk) in 1788. Beckett marked this passage with an exclamation mark and pencilled in the top margin: 'A. S. tried to be given birth to in England!' (I.143). Beckett underlined a few of the places where Schopenhauer stayed (such as Le Havre and Wimbledon) and marked the passages on the death of the philosopher's father in 1805 (I.147); his student years in Göttingen where professor Schulze told him to study Plato and Kant, before reading Aristotle and Spinoza (I.149); his moving to Berlin in 1811, attracted by the reputation of Johann Gottlieb Fichte (I.150). The importance of Fichte for Schopenhauer's philosophy (notably the notion of the Will) is undeniable, but to a large extent the impact worked *per negationem*.

Schopenhauer's sovereign attitude toward his teacher showed in his annotations and lecture notes. Frauenstädt mentions a college copybook ('Kollegheft'), the title page of which mentioned not only the title ('Über die Thatsachen des Bewusstseyns und die Wissenschaftslehre bei Fichte im Winter 1811–1812'), but also – next to the word 'Wissenschaftslehre' – the following comment: 'Vielleicht ist die richtige Lesart Wissenschaftsleere' (I.152). (Beckett had already applied a similar pun to the word 'Gelehrte' (scholars) in his 'Whoroscope' Notebook: 'Geleerte'.[39]) On the verso of the title page, Schopenhauer had written two mottoes, one by Kant and one by Goethe (I.152). Both of them are quoted by Frauenstädt. Beckett marked them as well as the passages on Schleiermacher (underlined), who could impress the young Schopenhauer as little as Fichte could (I.153); on Goethe, who initiated Schopenhauer in his colour theory (I.153); and on the orientalist Friedrich Majer, who introduced him to Indian philosophy.

During the period in Dresden in 1815, Schopenhauer wrote a poem on the 'Sistine Madonna' by Raphael (in the Galerie Alte Meister, Dresden), which Beckett read with enthusiasm, as the big exclamation mark in the right margin indicates (I.157). To some degree the exclamation mark is also an expression of recognition, for Beckett had seen the Dresden *Sistine Madonna*. He described it in his 'German Diaries' on 1 February 1937 as a depiction of 'Mary with Child on clouds, with left Pope Sixtus II & right St. Barbara' – 'The best Raphael I have seen', according to his comments. In particular the right hand of Pope Sixtus II was 'Wonderful'.

Frauenstädt mentions Schopenhauer's reading habits, such as the many pencil marks and marginal glosses in his books (I.175). Apart from the *Sämmtliche Werke*, Beckett's library also contains the fifth volume of *Der handschriftliche Nachlass*, completely devoted to Schopenhauer's marginalia ('Randschriften zu Büchern', ed. Arthur Hübscher, Frankfurt a.M.: Waldemar Kramer, 1968), possibly sent to Beckett by Barbara Bray.[40] One of the marginalia mentioned in this volume (54) is Schopenhauer's drawing on page 68 of his teacher's *System der Sittenlehre nach den Principien der Wissenschaftslehre*, where Fichte explains his general principle that the 'I' must 'posit itself' or 'set itself up' ('sich setzen') as an individual. As 'sich setzen' also simply means 'to sit down', Schopenhauer wittily expressed his critical distance by drawing a chair[41] in the left margin next to Fichte's solemn explanation of the central concept of his philosophy.[42] The drawing of the chair also expresses Schopenhauer's attitude toward reading in general. According to him, autonomous thinking ('Selbstdenken') was much more important than reading, because too much reading tended to smother or paralyse his own mental activity, as Frauenstädt notes.[43] The metaphor of 'smothering' and reading as a form of preventing one from breathing corresponds to Beckett's own attitude toward reading in relation to writing. In November 1931, Beckett had already told Thomas MacGreevy – with regard to his Joycean method of notesnatching: 'I have enough "butin verbal" to strangle anything I'm likely to want to say' (see Chapter 1; qtd. in *DN* xiv)

Beckett's alertness as a reader shows on the same page 175, where Frauenstädt writes that Schopenhauer was against excessive reading, including ephemeral newspaper articles. In the right margin, Beckett dryly comments: 'He read the Times every day' (I.175), implicitly referring to his earlier annotation on page 142. That he marked Schopenhauer's motto[44] and underlined the word 'Pudel' (I.178) indicates more than a merely trivial interest in Schopenhauer's daily walks with his poodle. Beckett had made extensive notes on *Faust* in August and September 1936 and was aware of the Mephistophelian background of Schopenhauer's choice of pet. A few pages further on, in a short paragraph evoking the austere interior of Schopenhauer's study, Beckett only marked the line about the poodle, lying on a black bearskin next to the sofa (I.181).

The biographical sketch is anything but hagiographical. Frauenstädt closes by stating in plain terms that in almost every respect Schopenhauer's life was at odds with his own theories. Beckett, however, does not seem to have passed judgment. He did not mark the fact that Schopenhauer arrogantly looked down upon other people; the only thing he underlined is the way the philosopher referred to the rest of humanity as mass-produced articles: 'Fabrikwaare der Natur' (I.197).

Beckett's interest in epistemology is reflected in his reading traces in Schopenhauer's *Schriften zur Erkenntnislehre*: in the introduction to 'Ueber die vierfache Wurzel des Satzes vom zureichenden Grunde' Beckett marked the way Schopenhauer stresses the importance of the principle of sufficient reason (Schopenhauer 1923, I.4), usually attributed to Leibniz. The principle that anything that happens does so for a reason is so important to Schopenhauer that he closes his introduction with it: 'Nichts ist ohne Grund worum es sei' (Schopenhauer 1923, I.5). Beckett not only marked it with grey pencil, but he also wrote the phrase in his 'Sottisier' Notebook between July 1979 and December 1980 (UoR MS2901, 13v).

In Schopenhauer's historical outline ('Geschichtliche Uebersicht', §7), Descartes' ontological proof of God's existence is shown to be based on a terminological confusion, which Beckett summarized in the left margin: 'Definition no proof of existence' (I.10). He also marked the philosophical consequences: Descartes' terminological confusion led to what Schopenhauer called Hegel's 'Philosophasterei' (I.12). In the next paragraph (§8) Spinoza's pantheism is presented as a continuation and realization of Descartes' ontological proof (I.14; marginal pencil line). The idea of something being generated within itself ('causa sui') is compared to Baron Münchhausen, pulling himself out of the water by his own hair. Beckett did not fail to mark this colourful description (I.15).

In the fourth chapter, Beckett highlighted a passage on the 'absurdity' of the so-called 'freedom of the Will' (I.48–9), as well as the corresponding footnote with two long quotations from Kant. Schopenhauer fulminates against the esteemed professors of philosophy, who have managed to ignore his work on this subject, deliberately failing to mention it, under the motto: 'Zitto, zitto, dass nur das Publikum nichts merke' [Hush, hush, so that the public does not notice]; I.50). The sentence is underlined in blue ink, with a note in the margin: 'Addenda Watt'. That these marginalia are written in blue ink may be an indication that this line was marked later than the other (pencil) marginalia. The 'Zitto' line is one of about a dozen addenda (including 'das fruchtbare Bathos' and 'die Merde hat mich wieder') that were not part of the manuscripts nor of the typescript of *Watt*.[45] Several of these derive from the 'Whoroscope' Notebook. So does the 'Zitto' passage. Not only as a 'marginalist' did Beckett mark this passage, he also noted it down in his capacity as an 'extractor'. In his 'Whoroscope' Notebook it follows immediately after an excerpt from an (unmarked) passage in §3, 'Nutzen dieser Untersuchung' (Schopenhauer 1923, I.3):

> 'la clarté est la bonne foi des philosophes' (Vauvenargues) quoted by Schopenhauer (Einleitung zu Vierfachen Wurzel)
>
> Zitto! Zitto! dass nur das Publikum nichts merke!
> (Conspiracy of silence against Schop^{er} V.W. p. 50) (WN 85r)

Against the background of the numerous publishers who refused *Murphy*, it is maybe understandable that Beckett noted this passage on the philosophy professors ignoring Schopenhauer's prize-winning essay on the freedom of the will. But it is remarkable that Beckett returned to this passage four decades later, when he reread Schopenhauer's *Concerning the Fourfold Root of the Principle of Sufficient Reason* and wrote in his 'Sottisier' Notebook: 'Sch. 'totgeschwiegen'' (UoR MS2901, 13v; qtd. in Hisgen and van der Weel 1998, 340).

Schopenhauer explains that the mind interprets the experiences of the body as effects of a cause, which it situates outside the organism (I.53). Apart from the underlined word 'ausserhalb', the passage is also marked with the word 'centrifuge' pencilled in the right margin (I.53). Another peculiarity of the mind, marked by Beckett, is the way it transforms the two-dimensional impression of external objects on the eye into a three-dimensional representation. According to Schopenhauer, the visual experience is planimetric, not stereometric; the stereometric elements are added by the mind (I.64). Alongside this passage, Beckett pencilled in the margin: 'Absurdity of stereometric film. Appropriateness of planimetri[c]'. Drawing a chair, for instance, involves a form of abstraction of that capacity of the mind (I.65; marginal pencil line).

The second volume of Schopenhauer's works – *Die Welt als Wille und Vorstellung* – only shows reading traces in the prefaces to the first and the second edition. In the 'Vorrede zur ersten Auflage' Beckett has drawn a pencil line next to the passage where Schopenhauer urges his readers to first read Immanuel Kant's major works, whose effect he compares to the overwhelming result of a successful cataract operation (II.xi). The first passage Beckett underlined in the 'Vorrede zur zweiten Auflage' is the line 'Wes Brod ich ess', des Lied ich sing' (II.xix), which Beckett also noted in his 'Sottisier' Notebook (UoR MS2901, 13v).

During his initial reading Beckett did not fail to notice Schopenhauer's antipathy against Hegel,[46] who serves as a contrastive background to the greatness of Immanuel Kant and the fundamental change Kant's philosophy causes in every mind that manages to understand it (II. xxiv). Beckett marked this long praise of Kant and the plea to read his works directly, rather than through the mediation of an introduction, for the ideas of such an extraordinary mind do not allow any form of filtering (II.xxv). The only other mark in the subsequent volumes of the complete works is again a reference to the 'all-shattering Kant'.[47] It is not implausible that these repeated pleas to read Kant incited Beckett to order the eleven volumes of Kant's *Immanuel Kants Werke*, which arrived on 5 January 1938. During the following months, Beckett also read another philosophical work that is one of the most surprising books in the extant library: Olga Plümacher's *Der Pessimismus*.

'THE PHILOSOPHY OF THE NINETEENTH CENTURY'

PLÜMACHER

Olga Plümacher (née Olga Marie Pauline Hünerwadel, 1839–95) grew up in Zürich and married a German sea captain, Eugene H. Plümacher. Olga was friends with the mother of the German writer Frank Wedekind (1864–1918). As a fervent supporter of Eduard von Hartmann, she introduced Wedekind to Hartmann's philosophy of the unconscious (1869) and to Schopenhauer's work. According to Gerald Izenberg,

> Wedekind's relationship with the remarkable Olga Plümacher, his 'philosophical aunt', was platonic but no less influential. A self-taught philosopher who had published books on Schopenhauer and Eduard von Hartmann, Olga schooled Frank's untutored speculative instincts, offering him what his traditional classical gymnasium education could not. It was she who introduced him to the most advanced philosophical currents of the day, not only to Hartmann's idea of the unconscious and the cosmic pessimism he had derived from Schopenhauer, but to the as yet little known Nietzsche (of whom she was critical for his attacks on Schopenhauer). (Izenberg 2000, 39)

On his seventeenth birthday, Wedekind received *Lichtstrahlen aus Eduard von Hartmanns sämtlichen Werken* (1881) from his 'philosophical aunt'. Around that period the Plümacher family with two children moved to Beersheba Springs, Tennessee. Olga Plümacher continued writing and completed three books: *Der Kampf ums Unbewußte* (Berlin 1881; second edition Leipzig: Friedrich, 1890), *Zwei Individualisten der schopenhauer'schen Schule [P. Batz and L. Hellenbach von Paczolay]* (Vienna, 1881) and *Der Pessimismus in Vergangenheit und Gegenwart: Geschichtliches und Kritisches* (Heidelberg: Georg Weiss Verlag, 1884; second edition 1888). But in anglophone philosophical and literary circles, hardly anyone knew her. Just how unknown she was in the Anglo-American world is evident from the 'Literary Notes' in *The New York Times*, 14 February 1879: 'The notable article on "Pessimism" by O. Plumacher in the January number of *Mind*, a voice out of the pessimistic camp raised in defense of its leader, Hartmann, supposed to be the work of an English writer sheltered under a nom de plume, is the production of a German-Swiss lady, Frau Olga Plumacher'.

Plümacher's *Der Pessimismus* is the only book in the library that has been interleaved. It is divided into two parts, the first of which is a historical survey of the philosophical concept of pessimism, whereas the second concentrates on the 'most recent reaction against pessimism'. The heavily marked chapters on Arthur Schopenhauer (124–33) and Eduard von Hartmann (134–60) immediately catch the eye. The interleaves are filled with translations and summaries (or a combination) in black ink. For instance, the first note on the interleaf facing the opening of the chapter on Schopenhauer (124) examines the untranslatable notion of 'Weltschmerz'. The opening passage is summarized and translated on the interleaf:

The title – 'Weltschmerz' is misleading. It might be supposed that in itself it constitutes Philosophy – or that it was the result of a particular Philosophy.

The analytical nature of this intensive reading shows in the summary of the next passage at the top of the interleaf, itemizing and numbering the reasons why Schopenhauer's work is labelled 'Philosophie des Weltschmerzes', while Plümacher's text does not make the numbers explicit:

Schopenhauer's Pessimism is called 'Weltschmerz'[48] on two grounds
1. It was the principal motive to philosophizing
2. The disposition between the Will of men & the [provision] for its satisfaction by nature is his only metaphysical assumption.

The red and blue underlinings in the printed text are probably the traces of the first reading stage. The next phase in the reading and assimilation process seems to have been the translation on the interleaves in black ink. Grey pencil marks constitute the next stage. On the interleaf facing page 130, the translation shows a blank space between brackets, to be filled in later – and indeed, at a later stage the word 'guilt' was added in pencil. On page 124, the grey pencil is used to analyse the structure of the argument, but also to complete the translation on the facing interleaf.[49]

Schopenhauer's Charge against Previous Philosophy

They did recognize Evil to a certlain extent but being inconsistent with their presupposition of a Wise^{'Allmighty [sic] & Perfect'} World-Cause they were forced to do violence to experience & at the most assign a secondary cause derived from Theology.

The addition '^{Allmighty & Perfect}' could indicate an attempt to complete the translation of the German 'Voraussetzung einer vollkommenen, weisen und allmächtigen Weltursache' (124; underlined with blue pencil). The possibility that the interleaved comments and translations are not Beckett's but someone else's cannot be excluded. The error in '^{Allmighty [sic] & Perfect}' and the capitals would be quite atypical if they were written by Beckett, and the same applies to the capitals in the translations in black ink. The copy could have been purchased in an antiquarian bookstore or Beckett may have received it from a friend, much in the same way as Brunschvicg's *Spinoza et ses contemporains* was lent to him by Brian Coffey or Descartes' *Choix de textes* by Beaufret. The lack of any inscription does not help to retrace the provenance, but the book does contain an interesting inserted booklet: one of only twenty copies in a manual impression of 'Das dichterische Element in unserer Zeit' – an excerpt from a lecture Hofmannsthal gave in Vienna in 1907 (see Chapter 4),[50] composed in Claudius-Fraktur by Axel Kaun[51] at the printing office Haag-Drugulin (Leipzig) in the autumn of 1937.[52] A few comments on the direct link between thought and language[53] in this lecture accord with Mauthner's *Beiträge zu einer Kritik der Sprache* and with Hofmannsthal's own fictitious letter, 'Ein Brief', one of the central texts in Austro-German literary *Sprachskepsis*. It is always possible that this pamphlet was accidentally inserted in Beckett's copy of Plümacher's book, but the link with the addressee of Beckett's famous German letter to Axel Kaun makes it plausible that *Der Pessimismus* entered Beckett's personal library in the wake of his journey to Germany.

Although Beckett's proteiform handwriting can take many shapes, the handwriting of the comments in black ink differs considerably from some of the notes in the 'Whoroscope' Notebook.[54] There are, however, a few reading traces that can plausibly be argued to be Beckett's: the pencil marks in the introduction and part I, chapter 1, first section ('Der Pessimismus im Brahmanismus und Buddhaismus', 18–27). The first marked passage (Plümacher 1888, 19) relates to the two cosmologies in Brahmanism, both of which are also mentioned in pencil on the facing interleaf: 'Emanationstheorie' and 'Illusionstheorie'. The latter comprises the theory of the deception of Maya ('Trug der Maja'). Plümacher explains how existence is not merely regarded as 'being' ('Sein') but as that which should or need not be, 'das Nichtseinsollende' (20, marginal pencil line). The Brahman who has understood that all phenomena, including the gods, are merely part of what Schopenhauer called the 'principium individuationis' ('blossen Trug der Maja'; 21), does no longer worship any gods and lives an ascetic life, superior to the gods (21; marginal pencil line). Whoever has torn apart the veil of Maya ('den Schleier der Maja zerrissen') practises asceticism, not to torment himself, but to show his independence from the illusion (22; marginal pencil lines). In the end, Brahmanism is not about acting in this or that way ('so oder so'), but about not acting at all (23; marginal pencil line).

Gautama Buddha drew the conclusions from the abstract monism of Brahmanism (24) and concluded that whatever lurked behind multiform existence had to be 'pure nothingness' ('so ist das was hinter dem vielheitlichen Sein ist, das reine Nichts'; 24, marginal pencil line). This nothingness or Nirvana, however, is only blissful *per negationem*, insofar as the world or Sansara is 'unblissful' (24; marginal pencil line). For a Buddhist, there is no knowledge beyond the earthly things. Since nothingness is all there is, all thirst for knowledge is vain. According to Buddhism (as portrayed by Plümacher) the world is an illusion, though not because it represents the eternal 'one-ness' in the form of individuals. As opposed to Brahmanism, Buddhism regards the world as that which should not be, because it actually emerged from nothingness ('dem Nichts entsprossen', 25; marginal pencil line). The section ends with a recapitulation of the link of these religions with pessimism, based on the idea that existence is worse than non-existence ('Nichtsein', 27; marginal pencil line).

These pencil marks are consistent with the reading traces that Beckett left in other philosophical works such as Kant's. The opening sentence of the introduction is already marked with a marginal pencil line next to Plümacher's working definition of pessimism as: the axiological judgment that the amount of pain exceeds the amount of pleasure and that the non-existence of the world would consequently be better than its existence (Plümacher 1888, 1). On the next page Plümacher suggests that the superlative 'optimism' should be replaced by the comparative 'meliorism', expressing the idea that existence is 'better' or more preferable than non-existence. This passage is marked and the word 'Pejorismus' is written in pencil on the facing (inter)leaf. The handwriting resembles that of the note 'pejorism / meliorism' (in black ink) on page 45v of Beckett's 'Whoroscope' Notebook.

The notes preceding the entry 'pejorism / meliorism' derive from Céline's *Bagatelles pour un massacre*. John Pilling has shown that these notes cannot have been taken before 28 December 1937, the date of publication of Céline's book (Pilling 2005, 42; 'achevé d'imprimer' 3 December 1937). On the second half of the facing page (46r), Beckett started making extensive excerpts from Fritz Mauthner's *Beiträge zu einer Kritik der Sprache* (WN 46r–58v).

A rough survey[55] of this intersection of reading traces (Kant, Plümacher, Mauthner, Sartre, Heimsoeth . . .) in the 'Whoroscope' Notebook gives an idea of the way Beckett jumped back and forth between philosophical texts in this period:

'Whoroscope' Notebook, page:

44r:	Bacon's 'De nobis ipsis silemus' taken by **Kant** as epigraph [cf. Cassirer XI.3]
45r:	Hyppasus; Pythagoras
45v:	Céline; pejorism / meliorism [**Plümacher**]
46r:	Mauthner, Der reine u. konsequente Nominalismus; III.615–16
46v:	Du holde Kunst [Schubert, 'An die Musik']
46r–48r:	Mauthner, Der reine u. konsequente Nominalismus (contd) III.615–16
48v:	Minchin's *Student's Dynamics*, etc.
49r:	**Kant**'s exact description of Westminster Bridge [cf. Cassirer XI.45–6]
49v–51v:	Mauthner, II.309
51v:	das fruchtbare Bathos der Erfahrung / (**Kant**) [cf. Cassirer XI.97]
52r:	Mauthner, II.506
52r–52v:	Mauthner, II.532
52v–53r:	Mauthner, II.533–4
53v–55r:	Mauthner, II.644–5
55r:	Mauthner, II.675
55r–55v:	Mauthner, II.689–90
55v–57v:	Mauthner, II.699–701
58r–58v:	Mauthner, II.714–15
59r:	**Kant**'s proof; hypothetical imperatives [see Cassirer XI.208–61]
59v:	Kant XI 294 [see Cassirer XI.294–5]
60r:	Art: 'Zweckmässigkeit ohne Zweck' (**Kant**) [see Cassirer XI.334]
60v:	Jules de **Gaultier**, *De Kant à Nietzsche* (1900); Dante, Inferno IV 103
61v:	'stultologie – applied by St Bernard at [Council] of Sens to theologie of **Abelard**'
	[based on Lasserre, *Un Conflit religieux*, 98; cf. supra]

62r: **'Leibniz to Locke**
        'Nihil est in intellectu quod non prius fuerit in sensu, <u>nisi ipse</u> <u>intellectus</u>.'
        noème, noèse
        the <u>geology</u> of conscience – Cambrian experience, Cainozoic judgments, etc. . .
        [see **Sartre**, *L'Imagination*, 34; 51; 141]
62v: Table of Geological Eras
62r, 63r: velocity of escape; 'Venus has a long day' [see Spencer Jones, 36–47].

The items on pages 62r and 63r derive from an article by Dr H. Spencer Jones, FRS (Astronomer Royal) regarding the question: 'Is there Life in Other Worlds?' The article was published in *Discovery: A Popular Journal of Knowledge* (New Series, Vol. II, No. 10, January 1939, 36–47). While it cannot be excluded that Beckett read this article several months after it was first published, the fact that it is part of a monthly rather than a book increases the probability that he made these notes in or around January 1939. The article indicates an astronomical interest of Beckett's that is less known (see Chapter 10) and it is important for the dating of the multifarious 'Whoroscope' notes. It serves as a *terminus a quo* for the notes on the subsequent pages, and if we may assume that Beckett read the article in this monthly journal around the time it came out and was available in bookshops and libraries, the excerpts can also (indicatively) serve as a *terminus ad quem* for the preceding notes, including the note based on Plümacher ('pejorism / meliorism', 45v). Within this interesting section of the 'Whoroscope' Notebook the Plümacher notes are to be situated at the beginning of the period between, on the one hand, the arrival of the eleven volumes on 5 January 1938 (or possibly the letter of 12 May, mentioning 'De nobis ipsis silemus') and, on the other hand, the notes from the January 1939 issue of *Discovery*.

If the reference to Kant's motto (Bacon's 'De nobis ipsis silemus') in the 'Whoroscope' Notebook (WN 44r) dates from the same period as the letter to Arland Ussher in which Beckett mentions 'Kant (de nobis ipsis silemus)' (12 May 1938; *LSB* 622), the Céline and Plümacher notes on page (45v) may have been entered slightly later than 'very late 1937 or relatively early in 1938' (Pilling 2006b, 164), closer to 'the late spring and early summer of 1938' (164) when Beckett's reading started alternating between Kant and Mauthner.

NIETZSCHE

De Gaultier's book (from which Beckett excerpted a fragment on page 60v[56] of the 'Whoroscope' Notebook, and on which he had already taken several notes in his 'Dream' Notebook, entries 1143–55) is not part of Beckett's library as far as it is still preserved in Paris. Nonetheless, Nietzsche *is* present, albeit not prominently, with a copy of *Le gai savoir* (1966 [1950]), showing several dog-ears.[57]

PHILOSOPHY IN THE TWENTIETH CENTURY

The pages in the 'Whoroscope' Notebook following immediately after the excerpts from the January 1939 article by Spencer Jones contain another reference to Kant. They also indicate that Beckett did not finish his study of the history of philosophy where Wilhelm Windelband left off:

63v: Deutéronome X.16
64r: Opening of Epistola ad Pisones [Horace]
      Dhan Gopal Mukerdji: *Brahmane et Paria.*[58]
64v–65r: 'Philosophy in 20th century [stresses] problem of cognition'
      (**Heimsoeth**) [see Heimsoeth, 574]
65r: cf. **Kant**'s definition of 'transcendental': 'Ich nenne alle
      Erkenntnis transzendental, die ... überhaupt beschäftigt.'
      (Kritik der reinen Vernunft, Einleitung VII; III. 49.)
65r–65v: 'Wissenschaftskritik' (**Heimsoeth**) [see Heimsoeth, 576].

The list of 'Books sent home' mentions the German version of Windelband's history, 'G[eschichte]. d[er]. Philosophie' (WN 18v), to which an extra chapter had been added in the 1935 edition: 'Die Philosophie im 20. Jahrhundert' by Heinz Heimsoeth. Beckett took notes from this chapter on pages 64v–65v (see Heimsoeth 1935, 574–6), noting an emphasis on the problem of cognition in the philosophy of the twentieth century.[59] The copy is still part of Beckett's library and contains only one annotation – on page 261 – in a small-print survey of medieval Arab and Jewish philosophy ('Übersicht über die arabische und jüdische Philosophie im Mittelalter'). The marginalia in the right margin enumerates the names of thinkers discussed in the text: 'Alkendi (†870) / Alfarabi (†950) / Avicenna (†1037) / Algazel (†1111) / Avempace (†1138) / Abubacer (†1185) / (Philosophus / autodidactus) / Averroës (†1198) / Ibn Chaldun (†1406) / Saadja Fajjumi (†942) / Avicebron (11th cent) / Maimonides (†1204) / Gersonides (†1344)' (Windelband 1935, 261).

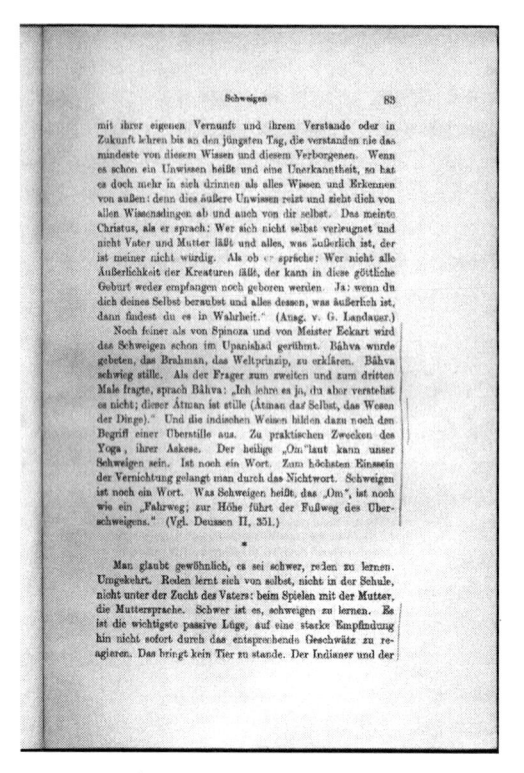

Figure 8 Fritz Mauthner, *Beiträge zu einer Kritik der Sprache* (1923), volume 1, page 83.

MAUTHNER

The beginning of this new century in the history of philosophy was marked by the publication of the first two volumes of Fritz Mauthner's *Beiträge zu einer Kritik der Sprache* (1901; the third volume appeared shortly afterward). After numerous attempts to assess Beckett's relation to Mauthner's work (see Chapter 1), Beckett's extensive excerpts from the *Beiträge* continue to raise questions, whose number only increases when the excerpts are compared with the more than seven hundred marked passages[60] in the copy of the *Beiträge* in Beckett's library. The marks are almost uniformly vertical, straight, single pencil lines, although there is a remarkable exception on page 83 (in volume 1), where the sentence regarding 'silence' and the Indian concept of an even more silent silence is marked with a double pencil line (see *Figure 8*).[61]

Philosophy

The sentence is part of a longer passage that is also marked (single pencil line) and contains the notion of the 'Nichtwort', reminiscent of Beckett's 'Literatur des Unworts' (*Dis* 54; see Van Hulle 1999, 159). The passage does not correspond with Beckett's notes, but it does correspond with one of the entries in Joyce's *Finnegans Wake* notebook VI.B.46, page 236.

The following table, juxtaposing the number of pages with the number of marked pages per chapter, visualizes the intensity with which the three volumes have been marked:

Fritz Mauthner, *Beiträge zu einer Kritik der Sprache*. 3 vols. Leipzig: Felix Meiner, 1923.
Volume 1

Chapter	Number of pages	Nr. of marked pages
Vorwort	16	4
Wesen der Sprache: Einleitung	7	1
Wesen der Sprache: I. Wesen der Sprache	16	2
Wesen der Sprache: II. Sprache und Sozialismus	18	4
Wesen der Sprache: III. Realität der Sprache	7	3
Wesen der Sprache: IV. Mißverstehen durch Sprache	19	14
Wesen der Sprache: V. Wert der Sprache	23	11
Wesen der Sprache: VI. Wortkunst	60	22
Wesen der Sprache: VII. Macht der Sprache	4	3
Wesen der Sprache: VIII. Wortaberglaube	21	13
Wesen der Sprache: IX. Denken und Sprechen	59	20
Zur Psychologie: Einleitung	13	4
Zur Psychologie: I. Seele und Leib	30	18
Zur Psychologie: II. Parallelismus	30	11
Zur Psychologie: III. Psychologische Terminologie	13	3
Zur Psychologie: IV. Seele und Sinne	32	26
Zur Psychologie: V. Zufallssinne	62	34
Zur Psychologie: VI. Subjektivität	33	13
Zur Psychologie: VII. Gedächtnis	93	38
Zur Psychologie: VIII. Aufmerksamkeit und Gedächtnis	67	38
Zur Psychologie: IX. Bewußtsein	29	10
Zur Psychologie: X. Verstand, Sprache, Vernunft	13	9
Zur Psychologie: XI. Ichgefühl	23	10
Zur Psychologie: XII. Erkenntnis und Wirklichkeit	26	15
Zur Psychologie: XIII. Möglichkeit der Philosophie	16	11
Zur Psychologie: Nachträge zur dritten Anflage	5	3

Volume 2

Chapter	Number of pages	Nr. of marked pages
I. Was ist Sprachwissenschaft?	30	16
II. Aus der Geschichte der Sprachwissenschaft	84	14
III. Sprachrichtigkeit	55	19
IV. Zufall in der Sprache	16	12
V. Etymologie	36	16
VI. Wurzeln	26	5
VII. Bedeutungswandel	29	8
VIII. Klassifikation der Sprachen	62	17
IX. Tier- und Menschensprache	36	6
X. Entstehung der Sprache	74	15
XI. Die Metapher	85	23
XII. Schrift und Schriftsprache	54	21
XIII. Sprachwissenschaft und Ethnologie	69	14
XIV. Ursprung und Geschichte von Vernunft	61	30

Volume 3

Chapter	Number of pages	Nr. of marked pages
Vorwort	7	4
Sprache und Grammatik: I. Unbestimmtheit des grammatischen Sinnes	54	6
Sprache und Grammatik: II. Das Verbum	28	3
Sprache und Grammatik: III. Das Substantivum	11	1
Sprache und Grammatik: IV. Das Adjektivum	8	1
Sprache und Grammatik: V. Adverbien – Raum und Zeit	30	0
Sprache und Grammatik: VI. Das Zahlwort	53	4
Sprache und Grammatik: VII. Syntax	38	8
Sprache und Grammatik: VIII. Situation und Sprache	38	16
Sprache und Logik: I. Begriff und Wort	33	8
Sprache und Logik: II. Die Definition	15	1
Sprache und Logik: III. Das Urteil	34	4
Sprache und Logik: IV. Die Denkgesetze	28	13
Sprache und Logik: V. Die Schlußfolgerung	77	14
Sprache und Logik: VI. Die Induktion	42	17
Sprache und Logik: VII. Termini technici der induktiven Wissenschaften	57	20
Sprache und Logik: VIII. Wissen und Worte	95	44
Sprache und Logik: Nachträge zur dritten Auflage	1	0

One of the first notions mentioned in Beckett's typed notes (TCD MS10971/5, corresponding to volume II, pages 473–9) is the veil of Maya, which he had already encountered in Schopenhauer and Plümacher. The notion occurs in the very first excerpted paragraph: before Mauthner starts his historical survey of philosophy, viewed as a slow self-undermining of the metaphorical, he regrets that he has to skip Indian philosophy, with its long tradition of viewing the phenomenal world ('das Wirklichkeitsbild') as the deception of Maya ('Blendwerk der Maya'), resulting from false analogies or metaphors (II.473). Several of Beckett's notes do not correspond with the marked passages in the book, but some of them do (especially toward the end of volumes II and III), as the following survey shows:

Beckett's Mauthner notes	corresponding page in Mauthner's *Beiträge*	pencil marks in the copy in Beckett's library
	Chapter VIII. Klassifikation der Sprachen	
WN 49v–51v	II.309	none
	Chapter XI. Die Metapher	
TCD MS10971/5	II.473–8	II. 474, 476, 477, 478
WN 52r	II.506	none
WN 52r–52v	II.532	none
WN 52v–53r	II.533–4	none
	Chapter XIII. Sprachwissenschaft und Ethnologie	
WN 53v–55r	II.644–5	none
	Chapter XIV. Ursprung und Geschichte von Vernunft	
WN 55r	II.675	none
WN 55r–55v	II.689–90	II.689
WN 55v–57v	II.699–701	II.699–701
WN 58r–58v	II.714–15	II.714–15
	Sprache und Logik: Chapter VIII. Wissen und Worte	
WN 46r–48r	III.615–16	III.615–16

The typewritten notes correspond with several pages in volume II, such as page 474, which is marked in the margin with one long, vertical pencil line covering the whole page. This page is part of the chapter on metaphors, which apparently interested James Joyce as well.[62]

Beckett's notes are verbatim excerpts. Their length seems to indicate that Beckett did not own a copy of the *Beiträge* himself when he made them. The Mauthner notes in the 'Whoroscope' Notebook were probably taken for his own literary project, however vague its contours still were at that point. The excerpts clearly differ from the ones he made for Joyce on another book, Heinrich Zimmer's *Maya, der indische Mythos*. Still, Beckett confirmed that he also skimmed through Mauthner *for Joyce*, the way he did with Zimmer. The difference, however, is that the copy of Zimmer's *Maya* is still preserved in Joyce's personal library in Buffalo, whereas the three-volume Mauthner is not.

In 1978, Linda Ben-Zvi wrote a letter to Beckett regarding Mauthner. Beckett replied (on 28 July) that he had not read Mauthner out loud to Joyce, but that – on Joyce's request – he had taken the volumes and read them himself, emphasizing however that the copies of Mauthner's *Beiträge* in his personal library were not the missing Joyce copies (Ben-Zvi 1984, 65).[63] A week later, Beckett wrote a letter to Ruby Cohn in which he repeated: 'My contact with his [Mauthner's] work was of the slightest [&] I have nothing to offer on the subject. My copy of the Beiträge is not the one I returned skimmed through to Joyce. I am sorry to disappoint her'. In the same letter, he dismissed the issue as 'a wild goose & a red herring' (qtd. in Pilling 2006b, 158). Beckett refrained from mentioning where his copy did come from and he insisted that the copy in his library was not Joyce's, so the insistence became a bit suspicious in itself, a Beckettian variation on Shakespeare's 'the Lady doth protest too much, methinks'.

So, to paraphrase *Watt* (*W* 74–5), six possibilities occurred in this connection:

1. Mr Beckett was responsible for the pencil marks in the three-volume Mauthner, and made these marks for Joyce, and knew that the book was Joyce's, but insisted that the book was not Joyce's, and was content.
2. Mr Beckett was not responsible for the pencil marks in the three-volume Mauthner, although he did read Mauthner for Joyce, in Joyce's copy, and knew that the book in his library was not Joyce's, and said so, and was content.
3. Mr Beckett was responsible for the pencil marks in the three-volume Mauthner, but did not make these marks for Joyce, and knew that the book was not Joyce's, and said so, and was content.
4. Mr Beckett was responsible for the pencil marks in the three-volume Mauthner, and did not make these marks for Joyce, and knew that the book was Joyce's, and insisted that it wasn't, and was content.
5. Mr Beckett was not responsible for the pencil marks in the three-volume Mauthner, although they were made for Joyce by another helper, and he knew that the book was Joyce's, but insisted that it wasn't, and was content.

6. Mr Beckett was not responsible for the pencil marks in the three-volume Mauthner, he did not make them for Joyce, he knew that the book was not Joyce's, and he said so, and was content.

Other possibilities occurred, in this connection, but they were put aside, for the time being. For as Beckett suggested, all these hypotheses may be just 'a wild goose & a red herring'. A letter to the German translator Hans Naumann of 17 February 1954 suggests that, at least in 1954, Beckett did not yet possess a copy of Mauthner's *Beiträge*: 'Parmi les livres que j'ai explorés pour Joyce il y avait Beiträge zu einer Kritik der Sprache de Fritz Mauthner qui m'a très fortement impressionné. J'ai souvent eu envie de le relire. Mais il semble introuvable' [Among the books that I explored for Joyce there was Beiträge zu einer Kritik der Sprache by Fritz Mauthner which greatly impressed me. I have often wanted to re-read it. But it seems impossible to find] (*LSB II* 462, 465). Whether Naumann subsequently provided Beckett with a copy of the *Beiträge* or whether Beckett later purchased or received a copy, for instance during one of his many visits to Germany to direct his plays (as with the copies of Wittgenstein's *Schriften*), are questions that still remain unanswered. According to Anne Atik, who was close friends with Mauthner expert Gershon Weiler, Beckett talked about Mauthner in 1961, shortly after he and Suzanne had moved into the apartment in Boulevard Saint-Jacques (Atik 2001, 19). In order to insert the explicit yet enigmatic reference to Mauthner in the manuscripts of *Pochade radiophonique* (1975),[64] Beckett certainly would not have needed to reread the *Beiträge*.

By the time he probably did have a copy to reread the *Beiträge*, the details of his original reading could understandably no longer be reconstructed with accuracy: 'I do not remember what passages I imagined as likely fodder for *FW*' (Ben-Zvi 1984, 66). The 'fodder' is not just an interesting expression to describe the reading notes for *Finnegans Wake*; as a metaphor it also suggests a link with his own novel *Watt*, which clearly shows signs of linguistic scepticism reminiscent of Mauthner's *Critique of Language*, as Jennie Skerl has demonstrated (Skerl 1974).

WITTGENSTEIN

This focus on language quickly raised the question among critics whether Beckett knew the writings of Ludwig Wittgenstein. Beckett told John Fletcher in 1961 that he had only read Wittgenstein's works 'within the last two years' (Fletcher 1964, 87–8). As John Pilling notes, Beckett told André Bernold on 20 May 1984 that he had read Wittgenstein (and about him) in recent years, unaided, because he had not been told about the Viennese philosopher during his university years in Dublin (Pilling 2006a, 223). The number of books by and on Wittgenstein in the library is considerable.

One of the first books on Wittgenstein that Beckett read was David Pole's *The Later Philosophy of Wittgenstein* (1958). On 21 December 1962, he mentioned in a letter to Barbara Bray that he was 'reading Pole on Wittgenstein again' (TCD MS10948/1/214). Most of the books by Wittgenstein in Beckett's possession were published in the 1960s:

- Wittgenstein, Ludwig, *Schriften*, 2 vols, Frankfurt a.M.: Suhrkamp, 1960.
- *Schriften; Beiheft* [mit Beiträgen von Ingeborg Bachmann, Maurice Cranston, Jose Ferrater Mora, Paul Feyerabend, Erich Heller, Bertrand Russell, George H. von Wright], Frankfurt a.M.: Suhrkamp, 1960.
- *The Tractatus Logico-Philosophicus*, transl. D. F. Pars and B. F. McGuinness, introd. Bertrand Russell, London: Routledge and Kegan Paul, 1961.
- *Tractatus Logico-Philosophicus; Logisch-philosophische Abhandlung*, Frankfurt a.M.: Suhrkamp, 1963.
- *Lectures and Conversations on Aesthetics, Psychology and Religious Beliefs*, ed. Cyril Barrett, Oxford: Basil Blackwell, 1966.
- *Letters from Ludwig Wittgenstein with a Memoir*, ed. Paul Engelmann, Oxford: Basil Blackwell, 1967.
- *Über Ludwig Wittgenstein*, Frankfurt a.M.: Suhrkamp, 1968.

The first two items in the list were given to Beckett by Renate Handke. The inscription in the two-volume *Schriften* reads 'Renate HANDKE, / to Samuel Beckett / Germany, 9–25–67'. The date suggests that Renate Handke gave the book(s) to Beckett the day before the premiere of *Endspiel* in Berlin. Beckett returned to Paris on 27 September 1967 'after 6 weeks [of rehearsals] in Berlin, *Endspiel* having opened the previous evening' (Pilling 2006a, 176). Probably the *Beiheft* with contributions by Ingeborg Bachmann, Bertrand Russell and others (inscribed: 'Renate Handke – 1961') was given to him during the same period of rehearsals. The marked passages in the *Schriften* and the *Beiheft* are underlined with a ruler, which would be a highly unusual practice for Beckett, judging from his other marginalia. It probably indicates that these are Renate Handke's reading traces. In the *Beiheft*, only the essays by Bachmann ('Zu einem Kapitel der jüngsten Philosophiegeschichte') and Russell ('Vorwort zum Tractatus logico-philosophicus') are marked – with underlinings in red and blue-black ballpoint, respectively on pages 8, 9, 10, 11, 12; and 68, 69, 70, 71, 72, 73, 74.

This pattern of traces is interrupted on two occasions by means of a marginal St Andrew's cross in red pencil, possibly added by Beckett. The first cross marks Bachmann's reference to the famous entry 6.44 in the

Tractatus, touching upon the mystical.[65] The second cross marks the title of Norman Malcolm's *Ludwig Wittgenstein: Ein Erinnerungsbuch* in the publisher's announcement at the back of the book. On 17 September 1967, shortly before the première of *Endspiel*, Beckett wrote to Barbara Bray that he had been given '(in German) Norman Malcolm's Wittgenstein' (TCD MS10948/1/402). The extant library does not contain this German edition, but it does feature the English version (*Wittgenstein: A Memoir*, 1967 [1962]), with the inscription 'For Sam / with love / from Mary / 1-1-71 / W's favourite / musical composer also / was Schubert...'. Beckett received it from Mary Hutchinson, whom he thanked on 20 January 1971: 'Wittgenstein book safely arrived. Very glad to have it'. Because there are no reading traces, it is hard to tell whether he read the German or the English version, but in the case of Bertrand Russell's introduction to the *Tractatus*, Beckett seems to have preferred the English version. Whereas the only traces in the German version of Russell's text in the *Beiheft* are the underlinings by Renate Handke, the English introduction in D. F. Pars and B. F. McGuinness's translation (*The Tractatus Logico-Philosophicus*, 1961) shows Beckett's characteristic pencil lines in the margins alongside more than a dozen passages.[66]

Russell's introduction was famously rejected by Wittgenstein as misleading. The interest in the early Wittgenstein's view on language ('Wittgenstein I') in these marked passages does not indicate to what extent Beckett was aware of the changed opinions of 'Wittgenstein II'. But the presence of David Pole's *The Later Philosophy of Wittgenstein* in the library suggests that he was familiar with the development of Wittgenstein's philosophy, even though the copy of Pole's book does not contain any marginalia. The irony of Wittgentstein's development is that it started off as an attempt to construct a critique of language '(though not in Mauthner's sense)', as his parenthesis in the *Tractatus Logico-Philosophicus* stressed (4.0031), whereas his later position as formulated in the *Philosophical Investigations* came 'much closer to Mauthner's than before' (Janik and Toulmin 1996, 232):

> Wittgenstein's later writing revived many positions and arguments already put forward by Mauthner in 1901 – for example, the view that the rules of language are like the rules of a game, and that the very word 'language' is itself a general abstract term, which we need to unpack by looking to see how, in actual practice, men put the expressions of their languages to use, within the context of all their varied cultures. (232)

Mauthner had indeed presented language as a mere convention, 'like a rule of a game: the more participants, the more compelling it will be. However, it is neither going to alter nor grasp the real world'.[67] This passage is not marked in the three-volume *Beiträge* in Beckett's library, but a pencil line on one of the subsequent pages does highlight what the idea of the language game comes down to: language is 'something between people' ('etwas zwischen den Menschen', Mauthner 1923, I.33).

'Wittgenstein II' realized that in the *Tractatus* he had paid insufficient attention to the ways in which language is put to *use*. Distancing himself from Augustine's theory of language, Wittgenstein opens his *Philosophical Investigations* by means of a language game to acknowledge the importance of the instrumental function of language, or what Richard Begam calls its performative effect: Wittgenstein II proposed that 'we think of language not as a blueprint for discovering the deep structure of reality but as a set of tools, games, or procedures for negotiating the day-to-day problems of life' (Begam 2007, 149). Without recourse to Wittgenstein, but with the help of Mauthner, Beckett had arrived at a similar critique of a constative or descriptive approach to language. Augustine's idea of language as a form of nomenclature, quoted at the beginning of Wittgenstein's *Philosophical Investigations*, is memorably questioned in Watt's 'pot' scene (*W* 67).

Given these affinities between Beckett and Wittgenstein II, it is remarkable that the single marginal red cross in Bachmann's essay marks a reference to Wittgenstein I (entry 6.44 of the *Tractatus*): 'Not *how* the world is, is the mystical, but *that* it is', usually related to the famous last entry: '7. Whereof one cannot speak, thereof one must be silent'. A possible answer to this enigma is Paul Engelmann's suggestion (in his edition of *Letters from Ludwig Wittgenstein with a Memoir*, 1967) to explain why Wittgenstein was mistaken for a positivist by his contemporaries: what he had in common with the positivists was that he drew a line between what we can and cannot speak about: 'The difference is only that they have nothing to be silent about. Positivism holds ... that what we can speak about is all that matters in life. *Whereas Wittgenstein passionately believes that all that really matters in human life is precisely what, in his view, we must be silent about*' (97). The page with this sentence in italics is the only one that is marked with a typically large dog-ear in Beckett's copy of Engelmann's book.

As early as 1950 Jacqueline Hoefer discussed the affinities between Beckett and Wittgenstein in an analysis of *Watt*. Marjorie Perloff recognized a reference to the last sentence of the *Tractatus* in the opening lines of 'Closed place': 'Closed place. All needed to be known for say is known. There is nothing but what is said. Beyond what is said there is nothing' (*TFN* 147). Perloff concludes: 'It is the lesson of Wittgenstein: "Wovon man nicht sprechen kann, darüber muss man schweigen"' (Perloff 1981, 207). It is certainly not impossible that Beckett's reading of Wittgenstein in the 1960s reverberates in some of the *Fizzles* ('Se voir' ['Closed place'] was written in 1968), but by that time Beckett did not need to take any lessons from Wittgenstein. He seems to have read him as a like-minded writer. As late as 1979, Beckett was still 'Reading the Wittgenstein with interest', as he told Barbara Bray (15 January 1979). No matter how late Beckett discovered Wittgenstein's writings, they did encourage him to continue looking for 'the nature of what has so happily been called the unutterable or ineffable' (*W* 52).

BACHELARD

Another non-positivist stance Beckett familiarized himself with was Henri Bachelard's. Critical of Auguste Comte's positivist perspective on science as a continuous progress, Bachelard suggested a discontinuous process, marked by 'epistemological breaks'. His non-Cartesian epistemology transpires in *L'Intuition de l'instant* (1932), a paperback version of which (1966) is still present in Beckett's library. Bachelard criticized Bergson's notion of the 'intuition of duration' against which he posited an intuition of the present instant. His main objection was that the intuition of duration affirms a form of continuity within oneself, while the human being is constantly faced with the discontinuity of his experience (42). In other words, what Bachelard criticizes is Bergson's immobile image of mobile time.

The notion of the 'image' became more important in Bachelard's later works. Notably the poetic or literary image was 'not merely a subjective phantasm, but a dynamic activity'; through its embodiment in language, the image has the ability to open up a vision of the world (Grimsley 1971, 56). An image only has aesthetic value when it attains a certain intensity, which happens only when the imagination establishes a relationship with an aspect of the material world – hence the notion of 'material imagination'. Literary imagination can 'form images that go beyond reality and change it' (57) and thus functions as a dynamic creative activity. In this respect, Bachelard's concept of imagination resembles that of Jean-Paul Sartre.

SARTRE

Although Sartre criticized Bachelard in *L'Être et le néant* for not having clarified the ontological implications of his principle of the material imagination, he did praise him for having introduced the principle in the first place. Sartre had already been writing about the imagination since the mid-1930s. Beckett possessed a copy of *L'Imagination* (1936), which is still part of the library.[68] In this small book, Sartre gives a survey of the ways in which imagination has been treated in philosophy and psychology since the seventeenth century. In rationalist philosophy, the imagination had a merely subordinate place. In Descartes's distinction between mind and matter, the imagination occupied an ambiguous position between the mind and the senses. As a consequence, Descartes and Pascal considered its products inferior to mental ideas. After an appraisal of the treatment of imagination throughout the following centuries, Sartre concludes that the subject was only approached properly by Husserl and phenomenology.

Beckett took a few notes on *L'Imagination* in the 'Whoroscope' Notebook, starting with 'Leibniz to Locke / "Nihil est in intellectu quod non prius fuerit in sensu, nisi ipse intellectus"' (WN 62r; Pilling 2005, 46). Beckett had already used the first part of this phrase in his 1929 essay on Joyce (*Dis* 24) and in his Mauthner notes it occurs as well (TCD MS10971/5; cf. Mauthner 1923, II.477). This guiding principle of empiricism was Mauthner's methodological starting point. It recurs frequently in the *Beiträge*, especially in the first volume (I.273; 324–5, 332–3) and again toward the end of the last one (III.639). In *L'Imagination*, Sartre introduced it in chapter 1 ('Les grands systèmes métaphysiques'), notably in the discussion of Hume's empiricism (Sartre 1936, 16), which partly overcame the rationalists' prejudice against the imagination by regarding the 'image' as a type of object that was explained as a weaker form of perception (Grimsley 1971, 46). But the famous empiricists' dictum did not account for the perception of the intellect itself. The mind does not 'appear' to itself, it is inferred from reflective analysis, according to Sartre. For that reason, Leibniz replied to Locke, completing the empiricists' dictum with: '*nisi ipse intellectus*', as Sartre notes on page 18. Six pages further on, Sartre comes back to the same reply: 'Ainsi Leibniz répondait jadis à Locke: *Nihil est in intellectu quod non prius fuerit in sensu nisi ipse intellectus*' (34).[69]

Ronald Grimsley points out that the importance of *L'Imagination* (1936) and *L'Imaginaire: Psychologie phénoménologique de l'imagination* (1940) was somewhat overshadowed by Sartre's later, existentialist publications. Beckett has often been associated with Sartrean existentialism. Yet, his works cannot be labeled 'existentialist'. One of the most important voices among Beckett readers who drew attention to the difference between Beckett and the existentialists was Theodor W. Adorno.

ADORNO

In his 'Versuch, das Endspiel zu verstehen', Adorno criticized the existentialist jargon that asserted the universally valid in a process of abstraction, blotting out particularity: 'To such unacknowledged abstraction, Beckett affixes the caustic antithesis by means of acknowledged subtraction' (Adorno 1982, 123–4). That was Beckett's 'answer to existential philosophy, which under the name of "thrownness" and later of "absurdity" transforms senselessness itself into sense' (128). Adorno dedicated the essay 'to S.B. in memory of Paris, Fall 1958'. Their first meeting had taken place in Paris on 28 November 1958. In memory of that long meeting 'until very late' (Tiedemann 1994, 23), Adorno gave Beckett a signed copy of his first volume of the 'Noten zur Literatur' (published in the same year): 'Für Samuel Beckett / zur Erinnerung an den / 28. November 1958 / herzlichst / T. W. Adorno / Paris – Frankfurt'.

Nine years later Beckett met Adorno in Berlin on a Saturday afternoon (23 September 1967), three days before the première of the *Endspiel* production by the Schiller Theater Berlin under Beckett's direction.[70] According to Adorno, they talked about Beckett's works, notably *Endgame*. As in a chess game, Beckett told Adorno, the play is 'already lost when it starts. After that one simply plays on' (Tiedemann 1994, 24). Beckett remembered that they talked mainly about music, notably Schönberg and Stravinsky. 'Afternoon saw Adorno', he wrote to Barbara Bray: 'Don't know why he likes me or why I like him' (TCD MS10948/1/403).

CIORAN

Another philosopher-essayist who frequently expressed his fondness for Beckett was E. M. Cioran. He showed his admiration on several occasions in his *Cahiers 1957–1972*, selected and translated by Thomas Cousineau (*The Beckett Circle*, 28.1, Spring 2005). Beckett told Barbara Bray on 5 October 1966 that he kept 'running into Cioran' (TCD MS10948/1/371) and his personal library contains a dozen books by the author. More than half of them are dedicated to Samuel and Suzanne Beckett. In December 1973 Cioran had spent an evening with Beckett, discussing the title *Sans*, its English version, *Lessness*, and the (im)possibility of translating the latter back into French. One of the dedications (in *De l'Inconvénient d'être né*, 1973) bears some traces of this evening: 'Paris le 9 Déc. 1973 . . . Merci pour la soirée de samedi. / J'ai cherché toute la nuit, bien entendu sans succès, un équivalent français de lessness'. Cioran notes that he returned home, without having found a solution. Both of them, independently, considered the option 'sinéité', but they eventually agreed that they would have to abandon their quest and accept that there was no French noun, capable of expressing absence as such (Cioran 1995, 1576). Cioran published his account of the quest in his *Exercices d'admiration* (1986) and sent a dedication copy in the year of its publication. The anecdote suitably illustrates Beckett's quest, which ended (and at the same time remained crucially incomplete) with 'what is the word'.

CHAPTER 8

Religion

Beckett's library contains some remarkable books on religious and theological matters, such as Pierre Lasserre's *Un conflit religieux au XIème siècle: Abélard contre Saint Bernard*[1] or J. B. Bouvier's *Dissertatio in Sextum Decalogi Praeceptum et Supplementum ad Tractatum de Matrimonio* (1852). The latter is mentioned in *Murphy*. Although Murphy is presented as 'a strict non-reader' (*Mu* 103), there was

> a relic of those sanguine days when as a theological student he had used to lie awake night after night with Bishop Bouvier's *Supplementum ad Tractatum de Matrimonio* under his pillow. What a work that was to be sure! A Ciné Bleu scenario in goatish Latin. Or pondering Christ's Parthian shaft: *It is finished.* (*Mu* 47)

The pages in the *Dissertatio* by Jean-Baptiste Bouvier (1783–1854) are not marked, but it is the source of several notes in the 'Dream' Notebook. In this notebook Beckett famously took notes on Pierre Garnier's *Onanisme seul et à deux sous toutes ses forms et leurs conséquences* (*DN* 422 and following notes). The verso pages of this cluster of notes are notes on a similar topic, but in the Bishop of Le Mans' 'goatish' Franco-Latin. Monseigneur Bouvier was also the author of such works as a treatise on indulgences (*Traité dogmatique et pratique des indulgences, des confréries, et du jubilé*) and on chastity (*Les mystères du confessionnal – Manuel secret des confesseurs suivi de la clé d'or et du Traité de chasteté*). Chastity is also the starting point on the opening pages of his *Dissertatio in Sextum Decalogi Praeceptum et Supplementum ad Tractatum de Matrimonio*: taking his cue from Aquinas, Bouvier distinguishes three categories, which Beckett translated as 'conjugal, vidual, virginal chastity' (*DN* 430).[2] On the next page, the bishop discusses the different threats to this chastity, starting with 'luxuria' (lust), which he defines as the inordinate appetite of venereal pleasure.[3] After having translated the first note, Beckett excerpted this definition in Latin. The first chapter, about 'luxuria' in general, is followed by a chapter on 'naturally consummated' lust,[4] including different forms of assault, rape or the 'unlawful deflowering of a virgin', according to Bouvier's definition ('stuprum', 'raptus violentiae' or 'raptus seductionis').[5] Beckett's translation 'hymen' for 'signaculum virginis' – which recurs notably in 'What a Misfortune' as 'th'imperforate hymen' and 'hymeneal insignia' (*DN* 434) – is based on another reference in Bouvier to Saint Thomas.[6] Beckett did not take any notes on the sections 'De adulterio', 'De incestu', 'De sacrilegio', nor on the first sections ('De bestialitate' and 'De sodomiâ') of chapter III, 'De speciebus luxuriae consummatae contra naturam'. But one of these unnaturally consummated kinds of 'luxuria' did catch his attention: section 3, 'De pollutione' (masturbation) – which explains the location of these notes (the verso pages of the excerpts from Garnier's *Onanisme seul et à deux*) in the 'Dream' Notebook. Martial's epigram 'Istud quod digitis, Pontice, perdis homo est' [what you lose with your fingers, Ponticus, is a human being] (*DN* 436) is quoted by Bouvier to prove that even pagans acknowledged that masturbation was evidently 'against nature'.[7] On the next verso page of the 'Dream' Notebook, Beckett translated one of Bouvier's pieces of advice, formulated in Q&A format:

Quaeritur I°   What shall he do who is aware that he is about to experience pollution?
R.   He shall elevate his mind to God, invoke him, signo crucis se munire [arm himself with the sign of the cross], abstain from all voluntary exoneration, renounce the delectation of voluptuousness. (*DN* 447)[8]

Beckett used the expression 'elevated his mind to God' in the story 'Echo's Bones'. His translation of 'nihil ad expellendum semen positive facere' [abstain from all voluntary exoneration] was probably inspired by the expression 'involuntary seminal exoneration', derived from Garnier, which Beckett used in a letter to MacGreevy (12 September 1931) to refer to two of the poems he had sent him, referred to as 'the Albas': 'Nothing is so attractive anyhow as abstention. A nice quiet life punctuated with involuntary exonerations (Albas). And isn't my navel worth 10 of anyone else's, even though I can't get a very good view of it' (*LSB* 88). As the letter indicates, Beckett's preoccupation with onanism had a complex poetical dimension as a metaphor for creative production, even though he preferred to present his poetry as involuntary, rather than voluntary, exonerations.

A trace of Bouvier's *Dissertatio* is also present in *Watt*. The very last part of Bouvier's work is an '*Abrégé d'embryologie sacrée*' (194), offering theological solutions to a few difficulties regarding baptism for premature babies, starting with the question when a foetus acquires a soul:

1.re Q. A quelle âge l'enfant est-il animé?

According to Bouvier, the foetus is 'animated' much earlier than one commonly assumes (195). The authority he refers to is 'L'auteur de l'*Embryologie sacrée*', a canon of Palermo, called '*Cangiamila*', who died in 1763, according to Bouvier (195, note 1). Beckett refers to him in one of the *Watt* Addenda (#17):

the foetal soul is full grown (Cangiamila's *Sacred Embryology* and Pope Benedict XIV's *De Synodo Diocesana*, Bk. 7, ch. 4, sect. 6.) (*W* 217)

Cangiamila claimed to have seen signs of life in a foetus of only 16 days old. His work had been acclaimed and praised in particular by 'Benoît XIV (*De Synodo diocesanâ*, l. XI ch. 7, n.° 13)' (Bouvier 195, note 1). If the delivery is extremely laborious, Pope Benedict XIV's advice was to baptize the baby inside the mother's womb by introducing lukewarm water manually or otherwise.[9] Although the Addenda in *Watt* refer to Cangiamila, the reference is taken from Bouvier's footnote: '*De Synodo Diocesanâ*, l. 7, ch. 4, n.° 6' (Bouvier 200, note 1).

BECKETT'S BIBLES

In order to 'elevate his mind to God', Beckett also had *A Little Manual of Liturgy* by the 'Most Rev.' Patrick Morrisroe (1926). Although he showed an interest in Brahmanism and Buddhism when he read Olga Plümacher's *Der Pessimismus* (see Chapter 7), and although he acquired a French copy of the Koran (*Le Coran*, 1970) toward the end of his life, his main focus of attention in terms of religion was the Bible.

In *How It Was*, Anne Atik writes that 'Beckett had several editions of the Bible – four in different languages (the *Family Bible, la Sainte Bible, L'Antico Testamento*, the Luther Bible) – as well as at least one concordance and the *Book of Common Prayer*' (71). There are even more bibles among the books in Beckett's Paris apartment. Apart from the *New Concordance to the Holy Scriptures* edited by John Eadie (1875), *The Prayer Book as proposed in 1928*, a *Comprehensive Teacher's Bible*, an *Authorized King James Version*, an Italian *Sacra Bibbia, ossia L'Antico e il Nuovo Testamento* (Roma: Societa Biblica Britannica e Forestiera, 1924), a German *Bibel, nach der Übersetzung von Martin Luther* (Stuttgart: Württembergische Bibelanstalt, 1970), there are also two French versions of the *Sainte Bible*.

Extensive studies have been published on religious themes and biblical allusions in Beckett's works (Ackerley 1999; Bailey 2009; 2010; Barry 2000;

Bryden 1998a; Locatelli 2001; Long 2000; Mercier 1978; 1989; Mooney 2000; Morrison 1983; Zeifman 1974). Iain Bailey notes that the passage 'Mene, mene' in *Endgame* is spelled 'Mané, mané' in *Fin de partie*. This spelling is to be found in the Port-Royal Lemaistre de Sacy translation (1696), but not in the two French versions in Beckett's apartment (Bailey 2010, 240). So, no matter how many Bibles Beckett possessed, he seems to have used even more Bibles than the ones that are still in his personal library.

BECKETT'S FIRST BIBLE

Indeed, one of the first Bibles Beckett studied intensively (in the sense of Roger Chartier's notion of 'intensive reading') is no longer in his apartment, but still carefully preserved: in the City of Dublin Public Library at Pearse Street, Dublin.[10] The text on the inside of the flyleaf reads:

> This Premium was adjudged to
> Samuel Beckett
> for Diligence and Attendance
> at
> Tullow Sunday School
> 13 of Dec. 1912
> Revd. G. W. N. Clark

It is a copy of *The Holy Bible, Containing the Old and New Testaments, Translated out of the Original Tongues and with the former Translations diligently compared and revised, by His Majesty's special command, Appointed to be read in Churches* (Oxford; printed at the University Press London: Henry Frowde, and distributed by the Association for Promoting Christian Knowledge, 37 Dawson Street, Dublin). The notion of 'Christian Knowledge' characterizes the way Beckett seems to have treated his Bibles, regarding them as books among other books, some of whose texts would later recur in his works, but usually in shards, like the numerous splinters of Christ's cross preserved as relics, scattered across the world.

The Old Testament is relatively sparsely annotated, with only a few tiny marks, such as a hyphen in pencil in the right margin next to chapter 18 of the Book of Genesis (page 17) or a black dot next to the First Book of Samuel, 30:9 (page 280). Deuteronomy 32:44 ('And Moses came and spake all the words of this song in the ears of the people, he, and Hoshea the son of Nun') is marked and in the margin the words 'Vigny's Moise' are inscribed in pencil, corresponding with Numbers 11:11–15, next to which the line 'LAISSEZ-MOI M'ENDORMIR DU SOMMEIL DE LA TERRE' from the poem 'Moïse' by Alfred de Vigny (1797–1863) is written in the margin.[11] Of all the books in the Old Testament, the Psalms have been read most intensively, judging from the number of stains and small dog ears. Yet, there are no marks next to 'The Lord upholdeth all that fall, and raiseth up all those that be bowed down' (Psalm 145:14), to which the title of Beckett's first radio play refers. Psalm 103 does show small dots next to lines 1, 7, 8, 14 and 15 – the last two referring to the vanity of all human endeavours and the 'dust thou art' theme that recurs so frequently in Beckett's works: 'For he knoweth our frame; / he remembereth that we are dust. / As for man, his days are as grass: / as a flower of the field, so he flourisheth. / For the wind passeth over it, and it is gone; / and the place thereof shall know it no more'.

This copy of the Bible may have gone through many hands, so the place of the book ribbon does not necessarily tell us anything about Beckett's reading. However, it is worth mentioning that it marks the opening of Ecclesiastes, chapter 12 of which is marked with a double-forward slash in blue-black ink before the first and after the fourth verse:

// Remember now thy Creator in the days of thy youth, while the evil days come not, nor the years draw nigh, when thou shalt say, I have no pleasure in them; while the sun, or the light, or the moon, or the stars, be not darkened, nor the clouds return after the rain: In the day when the keepers of the house shall tremble, and the strong men shall bow themselves, and the grinders cease because they are few, and those that look out of the windows be darkened. And the doors shall be shut in the streets, when the sound of the grinding is low, and he shall rise up at the voice of the bird, and all the daughters of music shall be brought low //

As the 'Dream' Notebook indicates, Beckett read Ecclesiastes together with the preceding book of Proverbs while preparing *Dream of Fair to Middling Women* (*DN* 549–72). He also made scattered notes on Genesis (*DN* 421, 750, 753), St. Paul's epistle to the Romans (*DN* 749), Leviticus (*DN* 751), Judges (*DN* 240), Zachariah (*DN* 243). John Pilling also refers to the passage 'marking the place where Lamentations ended and Ezekiel began' in 'What a Misfortune' (*DN* 571).

Regarding the New Testament, Anne Atik notes that Beckett's favourite Gospel was Luke (73), which is corroborated by the marks in his first Bible: apart from two short hyphens in black ink next to John 11:15 and 11:19, the only gospel that shows reading traces is Luke's, starting with Mary's visit to Elizabeth (Luke 1:39). The relevant passages are marked with different writing tools and different signs (vertical lines, crosses, dots, asterisks, hyphens and ticks):

Luke 1:39	| (pencil)
Luke 4:15	| (pencil)
Luke 4:16	| (pencil)
Luke 5 (title)	| (pencil)
Luke 5:32–3	| (blue crayon)
Luke 6:13–16	| (red crayon)
Luke 6:32	| (red crayon)
Luke 6:36	| (red crayon) + | (blue crayon)
Luke 7:18	| (blue crayon)
Luke 8	x (blue-black ink)
Luke 8:40–1	| (blue-black ink)
Luke 9:18	. (blue-black ink)
Luke 10 (title)	* (blue-black ink)
Luke 11 (title)	* (blue-black ink)
Luke 11:28	| (blue-black ink)
Luke 11:50	v (blue-black ink)
Luke 12:1	| (blue-black ink)
Luke 12:31	– (blue-black ink)
Luke 12:34	| (pencil)
Luke 12:54–7	| (pencil)
Luke 13 (title)	– (pencil)
Luke 14 (title)	– (pencil)
Luke 16 (title)	| (pencil)
Luke 16:31	| (pencil)
Luke 23 (title)	* (pencil)
Luke 23:34	x (blue-black ink)
Luke 24:32	x (blue-black ink)

Among the different signs, the double mark next to Luke 6:36 stands out because of its two different writing tools (red and blue crayon). The line sounds like a motto: 'Be ye therefore merciful, as your Father also is merciful'. Luke 23, and especially the marked verse 34, is not unimportant given the explicit reference to the scene of the two thieves in *Waiting for Godot*.[12] Beckett had already referred to this scene in a letter of 4 September 1936 (written from Cooldrinagh), reminding Arland Ussher that one of the thieves was saved.

Apart from the marginalia in the Acts (3:20; 22; 27; 42–5; 10:7–16), many of the marked passages in the last part of this copy of the Bible read like an ethical manual. The word 'LEARN.' in the margin next to

Corinthians 12:4–11 marks the 'intensity' with which some of these texts in the Bible were studied, in some cases as a sort of guideline for human conduct, for instance James 4:6 (pencil line) and James 3:13–17 (between black dots):

Who is a wise man and endued with knowledge among you? Let him shew out of a good conversation his works with meekness of wisdom. But if ye have bitter envying and strife in your hearts, glory not, and lie not against the truth. This wisdom descendeth not from above, but is earthly, sensual, devilish. For where envying and strife is, there is confusion and every evil work. But the wisdom that is from above is first pure, then peaceable, gentle, and easy to be intreated, full of mercy and good fruits, without partiality, and without hypocrisy.

The square brackets in black ink around James 4:14–16 mark the vanity of human ambitions again ('For what is your life? It is even a vapour, that appeareth for a little time, and then vanisheth away.')

The ticks in black ink next to Peter 2:20–1 urge the reader to follow in Christ's footsteps: 'because Christ also suffered for us, leaving us an example, that ye should follow his steps'. This guideline may have appealed to a young reader who happened to be born on a Good Friday, a coincidence which – as James Knowlson points out – 'was not created by Beckett' but 'assimilated by him into a view of life which sees birth as intimately connected with suffering and death' (Knowlson 1996, 2). The complex ironies of this assimilation reverberate in the ambiguous first line of *A Piece of Monologue*: 'Birth was the death of him'.

TEACHER'S BIBLE

In the Teacher's Bible in Beckett's apartment, the marked passages indicate an interest in more specialized 'Christian knowledge'. One of the first pencil marks in the Book of Genesis concerns the word 'imagination'. Chapter 6 deals with the way it 'came to pass, when men began to multiply on the face of the earth' and 'God saw that the wickedness of man was great in the earth, and that every imagination of the thoughts of his heart was only evil continually' (Gen. 6:5). The marked annotation explains that 'the Hebrew word signifies not only *the imagination*, but also *the purposes & desires*'.

Some of the highlighted verses in the Teacher's Bible seem to be marked because of their stylistic or formal quality, not only because of their content. For instance, toward the end of Genesis, chapter 10, three structurally similar verses are marked with a pencil line in the right margin:

Gen. 10:20: 'These are the sons of Ham, after their families, after their tongues, in their countries, and in their nations.'
Gen. 10:31: 'These are the sons of Shem, after their families, after their tongues, in their lands, after their nations.'
Gen. 10:32: 'These are the families of the sons of Noah, after their generations, in their nations: and by these were the nations divided in the earth after the flood.'

These marked passages partially account for Beckett's unusually fierce reaction when he 'became a little angry' (Siegfried Unseld, qtd. in Knowlson 1996, 479) after Theodor Adorno's suggestion that the name of *Endgame*'s 'central' character could be related to Shakespeare's Hamlet. Against the background of the way things were divided on the earth after the flood, according to the Book of Genesis, Hamm does indeed appear as a Ham (Genesis 10:20), not so much as a derivative Hamlet, but as a counterpart to Shem (Genesis 10:31), reminiscent of, and on a par with, Joyce's 'Shem the penman'. In a letter to Pamela Mitchell, Beckett wrote on 7 February 1955 that he had 'been reading in your grand Baudelaire and in the Holy Bible the story of the Flood and wishing the Almighty had never had a soft spot for Noah' (*LSB II* 522; see also Chapter 3) – which may be an indication as to the dating of the marginalia in Genesis 10.

A trace of the intensity in the sense of Chartier's 'intensive reading' is the underlining of the word 'spokesman' in Exodus 4:16: 'And he [Aaron] shall be thy spokesman unto the people'. A pencil note ('vi:1') in the left margin refers to Exodus 6:1, where the word prophet is underlined as a synonym for spokesman: 'Aaron shall be thy prophet' (41). A similar system as the intratextual references in Beckett's works is made explicit in the margins of this copy of the Teacher's Bible. For instance, alongside Judges 7:25 ('And they took two princes of the Midianites, Oreb and Zeeb; and they slew Oreb upon the rock Oreb, and Zeeb they slew at the winepress of Zeeb, and pursued Midian, and brought the heads of Oreb and Zeeb to Gideon on the other side Jordan.') the pencilled marginalia refer to 'Isaiah iv:4',[13] where the words 'in the day of Midian' are underlined, and the marginalia refer back to 'Judges vii.25'. Apart from marks, the Teacher's Bible also contains a small black-and-white photograph postcard of Rafaello's 'Saint John preaching in the desert' (Galleria degli Uffizi, Firenze) inserted at Ecclesiastes 7 (page 426).

The marked passages in the *Teacher's Bible* do not correspond to the notes in the 'Dream' Notebook. For instance, the marked passages in chapter 9 of Leviticus (4; 6; 22–4) differ from note 751 in the 'Dream'

Notebook, derived from Leviticus 20:18: 'A woman having her sickness – he hath discovered her fountain & she hath uncovered the fountain of her blood'. The line 'They shall be one flesh' (Genesis 2:24; *DN* 753) is not marked in the Teacher's Bible, which shows no traces of any special interest in the Proverbs corresponding to the extracted proverbs in the 'Dream' Noteboook (*DN* 549–57; 566–70).

Above the title of each of the gospels, the number of quotations from the Old Testament is noted in pencil: 'Over 100 quotations from 20 of the books of O.T.' in Matthew; '15 quotations from 13 books of O.T.' in Mark; '34 from 13 books of O.T.' in Luke; and finally, above the title 'The GOSPEL according to St. JOHN': '11 quotations from 6 books of O.T.', followed immediately by the sum total: 'in the 4 gospels 160 quotations' (page 64).

Several verses contain underscored words,[14] but these underlinings are not necessarily Beckett's. On page 165, for instance, next to Joshua 21:43–5,[15] the marginalia read: 'May 24th 189[2] Bath'. Whether the inscription simply marks a date of reading or perhaps a moment of identification (not unlike the 'Mail boat' identification in Beckett's marginalia in Proust's *À la recherche du temps perdu*; see Chapter 3), it was certainly written by a reader of an older generation. This annotator seems to have been familiar with the German language,[16] for toward the end of the first epistle of John (page 175),[17] the word 'understanding' is underlined and annotated in the right margin by means of the German word 'Sinn'. And in Psalm 37, next to the seventh verse – 'Rest in the Lord, and wait patiently for him' – a pencil cross refers to a note in the bottom margin with an alternative translation, based on Luther's German translation: '"Lie still & let Him mould thee" – Luther's translation' (page 372).

FRENCH BIBLES

The two French Bibles in Beckett's library are *La Sainte Bible, qui contient le vieux et le nouveau testament, revue sur les originaux par David Martin* (New York: Société Biblique Américaine, 1874) and *La Sainte Bible, qui comprend l'ancien et le nouveau testament traduits sur les textes originaux hébreu et grec par Louis Segond, nouvelle édition revue* (Paris: [58, rue de Clichy], 1921). The German and French Bibles are not annotated, but the translation by David Martin does contain two scraps of paper, inserted at pages 131 (Numbers 5) and 191 (Deut. 23–4). The latter marks Beckett's reading of Deuteronomy in French. The note 'Circoncisez donc le prépuce de votre cœur et ne roidissez plus votre cou' (Deutéronome X.16)' in the 'Whoroscope' Notebook (63v) is an indication that Beckett read Deuteronomy in the translation by David Martin early in 1939.[18]

Beckett's use of his French Bibles is sometimes eclectic. In the second manuscript of *Pas moi*, Beckett was seeking the correct translations for these three fragments:

God is love ... tender mercies ... new every morning ...

The English version is a combination of 1 John 4:8 ('God is Love'), Psalm 25:6 ('Remember, O LORD, thy tender mercies'), and Lamentations 3:22–3 ('his compassions fail not. *They are* new every morning'; Lamentations 3:22–3, King James Version). In the manuscript of Beckett's French translation, he first wrote 'Dieu c'est l'amour..plein de miséricorde' (UoR MS1396/4/26, 6r) with a reference to James 5:11 in the translation by Louis Segond: 'le Seigneur est *plein de miséricorde* et de compassion.' Beckett then probably checked his Bibles and wrote in the left margin: '1re Epitre Jean.IV.8', changing 'Dieu c'est l'amour' into the Segond version 'Dieu est amour' (Louis Segond).[19] He also changed 'plein de miséricorde' into 'bonté intarissable ... renouvelée chaque matin ...', this time based on the Martin translation 'ses compassions ne sont point taries. Elles se renouvellent chaque matin'.[20] On the next page, with the same passage, Beckett has added in the margin 'Lamentations III 22–23' (UoR MS1396/4/26, 7r).

GERMAN AND ITALIAN BIBLES

The German Bible 'nach der Übersetzung Martin Luthers' is of a more recent date (1970). It is unmarked, but Beckett used it to look up the precise wording of biblical references in his own works. For instance, in the margin of the bilingual (English/German) edition of *Eh Joe* used by Rick Cluchey, Beckett wrote: 'Den[n] du bist Erde und sollst zu Erde werden (Luther)' (UoR MS3626), related to the line 'Mud thou art'. The German equivalent, 'Dreck bist du', is followed by a note indicating the source: 'Genesis III 19' (UoR MS3626) – 'for dust thou art, and unto dust shalt thou return' in the King James version.

Unlike this German Bible, the 1924 edition of the Italian Bible dates from his student days and features the inscription 'S. B. Beckett / Trinity College / Dublin'. The sea on the map of 'La Terra Santa' at the back of this Bible is as pale blue as on the map of 'The Holy Land' in the Teacher's Bible – as pale as in Gogo's description in *Waiting for Godot* (*CDW* 13; see Chapter 1). Gogo's reminiscence is his reply to Didi's question if he ever read the Bible and if he remembers the Gospels. His subsequent remarks regarding the two thieves, crucified at the same time as Jesus Christ, focus on the discrepancies between the accounts of the Evangelists: 'The four of them were there – or thereabouts – and only one speaks of a thief being saved' (*CDW* 14).

Beckett himself, however, may have read more than just the Gospels to write this scene. His copy of *Curiosités littéraires* by Ludovic Lalanne contains a discussion of the Gospels and their mutual discrepancies (173–6). Although this discussion shows no direct reading traces, the marked sentence immediately following it indicates a remarkable philological interest in the text of the Bible. The passage concerns the famous verse about the holy trinity, the so-called Comma Johanneum, which had been fiercely debated, especially since the beginning of the sixteenth century.[21] Given this debate, it is remarkable – Lalanne notes – that the passage appears neither in the earliest manuscripts, nor in any of the Greek manuscripts predating the sixteenth century.[22] A marginal pencil line marks this textual history of the Trinity.

In Trinity College, Beckett's method of Bible reading seems to have changed from an 'intensive' to a more 'extensive' approach (see Chapter 1). His Italian Bible (with the inscription 'S.B. Beckett / Trinity College / Dublin') shows many marks in the book of Proverbs ('I Proverbi', page 816). Several proverbs are marked with a vertical pencil line: 3:13–17; 6:4–5; 7:16–19; 11:22; 21:19, but not 13:12, 'Hope deferred maketh the heart sick', referred to in *Waiting for Godot* (*CDW* 12). The marked proverbs do not form a pattern that corresponds with the notes on Proverbs in the 'Dream' Notebook, but the pencil line marking 11:22 ('Una donna bella, ma senza giudizio, è un anello d'oro nel grifo d'un porco') does correspond with note 554: 'jewel of gold in a swine's mouth (fair woman – discretion)'. The following proverbs are underscored in pencil in the Italian Bible:

1:7 Il timore dell'Eterno è il principio della scienza
3:17 Le sue vie son vie dilettevoli, e tutti i suoi sentiei sono pace
   Marginalia in grey pencil: 'All her paths are peace'
4:17 bevono il vino della violenza
5:19 Cerva d'amore, cavriola di grazia
   Marginalia in grey pencil: 'Loving hind & pleasant roe'

These marks of intensive reading contrast with traces of extensive reading in blue ink. In the same Italian Bible, Beckett underlined and marked several passages in the most diverse sections, jumping from Ezekiel and Hosea to

Genesis. The blue ink of the marks, annotations and abbreviations 'L. d'A' or 'L. d'Am.' indicates that they belong together and suggests an explanation for their scattered nature. Voltaire's *Lettres d'Amabed*, notably the footnotes to the *Troisième lettre du journal d'Amabed*, offers the key to the reading pattern. In Voltaire's text, the non-Christian reader's amazement at the content of the Old Testament is concisely summarized in a few paragraphs, recounting a reading experience. The Franciscan chaplain Fa molto has read 'des choses merveilleuses' in the Bible. For instance, the god of these people – 'le dieu de ces gens-là' – makes one of the prophets butter his bread with cow's dung and another sleep with prostitutes. Voltaire enumerates an impressive list of the dubious behaviour with extensive references to several instances in the Bible:

Ce qui me fait le plus de peine, à moi qui me pique de propreté et d'une grande pudeur, c'est que le dieu de ces gens-là ordonne à un de ses prédicateurs[a] de manger de la matière louable sur son pain; et à un autre, de coucher pour de l'argent avec des filles de joie[b], et d'en avoir des enfants.

Il y a bien pis. Ce savant homme nous a fait remarquer deux sœurs, Oolla et Ooliba[c]. Tu les connais bien, puisque tu as tout lu. Cet article a fort scandalisé ma femme: le blanc de ses yeux en a rougi. J'ai remarqué que la bonne Déra était tout en feu à ce paragraphe. Il faut certainement que ce franciscain Fa molto soit un gaillard. Cependant il a fermé son livre dès qu'il a vu combien Charme des yeux et moi nous étions effarouchés, et il est sorti pour aller méditer sur le text.

Il m'a laissé son livre sacré; j'en ai lu quelques pages au hasard. O Brama! ô justice éternelle! quels hommes que tous ces gens-là[d]! ils couchent tous avec leurs servantes, dans leur vieillesse. L'un fait des infamies[e] à sa belle-mère, l'autre à[f] sa belle-fille. Ici c'est une ville tout entière qui veut absolument traiter un pauvre prêtre comme une jolie fille[g]; là deux demoiselles de condition enivrent leur père[h], couchent avec lui l'une après l'autre, et en ont des enfants.[23]

[a] Voyez Ézéchiel, chapitre IV.
[b] Osée, chapitre 1er.
[c] Ézéchiel, chapitre XVI. 'Tes tétons ont paru, ton poil a commencé à croître; je t'ai couverte, tu as ouvert tes cuisses à tous les passants..., etc.' et chapitre XXIII: 'Elle a recherché ceux qui ont le membre d'un âne, et déch...... comme des chevaux.'
[d] Voyez l'histoire d'Abraham, de Jacob, etc.
[e] Le patriarche Ruben couche avec Bala, concubine de son père; *Genèse*, chap. XXXV.
[f] Le patriarche Juda couche avec Thamar, sa bru; Genèse, ch. XXXVIII.
[g] ... *Juges*, chapitre XIX.
[h] Les filles de Lot: *Genèse*, chapitre XIX.

Beckett's reading of Voltaire clearly aroused his curiosity. He systematically looked up the references in the footnotes[24] and marked the corresponding passages in his *Sacra Bibbia*:

[^a^] Ezechiele 4: 12–15 marked in blue ink; marginalia: 'Lettres d'Amabed' in left margin. The following passage is underlined in blue ink:
Guarda, io ti do dello sterco bovino, invece d'escrementi d'uomo; sopra quello cuocerai il tuo pane!

[Then he said unto me, Lo, I have given thee cow's dung for man's dung, and thou shalt prepare thy bread therewith. (King James Bible, Ezekiel 4:15)]

[^b^] Osea 1:2; marginalia at the bottom of the page: 'Lettres d'Amabed'.
'Va', prenditi per moglie una meretrice, e genera de' figliuoli di prostituzione

[And the LORD said to Hosea, Go, take unto thee a wife of whoredoms and children of whoredoms (King James Bible, Hosea 1:2)]

Osea 1:6: the word 'Lo-Ruhama' is underlined.[25]
Osea 2:1: the words 'Ammi' and 'Ruhama' are underlined.

Beckett spelled the name 'Lo-Ruhama' in the same way as in the Italian Bible when he included it in the poem 'Text', one of the four poems published in *The European Caravan: An Anthology of the New Spirit in European Literature*, published on 13 November 1931 (Pilling 2006a, 34). In this case, Beckett did not limit himself to the line referred to in the footnotes of the *Lettres d'Amabed*. The context suggests that he was struck by the notion of 'compassione': 'E l'Eterno disse ad Osea: "Mettile nome Lo-Ruhama; perchè io non avrò più compassione della casa d'Israele in guise da perdonaria. Ma avrò compassione della casa di Giuda ..."' (Osea 1:6–7). In 'Text', the lines 'Lo-Ruhama Lo-Ruhama / pity is quick with death' translate the 'compassione' into the 'pity' ('pietà') that is also central in 'Dante and the Lobster' (see Chapter 5), suggesting a contemporaneous date of composition.

In Voltaire's text, some of the passages that both scandalized and excited especially the female audience during the chaplain's reading are excerpted in the footnotes. Beckett has checked the titillating French version against the Italian, writing the French version in the bottom margin of his Italian bible:

[^c^] Ezechiele 16:7: passage underlined in blue ink and French translation added at the bottom of the page:
ma tu eri nuda e scoperta.

Marginalia: 'Tu as ouvert tes cuisses à tous les passants. (Lettres d'Amabed)'

[I have caused thee to multiply as the bud of the field, and thou hast increased and waxen great, and thou art come to excellent ornaments: *thy* breasts are fashioned, and thine hair is grown, whereas thou *wast* naked and bare. (King James Bible, Ezekiel 16:7)]

Ezechiele 23:20: passage underlined in blue ink and French translation added at the bottom of the page:
e s'appassionò per quei fornicatori dale membra d'asino, dall'ardor di stalloni

Marginalia: 'Elle a recherché ceux qui ont le membre d'un âne, et déchargent comme des chevaux. (L. d'Am.)'

[For she doted upon their paramours, whose flesh *is as* the flesh of asses, and whose issue *is like* the issue of horses. (King James Bible, Ezekiel 23:20)]

The woman to whom this passage refers is 'Oholiba' according to the spelling of the Italian Bible, which Beckett adopted in the opening line of another poem published in *The European Caravan*, 'Hell Crane to Starling',[26] whose closing word ('Tsoar') also derives from the cluster of biblical obscenities inspired by Voltaire (Genesis 19:30; footnote h):

[e] Genesi 35:8: 'Allon-Bacuth' underlined in blue ink
Genesi 35:18: 'Ben-Oni' underlined in blue ink
Genesi 35:22: passage underlined in blue ink; marginalia in right margin:
(L. d'A.) Ruben andò e si giacque con Bilha, concubina di suo padre. E Israele lo seppe. [Reuben went and lay with Bilhah his father's concubine: and Israel heard it.]
[f] Genesi 38:14–21: marked with a line in blue ink; marginalia: 'L. d'A.'.
[h] Genesi 19:30–5: marked with a line in blue ink, starting with 'Lot salì da Tsoar'; marginalia: 'L. d'A.'.

If 'intensive' reading was inspired by the Protestant practice of studying the Bible, as Roger Chartier suggests (see Chapter 1), this 'extensive' reading experience reflects an act of rebellion of a reader with a rigorous Protestant background inspired by a satirical critic of Catholicism. Still, the reading is not entirely extensive in that the marginalia do not so much describe intertextual references, emanating from the Bible to Voltaire's text, but the other way round. In this case, Beckett used the Bible as a reference work, not just to double-check the footnotes in Voltaire's *Lettres d'Amabed*, but also to enrich the text in his copy of the Bible with translations. In this particular case, Beckett used this cluster of Biblical obscenities to write his poem 'Hell Crane to Starling'.[27] Still, the notes in the margins of the Italian Bible do not serve as a draft for this poem. The margins mark the boundaries of what Raymonde Debray Genette termed 'exogenesis'. And although it is often extremely difficult to draw a clear boundary between exo- and endogenetics, Beckett's reading and writing habits seem to respect the integrity of the printed text, including its margins, as part of the exogenetic space. The act of writing in the margin is oriented toward the text he is reading rather than to his own writing. In this respect, the French translations in the margins of his Italian Bible have a similar function as the translation 'She's not heavy enough to hang herself' in the margin of Beckett's copy of Renard's journal. Only after he had copied this translation in his 'Dream' Notebook did it become part of the endogenetic realm.

Beckett's multilingual approach to the texts of the Bible is also recognizable in his activities as an 'extractor'. In his 'Whoroscope' Notebook (21r–22r) he quotes from Luke 16:24–6:

Luke XVI: Dives – Lazarus, prayer from virtual to actual in entelechy, [or] petites perceptions to apperceived in monad – poem (qtd. in Nixon 2011, 210).

   Père A., aie pitié de moi, et envoie Lazare, afin qu'il trempe dans l'eau le bout de son doigt, pour me rafraîchir la langue; car je suis extrêmement tourmenté dans cette flamme. / Mais A. lui répondit: Mon fils, souviens-toi que tu as eu tes biens dans ta vie, et Lazare y a eu des maux; et maintenant il est consolé, et tu es dans les tourments. / Outre cela, il y a un grand abîme entre vous et nous, de sorte que ceux qui voudraient passer d'ici vers vous ne le peuvent, non plus que ceux qui voudraient passer de là ici.

   Padre Abramo, abbi pietà di me e manda Lazzaro a intingere la punta del dito nell'acqua per rinfrescarmi la lingua, perchè sono tormentato in questa fiamma. / Ma A. disse: Figliuolo, ricordati che tu ricevesti i tuoi beni in vita tua, e che L. similmente ricevette i mali; ma ora qui egli è consolato, e tu sei tormentato./ E oltre a tutto questo, fra noi e voi e posta una gran voragine, perchè quelli che vorrebbero passar di qui a voi non possano, nè di là si passi da noi. ~~Ed egli disse:~~

[the King James version reads: 'Father Abraham, have mercy on me, and send Lazarus, that he may dip the tip of his finger in water, and cool my tongue; for I am tormented in this flame. But Abraham said, Son, remember that thou in thy lifetime receivedst thy good things, and likewise Lazarus evil things: but now he is comforted, and thou art tormented. And beside all this, between us and you there is a great gulf fixed: so that they which would pass from hence to you cannot; neither can they pass to us, that would come from thence]

In 'Intercessions by Denis Devlin' (*Dis* 92), published in *transition*, April–May 1938, Beckett employed the word '*gulf*' (as in the King James version) as the equivalent for 'abîme' / 'voragine': 'both here and there *gulf.* The absurdity, here or there, of either without the other, the inaccessible other' (92). But to explain the 'Dives–Lazarus symbiosis' he claimed to adopt the Concise New Oxford Dictionary example (the symbiosis of fungoid and algoid in lichen) instead of referring to the Bible. The French quotation derives from the Ostervald version (the translation made by the Swiss Protestant pastor Jean-Frédéric Ostervald [1663–1747]); the Italian quotation is taken from the Riveduta version. The Italian Bible in Beckett's library is a copy of the Riveduta version, but there are no marks next to Luke

16:24–6. This extract further illustrates Beckett's 'extensive' reading of the Bible. Apparently, Beckett carefully copied the story in two languages as an illustration of Leibniz's monad theory, notably his concepts of virtuality and 'petites perceptions'. Matthew Feldman suggests that Leibniz 'may well be the link between Beckett's philosophical and psychological readings' (Feldman 2006a, 97).[28] Beckett's extensive reading of the Bible thus turns the parable of Dives and Lazarus into an illustration of an epistemological issue on the interface between philosophy and psychology.

THEOLOGICAL CURIOSITIES

A few pages further on in the 'Whoroscope' Notebook (24r), Beckett noted: 'sudarium (Veronica's cloth)'.[29] The same subject drew his attention when he read one of the most remarkable books in his personal library, the *Curiosités théologiques par un bibliophile* (Paris: Garnier Frères, nouvelle edition, [1884]). The anonymous bibliophile appears to have been Pierre Gustave Brunet (1805–96), and the book, originally published by Adolphe Delahays in 1861, is a collection of apocryphal stories relating to characters in the Old Testament, notes on relics, different kinds of superstition and bizarre legends of saints.

The book contains several marks, underlinings and some marginalia. For instance, a marginal annotation on page 73 notes (in the same language as the main text) that the story of Saint Maclou or Saint Malo, saying mass on the back of a whale, which he took for an island, is also attributed to Saint Brendan.[30] 'Saint Maclou célébrant la messe sur le dos d'une baleine' is also mentioned on page 168, and again the (French) pencil marginalia mention 'comme S. Brendan'.

Several examples in the chapter on 'Superstitions' are marked in the margin. One of these marked passages is in Latin[31] and contains the expression 'Christi pietate' – which is misprinted: 'Christi pictate'. Whether or not Beckett's preoccupation with the ambiguity of 'pietà' in 'Dante and the Lobster' made him extra alert to this word, he did notice the misprint and corrected it by crossing out the 'c' and penciling an 'e' in the left margin.

On pages 57 and 58, a few passages on the veronica are marked in the margin, with some extra underlinings.[32] The 'vera icon' – which appears as the 'veronica mundi / veronica munda' in 'Enueg II' and as a motif in 'What a Misfortune' – was added to the text of *Watt* at a late stage in the composition process, as Chris Ackerley points out. By means of this addition, Beckett applied his 'vaguening' technique[33] and made the word 'station' more ambiguous by suggesting the extra meaning of a station of the Cross:

> Watt, faithful to his rule, took no more notice of this aggression than if it had been an accident. This he found was the wisest attitude, to staunch, if necessary, inconspicuously, with the little red sudarium that he always carried in his pocket, the flow of blood, to pick up what had fallen, and to continue, as soon as possible, on his way, or in his station, like a victim of mere mischance. (*W* 25)

As one of the many references to Christ's suffering, the sudarium was to reappear in later works such as *Fin de partie* and *Nacht und Träume*. It is also conspicuously present in 'Ernest et Alice'. Although Ruby Cohn prefers to consider 'Ernest et Alice' as 'an odd fragment, unrelated to *Fin de partie*' (2001, 220), the handkerchief hiding the face of Ernest, who is fastened to a cross, is clearly a motif which the 'odd fragment' and the famous play have in common. According to the legend, Veronica wiped Jesus's face (sixth station of the cross). Whereas Christ presumably did not explicitly ask her to do so, Ernest shouts at Alice, after she has washed his hands and feet: 'Ma figure. Tu n'as pas fait ma figure!' Eventually, his mother says she will take care of his face, calling it 'cette jolie petite frimousse!' and noting how he increasingly resembles his father: 'comme il tient de son papa. De plus en plus' (UoR MS1227/7/16/2).

The book *Curiosités théologiques* adds an extra element to this motif: the multiple imprint of Christ's face turns the 'vera icon' into a Warhol portrait *avant la lettre*. If the Veronica was not an invention or a product of the flourishing medieval relic business, its multiplication certainly was. But even this miraculous multiplication was explained away as divine 'Providence', designed to maintain the devotion of the faithful, as the marked passage in the final paragraph of the chapter on relics suggests.[34] Perhaps more remarkable than the 'miraculous' multiplication of relics are the sophisms that were concocted to explain this miracle. The case of the Veronica may be just a detail, but it is paradigmatic of Beckett's interest in the way human beings always seem to have managed to convince themselves they understood the universe and to come up with rational explanations for irrational behaviour, which Beckett notably satirizes in *Watt*.

The *Curiosités théologiques* proved an excellent source of inspiration for this form of satire. When Watt meets Mr Spiro in the train, who tells him about the prize competitions in his Catholic monthly *Crux*, the editor also gives an example of a typical question: '*What do you know of the adjuration, excommunication, malediction and fulminating anathematization of the eels of Como, the hurebers of Beaune, the rats of Lyon, the slugs of Mâcon, the worms of*

Como, the leeches of Lausanne and the caterpillars of Valence?' (21). What Beckett knew of these adjurations and excommunications was based on what he had read in the *Curiosités théologiques*.

Mary Bryden notes about the *Watt* manuscripts at the Harry Ransom Center: 'At the draft stage, Beckett has not yet suppressed his source' when he mentions all the bibliographical details regarding the anathematization of 'the flies of Lyon, the slugs of Mâcon, the worms of Como, the hurebers of Beaune and the eels of Lake Leman, as recorded by the egregious jurisconsult Barthélémy de Chassanée, in the fifth part of his first consultation, Lyon, in-folio, 1531' (Bryden 1998a, 81). Mary Bryden suggests that Beckett may have had access to the original work or to a facsimile: '(There would, for instance, have been a copy of it in the Royal Court and State Library of Munich when Beckett visited Munich in 1937)' (Bryden 1998a, 81). But Beckett did not need to consult the original. His mention of the bibliographic reference – with all its pedantry – is part of the satire on the 'loutishness of learning'. All the information he mentions (both at the draft stage and in the published version), including details such as 'in-folio' and the exotic word 'hurebers', derives from the chapter on 'Excommunication' in the *Curiosités théologiques*.[35] The case thus nicely illustrates the way Beckett (not unlike Joyce, from whom he learned many writing skills) often obtained information through mediation rather than from the primary source.

In the *Curiosités théologiques*, the five parts of Chassanée's *De excummunicatione animalium insectorum* are briefly summarized. At the draft stage of *Watt*, Beckett explicitly mentioned 'the fifth part of his first consultation', which is treated much more extensively in the *Curiosités théologiques* than the other parts and indeed contains most of the examples. The opening paragraph, marked with a pencil line in the right margin, describes how Chassanée enumerates the crimes committed by judges, lawyers, notaries, clergymen, women, young persons and elderly people.[36]

This procedure of enumerating becomes a narrative strategy in *Watt*, possibly inspired by the system of exhaustive enumeration as a critical perversion of the Enlightenment project in the Marquis de Sade's *Les 120 Journées de Sodome*. At the same time, the human being's pride in his rational capabilities is satirized by means of inconsistencies in the logic of his argumentation. As Mary Bryden points out, animals cannot be excommunicated, strictly speaking, 'since they are not legitimate communicants in the first place, but this term does seem to have been used alongside that of anathematization' (Bryden 1998a, 78). In the *Curiosités théologiques*, the bibliophile author notes that Chassanée's fulminations against the excommunication of animals may have had a reverse effect.[37] Several of his examples show indeed that the excommunication seems to have had the desired effect – and these are the examples Beckett refers to in *Watt*. The French version reads as follows: '*Dites ce que vous savez de l'adjuration, excommunication, malédiction et anathématisation foudroyante des anguilles de Côme, hurebers de Beaune, rats de Lyon, limaces de Macon, vers de Côme, sangsues de Lausanne et processionnaires de Valence*' (Beckett 2001, 29).[38] In the latter case, the caterpillars did not obey and the vicar-general was determined to take legal action against them by means of excommunication. Two jurisconsults and two theologians were consulted and they were able to change the vicar-general's mind; as a result only invocations, prayers and holy water were used. When the animals eventually disappeared, the miracle was attributed to these devotions, which had lasted several months – longer than the average life of a caterpillar.

Whether the enumeration of these curiosities would have been enough to win Mr Spiro's prize competition in *Crux* remains to be seen, but this is what we '*know of the adjuration, excommunication, malediction and fulminating anathematization*' of the animals mentioned in *Watt* (*W* 21).

These examples, however, are 'non-marginalia': they found their way into the text of *Watt*, but they are not marked in Beckett's copy of *Curiosités théologiques*. On the other hand, there is also an interesting paragraph, which is marked but did not make it into the text of *Watt*.[39] The mark next to this passage seems to indicate the reader's interest in a non-anthropocentric position and a form of sympathy with this strange character of Chassanée, standing up for the rights of animals. Based on E. P. Evans's *The Criminal Prosecution and Capital Punishment of Animals* (1906, rpt. London: Faber, 1987),[40] Mary Bryden also relates Chassanée's consultations to Mr Spiro's reading of the letter to the editor, concerning the following issue:

A rat, or other small animal, eats of a consecrated wafer.
1) *Does he ingest the Real Body, or does he not?*
2) *If he does not, what has become of it?*
3) *If he does, what is to be done with him?* (22)

According to the text of *Curiosités théologiques*, Chassanée does indeed mention a request by the inhabitants of a parish, ravaged by rats. But the matter of the rat and the consecrated wafer is most probably derived from another case, disclosed (some eighty pages) further in the *Curiosités théologiques* under the heading 'Dissertation sur une question étrange'. The bibliophile inclination of the anonymous compiler of these curiosities – Pierre Gustave Brunet – cannot help mentioning all the bibliographic details of his source text: 'un volume composé par Wilhelm Horder, ministre à Stuttgardt, superintendant général, etc. Dirigé contre les jésuites d'Ingolstadt, ce livre a, selon l'habitude de l'époque, un titre bizarre: *Mus exenteratus, hoc est tractatus valdè magistralis...* Le Rat éventré, ou Traité superlativement magistral sur une certaine question théologale, épineuse et des plus subtiles. Tubingue, 1593, in-4°.' ([Brunet 1884], 178) In the drafts (*Watt* Notebook 2, 15; TS 99–103.) the Latin title of Horder's work is adapted to *Mus eventratus mcgilligani*, and the story of Matthew David McGilligan's theological thesis is given at length:

Curiosités théologiques, 179–81 'Dissertation sur une question étrange'	*Watt* Notebook 2, 15; TS 99–103. (transcription by Chris Ackerley 2005, 45–6):
Il [Horder] se pose d'abord cette question: « Si un rat ou tout autre animal ronge ou mange une hostie consacrée, ronge-t-il ou mange-t-il le corps même de Jésus-Christ, et, dans le cas négatif, que devient ce corps? »	If a rat gnaws or nibbles a consecrated host, does he gnaw or nibble the Real Body? If he do not, what has become of the Body? If he do, what is to shall be done with the rat?
Sur cette question première, il se livre à une foule de recherches appuyées sur les dires et opinions pour et contre des théologiens les plus renommés, saint Thomas d'Aquin, saint Bonaventure, Pierre Lombard, Alexandre de Hales et bien d'autres. . . .	To the first of these questions McGilligan replied that the rat did indeed gnaw or nibble the Real Body, and this conclusion he supported with quotations from the works of Saint Thomas Aquinas, Saint Bonaventura, Peter Lombard, Alexander of Hales, the Four Great Doctors of the West, the Four Great Doctors of the East Middle-West, Sanchez, Suarez, Henno, Soto, Diana, Concina, Dens, O'Dea and others.
Holder [sic] examine d'abord les arguments de ceux qui soutenaient que le rat dévorant ne mangeait pas le corps de Jésus-Christ. Il expose ensuite la raison de ceux qui soutenaient la thèse opposée.	To the second question McGilligan contented himself with simply replying that the Body being consubstantial with the Host, as much of the former was in the rat as he had gnawed or nibbled of the latter, and as much still in the latter as he had not gnawed or nibbled thereof.
Cette dernière opinion prévalant, on devait sévir contre le rat sacrilège avec toute la rigueur des droits canoniques et des décrets pontificaux.	To the third question McGilligan replied that the rat, when caught, should be pursued with all the rigour of the canon laws and pontifical decrees, adding that in this connexion a number of difficulties arose . . .
Cependant, disaient quelques théologiens, il faut procéder avec prudence, dans la crainte de tomber sur un rat innocent.	'Pint wan: Wance yis'v cotta howlt on de rat, howwa yis ter know wuddit be de roight rat yis've cotta howlt on, ower wuddent it.

Toutefois, on reconnaissait encore que, dans le doute, le prêtre pouvait exorciser le rat ainsi que les décrets le permettent....

Au contraire, si l'on était sûr du fait, si le rat capturé pouvait être convaincu d'avoir dévoré l'hostie consacrée, alors on devait procéder à des recherches minutieuses; et d'abord s'élevait une question nouvelle et préliminaire: devait-on ou non adorer l'hostie consacrée que le rat venait de manger et qu'il s'apprêtait à digérer?...

Le rat étant pris et convaincu du crime, l'adoration de l'hostie étant, nous supposons, convenue en principe, que devait-on faire?

Saint Antonin, archevêque de Florence, dit, dans sa Somme théologique, que le rat doit être solennellement brûlé. Mais, répondait-on, si vous brûlez le rat, vous brûlez aussi l'hostie cansacrée. Là-dessus disputes nouvelles.

Quelques-uns voulaient que le rat fût égorgé, puis éventré; que l'hostie fût retirée de son corps et rétablie à l'usage des fidèles, après avoir été lavée et nettoyée. D'autres ajoutaient que si les fidèles répugnaient à avaler une hostie déjà mangée par un rat, cette hostie devait être déposée dans le tabernacle et y rester jusqu'à ce qu'elle tombât en poussière....

Si, lors de la capture du rat, il était trop tard pour en substance dans son corps, que devait on penser?

'Pint tew: Sewposin tis de roight wan, wud it be me jewity tew adower de bitta d'host what he's afther swallyin up.

'Pint thray: Sewposin tis me jewity so tew dew, what are yis tew dew wid d'ould rat? Are yis tew burren him? Thin yis burren de Rale Body. Are yis t'open him up an levvy it owit de bist way yis can? For tew putt it back in de kiebowerium, ower fer tew et it yerself, seeance teenent?

'Pint fower: Sewposin yes doant ketch a howlt on d'ould rat unthil afther what he's bane an – afther what he's bane – bane an done his doolies, purissimavirgoemenda-cormuemetcarnemmeam, thin whire are yis?

These passages of *Curiosités théologiques* are not marked in Beckett's copy, but a comparison with the text of the draft shows how important these 'non-marginalia' were at an early stage of the composition process and how closely Beckett followed the text of *Curiosités théologiques*. Although this particular scene did not make it into the published text of *Watt*, its source text is not irrelevant. Brunet notes that the purpose of Horder's book was to mock certain views that pushed the interpretation of religious doctrine to ridiculous extremes.[41] Applied to rationalism and the Enlightenment project, this description – pushing dogmas to ridiculous extremes – can serve as an adequate description of the programme of *Watt* and of Beckett's early poetics.

CHAPTER 9

Dictionaries and Reference Works

When Beckett told James Knowlson in 1973 that his library contained merely 'reference books and a few old chestnuts' (24 August 1973; JEK B/1/39), he was, at least partly, telling the truth. Beckett's library contains a vast array of dictionaries and reference books, in many languages, and many of them bear reading traces. Like Joyce and other writers, Beckett not only consulted dictionaries, but read them avidly. At times he did so to find 'hard' words, obscure details and simple curiosities, and at other times he turned to dictionaries and other reference books for their 'authority', whether in citing the use of words by other authors or simply to check grammatical or philological accuracy. As the Dean in Joyce's *Portrait of an Artist* states with regard to the word 'tundish': 'That is a most interesting word. I must look that word up. Upon my word I must' (Joyce 1992, 204).

ENCYCLOPAEDIA BRITANNICA

Already in the 1930s, Beckett consulted and took notes from the famous *Encyclopaedia Britannica*, excerpting for example material on Greek mythical figures (WN 31r–33r; see Chapter 6). The so-called 'Trueborn Jackeen' notes on Irish history, kept with a potential creative work in mind, also derive from this source (TCD MS10971/2). Beckett possessed the 11th edition (1910–11) of the *Encyclopaedia Britannica*, which was given to him by the manuscript dealer Jake Schwartz. Thanking Schwartz for the 'beautiful edition', Beckett wrote that he was 'not yet quite sure whether I shall keep it here or take it to the country, probably the latter, since most of my work now is done there and I have more room there. I know I shall have great pleasure from it, and instruction, in the years to come – if they do' (letter to Jake Schwartz, 15 March 1958). In the event, he did take it to Ussy, as a further letter to Schwartz (25 March 1958) shows: 'The EB very handsome on my shelves here in the wilderness. I have been dipping into it with the greatest satisfaction'. Beckett may have been 'dipping' into the volumes, but he does not appear to have embarked on any extensive encyclopaedic reading enterprise. When he told Jacoba van Velde in April 1958 that he had been given the *Encyclopaedia*, his only comment was that it came too late (see Chapter 1). By 1961, Beckett was telling Barbara Bray with a sense of dismay that he had 'read all books here [in Ussy] and have been reduced to En. Brit'. (16 August 1961; TCD MS10948/1/158).

The twenty-eight volumes of the *Encyclopaedia Britannica* – it is missing the final volume containing the index – shows some reading traces, although it is difficult to determine whether they were made by Beckett or someone else. The entry on Manichaeism was clearly marked by Beckett (see Chapter 1), but other pages that bear dog-ears do not as easily correspond to what we know of his interests. Thus the page with the entry on D. G. Rossetti has been folded over, and there are red pencil marks beside the population estimate of Oil City in 1906 and the age of eligibility for pensions in France. The folded page marking the entry on the 'Brain' could conceivably have interested Beckett.[1]

A DICTIONARY OF THE ENGLISH LANGUAGE BY SAMUEL JOHNSON

Beckett owned an antiquarian edition of Johnson's famous precursor to the modern English dictionary, the *Dictionary of the English Language*, published in two volumes in 1799 (8th edition).[2] The edition itself contains no marginalia, but was clearly used by Beckett. Anne Atik for example relates the story that Beckett was delighted by one of Johnson's definitions: 'Just read this in Johnson's Dictionary – his definition of "lamentation": "audible wail"' (Atik 2001, 77). Beckett considered drawing on Johnson's dictionary in *Krapp's Last Tape*, as Krapp tries to remind himself of the meaning of the word 'viduity', which he used in younger years but has now forgotten. As Beckett notes in a manuscript version of the play, 'or Johnson's dictionary and quotes example' (Knowlson 1980, 21). Beckett himself continued to turn to Johnson when verifying the source of words, as a letter to Barbara Bray (26 July 1977; TCD MS10948/1/616) reveals (possibly after re-reading Johnson's 'Vanity of Human Wishes', in which the queried word appears): 'Looking up "pest" in Johnson I came upon the following: "Pessary: an oblong form of medicine, made to thrust up into the uterus upon some extraordinary occasions"'. Beckett was sufficiently struck by the oddity of the word (and its meaning) to enter it that same month into his 'Sottisier' Notebook (UoR MS2901, 8r).

In many ways, what is at stake here is the accuracy of definition and the tradition of usage. For a writer who is notorious for questioning and 'misusing' language, Beckett surprisingly often turned to dictionaries for their 'authority', and that of his literary precursors, to legitimize the use of particular words and expressions.

THE *OXFORD ENGLISH DICTIONARY*

The *OED* served as one such source. Beckett appears to have come to the *Oxford English Dictionary* rather late in life, as no citation from or reference to the dictionary appears until after 1945. He thus did not possess an actual edition of the first *OED*. Indeed, by the time Beckett used the *OED*, his own use of words had been added in the second supplements to the dictionary. Just as James Murray established the *OED* by citing the authority of the 'great writers', his successor in reshaping the dictionary, Robert Burchill, sought to incorporate usage (and coinage) of words by modern writers. As the preface to the second Supplement to the *OED* acknowledges, the dictionary introduced words found in the work of Joyce (who, in the fullness of time, would contribute 1,838 quotations to the second edition of the *OED*, published in 1989), Virginia Woolf, W. B. Yeats, T. S. Eliot, D. H. Lawrence and W. H. Auden, to name but these, as well as Samuel Beckett (xiv). Beckett's library contains three shorter versions of the *OED*: the *Pocket Oxford Dictionary* (1947), the *Shorter Oxford English Dictionary* (2 vols, 1972) and the *Concise Oxford Dictionary* (1983). However, it also contains the 'real thing', but in the *Compact Edition* published 'micrographically' in two volumes in 1971. As Beckett told Bray, 'Toy with thought of acquiring OED microscopic edition' (18 October 1971; TCD MS10948/1/496). As the letter indicates, Beckett's motivation for acquiring this particular edition appears to have been rooted in his struggle to find the adequate definition for the French expression 'grimpeur indélicat', which he thought was not the same as 'indelicate', 'not a gallicism', but rather 'unprincipled' or 'inconsiderate'. Having acquired this particular edition, he would use it to settle his own queries regarding the use of particular words, as is evident in a letter to Avigdor Arikha of 4 November 1983: 'Thank you for feat (adj.) examples. Few of adverbial use. My compact OED gives, from The Lovers's Complaint, "With sleaved silk feat and affectedly enswath'd"' (qtd. in Atik 2001, 56). Beckett had used the word 'feat' in *Footfalls* (1976): 'Watch how feat she wheels' (*CDW* 401).

Beckett similarly used French language dictionaries when justifying the use of particular expressions. For example, in a 1953 letter to Mania Péron, Beckett wrote that 'Ma Grammaire Larousse recommande l'accord pour se douter' (undated [postmark is 24 April 1953]). And, in choosing the word

Dictionaries and Reference Works 195

'foirade' for the title of the book collecting his 'Fizzles' (written intermittently between 1955 and 1972), he called upon the *Petit Robert* to explain his choice of title:

Foirade: Le fait de foirer.
Foirer: rater, échouer lamentablement (Robert) (letter to John Kobler, 5 March 1973; qtd. in *TFN* xix)

Beckett owned two 'standard' *Larousse* dictionaries, and two editions of the *Petit Robert* (1967 and 1972).[3] As Beckett told Bray with regard to the later edition of the *Petit Robert*: 'Indulged in a Petit Robert at lexicographic expense' (letter to Barbara Bray, 8 September 1979; TCD MS 10948/1/649).

ETYMOLOGIES

Given Beckett's interest in the fundamental particles of language – words – it is not surprising to find etymological dictionaries in his library. The earliest volume is Ernest Weekley's *A Concise Etymological Dictionary of Modern English* (1924), which Beckett bought, as the inscription shows, in February 1936 in Dublin. Beckett also possessed the standards of French and German etymologies, Albert Dauzat's *Dictionnaire étymologique* (1938) and Friedrich Kluge's *Etymologisches Wörterbuch der Deutschen Sprache* (1960).

Beckett's library also contains many language dictionaries, which he acquired throughout his life. Several of them he would have used as a student studying the Romance languages, others may have been kept with a view to advising on translations of his work into various languages.

ENGLISH LANGUAGE DICTIONARIES AND GRAMMARS

Beyond the English dictionaries mentioned above, Beckett owned several books dealing with the proper usage of the English language and grammar. The standard reference works are all present, such as *Fowler's Dictionary of Modern English Usage* (1930 [1926]), probably acquired in the 1930s as it carries the Dublin booksellers' Greene & Co. sticker, and H. W. Fowler and F. G. Fowler's *The King's English* (1962 [1931]). There is also a French book on English grammar, L. Carré's *Eléments de grammaire anglaise* (1928), and two editions of Webster's dictionary (one of them the *New World Dictionary of the American Language*). Beckett also possessed a copy of *Roget's Thesaurus*, although he appears to have found it less useful: 'Can't imagine anyone [feasting?] on Roget. Haven't got a tip from it yet' (letter to Barbara Bray, 16 August 1961; TCD MS10948/1/158).[4]

FRENCH LANGUAGE DICTIONARIES AND GRAMMARS

Beyond the six French dictionaries (French only, French–English and French–Italian) in the library, Beckett acquired several volumes dealing with proper French usage in the 1950s and 1960s, following his transition from writing in English to writing in French and his decision to translate his own works between the two languages. The library contains René Bailly's *Dictionnaire des Synonymes* (1947), the *Dictionnaire de l'argot moderne* (1953), Maurice Rat's *Dictionnaire des locutions françaises* (1957) as well as Maurice Grevisse's *Le Bon Usage: grammaire française* (1969). Only the Larousse *Grammaire supérieure* shows any kind of marginalia, which may or may not be by Beckett; beside the chapter title 'L'interjection' the reference 'voir p.50' has been scribbled (135), and the definition of 'interjection' is indeed marked on that page (50); furthermore, the chapter on 'Le nom' is appended by an asterisk.

ITALIAN LANGUAGE DICTIONARIES AND GRAMMARS

As noted in Chapter 5, many of Beckett's copies of Italian literature dating from his undergraduate days contain translations of words with which the young student was arguably unfamiliar. These undoubtedly derive from *Melzi's Italian–English / English–Italian Dictionary*, which he bought in the first year of his studies; the inscription reads: 'S.B Beckett / Trinity College, Dublin / 1924', and is still in his library. Surprisingly, however, no Italian grammar survives. Yet in 1955 Pamela Mitchell sent Beckett Nicola Zingarelli's *Vocabolario della Lingua Italiana*, published a year earlier.

Thanking her, Beckett wrote that he had 'been reading in your big magnificent Zingarelli with much satisfaction and wishing he was more explicit about the difference between the s's of cosa and rosa and the zz's of mezzo and pazzo' (letter to Pamela Mitchell, 17 February 1955; LSB II 525).[5]

GERMAN LANGUAGE DICTIONARIES AND GRAMMARS

Beckett's library contains no less than nine dictionaries of the German language, in which he was self-taught but, by 1936 at least, proficient (see Chapter 4). Beyond translation dictionaries, the library contains three books on grammar as well the German equivalent of the *Oxford English Dictionary*, *Der Sprach-Brockhaus* (7th edition, 1958 [1951]).

SPANISH AND PORTUGUESE DICTIONARIES AND GRAMMARS

There is evidence that Beckett started to teach himself Spanish in the early 1930s, and that he envisaged a trip to the country, which never materialized. As he told MacGreevy on 22 June 1933: 'I started to work hard at Spanish, and though the occasion to use it has receded I suppose I may as well keep it on' (22 June 1933, TCD MS10402/51). It does not appear as if he pursued this project for very long, although his knowledge was good enough (even if not in his own estimation) to translate the *Anthology of Mexican Poetry* (1958). Published too late to be of any use in such translation exercises, the library contains three Spanish dictionaries and a grammar (L. D. Collier's *Everyday Spanish*; 1982), all dating from the 1980s.

Beckett did, however, make a serious attempt to teach himself Portuguese, and, by his own admission, got to a level that enabled him to read Agatha Christie. His motivation in acquiring Portuguese undoubtedly stemmed from the fact that he was increasingly travelling to Portugal. On 11 December 1968 (TCD MS10948/1/415), writing from Funchal, he told Barbara Bray that he had bought a Portuguese grammar. The book, Jose Nunes de Figueiredo and Antonio Gomes Ferreira's *Compêndio de Gramàtica Portuguesa* (1968), is still in his library. At first he thought it did not 'look too formidable', but confessed twenty days later that he was 'plod[ding] dully through Compendio de Gramatica' (TCD MS10948/1/419). There are minor annotations and corrections on nine pages, which show that Beckett studied the book carefully. Moreover, he found the last chapter 'on what is literature, with examples', to be 'wonderful' (letter to Barbara Bray, 7 January 1969; TCD MS10948/1/420). The chapter in question, 'A língua como expressão literária', is divided into two parts. The first part deals with 'Linguagem corrente e linguagem literária', with sections on figures of speech and style. It includes two examples of manuscript revisions, one by Miguel Torga and one by Aquilina Ribeiro, and argues that 'higher artistic value' can be obtained by means of revision.[6] The second part of the chapter is entitled 'Géneros literários', and discusses the difference between prose and poetry ('prosa e verso'): 'A poesia é uma linguagem muito *mais ritmada* do que a prosa'. The second example, showing that 'a poesia, porque fundada neles, excita a *imaginação*, e provoca a *sugestão*, o *sonho*', is taken from Fernando Pessoa:

> Ó mar salgado, quanto do teu sal
> São lágrimas de Portugal.

This was probably not the only guide he bought that year, as his library also contains copies of a *Dictionnaire Français–Portugais / Português–Francês* and J. W. Barker's Teach Yourself Portuguese – all three volumes published in the same year, 1968).

DICTIONARIES OF QUOTATIONS

As previously indicated in this book, Beckett was not only interested in the way that other writers used words, but was also always on the lookout for lines and phrases that he could appropriate, and make his own. His library thus contains dictionaries of quotations. Chief among these is, naturally enough, Bartlett's *Familiar Quotations*, of which he owned an 1885 edition that he had received from his father, but which is now in private hands.[7]

The library also contains a copy of *The Penguin Dictionary of Quotations* (1972 [1960]), which Barbara Bray sent to Beckett after he had asked her to send it to him 'to supplement my dear old family Bartlett' (16 August 1961; TCD MS10948/1/158), as well as Pierre Oster's *Nouveau Dictionnaire de citations françaises* (1970) and P. Dupré's *Encyclopédie des citations* (1961 [1959]); the latter of these was presented to Beckett by the critic Lawrence Harvey (and his wife) in March 1962. One would expect either of the two French dictionaries of citations to be the source of three quotations using the word 'blanc' which Beckett sent to Bray on 19 July 1962 (TCD MS10948/1/184), but instead he took them from his edition (in seven volumes) of *Littré, Dictionnaire de la langue française en 7 volumes* (1959; I.1054):

> "Mais elle met du blanc et
> veut paraître belle"
>
> (Misanthrope)

> "Loin, ces études d'œillades,
> Ces eaux, ces blancs, ces pommades,
> Et mille ingrédients qui font des teints fleuris. "
>
> (Ecole des Femmes)

> "Point d'autre rouge sur son visage
> que celui que causait la pudeur,
> ni de blanc que celui que donne
> l'abstinence"
>
> (Bossuet: Pensées Chrétiennes)

OTHER DICTIONARIES

It should be noted that Beckett possessed various dictionaries that are not related to language, such as Donald Attwater's *The Penguin Dictionary of Saints* (1966 [1965]), C. H. McDowell's *A Short Dictionary of Mathematics* (1957), *The Nurse's Dictionary of Medical Terms and Nursing Treatment* (n.d. [1895?]), R. Farquharson Sharp's *Biographical Dictionary of Foreign Literature* (1933) and Richard and Maisie Fitter's *The Penguin Dictionary of British Natural History* (1967).[8] All of these volumes attest, as the library generally does, to Beckett's wide-ranging interests, and should be viewed alongside the extensive notes he took from various fields of knowledge in the 1930s. A rather more curious volume, as its title suggests, is *Everybody's Scrapbook of Curious Facts: a Book for Odd Moments*, edited by Don Lemon and published in 1890. Beckett acquired the volume in February 1936 in Dublin (as the inscription shows), and dog-ears within the book show that he spent time looking through or even reading it.

But it is the sheer volume of language dictionaries and grammars that define the nature of Beckett's writing – polyglot and linguistically accurate. This love of language is encapsulated in a line from Beckett's 'From an Abandoned Work': 'I love the word, words have been my only loves, not many' (*TFN* 64).

CHAPTER 10

Science

The most important scientific work in Beckett's library is an edition of Charles Darwin's *On the Origin of Species by Means of Natural Selection or the Preservation of Favoured Races in the Struggle for Life*. Beckett's copy is volume XI of the series 'The World's Classics' ('The Works of Charles Darwin I: *On the Origin of Species*'), published by Grant Richards (London, 1902), based on the text of the second edition (1860).

BIOLOGY: DARWIN (FIRST READING)

In a letter to Thomas MacGreevy, Beckett wrote on 4 August 1932: 'I bought the Origin of Species yesterday for 6d and never read such badly written catlap. I only remember one thing: blue-eyed cats are always deaf (correlation of variations)' (*LSB* III). This account corresponds with one of the very few marginalia in his copy of Darwin's *Origin of Species*. On page 11, in the first chapter (on 'Variation under Domestication'), Beckett has marked and underscored the passage 'cats with blue eyes are invariably deaf' (with an undulating line in grey pencil). As Beckett indicates in his letter, the line is taken from the passage on correlations between variations. Darwin sums up a whole series of examples:

Breeders believe that long limbs are almost always accompanied by an elongated head. Some instances of correlation are quite whimsical; thus cats with blue eyes are invariably deaf; colour and constitutional peculiarities go together, of which many remarkable cases could be given amongst animals and plants. . . . Hairless dogs have imperfect teeth; long-haired and coarse-haired animals are apt to have, as is asserted, long or many horns; pigeons with feathered feet have skin between their outer toes; pigeons with short beaks have small feet, and those with long beaks large feet. (Darwin 1902, 11)

At this point, Beckett does not seem to have been particularly interested in the more theoretical point about the unconscious side effects of breeding

Darwin tried to make, but simply picked out a very concrete example. He did mention the blue-eyed cats in 'What a Misfortune', but he makes the 'colossal Capper' quote Darwin's line 'for no other reason than that the phrase had been running in his mind and now here was a chance to discharge it on a wit' (*MPTK* 125).

The only other pencil mark in the book also concerns a concrete example: in the first part of the important chapter III, on the 'Struggle for Existence', Darwin explains how his theory is in fact 'the doctrine of Malthus applied with manifold force to the whole animal and vegetable kingdoms' (Darwin 1902, 59). In Thomas Malthus' *Essay on the Principle of Population*, Darwin had read that the human population, when unchecked, goes on doubling itself every twenty-five years, or increases in a geometric ratio. Based on this passage, he expounded the principle of the 'struggle for existence' and applied it, not only to human beings, but to all living organisms:

> There is no exception to the rule that every organic being naturally increases at so high a rate, that if not destroyed, the earth would soon be covered by the progeny of a single pair. Even slow-breeding man has doubled in twenty-five years, and at this rate, in a few thousand years, there would literally not be standing room for his progeny. (Darwin 1902, 59)

Darwin subsequently did what he described earlier on: he applied this Malthusian insight to flora and fauna. With reference to flora, Linnaeus had already calculated that an annual plant, producing only two seeds whose seedlings would in their turn produce two seeds the next year etc., would be responsible for a million plants after only twenty years. With reference to fauna, Darwin studies the slowest-breeding animal, and that is the example Beckett has marked with a grey pencil in the margin:

> The elephant is reckoned the slowest breeder of all known animals, and I have taken some pains to estimate its probable minimum rate of natural increase: it will be under the mark to assume that it breeds when thirty years old, and goes on breeding till ninety years old, bringing forth three pairs of young in this interval; if this be so, at the end of the fifth century there would be alive fifteen million elephants, descended from the first pair. (Darwin 1902, 60)

Again, it is a concrete example, which confirms the impression that Beckett was mainly interested in particulars – at least at that moment, in August 1932, shortly after finishing *Dream of Fair to Middling Women*.[1] One year after he had written to MacGreevy that he was 'soiled … with the old demon of notesnatching' (early August 1931, qtd. in Pilling 1999, xiii), and a month after he had vowed he would get over the Joycean influence (28 June

1932, *LSB* 108), the habit of looking for immediately usable phrases (according to Joyce's writing method) still made itself felt.

But the two pencil marks in *The Origin of Species* are merely the first traces of his immediate response to Darwin's theory, which did make a more lasting impression than the qualification 'badly written catlap' may suggest. Apart from the two underlined passages, there is also an instance of what Axel Gellhaus termed 'non-marginalia' (see Chapter 1). This category applies to Darwin's caterpillar, which recurs not just in *Murphy*, but also in *Watt* (see Ackerley and Gontarski 2004, 125–6) and in the story 'Echo's Bones', unpublished in Beckett's lifetime.

In 'Echo's Bones', Belacqua is talking to Doyle, a 'natural man of the world'. They digress and Doyle reminds Belacqua that he was saying 'but' and did not finish his sentence. Belacqua replies that he needs a better cue than that, otherwise he will have to go back to where he started, like the caterpillar: 'My memory has gone to hell altogether' said Belacqua. 'If you can't give me a better cue than that I'll have to be like the embarrassed caterpillar and go back to my origins' (EB 23). With the word 'origins', Beckett obliquely referred to his source text. And no matter how 'badly written' the 'catlap' was, he evidently had a keen interest in Darwin's style and rhetoric, as the use of the word 'embarrassed' suggests. The allusion is to Chapter VII ('Instinct') in the *Origin of Species*, where Darwin – who is usually careful with anthropomorphisms – writes about his colleague P. Huber's description of a caterpillar that was 'much embarrassed':

> if he took a caterpillar which had completed its hammock up to, say, the sixth stage of construction, and put it into a hammock completed up only to the third stage, the caterpillar simply re-performed the fourth, fifth, and sixth stages of construction. If, however, a caterpillar were taken out of a hammock made up, for instance, to the third stage, and were put into one finished up to the sixth stage, so that much of its work was already done for it, far from deriving any benefit from this, *it was much embarrassed*, and in order to complete its hammock, seemed forced to start from the third stage, where it had left off, and thus tried to complete the already finished work. (Darwin 1902, 187; emphasis added)

But there are no markings, not even dog-ears, on the corresponding page in Beckett's copy of *On the Origin of Species* (187). As in the case of the rat and the consecrated wafer in *Curiosités théologiques*, which found their way into *Watt* (see Chapter 8), the most 'useful' passages for Beckett were often non-marginalia, such as the sentence 'Even Ireland has a few animals, now generally regarded as varieties, but which have been ranked as species by some zoologists' in 'Draff' (*MPTK* 171), which is taken integrally from chapter II ('Variations under Nature') in Darwin's *Origin of Species*.[2]

BIOLOGY: DARWIN (SUBSEQUENT READINGS)

After Beckett's initial, somewhat hasty conclusion about Darwin's work, the different kinds of 'marginalia' (pencil marks and dog-ears) suggest that he later reread the book. The different types of reading traces indicate that Beckett must have read the text in bits and pieces, yet they do add up to form a reading pattern that covers the entire book.

In order to map this pattern, the following analysis is an attempt to approach the matter from a bibliographical perspective. Apart from the pencil marks, Beckett's copy also shows signs of remarkably large dog-ears. They occur throughout the book, even in the last chapter:

1) pp. 57–8: opening pages of chapter III, 'Struggle for Existence'
2) pp. 179–80: latter part of chapter VI, 'Difficulties on Theory'
3) pp. 275–6: latter part of chapter IX, 'Imperfection of the Geological Record'
4) pp. 281–2: opening paragraphs of chapter X: 'On the Geological Succession of Organic Beings'
5) pp. 293–4: chapter X, 'On the Geological Succession of Organic Beings'
6) pp. 405–6: chapter XIII: 'Mutual Affinities of Organic Beings: Morphology: Embryology: Rudimentary Organs', subsection 'Rudimentary, atrophied, or aborted organs'

Apart from the first, fourth and sixth dog-ears (marking the opening pages of new chapters or subsections), the function of the other dog-ears is rather enigmatic. Nonetheless, they have one characteristic in common: each contains an expression of the limitations of human knowledge. One of the paragraphs in the section marked by the second dog-ear opens with a very explicit admission of ignorance: 'We are profoundly ignorant of the causes producing slight and unimportant variations' (178).

A similar admission characterizes the following passage on the pages marked by the third dog-ear, relating to the imperfection of the geological record: 'To the question why we do not find records of these vast primordial periods, I can give no satisfactory answer' (313). The passage marked by the fifth dog-ear again features a sentence that exposes human ignorance: 'We know not at all precisely what are all the conditions most favourable for the multiplication of new and dominant species' (292). This focus on ignorance, which later became a cornerstone of Beckett's poetics, accords with the epistemological scepticism in his notes on Geulincx and Mauthner (see Chapter 7).

Between the second and the third dog-ear, there is a gap of almost one hundred pages. Nonetheless, Beckett did read those pages, and made notes on them in his 'Whoroscope' Notebook, notably on chapters VII ('Instinct') and

VIII ('Hybridism'). Among the notes 'FOR INTERPOLATION' at the back of the 'Whoroscope' Notebook, the entry 'Darwin poring over the aphides' (WN 145v) most probably refers, as John Pilling has suggested (Pilling 2006c, 211), to a passage from chapter VII on instincts. Darwin mentions the aphids, voluntarily yielding their sweet excretion to ants, as one of the most remarkable instances of an animal apparently performing an action for the sole good of another. According to Darwin, this is only 'apparently' the case, for after an experiment, involving his tickling and stroking the aphids in the manner of an ant, he concludes that it is not an example of pure altruism after all: 'as the excretion is extremely viscid, it is probably a convenience to the aphides to have it removed; and therefore probably the aphides do not instinctively excrete for the sole good of the ants' (Darwin 1860, 211).

On page 80r of the 'Whoroscope' Notebook, Beckett jotted down 'danger-chuckle of hen / (Origin of Species 194)', corresponding to a passage on the loss of fear. The next entry on page 80r, 'Mr. Pistil and Miss Stamen', seems to be a short relapse into Joycean-style 'notesnatching', but it is followed by two more serious, academic notes with page references: 'American cuckoo makes her own nest (Ib. 195)' and 'slave-making ants (FORMICA rufescens – European & Formica sanguinea – British.). The slave Formica fusca (Ib. 196 sqq.)'. After a short interruption ('613 commandments of the Jews'), Beckett's notes on Darwin continue in brown pencil:

> hybrid = offspring of crossed species
> mongrel = "   "   "   varieties[3]

He then proceeded to copy out the following passage

> I think those authors right, who maintain that the ass has a prepotent power over the horse, so that both the mule & the hinny more resemble the ass than the horse; but that the prepotency runs more strongly in the male-ass than in the female-ass, so that the mule, which is the offspring of the male-ass & mare, is more like an ass than is the hinny, which is the offspring of the female ass & stallion. (Darwin 1902, 246)

At this point in the 'Whoroscope' Notebook, the Darwin material is interrupted by one of Beckett's favourite lines from Dante's Inferno:

> hoarse from long silence: Virgil to Dante
> (chi per lungo silenzio parea fioco; Inf I) (qtd. in Caselli 2005, 153)[4]

Still, Darwin continued to be on his mind. The excerpt regarding asses and horses derived from page 246. Fewer than forty pages further on (281–2), Beckett's copy of *The Origin of Species* features the traces of another typically large dog-ear, followed by another one on pages 293–4. The next entry in the 'Whoroscope' Notebook (WN 81r) is the word 'Inosculation' (etymologically derived from Lat. 'inosculare', to kiss), which possibly derives from Darwin. It occurs only once in *On the Origin of Species*, in chapter XII ('Geographical Distribution – continued', 345),[5] about fifty-five pages after the dog-ear on pages 293–4 and about sixty-five pages before the last dog-ear on pages 405–6.

According to John Pilling it is 'virtually certain' that all of the notes 'FOR INTERPOLATION' at the back of the 'Whoroscope' Notebook were entered 'before *Murphy* was brought to its "first end" (as described in a letter to Thomas MacGreevy of 9 June 1936)' (Pilling 2006c, 205). The Darwin entry among these notes (WN 145v) at the back of the notebook derives from chapter VII, a mere five pages before the passage on which the 'danger-chuckle of hen' (WN 80r) is based. The following chart maps the distribution of the notes:

Darwin, *Origin of Species* page	Beckett as marginalist		Beckett as extractor 'Whoroscope' Nb.	
	pencil marks	dog-ears	front to back	back to front
11	x			
57–58		x		
60	x			
176–80		x		
190				x [145r]
194			x [80r]	
195			x [80r]	
196			x [80r]	
244			x [80r]	
246			x [80r]	
275–6		x		
281–2		x		
293–4		x		
345			x [81r]	
405–6	x			

But even though the 'distance' between the passages on the aphids and the danger-chuckle is only four pages in Darwin's text, the interruption of Beckett's reading may have amounted to several years. The location of Beckett's jottings from the January 1939 article 'Is There Life in Other Worlds?' by H. Spencer Jones[6] on pages 62r and 63r suggests that the subsequent notes, including the Darwin notes on page 80r, date from later than January 1939.

If the notes 'FOR INTERPOLATION' were written in the first half of 1936; if the order of the other notes reflects the chronology in which they were jotted down; and if the notes from *Discovery* (January 1939) serve as a *terminus a quo*, there may have been a gap of almost three years between the note on the aphids (145v) and the other Darwin notes (80r–81r). And in between, Beckett may also have read the *Voyage of the Beagle*, since he wrote in the 'Whoroscope' Notebook: '– as the Diodon eats its way out of the shark (Voyage of the Beagle 27–28[)]' (WN 73v).

Apart from the embarrassed caterpillar, Beckett's use of his notes on Darwin in his later works is less explicit. In the original manuscript of Beckett's translation of *Fin de partie*, for instance, Hamm's exclamation with regard to the flea was more explicit in its reference to the theory of evolution as the verb was to 'evolve' instead of the variant 'start' in the published text: 'A flea! But from there humanity might [evolve] all over again!' (HRC MS215, 31r). Darwin proved to be just as useful for Beckett's 'decreation' as the Book of Genesis, which he had been rereading in preparation of *Fin de partie*, 'wishing the Almighty had never had a soft spot for Noah' (qtd. in Knowlson 1996, 406; see chapters 3 and 8).

Apart from the *Origin of Species*, the library contains a few books on biology and 'natural history', such as Richard and Maisie Fitter's *Penguin Dictionary of Natural History* (1967), the two-volume Larousse edition of *La Vie des animaux* (1952), Konrad Z. Lorenz's *King Solomon's Ring: New Light on Animal Ways* (1965) and Jean Rostand's *Inquiétudes d'un biologiste* (1967), which Beckett read in Tangier on 12 February 1978. On the inside of the back cover, Beckett has noted page numbers '29–30' and '67 dieux ahuris', corresponding with Rostand's remark that science may explain everything without however making us more enlightened; it will turn us into bewildered gods.[7] From the preceding page, Beckett excerpted the following line in his letter to Barbara Bray of 12 February: 'Le biologiste passe, la grenouille reste', followed by the laconic comment: 'Ask the grenouille' (TCD MS10948/1/626).

PHYSICS, ASTRONOMY

Not all the scientific books Beckett once read have been preserved. For instance, the library does not contain Minchin's *Student's Dynamics* or Poincaré's *La Valeur de la science*, from which he took notes in his 'Whoroscope' Notebook in 1938, shortly before he read the article by

Spencer Jones, 'Is There Life in Other Worlds?' The content of this article reflects an interest of Beckett's in stars and planets, which was already apparent in the notes in the 'Dream' Notebook based on Sir James Jeans's chapter 'Exploring the Sky' from *The Universe Around Us* (1929; *DN* 1040–67), notably the references to Venus in the 'Dream' and 'Whoroscope' notebooks:

<u>Venus</u>: <u>Morning</u>   <u>Evening</u>
        Phosp[h]orus Hesperus
        Lucifer

(*DN* 1046)

<u>Venus</u>.
'Venus has a long day' –
about 30 of ours.
Temp. of sunlit face = 80° or 90° F.
————dark   "   = 40°   "
Covered with dense permanent layer of clouds.
Scarcity of oxygen, abundance of carbon dioxide – as at beginning of life on earth.
Venus [cooling] planet where life may be present when on Earth extinct.

(WN 63r)

For instance, Spencer Jones suggests that 'when life on the Earth may be nearing extinction, Venus may be the home of higher and higher types of life' (44). Beckett's note on the 'planet where life may be present when on Earth extinct' reads as a strikingly positive counterpart to Hamm's fear that humanity might evolve all over again from a single flea.

Together with the presence in Beckett's library of books such as Bruno H. Bürgel's *Les Mondes lointains* (1944) and Pierre Rousseau's *Explorations du ciel* (1939), the notes on Jeans and Spencer Jones mark a preoccupation that kept surfacing as late as the last decade of Beckett's career, during the composition of *Mal vu mal dit / Ill Seen Ill Said* ('From where she lies she sees Venus rise'; *CIWS* 45) and *Stirrings Still / Soubresauts* ('the thought of one hastening westward at sundown to obtain a better view of Venus'; *CIWS* 111).

In Rousseau's *Explorations du ciel*, two marginal pencil lines on page 33 (in the chapter on 'La Famille des planètes') mark the distance to the moon '384 000 kilomètres (Fig. 6)' and the way to calculate it, making use of the parallax (see *Figure 9*).

Figure 6 (with the caption 'Comment on mesure la distance de la lune') illustrates this 'parallax'. It is not unlikely that this notion may have reminded Beckett of Leopold Bloom's ruminations on the same concept in Joyce's *Ulysses*. Bloom knows the word from one of the items on his own

208   Samuel Beckett's Library

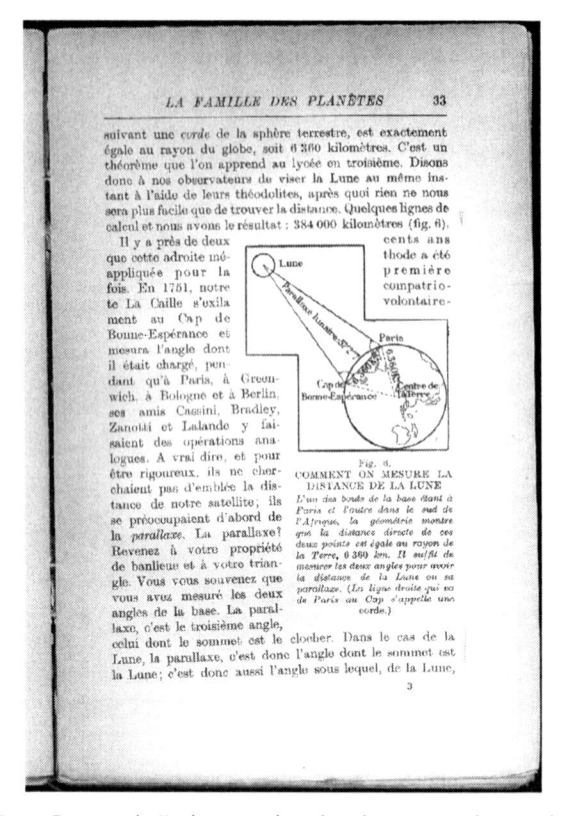

Figure 9 Pierre Rousseau's *Explorations du ciel*, with Fig. 6, explaining the notion of 'parallax' and the way to measure the distance from the moon.

bookshelf: Sir Robert Ball's *The Story of the Heavens*. In an effort to explain his branch of science to a general audience, Ball notes that 'it is by parallax that the distance of the sun, or, indeed, the distance of any other celestial body, must be determined'. He then invites his readers to do a small experiment:

Stand near a window whence you can look at buildings, or the trees, the clouds, or any distant objects. Place on the glass a thin strip of paper vertically in the middle of one of the panes. Close the right eye, and note with the left eye the position of the strip of paper relatively to the objects in the background. Then, while still remaining in the same position, close the left eye and again observe the position of the strip of paper with the right eye. You will find that the position of the paper on the background has changed. … This apparent displacement of the strip of paper, relatively to the distant background, is what is called parallax. (Ball 1892, 151)

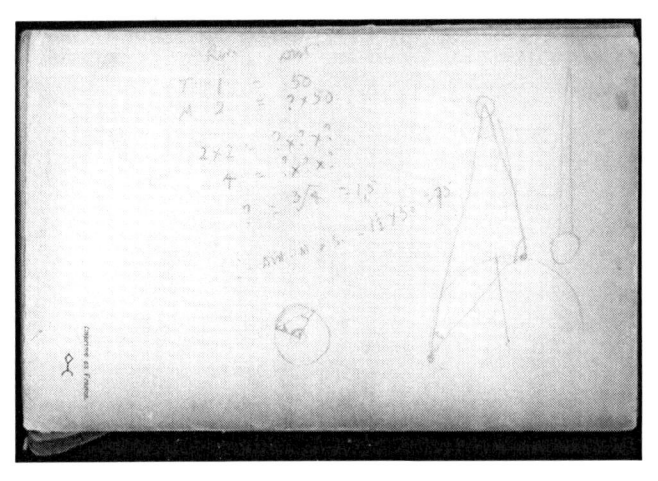

Figure 10 Back cover of Pierre Rousseau's *Explorations du ciel*

The passage is part of chapter VIII, 'Venus', for the parallax is used as part of Halley's method of finding the distance of the sun by means of the transit of Venus. Not unlike Joyce, in whose work the notion of parallax serves as a metaphor for modernist perspectivism, Beckett seems to have taken a similar metaphorical interest in the concept. On the back cover of Rousseau's *Explorations du ciel* he has drawn a sketch, similar to Fig. 6, and made some calculations to measure the 'Dist. M. à S. = 1 ½ x 50 = 75' (see *Figure 10*).

Whereas Joyce's 'parallax' consisted of different pairs of eyes looking at the same object, such as Stephen and Bloom looking at the same cloud respectively from positions in Sandycove and Dublin, resulting in different, yet equally gloomy thoughts on a sunny day, Beckett applied the concept to a more reflexive form of perspectivism. The drawing of Fig. 6 resembles the sketch in the stage directions of the television play . . . *but the clouds* . . ., and the cube root of four next to Beckett's parallax drawing on the back of Rousseau's *Explorations du ciel* suggests that Beckett, not unlike Mr. Nackybal in *Watt* and 'V' in . . . *but the clouds* . . ., used to busy himself with 'something more rewarding, such as . . . such as . . . cube roots, for example' (*ATF* 140).

In *L'Innommable*, Malone is compared to a planet revolving in an orbit. The Unnamable speaks of 'the transit of Malone' and suggests he can 'work out to within a few inches the orbit of Malone, assuming perhaps erroneously that he passes before me at a distance of say three feet' (9). The reference to the transit of Venus suggests an analogy between the heliocentric 'I' and the sun: 'I like to think I occupy the centre' and Malone 'wheels ... about me, like a planet about its sun' (5). He 'appears and disappears with the punctuality of clockwork, always at the same remove' (4) – 'toujours à la même distance de moi' (Beckett 1953, 13) in the French version. More than forty years later, Beckett started the first draft of what was eventually to become *Stirrings Still / Soubresauts* with the same line: 'tout toujours à la même distance' (UoR MS2933/1, 1r; BDMP1), and on the verso side of the manuscript, he drew a sketch that shows some resemblance to the parallax drawing. The sketch is followed by the caption 'In the mind too – Too?' (UoR MS2933/1, 1v;[8] Van Hulle 2011, 53).

PSYCHOLOGY

Applying the notion of parallax to the mind, possibly as a means to determine the distance to the self, is part of Beckett's way of discovering dramatic and narrative potential in philosophical, psychological or scientific images. A similar case is the entry 'the geology of conscience – Cambrian experience, cainozoic judgments, etc.' in the 'Whoroscope' Notebook, based on a passage in *L'Imagination* (141, 144ff) where Jean-Paul Sartre speaks of 'a 'géométrie' in Husserl' (Pilling 2005, 46; see also Chapter 7). The last chapter of Sartre's book is completely devoted to Edmund Husserl's phenomenology. From Husserl, Sartre derived the notions of 'noème' and 'noèse' (respectively denoting the object of thought and the act of thought; Sartre 1936, 51),[9] noted down by Beckett in the 'Whoroscope' Notebook (WN 62r). The next note corresponds with a passage in the last chapter (Sartre 1936, 141; 144ff.), where Sartre compares Husserl's phenomenology to geometry. Beckett seems to have been inspired by Sartre's suggestion and, after changing 'géométrie' into 'the geology of conscience – Cambrian experience, cainozoic judgments, etc.', he drew a 'Table of Geological Eras' on the back of the page (62v). As John Pilling notes, Beckett here employs the word 'conscience' in the French sense, meaning sensibility or consciousness (Pilling 2005, 46). The order of the notes (62r: Sartre; Spencer Jones / 62v: Table of geological eras / 63r: Spencer Jones – contd.) suggests that Beckett read Sartre in the autumn of 1938 or around January 1939, when Spencer Jones' article was published in *Discovery*.[10] A palpable trace of this reading is a postcard inserted on page 18, showing the Sugar Loaf Mountains, Greystones (see *Figure 11*). Greystones is the place where Beckett's father was buried.

Figure 11 Postcard of the Sugar Loaf Mountains, Greystones, inserted in Sartre's *L'Imagination*

Beckett did not fully develop the idea of the 'geology' of consciousness, but he did refer to it in the second *Watt* notebook. The material circumstance of Beckett's reading and the inserted postcard becomes thematic:

'Never mind that now' cried Arsene. 'Dig! Delve! Deeper! Deeper! The Cambrian! The uterine! The pre-uterine!'
'The pre-uterine' we said. 'No. That reminds us of the rocks at Greystones.'

(qtd. in Nixon 2011, 53)

Beckett's own idea of a geology of consciousness is implicitly rejected because of the reminder of the father – the pre-uterine era. This Beckettian variation on Ariel's 'full fathom five' is a complex comment on the theme of depth that runs through the 'Whoroscope' Notebook, including 'das fruchtbare Bathos der Erfahrung (Kant)' with its explanation 'Bathos = deep (Gr.) !' at the bottom of page 51v. Beckett made this self-criticism more explicit in *L'Innommable / The Unnamable*: 'Y a-t-il d'autres fonds, plus bas? Auxquels on accède par celui-ci? Stupide hantise de la profondeur'. (Beckett 1953, 11) / 'Are there other pits, deeper down? To which one accedes by mine? Stupid obsession with depth' (*Un* 3). And even in the later work, Beckett seems to mock his earlier self's preoccupation with depth, for instance in ... *but the clouds* ..., where 'V' mentions 'case nought', 'deep down into the dead of night', when he busied himself 'with nothing': 'busied myself with nothing, that MINE' (*ATF* 140). The pun on 'mine' (see Chapter 5), suggesting a connection between the 'I' and a mine shaft through different layers not only shows congruence with the geology of consciousness, but also with one of Sigmund Freud's favourite metaphors: the 'archaeology' of the mind.

Beckett's interwar psychology notes (Feldman 2006a; Frost and Maxwell 2006) seem to have been based on borrowed books. The few psychology-related books in his personal library date from much later, the earliest one from 1953: Ernest Jones's *Sigmund Freud: Life and Work* (3 vols, 1953). In a letter of 7 May 1934 to Con Leventhal, Beckett wrote: 'There seems to be no limit to my redemption. There's a great article in Freud called "displacement upward", a neurotic device of great popularity' (qtd. in Nixon 2011, 41; see also Pilling 2006a, 46). Pilling notes that Beckett had read about this concept in Ernest Jones's *Papers on Psychoanalysis*. It also occurs in *Sigmund Freud: Life and Work*. In volume 2 – 'Years of Maturity 1901–1919' – Jones mentions Freud's suggestion that 'stammering could be caused by a displacement upwards of conflicts over excremental functions' (II.183).

The other books relating to Freud all date from the 1960s and 1970s. They deal with biography rather than psychoanalysis: Sigmund Freud, *Briefe 1873–1939* (1960), Octave Mannoni's *Freud* (1968) and *The Freud-Jung Letters: The Correspondence between Sigmund Freud and C.G. Jung* (ed. William McGuire, transl. Ralph Manheim and R. F. C. Hull, 1974). None of them contain marginalia. Nevertheless, Beckett did enjoy reading about Freud. After having thanked Barbara Bray on 26 June 1959 for 'the Freud' [Ernest Jones's *Sigmund Freud*], which he was 'delighted to have' (TCD MS10948/1/37), he told her on 7 August that he had 'Read the Freud with great enjoyment – incredible [suffering] and [fortitude] of last fifteen years. Amazing story of his strictures on Céline's Voyage which Marie Bonaparte sent him and he tried to read to please her' (TCD MS 10948/1/41). The passage Beckett was struck by is a letter from 26 March 1933, in which Freud tells Marie Bonaparte that he is half-way through Céline's *Voyage au bout de la nuit* and that he is only reading it because she wished him to: 'I have no taste for this depicting of misery, for the description of the senselessness and emptiness of our present-day life, without any artistic or philosophical background. I demand something other from art than realism' (Jones 1953, 3.188).

Freud is also 'marginally' present in the library, in Cassirer's essay on Kant (see Chapter 7). Next to the marked passage 'Der "bestirnte Himmel über mir und das moralische Gesetz in mir"' (Cassirer in Kant XI.284), Beckett wrote in the left margin (grey pencil): '"The stars are undoubtedly superb ..."'. This is the line referred to by 'B.' in the second of the *Three Dialogues with Georges Duthuit*: 'The stars are undoubtedly superb, as Freud remarked on reading Kant's cosmological proof of the existence of God' (*Dis* 141). According to David Hatch, the passage mentioned by 'B.' derives from the 1932 essay 'The Dissection of the Psychical Personality', in which Freud discusses the formation of the super-ego and the origin of conscience. Freud refers to the conclusion of the *Critique of Practical Reason*, in which Kant claims that there are two things that imbue the mind with a feeling of admiration and reverence: the star-clad sky above us and the moral law within ourselves. Freud's response to Kant's statement is that the stars are undoubtedly superb, but with regard to conscience God has done an uneven and careless piece of work (Baker 1997; Hatch 2003, 62–3). Phil Baker first traced Freud's line to the chapter 'Anatomy of the Mental Personality' in his *New Introductory Lectures on Psychoanalysis* (Baker 1997, 177) and as Matthew Feldman has shown, Beckett typed out the following passage among his psychology notes, under the heading 'Id, Ego & Superego': 'The philosopher Kant once declared that nothing proved to him the greatness of God more convincingly than the starry heavens and the moral conscience within us. The stars are unquestionably superb...' (TCD MS10971/7, 6r; Feldman 2006a, 30). Apart from the variant ('undoubtedly' instead of 'unquestionably') the marginalia in Cassirer ends with the same, telling ellipsis.

CHAPTER 11

Music and Art

In his critical essays, Beckett frequently stated that literature lagged behind music and the visual arts in its capacity to express the human condition. In his letter to Axel Kaun of 9 July 1937 he stated that literature was 'left behind on that old, foul road long ago abandoned by music and painting' (*LSB* 518). Beckett's library bears witness to his love of art and music.

MUSIC

Unlike in other fields of knowledge, Beckett does not appear to have studied the history of music in any concerted way, although his library does contain Percy A. Scholes' *The Oxford Companion to Music* (1944 [1938]) and the *Larousse de la Musique* in two volumes (1957).[1] Instead, as his letters show, Beckett avidly attended concerts and listened to music on the radio. Moreover, he was a good pianist and had pianos in both Ussy and in Paris; numerous piano scores that he used survive. Beckett's taste in music was varied, ranging from the more traditional to contemporary, dodecaphonic music. In particular, he admired romantic music and German *Lieder*, especially those composed by Schubert. Beckett's deep engagement with classical music influenced his work both thematically in the form of references and structurally through the employment of techniques drawn from music. Moreover, Beckett also read more theoretical and philosophical studies of music, such as Schopenhauer's chapter on music in *Die Welt als Wille und Vorstellung* (letter to MacGreevy, July 1930). And in 1960, Theodor Adorno sent Beckett his study of Mahler (TCD MS10948/1/111), although it is not clear whether he read it or not.

BEETHOVEN

The German composer Ludwig van Beethoven is present throughout Beckett's work, and played an important part in his aesthetic thinking. Beckett's exposure to Beethoven's work came, unsurprisingly, by hearing the music played in concerts. His response was, at first, not always positive, and a 1931 letter shows that he felt that 'Beethoven's Quartets are a waste of time' (letter to MacGreevy,

24 February 1931; *LSB* 68). By 1934, however, his opinion of the String Quartets had changed considerably, especially after attending two of the six concerts played by the Busch Quartet in February and March 1934. In particular, he was drawn to Beethoven's last quartet, Opus 135 in F Major, which was constructed around 'Der schwergefasste Entschluss' [the difficult decision] in the form of the line 'Muss es sein? Es muss sein! Es muss sein!' In anticipation of hearing the Quartet played on 17 March 1934, Beckett discussed the piece in a letter of 4 March 1934 to Morris Sinclair and noted down part of the score (*LSB* 194).[2] The reference to the inevitability of death (perhaps unsurprisingly) reappears in Beckett's poem 'Malacoda' – 'must it be it must be it must be' – written shortly after his father's death.

Beckett's knowledge of Beethoven's work and life also derives from his reading, in the first instance of Romain Rolland's *Vie de Beethoven*, from which he took six entries in the 'Dream' Notebook (1105–10). Beyond showing an interest in Beethoven's piece 'An die ferne Geliebte', Beckett was struck by Beethoven's own description of the Seventh Symphony as being 'aufgeknöpft' (unbuttoned). In 'What a Misfortune', Belacqua connects happy recollections of Lucy with 'the first movement of the Unbuttoned Symphony' (*MPTK* 131). Moreover, Beckett combines this phraseology with the composer's relationship with Teresa of Brunswick ('another unsterbliche Geliebte', *DN* 1106), as in his reference in *Dream* to a 'Beethofen' who 'unbuttons himself to Teresa' (138).

Beckett's first novel *Dream of Fair to Middling Women* could be seen as an attempt to textually 'score' Beethoven's music, in that it tries to inscribe his aesthetic thinking about silences and pauses. This is most obvious in Belacqua's statements of artistic intent, which refer to Beethoven's 'vespertine compositions eaten away with terrible silences':

I think of his [Beethoven's] earlier compositions where into the body of the musical statement he incorporates a punctuation of dehiscence, flottements, the coherence gone to pieces. (*Dream* 138–9)

In formulating this poetics of 'dehiscence', Beckett harnessed a particular identification of Beethoven's music as expressing an 'incoherent continuum' (*Dream* 102). He returned to the same idea repeatedly in the 1930s, as when he told MacGreevy that in *Thorns of Thunder*, an English selection of Eluard's poetry, 'no attempt seems to have been made to translate the pauses', comparing this failure to 'Beethoven played strictly to time' (17 July [1936]; *LSB* 359). It finds a more elaborate expression in the letter to Axel Kaun of July 1937, in which Beckett invokes Beethoven's Seventh Symphony ('the dearest of the nine'; letter to MacGreevy, 19 October 1958) to express his feelings of dissatisfaction with language:

Gibt es irgendeinen Grund, warum jene fürchterlich willkürliche Materialität der Wortfläche nicht aufgelöst werden sollte, wie z.B. die von grossen schwarzen Pausen gefressene Tonfläche in der siebten Symphonie von Beethoven, so dass wir sie ganze Seiten durch nicht anders wahrnehmen können als etwa einen schwindelnden unergründliche Schlünde von Stillschweigen verknüpfenden Pfad von Lauten?

[Is there any reason why that terribly arbitrary materiality of the word surface should not be dissolved, as for example the sound surface of Beethoven's Seventh Symphony is devoured by huge black pauses, so that for pages on end we cannot perceive it as other than a dizzying path of sounds connecting unfathomable chasms of silence?] (*LSB* 514, 518–19)

Beckett's early encounter with Beethoven's work via Rolland's study threw a long shadow. When he came to translate Georges Duthuit's essay on the American painter Sam Francis into English for the journal *Nimbus* (June–August 1953 issue), he recalled Beethoven's claim in a letter to Franz von Brunswick that 'Mein Reich ist in der Luft' [My kingdom is in the air] (*DN* 1110). In his essay, Duthuit states that 'Sam Francis is concerned with air itself', and expands this theory through several paragraphs. In translating these passages, Beckett inserted the reference to Beethoven (UoR MS2926, 21r). Georges Duthuit was not pleased, as a letter to Mary Hutchinson reveals: 'Dans l'article sur Sam Francis veuillez enlever la phrase sur Beethoven et le Kingdom of the air. C'est Beckett qui l'a ajoutée pour s'amuser, mais ça ne va pas' (7 February 1953).[3]

If Rolland's book on Beethoven does not survive in the library, two other books on 'vénérable Ludwig' do (letter to Morris Sinclair, 4 March 1934; *LSB* 194). Both books, Leopold Schmidt's *Beethoven, Werke und Leben* (1924) and the volume *Beethoven im Gespräch* (1959), show reading traces in the form of dog-ears. In the latter, one of the pages (64) that has been folded down at some point describes Beethoven's feelings of happiness (he feels 'aufgeknöpft'). Another is on page 77, at the point when the essay covering the relationship between Beethoven and Schubert begins.[4]

SCHUBERT

Beckett's attraction to the musical form of the *Lied* is well known, as is his admiration of the composer Franz Schubert. In the confluence of text and music, mood and tone, Beckett found an expression of suffering and of *Schwermut* with which he could identify. As Miron Grindea has noted, the 'composer who spoke most to him was Schubert, whom he considered a friend in suffering' (qtd. in Bryden 1998b, 183). As already discussed (Chapter 4), Beckett's engagement with Schubert's *Lieder*, and the texts that underlie them,

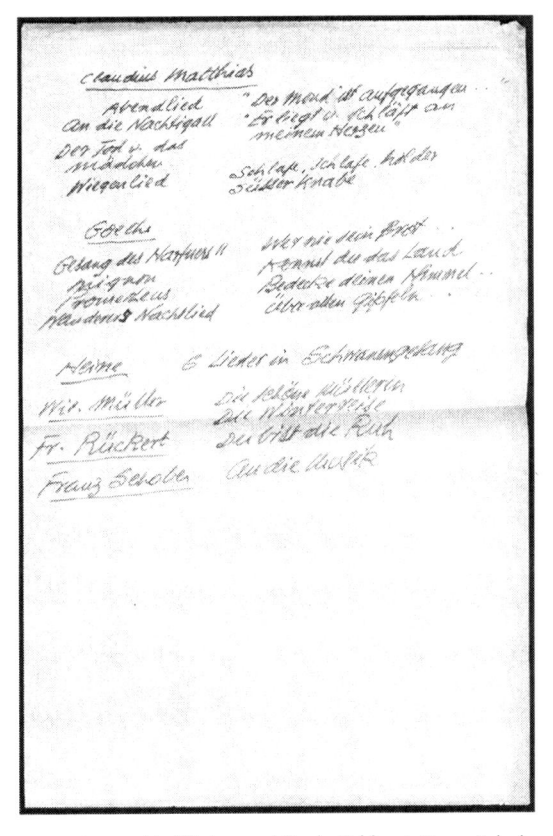

Figure 12 *Loose page inserted in Walter and Paula Rehberg's* Franz Schubert, sein Leben und Werk *(1947[1946])*

is evident from his copy of Walter and Paula Rehberg's *Franz Schubert, sein Leben und Werk* (1947[1946]). Beckett bought the book in 1969: 'stood myself I fear a dull life & work of Schubert of bisexual Swiss authorship' (letter to Barbara Bray, 2 September 1969; TCD MS10948/1/432). Six weeks later he told her, while in Nabeul, that 'Schubert biography (poor) nearly ausgelesen [finished reading]' (17 October 1969; TCD MS10948/1/444). The book contains interesting reading traces: having marked the names of specific poets and particular texts in the index of the book, Beckett proceeded to copy out the titles and first lines of various poems set to music by Schubert on a separate piece of paper (see *Figure 12*).

Leaving aside the *Lieder* of poems by Claudius, Goethe and Heine (as discussed in Chapter 4), we find evidence here of Beckett's favourite cycles and songs. Thus, for example, Beckett marks Schubert's setting of Franz Schober's poem 'An die Musik', which he had copied out, with musical score, in the 'Whoroscope' Notebook (WN 46v). Beckett referenced the piece in 'Walking Out', as the short story closes with Belacqua listening to 'An die Musik' with Lucy on the 'gramophone' (*MPTK* 105).[5] He also notes down the *Lied* 'Du bist die Ruh' by Franz Rückert, which he would praise in conversation with Anne Atik and Avigdor Arikha in the 1960s (Atik 2001, 67). More importantly, he annotates the two substantial Schubert *Lieder* cycles, *Die schöne Müllerin* and *Winterreise*. Both set to music texts by Wilhelm Müller, a writer who died at the age of 33 as Schubert was working on the latter cycle. Indeed, Schubert himself would not see the publication of the second volume of the twenty-four songs of *Winterreise*, which was published in 1828.

Beckett was already familiar with Schubert's *Lieder* as a young man (see, for example, his letter to MacGreevy of 24 February 1931), and *Winterreise* in particular formed a subtext, or rather a musical background, to many of his works. In 1956 he heard the famous interpreter of Schubert's *Lieder*, Dietrich Fischer-Dieskau, sing *Winterreise* in Paris (letter to Robert Pinget, 8 March 1956; *LSB II* 604), and in July of the same year expressed his hope of acquiring a recording (letter to Thomas MacGreevy, 30 July 1956; *LSB II* 640). The symbolic 'winter journey' crops up in several of Beckett's texts, from the *Textes pour rien* through to *What Where* ('It is winter. Without journey'; *CDW* 476).[6] Beckett's most profound use of one of Schubert's *Lieder* occurs in the TV play *Nacht und Träume* (originally called *Nachtstück*), which uses the last seven bars of Schubert's late *Lied* of the same name (with words by Matthäus Casimir von Collin).[7]

Mirroring Beckett's interest in Schubert, the library contains three further works beyond the one by the Rehbergs, Annette Kolb's biography *Franz Schubert: Sein Leben* (1968 [1941]), *Schubert: Die Dokumente seines Lebens*, edited by Otto Erich Deutsch (1980 [1964]), and Gerald Moore's *The Schubert Song Cycle and Thoughts on Performance* (1975), none of which contains any marginalia.

Although Beckett favoured Schubert, he also admired the *Lieder* of Robert Schumann, in particular his cycle *Dichterliebe*, setting poems by Heinrich Heine.

SCHOENBERG

Although Beckett's musical tastes were firmly rooted in traditional classical music, he did take an interest in contemporary composers, particularly in the 1950s. As Avigdor Arikha recalls, 'We had a period during which we listened to quite a bit of dodecaphonic music – Schoenberg, Berg, Webern (before 1959)' (qtd. in Knowlson 1996, 496). By all accounts he thought that the work of the Austrian composer Arnold Schoenberg, whose innovative experiments in atonality led to his development of the twelve-tone row, was particularly interesting. Beckett possessed H. H. Stuckenschmidt's book *Arnold Schoenberg: His Life, World and Work*, published in an English translation by Calder in 1959. As Beckett told Barbara Bray, he read the book in 1963 (20 August 1963; TCD MS10948/1/243). A further book in the library testifies to Beckett's interest in contemporary music, André Hodeir's study *Since Debussy: A View of Contemporary Music* (1961).

VISUAL ARTS

Given Beckett's profound interest in painting and other visual arts, the sparse collection of books in his library is surprising. However, Beckett gave the bulk of his art catalogues and books on art to his friend, the painter Avigdor Arikha, including his copy of Vasari's *Lives of the Painters* and an annotated copy of Poussin's letters (*Lettres et propos sur l'art*, 1964) he had in fact received from Arikha (Atik 2001, 100). Among the books Beckett gave to Arikha were also the art catalogues he had bought during his *Kunstreise* through Germany from October 1936 to April 1937, during which he viewed and took notes on literally hundreds of paintings and art objects in his 'German Diaries'.[8]

The art books which are extant in his library are mostly exhibition catalogues of painter friends, many of which are inscribed. There are thus more than 20 catalogues and books by Avigdor Arikha in the library, as well as volumes by Louis Le Brocquy, Bram and Geer van Velde and Henri Hayden. There are also presentation copies of catalogues by other artists such as Anne Madden, or Vadim Sidur, whose sculpture stood on the window-ledge outside the window of Beckett's office in the Boulevard St Jacques. The only exceptions to this rule are copies of C. R. Leslie's *Memoirs of the Life of John Constable* (1980 [1951]), the *Zeichnungen von Sandro Botticelli zu Dantes Göttlicher Komödie* in an 1896 edition and a catalogue of Hercules Seghers' *Grafiek* from an exhibition in Amsterdam in 1967.

The only book on the visual arts containing marginalia in the library is the volume *Jack B. Yeats, a Centenary Gathering*, edited by Roger McHugh and published by the Dolmen Press in 1971. The book contains Beckett's two essays, 'MacGreevy on Yeats' and 'Hommage a Jack B. Yeats', and is heavily annotated in pencil. However, the marginalia are presumably not by Beckett, especially as one of the handwritten notes reads 'Beckett?' The library also contains a copy of Hilary Pyle's biography of Jack Yeats (1970), which was presented to Beckett by Alan Clodd.

Concluding Marginalia

> No poet, no artist of any art, has his complete meaning alone. His significance, his appreciation is the appreciation of his relation to the dead poets and artists. You cannot value him alone; you must set him, for contrast and comparison, among the dead. (T. S. Eliot, 'Tradition and the Individual Talent')

A remarkable book in Beckett's library is Ludovic Lalanne's *Curiosités littéraires* (see Chapter 3). It provided Beckett with a comprehensive survey of the extent to which intertextuality (before the term had been coined) marks all forms of literature, even the most celebrated works by the most 'original' minds of all ages, such as Dante, Shakespeare and Milton. The interconnections are not 'invisible threads' but 'powerful links', according to Lalanne (1857, 112).

Beckett was painfully aware of these links and he was uncomfortable when he felt too close to the writings of his contemporaries. In his letter to Hans Naumann of 17 February 1954, for instance, he claimed he had stopped reading Kafka's *Das Schloss* toward the end, because he felt too much at home – 'je m'y suis senti chez moi, trop' (*LSB II* 462). The extant library reflects this wariness of literary domesticity: it is remarkable how many of the books that are preserved are by 'old masters', often in other languages than English. It was easier to keep a distance from Walther von der Vogelweide than from Kafka. To some extent the distance in time, as well as in space, seems to have served as a warranty, guaranteeing the books' foreignness, a safeguard against too close proximity. The many references to passages in foreign languages in this book reflect this characteristic aspect of Beckett's multilingual reading experience.

Paradoxically, Beckett tended to return to the 'old chestnuts' because they gave him more clues as to the future of literature than did contemporary or 'modern' literature. Beckett especially appreciated their know-how, or '*vieilles compétences*', as recorded by Anne Atik:

All writing is a sin against speechlessness. Trying to find a form for that silence. Only a few, Yeats, Goethe, those who lived for a long time, could go on to do it, but they had recourse to known forms and fictions. So one finds oneself going back to *vieilles compétences* – how to escape that. One can never get over the fact, never rid oneself of the old dream of giving a form to speechlessness. (Atik 2001, 95)

He applied techniques he appreciated, such as the monologues in Racine's plays, and when he reread the old masters he retroactively recognized the correspondence. More than two decades after having lectured on Racine's complexity at TCD, Beckett still appreciated Racine's plays for the same reasons. After having heard 'a marvelous Bérénice on the air', Beckett wrote to Thomas MacGreevy on 27 September 1953: 'There too nothing happens, they just talk, but what talk, and how spoken' (*LSB II* 407). And on 4 June 1956 he told MacGreevy: 'I read Andromaque again with greater admiration than ever and I think more understanding, at least more understanding of the chances of the theatre to-day' (*LSB II* 624).

Whenever Beckett referred to his 'old chestnuts', the expression implied an interest both in the works and in the lives of his favourite writers and artists of the past. The library contains dozens of biographies, from Henri Dauphin's *Vie du Dante* and Passerini's *Le Vite di Dante* to Bacharach's *Lives of the Great Composers*. He even took Sainte-Beuve's biographical approach to literature to a meta-level, by reading Michaut's biography of Sainte-Beuve. Evidently, many lives are missing from the library. Augustine, for instance, is conspicuous by the absence of his *Confessions*.

Whether the lacunae in the library imply that Beckett may have tried to erase some of his traces to conceal some of the influences on his work is unlikely. In the same letter to Naumann, following the paragraph on Kafka, Beckett candidly indicated that he was not resistant to influence. He also openly admitted, for instance, that Fritz Mauthner greatly impressed him, even though he did not have a copy of the *Beiträge zu einer Kritik der Sprache* at that moment. Later on, this gap was filled, as were other lacunae, such as his initial unfamiliarity with Wittgenstein's work – a hiatus that was compensated with more than half a dozen of books by and on the philosopher.

Beckett also told Naumann that he had always been 'a poor reader, incurably inattentive, on the look-out for an elsewhere' ('à l'affût d'un ailleurs'), and that the reading experiences that had affected him most were those that had been best at 'sending' him to that elsewhere (*LSB II* 462; 465). This 'elsewhere' can be interpreted as an imaginary space where he could develop his own work, but it could also be the surrounding intertextual web. While reading Proust, for instance, he was reminded of Dante's line 'state contenti, umana gente, al quia'; while reading de Sanctis's quotation from Guarini's *Il Pastor fido*, he was 'sent' to Marcel Schwob's 'Béatrice'. And

Beckett sometimes travelled through his library like a cultural globetrotter: 'I have been reading wildly all over the place', he wrote to MacGreevy on 25 March 1936, after having dipped into German, French, English and Italian literature in short succession, from Goethe to Racine, Chesterfield, Boccaccio, Fischart, Ariosto and Pope (*LSB* 324).

But despite Beckett's characterization of himself as a 'poor reader', his 'extensive' reading method was more than a literary equivalent of the 'grand tour'. Some of his readings were extraordinarily 'intensive', in Roger Chartier's sense, and the reading traces indicate a huge respect for the integrity of other authors' texts (sometimes even with an almost pedantic care for typographical errors). The margins may have served as pathways to other literatures, an 'elsewhere', but they also remained the thresholds of the text he was reading. These border zones were a form of no-man's land with special characteristics. Unlike contemporary authors such as Paul Celan, Beckett did not start writing his own texts in the margins, in close proximity of another writer's text. At the same time, the margins did provide enough space, for instance, to shout 'Balls' to Proust (see Chapter 1), from a safe distance and yet 'within earshot'.

Instead of 'notesnatching', which Beckett tried his hand at in the early 1930s in Joyce's wake, he discovered that he did not have to steal phrases; the phrases rather imposed themselves upon him. Some of them even kept 'stalking' his mind for the rest of his life. Walther von der Vogelweide's incipit 'Ich saz ûf eine steine'; Dante's account of the way Virgil's figure appeared, 'fioco' from long silence; Petrarch's observation that he who knows he is burning is burning in a small fire – all these evocative lines kept 'rustling' in his mind like the Dante quotation that rustles in Mercier's head (Beckett 1970, 100) or like the 'dead voices' in *Waiting for Godot*, which also 'rustle', according to Gogo, who insists that they make a noise like leaves.

All the books in Beckett's library amount to many thousands of leaves. Some of them show traces of reading, left by Beckett. These traces have an effect on the texts they relate to. Beckett's notes on Geulincx, for instance, have had an impact on the reception of the *Ethica*. Thanks to Beckett, Geulincx's work, with its insistence on ignorance, is rediscovered as a philosophy with 'proto-Beckettian' elements, and we partially owe it to Beckett's notes that the *Ethica* was recently translated into English. Although not all of Beckett's notes and marginalia have an equally radical effect, they do have an impact on our perception of his predecessors. As the exploration of the library may have shown, the 'old chestnuts' have not just had an influence on Beckett; Beckett's reading of them is like a cool breeze, which has left a trace, 'like air leaves among the leaves' (*TFN* 51).

Notes

INTRODUCTION

1. As John Pilling has pointed out (2011, 141), Beckett took the line from Boswell's *Life of Johnson*; it appears in a letter to MacGreevy on his reading of Goncharov's *Oblomov* (21 January 1938; *LSB* 590), in the 'Whoroscope' Notebook (19r), in the 25th Addenda to *Watt* and (amended) in two letters to Barbara Bray of October 1971.
2. This letter is cited in the catalogue of the book dealer Michael Silvermann, August 2011.
3. It is, for example, not possible to give a full account of all the chess books in Beckett's library, of which there are nineteen. Beckett's love of chess is well known; not only did he play against various friends and fellow artists such as Marcel Duchamp, Bram van Velde and Max Frisch, he would also study chess games and puzzles in books. One example is Alexander Alekhine's *My Best Games of Chess 1924–1937* (1949 [1939]): Beckett ticked off the games as he worked his way through the book. As he told Pamela Mitchell on 23 February 1955: 'Now a game of chess from your Alekhine book … & then bed' (UoR MS5060).

CHAPTER 1

1. 'pour exprimer ces impressions pour écrire ce livre essentiel, le seul livre vrai, un grand écrivain n'a pas dans le sens courant à l'inventer puisqu'il existe déjà en chacun de nous, mais à le traduire. Le devoir et la tâche d'un écrivain sont ceux d'un traducteur' (Proust, 16.41).
2. This plan did not materialize, although 'Casket of Pralinen for a Daughter of a Dissipated Mandarin' features Proustian elements such as the 'Balbec express' and 'memory's involuntary vomit'.

CHAPTER 2

1. Beckett's intense engagement with Chaucer's work is evident in his first novel *Dream of Fair to Middling Women*, which contains several references and allusions. His 'Dream' Notebook contains several excerpts from the *Canterbury Tales* (1161–76).

2. John Pilling also dates the notes to this period (2006a, 233).
3. However, letters to MacGreevy reveal that Beckett was reading Jonson extensively in January and February 1935.
4. An interesting correction, in purple pen, is made in the entry on the Irish writer George Darley. Beckett corrects the title of the poem 'It is not beauty I demand', which had been cited as appearing in Palgrave's *Treasury* with the word 'desire' instead of 'demand'. This correction must have been made at the same time as a correction, also in purple pen, in Beckett's copy of Palgrave's anthology. Here the attribution of the poem 'Second' to *Anon.* is replaced by the entry 'George Darley, 1795–1846!' It is possible that Beckett made these changes after receiving a copy of A. J. Leventhal's memorial lecture on this neglected Irish author. The book is entitled 'George Darley 1795–1846' and was published in 1950.
5. When citing the line again a year later, Beckett mistakenly thought it derived from Marston's *Antonio's Revenge*: 'I feel more and more the sullen sot, always brooding and never thinking, of the somebody's Revenge by Marston is it' (letter to MacGreevy, 18 October 1956; *LSB II* 663).
6. Beckett's 1869 edition of *Mottoes & Aphorisms from Shakespeare*, which was most probably his source for many Shakespearean allusions in his early work, is unfortunately in private hands and cannot be consulted. There are two critical studies: Jean-Jacques Mayoux's *Shakespeare* (1982), which Beckett clearly read, and W. W. Greg's *The Editorial Problem in Shakespeare; The Clarke Lectures* (1962 [1942]).
7. The reference also appears in the dramatic fragment 'The Gloaming' (1956), which was abandoned but anticipates 'Rough for Theatre I'.
8. However, there is a single entry from Smollett's novel in the 'For Interpolation' section of the 'Whoroscope' Notebook (WN, page 23 from back).
9. Beckett read *Persuasion*, as he told Bray, in February 1963 (TCD MS10948/1/221).
10. As letters to MacGreevy (8 October 1932, 4 and 11 November 1932), A. J. Leventhal (7 May 1934) and Nuala Costello (10 May 1934) show, Beckett read Fielding's *Amelia*, *Tom Jones* and *Joseph Andrews*.
11. Beckett spoke of *Tristram Shandy* in conversation with Avigdor Arikha and Anne Atik, as for example on 23 December 1984 (see Atik 2001, 57 and 120).
12. See letter to MacGreevy, 5 June 1937: 'The only thing resembling work has been in the library on Johnson' (*LSB* 504).
13. Beckett gives the bibliographical details of the book in a letter to Ruby Cohn dated 17 November 1986.
14. Curiously, the book contains the bookseller stamp of Greene & Co. in Dublin, where Beckett bought so many of his books in the 1930s. The six volumes in the library, however, do seem to be the ones mentioned in Beckett's letter as having been purchased in Brighton.
15. As a result of Cohn's queries, Beckett took out his old notes on Johnson, and eventually gave her all of his manuscript material of *Human Wishes*. Cohn subsequently presented this material to the Beckett International Foundation at the University of Reading.

16. Beckett's library also contained Johnson's *The Complete English Poems* (1971) and a copy of *Dr Johnson by Mrs Thrale: 'The Anecdotes' of Mrs. Piozzi in their Original Form* (1984). Beckett gave Noga Arikha his 1785 edition of *The Poetical Works of Samuel Johnson, LL.D.* in 1982.
17. Beckett read Pepys throughout February 1978, despite admitting that he was 'bored to death' with him. Quotations from Pepys's diaries already appear in the 1930s 'Whoroscope' Notebook (WN 72r).
18. Beckett's copy of Yeats' *The Wind among the Reeds* (1943?) does contain marginalia, but most certainly not by Beckett. The copy was presented to Beckett by Katharine Worth in 1986.
19. However, Beckett thought that a study by Ellmann (*Yeats: The Man and the Masks*, which is still in the library) 'labours ... the subsidiary' (letter to H. O. White, 15 April 1957). In the same letter he stated that he had been rereading Yeats' poems.
20. The sticker on the inside of the cover gives Joyce's address from April to October 1939, 34 Rue des Vignes in Paris. There were 3,400 copies printed, of which 950 were, however, destroyed. Although not signed, the copy is scarce due to the sticker carrying Joyce's address.
21. A copy of the programme of Pinter's production at the Mermaid Theatre survives in the library.
22. James Stern's dedication is representative: 'For Sam Beckett / from Jimmy Stern / in admiration / & in memory of Paris / days – indeed of the / Epiphanist Himself! / London / March 1957'.
23. The library also holds a copy of *The Dublin Diary of Stanislaus Joyce*, and Beckett was struck by the memory of Joyce's father stating 'I'll break your bloody hearts but I'll break your stomachs first' (letter to Barbara Bray, 21 September 1962; TCD MS10948/1/198).
24. As critics began to send Beckett their studies of his own work, he must have realized that he could not escape their attention. He tended to respond in a bemused manner, as in the statement 'Highly gratified to learn that I'm a symbolist & moralist' after reading an essay sent by Jean-Jacques Mayoux (letter to Ruby Cohn, 25 June 1971).
25. Warner's inscription alerts Beckett to the fact that 'page 4, for some unknown reason, has been suppressed by the régime'. The translation of chapter 3 of *Finnegans Wake* was made by M. S. Lourenço, and it was published in the Catholic journal *O tempo e o modo*. As João Dionisio suggests (personal correspondence, 9 April 2010), the sexual allusions on the page in question were possibly 'overtranslated' and made more explicit by Lourenço. As Dionisio also points out, Lourenço made an English translation of Beckett's short text 'Sans'. Lourenço claims Beckett sent him, through Warner, an algorithm which helped him in the process of translating 'Sans'.
26. The word 'quaqua', related to the 'voice', appears throughout Beckett's novel *How It Is*.
27. David Gullette, recording his meeting with Beckett in 1972, records Beckett's opinion that there was too much 'symbol-chasing going on in the States, but that Melville "still has a lot to say to us"'.

28. Beckett was also impressed by Salinger's collection of short stories, *For Esmé with Love and Squalor* (January 1955; Pilling 2006a, 126).

CHAPTER 3

1. Montaigne is mentioned in a letter to Thomas MacGreevy (30 August 1932).
2. With many thanks to Thomas Hunkeler for his clarifications with regard to Scève's poetry and Parturier's introduction.
3. *Nicomède*, Act I, Scene 5, lines 313–14: 'L'espoir d'en voir l'objet entre ses mains remis / A pratiqué par lui le retour de mon fils'.
4. 'Mon cœur en même temps se retient et s'excite' (line 1378, page 68).
5. Line 1213 in Act IV, Scene 5 ('Celle que nous aimons jamais ne nous offense') is annotated professionally in the left margin: 'Cp. 'Le Misanthrope' / Line 1265: / 'Une coupable / aimée est / bientôt innocente' (black ink).
6. 'Chez Racine, la foi et l'ambition commandent souvent la même attitude. La peur de Dieu et le goût du monde lui donnent les mêmes inspirations.' (Mauriac 1928, 169).
7. 'L'héroïne racinienne relève la tête, se dresse contre l'aigle menaçant et prêt à fondre; Athalie fait la brave contre Dieu' (Mauriac 1928, 195).
8. Act I, scene 1: 'bien que mon sort touche à ses derniers soleils' (II.206).
9. Marginalia in the right margin (black ink), next to the line: 'Et ce passage offrit la Princesse à mes yeux' (Act I, scene 1; II.207).
10. 'le prince de Messène est celui de qui le mérite s'est attiré mes vœux' (Molière n.d., II.234).
11. Monsieur Tibaudier's line 'je vous ferai voir que je suis au poil et à la plume' (Molière n.d., V.148), meaning to be fit to hunt hares and partridges, to be fit for anything.
12. Moron's line 'il n'est pas généreux, mais il est de bon sens' (Molière n.d., I.212).
13. 'Fort bien: c'est un recours où je ne songeais pas / Vous n'avez qu'à mourir pour sortir d'embarras; / Le remède sans doute est merveilleux. J'enrage / Lorsque j'entends tenir ces sortes de langage' (Molière n.d., II.268).
14. 'Les hommes la plupart sont étrangement faits! / Dans la juste nature on ne les voit jamais; / La raison a pour eux des bornes trop petites; / En chaque caractère ils passent ses limites; / Et la plus noble chose, ils la gâtent souvent / Pour la vouloir outrer et pousser trop avant.' (Molière n.d., II.257).
15. In the marked passage, the following lines are underscored (blue ink): 'Et leur dévotion est humaine, est traitable' (Molière n.d., II.258); 'Et ne veulent point prendre, avec un zèle extreme, / Les intérêts du Ciel plus qu'il ne veut lui-même' (Molière n.d., II.259).
16. In the marked passage, the following two lines are underscored: 'Chez elle jamais rien ne surprend trop d'accès, / Et sa ferme raison ne tombe en nul excès' (Molière n.d., II.314).
17. 'Bien que *le Cocu* fût joué en plein été, durant les fêtes d'un mariage royal, il fallut le donner quarante fois de suite' (Lafenestre 1909, 34); 'Lorsque *le Cocu* se présenta à la cour, il n'effaroucha pas davantage son noble auditoire' (35);

'Comme *les Précieuses*, *le Cocu* est de suite imité, parodié, critiqué, accusé de plagiat' (35); 'Ce fut par *le Cocu* que s'inaugura, le 20 janvier 1661, la salle du Palais-Royal' (36).

18. For instance Molière, *Sganarelle; ou, Le mari qui se croit trompé*. Arrangé avec des scènes nouvelles, un nouveau dénouement, et mise en un acte par J. A. Gardy (Paris: Fages, 1802).

19. Marked pages: 50, 52, 53, 54, 55, 56, 58, 62, 63, 64, 65, 66, 67, 68, 69, 70, 71, 72, 79, 82, 86, 87, 94, 108, 109, 115, 120, 127, 128, 129, 130, 131, 135, 154, 156, 157, 158, 159, 160, 161, 165, 166, 167, 168, 169, 170, 171, 172, 174, 175, 176, 177, 178, 179, 180, 181, 182, 183, 184, 186, 187, 188, 189, 191, 192, 193, 195, 196, 206, 207, 208, 209, 210, 211, 212, 213, 214, 215, 217, 219, 221, 222, 223, 224, 226, 227, 229, 232, 233, 234, 236, 237, 238, 239, 242, 243, 244, 245, 246, 248, 257, 258, 262, 263, 264, 265, 267, 271, 272, 273, 274, 275, 277, 279, 280, 283, 284, 286, 287, 288, 289, 290, 291, 292, 293, 294, 295, 296, 297, 298, 299, 302, 303, 304, 305, 308, 311, 312, 313, 314, 315, 320, 321, 323, 324, 325, 326, 327, 328, 330, 331, 332, 337, 339, 341, 342, 343, 345, 346, 347, 348, 351, 354, 356, 357, 358, 361, 362, 363, 364, 366, 368, 369, 371, 372, 374, 375, 376, 377.

20. For instance: 'On se voit d'un autre oeil qu'on ne voit son prochain' (54).

21. For instance: 'Le chêne et le roseau' (72), 'Le lion et le rat' (87), 'La colombe et la fourmi' (87), 'Le cygne et le cuisinier' (115), 'La belette^{weasel} entrée dans un grenier' (120), 'Le lièvre et la tortue' (184), 'La laitière$^{\text{milk-maid}}$ et le pot au lait' (215), 'L'huitre^{oyster} et les plaideurs^{pleaders}' (288), 'Le chat et le renard' (293).

22. See also Beckett's notes from 'R. de d'A.' in the 'Dream' Notebook (*DN* 965), including 'The swarm of bees (continuous & contiguous)', to which Moran's bees in *Molloy* may be an intertextual reference.

23. 'You know what the rose said to the rose?'
    No, she did not seem to have heard that one.
    '"No gardener has died within the memory of roses."'
    'Very neat' she said 'very graceful. Adios.' (*Dream* 175)

24. HRC Typescript, 'Leventhal Collection', 19 ; see also Atik 2001, 87.

25. 'Rassasié de gloire, vous vivez au sein de l'abondance, et vous ne trouvez que mal sur la terre; moi obscure, pauvre, je trouve que tout est bien' (qtd. in Chuquet 1893, 54).

26. 'Vivre est une maladie dont le sommeil nous soulage toutes les seize heures. C'est un palliatif ; la mort est le remède. [sleep till death / healeth / come ease / this life disease]' (*SP* 172–3); the other one reads: 'Je ne conçois pas de sagesse sans défiance. L'Écriture a dit que le commencement de la sagesse était la crainte de Dieu; moi, je crois que c'est la crainte des hommes' (Chamfort 1950, 35).

27. The copy of Pascal's *Pensées* (published by Flammarion) in Beckett's library is not annotated.

28. A piece of cardboard is inserted on page 17 and an envelope on page 27 of the copy of Arnaud's *Chamfort*.

29. Beckett quoted the same lines many years later, in a letter to George Reavey, 8 July 1948.

30. 'un accent traînard' (2), 'l'atmosphère empestrée' (3), 'quarante toises de long' (5), 'dépôt de mendicité' (10), 'calèche' (11), 'chemin de hallage' (14), 'incidenter' (19),

'prévenances' (31), 'préséance' (37), 's'astreindre' (62), 'estafette' (97), 'une avanie' (100), 'bourbier' (101), 'une *chapelle ardente*' (107), etc.

31. 'je soigne mes plaisirs, et c'est ce qui doit passer avant tout' (Stendhal 1925, 213). Other passages marked as 'Beylisme' are: 'Car il faut s'amuser, continua le marquis, il n'y a que cela de réel dans la vie' (275); 'Ma foi! dit Julien, qui veut la fin veut les moyens; si, au lieu d'être un atome, j'avais quelque pouvoir, je ferais pendre trois hommes pour sauver la vie à quatre' (296).

32. See *Le Rouge et le Noir*, 213: 'S'il n'était qu'un simple religieux, il serait déjà *in pace*.'

33. The underlined passage to which this marginalia refers reads as follows: 'L'amour de tête a plus d'esprit sans doute que l'amour vrai, mais il n'a que des instants d'enthousiasme; il se connaît trop, il se juge sans cesse; loin d'égarer la pensée, il n'est bâti qu'à force de pensées' (358).

34. Written in the margin next to the line 'Son premier devoir était la discrétion; il le comprit' (360). Beckett refers to this interplay between text and marginalia in his letter to Thomas MacGreevy of 16 September 1934: 'Alas that Stendhal's thesis that the world had lost its energy when it substituted the devoir de discrétion for the folie pour rien should be so true now: "La vie d'un homme était une suite de hasards. Maintenant la civilization a chassé le hasard, plus d'imprévu"' (*LSB* 228).

35. As late as 1965, Beckett was still reading Stendhal, as he mentioned to Barbara Bray: 'Trying to read Henri Brulard' (TCD MS10948/1/320).

36. Note [917] corresponding to 'La profondeur, l'inconnu du caractère de Julien' (Stendhal 1925, 320).

37. Notes [905], [906] and [920], corresponding respectively to pages 314, 329 and 448. Next to the latter passage, Beckett has written in the margin: 'abdication de l'audace correspond avec un retour au naturel de l'imprévu' (448, left margin).

38. On 29 April 1951, Beckett wrote to Mania Péron: 'J'ai lu la vie de Balzac de Billy, 2 gros volumes remplis de chiffres, et le terrible récit de Mirbeau sur la mort' (*LSB II* 247).

39. Postcard to Barbara Bray, 16 March 1973, from El Jadida (TCD MS10948/1/530). Shortly afterwards he told her: 'Trying to read Les Illusions perdues. Not a hope' (TCD MS10948/1/542).

40. 'sans parler des deux cons tout court, celui maudit qui m'avait lâché dans le siècle et l'autre, infundibuliforme, où j'avais essayé de me venger, en me perpétuant' [not to mention the two cunts into the bargain, the one for ever accursed that ejected me into this world and the other, infundibuliform, in which, pumping my likes, I had tried to take my revenge] (Beckett 1953, 73).

41. Pages 51 and 241 of *Les Fleurs du mal* (ed. Jean-Paul Sartre) are folded down.

42. 'Worked with the Penman last night. He recited Verlaine and said that poetry ought to be rimed...' (Beckett to Thomas MacGreevy, 1 March 1930; *LSB* 19).

43. In the margin of a typescript of *Happy Days* Beckett noted the instruction 'vaguen' to himself (Pountney 1988, 149).

44. 'Je me souviens des heures en allées; pieds nus sur les dalles; j'appuyais mon front au fer mouillé du balcon; sous la lune, l'éclat de ma chair comme un fruit

merveilleux à cueillir' (Gide 1932, II.213). The capital (V.) and (G.) preceding the two literary quotations containing the expression 'en allé' could also indicate that Beckett may have consulted a dictionary such as his *Littré*.
45. 'Black A, white E, red I, green U, blue O – vowels / Some day I will open your silent pregnancies' (see Knowlson 1996, 686; Pilling 2006a, 225).
46. In an undated letter to Mania Péron, '[? After 18 October 1955]', Beckett defended his use of the word 'malinement' (for which Mania Péron had suggested the correction 'malignement') by quoting the first stanza of Rimbaud's 'Comédie en trois baisers' (*LSB II* 558).
47. Lines marked in pencil: 'Comme je descendais des Fleuves impassibles' (page 84); 'Porteur de blés flamands ou de cotons anglais' (84); 'La tempête a béni mes éveils maritimes' (85); 'Et l'éveil jaune et bleu des phosphores chanteurs' (86); 'Sans songer que les pieds lumineux des Maries / Pussent forcer le mufle aux Océans poussifs.' (87); 'Mêlant aux fleurs des yeux de panthères aux peaux / D'hommes, des arcs-en-ciel tendus comme des brides' (87); 'Quand les Juillets faisaient crouler à coups de triques / Les cieux ultramarins aux ardents entonnoirs' (89); '... vers le crépuscule embaumé' (90); 'Je ne puis plus, baigné de vos langueurs, ô lames, / Enlever leur sillage aux porteurs de cotons, / Ni traverser l'orgueil des drapeaux et de flammes ...' (90).
48. His translation, 'Drunken Boat', was sold to Edward Titus in 1932 for publication in *This Quarter*, but the literary review ceased publication shortly afterward (*SP* 192).
49. Beckett was familiar with Rimbaud's letters, as an entry in the 'Dream' Notebook suggests: 'Je ne peux t'écrire plus longuement la contemplostate de la nature xxx m'obsorculant tout entier' (*DN* 1078), derived from a letter to Ernest Delahaye (May 1873).
50. 'Et pour des visions écrasant l'oeil darne' (qtd. in Pilling 2000, 20).
51. 'Dans un grand nonchaloir chargé de souvenirs' (TCD MS10948/1/275).
52. 'Chantons durant des siècles la vanité de vivre et la force invincible du néant et de la mort, nous ferons passer sous nos yeux des tristesses qui deviendront plus monotones à mesure qu'elles se rapprocheront davantage de la dernière vérité. Essayons au contraire de varier l'apparence de l'inconnu qui nous entoure et d'y découvrir une raison nouvelle de vivre et de persévérer, nous y gagnerons du moins d'alterner nos tristesses en les mêlant d'espoirs qui s'éteignent et se rallument. Or, dans l'état où nous sommes, il est tout aussi légitime d'espérer que nos efforts ne sont pas inutiles, que de penser qu'ils ne produisent rien. La vérité suprême du néant, de la mort et de l'inutilité de notre existence, où nous aboutissons dès que nous poussons notre enquête à son dernier terme, n'est, après tout, que le point extrême de nos connaissances actuelles. Nous ne voyons rien par delà, parce que là s'arrête notre intelligence. Elle paraît certaine, mais en définitive rien en elle n'est certain que notre ignorance. Avant que d'être tenu de l'admettre irrévocablement, il nous faudra longtemps encore chercher de tout notre cœur à dissiper cette ignorance et faire ce que nous pourrons pour trouver la lumière'. (Maeterlinck 1939, xii; Beckett's underscoring).

53. Letter to MacGreevy, 25 January 1931 (*LSB* 62).
54. On 24 February 1931, Beckett wrote to Thomas MacGreevy: 'I am reading 'Journal Intime de Jules Renard' ... Odd things' (*LSB* 69).
55. 'honour your father, your mother and Göthe', corresponding with Jules Renard, *Journal*, volume 1, page 59, 22 février 1890: 'Insupportable comme un homme qui vous parle du « divin Virgile ». Ah! elle est bien là tout entière, la tradition! Honore ton père, et ta mère, et Virgile' (see *DN* 214).
56. Letter to Thomas MacGreevy, 11 March 1931: 'I've been reading nothing but Rimbaud – tired out by Renard. Oh a good name – foxy foxy. I'll come back to him' (*LSB* 73).
57. The line corresponds with Renard's entry 'Le vol d'un pigeon qui se pose sur une branche trop faible. De l'aile, il aide la branche' (16 April 1908).
58. In *La Fin / The End*, he chose a crocus, but at one point it seems interchangeable with a hyacinth: 'I would have liked to have a yellow crocus, or a hyacinth, but there, it was not to be. She wanted to take it away, but I told her to leave it' (*ECEF* 43).
59. 'Je trouve cette jacinthe admirable. Elle n'a pas besoin d'amour. Elle ne se nourrit que d'eau fraîche. Car, enfin, si l'on te mettait comme elle dans un pot, tu n'irais pas loin' (Renard 1.202).
60. I.465, corresponding to '*8 mars 1898* Si mignonne que, si vous vouliez vous pendre, vous n'auriez pas le poids'.
61. John Pilling mentions the entry for 11 February 1902 (on the pleasures of being unknown), and the entry for 11 August 1900 (regarding insomnia), both of them in Beckett's correspondence with André Bernold (Pilling 2006a, 226, 228).
62. Bair's information is based on an essay by Thomas Wall in tribute to Thomas MacGreevy, *Capuchin Annual* (Dublin, 1967), page 293 (Bair 1990, 115, endnote 56).
63. 'ce serait donc une vraie mort de nous-même, mort suivie, il est vrai, de résurrection, mais en un moi différent et jusqu'à l'amour duquel ne peuvent s'élever les parties de l'ancien moi condamnées à mourir' (Proust 1928, 4.99).
64. 'Quand je voyais un objet extérieur, la conscience que je le voyais restait entre moi et lui, le bordait d'un mince liséré spiritual qui m'empêchait de jamais toucher directement sa matière; elle se volatilisait en quelque sorte avant que je prisse contact avec elle, comme un corps incandescent qu'on approche d'un objet mouillé ne touche pas son humidité parce qu'il se fait toujours précéder d'une zone d'évaporation' (Proust 1928–9, I.124; trans. C. K. Scott Moncrieff and Terence Kilmartin, *Remembrance of Things Past*, vol. 1 [London: Penguin, 1989], 90).
65. 'Dans l'espèce d'écran diapré d'états différents que, tandis que je lisais, déployait simultanément ma conscience, et qui allaient des aspirations les plus profondément cachées en moi-même jusqu'à la vision tout extérieure de l'horizon que j'avais, au bout du jardin, sous les yeux, ce qu'il y avait d'abord en moi, de plus intime, la poignée sans cesse en mouvement qui gouvernait le reste, c'était ma croyance en la richesse philosophique, en la beauté du livre que je lisais,

et mon désir de me les approprier, quel que fût ce livre' (I.124). Beckett's marginalia read: 'emersive tendency / to be replaced by an immersive necessity'.
66. The phrase 'zone of evaporation' also occurs in Rachel Burrows's notes and surfaces again in Beckett's contribution to Ralph Mannheim's translation of Georges Duthuit's book, *The Fauvist Painters* (New York: Wittenborn, Schultz Inc., 1950), 75; with many thanks to John Pilling.
67. Beckett's marginal note reads: 'Negatives of experience / developed by intelligence' (Proust 1928-9, 16.46).
68. 'le talent d'un grand écrivain ... n'est qu'un instinct religieusement écouté au milieu du silence, imposé à tout le reste' (16.46).
69. 'pour exprimer ces impressions pour écrire ce livre essentiel, le seul livre vrai, un grand écrivain n'a pas dans les sens courant à l'inventer puisqu'il existe déjà en chacun de nous, mais à le traduire. Le devoir et la tâche d'un écrivain sont ceux d'un traducteur'. (16.41).
70. Later, in 1934, Beckett read Albert Feuillerat's *Comment Proust a composé son roman*. His review 'Proust in Pieces' appeared in the *Spectator* on 23 June 1934.
71. 'la vérité ne commencera qu'au moment où l'écrivain prendra deux objets différents, posera leur rapport ... et les enfermera dans les anneaux nécessaires d'un beau style ..., il dégagera leur essence en les réunissant l'une et l'autre pour les soustraire aux contingences du temps, dans une métaphore' (16.40).
72. 'Bien plus, une chose que nous vîmes à une certaine époque, un livre que nous lûmes ne restent pas unis à jamais seulement à ce qu'il y avait autour de nous; il le reste aussi fidèlement à ce que nous étions alors; si je reprends dans la bibliothèque *François le Champi*, immédiatement en moi un enfant se lève qui prend ma place' (16.34).
73. In November 1956 Richard Roud asked Beckett about the origin of this quote; on the 28th of that month, Beckett replied that he thought it was 'probably Francesco de Sanctis' (*LSB II* 677).
74. 'Pour Franck / Ce n'est pas un motif qui reprend, c'est une névralgie qui recommence' (Proust 1993, 588).
75. Based on his study of the writing process, Feuillerat presented a Proust that did not fit in with Beckett's view on the *Recherche*. To some extent, Beckett was reading the 'dribs and drabs' into the *Recherche*, thus applying Proust's notion of *contresens* to his own work.
76. The poem is also mentioned in 'Intercessions by Denis Devlin' (*Dis* 93).
77. The only stanza he marked (with a vertical line in the left margin, in black ink) is the following:

>   Voie lactée ô sœur lumineuse
>   Des blancs ruisseaux de Chanaan
>   Et des corps blancs des amoureuses
>   Nageurs morts suivrons-nous d'ahan
>   Ton cours vers d'autres nébuleuses (Vaissière 1923, 13)

78. Letter to Kay Boyle, 7 January 1983: 'A la Santé, V / Que lentement passent les heures / Comme passe un enterrement // Tu pleureras l'heure où tu pleures / Qui

passera trop vitement / Comme passent toutes les heures'. The next month (1 February 1983) he sent her the last stanza of the last section of 'A la Santé' (VI): 'Le jour s'en va voici que brûle / Une lampe dans la prison / Nous sommes seuls dans ma cellule / Belle clarté chère raison'.

79. Beckett had a copy of André Billy's *Apollinaire* (Paris: Seghers, 1956).
80. John Pilling (2006a, 77) thinks Atik's conjecture that 'les joues rouges' was Beckett's first poem in French is less plausible than the suggestion that one of the *Poèmes 38–39* (as published in 1946) is the first.
81. 'que les longues heures / vont ~~peu à peu~~^lentement lui enlever / ~~peu à peu~~^lentement les blanches heures'.
82. *L'Œuvre du Divin Arétin*, 2 vols. (1933) and *L'Œuvre du Marquis de Sade* (1909).
83. Guillaume Apollinaire, *Zone*, transl. Samuel Beckett (Dublin: Dolmen Press, 1972).
84. On 27 March 1949, Beckett wrote to Thomas MacGreevy: 'I translated Apollinaire's Zone (first poem of Alcools) for Duthuit. There are some admirable passages' (*LSB II* 146).
85. The inscription reads: 'À Samuel Beckett / le plus grand / son ami / Maurice Nadeau'. The book is still part of Beckett's library.
86. Letter to Thomas MacGreevy, 26 May 1938 (*LSB* 626).
87. The corners of the following pages have been folded down: 9, 13, 23, 27, 31, 33, 37, 87.
88. 'Beckett could not have read Céline's *Bagatelles pour un massacre* before December 28, 1937, the date of its publication in Paris' (Pilling 2005, 42).
89. Céline, *Bagatelles pour un massacre* (1937): 'Je donne à tout ce bavardage une sorte d'"éjaculation" ... Je l'ai toujours là dans ma poche ... dans un petit bout de papier' (70).
90. Corresponding to Céline's *Bagatalles*: 'La pire des épreuves pour les grands "Céphalo-Bills", c'était le moment des adieux' (71) and 'Toutvabienovitch avait des élèves dans le coin' (78).
91. Beckett told Ruby Cohn on 16 February 1962 that he had read Céline before the war (Pilling 2006a, 158).
92. Only one passage in Jaspers's book is marked: 'toute spiritualité se convertit en affairisme ou en institutions officielles, où la volonté ne s'exerce qu'en vue d'obtenir un certain genre d'existence, où tout est fabriqué en prévision d'un rendement, où la vie est un cabotinage, en un temps où l'homme ne perd jamais de vue ce qu'il est, où la simplicité même est voulue, où l'ivresse dionysiaque est factice, aussi bien que la discipline qui la stylise, et où l'artiste en est à la fois trop conscient et trop satisfait de l'être' (275).
93. 'L'auteur de *Madame Edwarda* a lui-même attiré l'attention sur la gravité de son livre. Néanmoins, il me semble bon d'insister, en raison de la légèreté avec laquelle il est d'usage de traiter les écrits dont la vie sexuelle est le thème. ... je demande au lecteur de ma préface de réfléchir un court instant sur l'attitude traditionnelle à l'égard du plaisir ... et de la douleur (que la mort apaise, il est vrai, mais que d'abord elle porte au pire). Un ensemble de conditions nous conduit à nous faire

de l'homme (de l'humanité), une image également éloignée du plaisir extrême et de l'extrême douleur: les interdits les plus communs frappent les uns la vie sexuelle et les autres la mort, si bien que l'une et l'autre ont formé un domaine sacré, qui relève de la religion. Le plus pénible commença lorsque les interdits touchant les circonstances de la disparition de l'être reçurent seuls un aspect grave et que ceux qui touchaient les circonstances de l'apparition – toute l'activité génétique – ont été pris à la légère. Je ne songe pas à protester contre la tendance profonde du grand nombre: elle est l'expression du destin qui voulut l'homme riant de ses organes reproducteurs. Mais ce rire, qui accuse l'opposition du plaisir et de la douleur (la douleur et la mort sont dignes de respect, tandis que le plaisir est dérisoire, désigné au mépris), en marque aussi la parenté fondamentale. Le rire n'est plus respectueux, mais c'est le signe de l'horreur. Le rire est l'attitude de compromis qu'adopte l'homme en présence d'un aspect qui répugne, quand cet aspect ne paraît pas grave. Aussi bien l'érotisme envisagé gravement, tragiquement, représente un entier renversement.

Je tiens d'abord à préciser à quel point sont vaines ces affirmations banales, selon lesquelles l'interdit sexuel est un préjugé, dont il est temps de se défaire. La honte, la pudeur, qui accompagnent le sentiment fort du plaisir, ne seraient elles-mêmes que des preuves d'inintelligence. Autant dire que nous devrions faire enfin table rase et revenir au temps de l'animalité, de la libre dévoration et de l'indifférence aux immondices. . . . il nous est loisible de revenir – en partie – sur une vue que le rire seul introduisit.

C'est le rire en effet qui justifie une forme de condamnation déshonorante. Le rire nous engage dans cette voie où le principe d'une interdiction, de décences nécessaires, inévitables, se change en hypocrisie fermée, en incompréhension de ce qui est en jeu. L'extrême licence liée à la plaisanterie s'accompagne d'un refus de prendre au sérieux – j'entends: au tragique – la vérité de l'érotisme.

La préface de ce petit livre où l'érotisme est représenté, sans détour, ouvrant sur la conscience d'une déchirure, est pour moi l'occasion d'un appel que je veux pathétique. Non qu'il soit à mes yeux surprenant que l'esprit se détourne de lui-même et, pour ainsi dire se tournant le dos, devienne dans son obstination la caricature de sa vérité' (Bataille 1979, 9–12).

94. The handwritten dedication reads: 'pour Samuel Beckett / en témoignage de / vive admiration, ces / écarts de langage / Ludovic Janvier'. The subsequent titles are: *Pour Samuel Beckett* (1966), *La baigneuse* (1968) – which Janvier calls 'une approximation encore très lointaine' in his dedication – *Face* (1975), *Naissance* (1984), *La Mer à boire: poèmes* (1987).
95. The inscription reads: 'mon cher Sam / encore un signe de / vie et ma voix d'ami / à bientôt? / Ludovic / 12.2.88'.
96. On 28 February 1953 Beckett also mentioned having received a dedication copy of Robbe-Grillet's *Les Gommes* (Pilling 2006a, 118).
97. Robert Pinget, *The Inquisitory*, trans. Donald Watson (London: Calder, 1982), 66. With many thanks to John Pilling.

236 *Notes to pages 81–92*

98. See Beckett's letter to Barbara Bray, 21 September 1960: 'From one Martin Esslin today his chapter on my plays from his book on the "Theatre of the Absurd" in which he deals also with Ionesco, Adamov, Genet, Pinter, Simpson and others' (TCD MS10948/1/111).
99. Handwritten inscription in Arrabal's *Lettre à Fidel Castro: an "1984"* (1983).

CHAPTER 4

1. The fact that the book was written before the Nazis' assumption of power ('Machtübernahme') in 1933 was important to Beckett, as he was aware that any book published afterwards would be 'ideologically' inflected. See also his comment after a visit to a bookshop in Hamburg: 'Everything in way of history of literature, art, m.[usic] etc., prior to Machtübernahme, disparaged' (GD, 22 October 1936; qtd. in Nixon 2011, 89).
2. Beckett had renewed his reader's ticket at the British Library in February 1934. Cf. also Beckett's reference to the medieval 'Meistergesang' in his review of MacGreevy's *Poems*, entitled 'Humanistic Quietism' and published in July 1934 (*Dis* 68).
3. 'I sat upon a stone / One leg across the other thrown / One hand I propped my elbow in, / And in the other hand my chin / And half my cheek was hidden' (Vogelweide 1938, 49).
4. Their purchase is recorded in the 'German Diaries', entries for 12 and 14 November 1936.
5. 'You are mine, I am yours / Of that you may be sure. / You're locked away / Within my heart. / The little key is lost / So there you'll ever stay!'
6. Beckett again mentioned reading Claudius in a further letter to Bray, 1 October 1961).
7. Anne Atik recounts how Beckett and Arikha would frequently recite Claudius's poem 'Der Tod und das Mädchen' (66).
8. See for example the line 'Mein Ruh ist hin mein Herz ist schwer ich finde Sie nimmer und nimmer mehr' (Goethe's *Faust*) in 'The Smeraldina's Billet-Doux' (*MPTK* 146); more particularly, the line is from 'Gretchen am Spinnrade' in *Faust*.
9. Marion Fries-Dieckmann, 'Fragments of German Literature in the German Translations of Beckett's Work', paper given at the 'Beckett und die deutsche Kultur' conference in Darmstadt, September 2011.
10. Beckett was fond of quoting the last line from this poem ('Alle Schuld rächt sich auf Erden' [The debt all guilt exacts from mortal men]) in his correspondence; cf. for example letter to Ruby Cohn, 24 May 1981 (UoR MS5100).
11. A further example of such an intertextual 'rearrangement' in translation is Beckett's use of Grillparzer's 'long joys of summer' in *Malone Dies* (58).
12. 'Zuweilen regte noch sich eine Geisteskraft in mir. Aber freilich nur zerstörend! Was ist der Mensch? konnt ich beginnen; wie kommt es, dass so etwas in der Welt ist, das, wie ein Chaos, gärt, oder modert, wie ein fauler Baum, und nie zu

einer Reife gedeiht? Wie duldet diesen Heerling die Natur bei ihren süssen Trauben?' (Hölderlin n.d., 469).
13. 'Es gibt ein Vergessen alles Daseins, ein Verstummen unsers Wesens, wo uns ist, als hätten wir alles gefunden. Es gibt ein Verstummen, ein Vergessen alles Daseins, wo uns ist, als hätten wir alles verloren, eine Nacht unsrer Seele, wo kein Schimmer eines Sterns, wo nicht einmal ein faules Holz uns leuchtet. Ich war nun ruhig geworden. Nun trieb mich nichts mehr auf um Mitternacht. Nun sengt ich mich in meiner eigenen Flamme nicht mehr' (Hölderlin n.d., 466–7).
14. See also Beckett's awareness of wider political and cultural contexts, as his marginal note on the following passage in *Hyperion* as being 'fit for Das I.R.' indicates: 'Von ihren Taten nähren die Söhne der Sonne sich; sie leben vom Sieg; mit eignem Geist ermuntern sie sich, und ihre Kraft ist ihre Freude' [The children of the sun live by their deeds; they live by victory; their own spirit rouses them, and their strength is their joy] (Hölderlin n.d., 453; 1990, 21). *Das Innere Reich* was a literary journal, published in Nazi Germany, that advocated the stance of 'Innere Emigration'. Beckett met one of its editors, Paul Alverdes, in Munich in spring 1937.
15. 'You graceful views in the valley, / For instance garden and tree / And then the footbridge, the narrow, / The stream one can hardly see' (Hölderlin 1967, 576–7). Beckett also underlined the word 'schmaler' [narrow] at the end of the poem 'An Landauer' (Hölderlin n.d., 62).
16. Anne Atik sees a further reference to the poem in *Eh Joe*, with the lines 'The green one, the narrow one' alluding to Hölderlin's 'Und dann der Steg, der schmale' (67). She also comments that Arikha and Beckett would frequently recite the poem 'Die Titanen', with the closing line 'Ich aber bin allein' (Atik 2001, 61). A further book by Hölderlin in the library is *Werke, Briefe, Dokumente* (1977[1963]), which was presented to Beckett by the production team and cast of *Was Wo* in Stuttgart in June 1985.
17. IMEC, Fonds Calder, Dossiers Beckett N° 3 in CAL2 C51 B2 [1–4].
18. 'In younger days each morning I rose with joy, / To weep at nightfall; now, in my later years, / Though doubting I begin my day, yet / Always its end is serene and holy' (Hölderlin 1967, 41).
19. André Bernold (31–2) sees a connection between the lines 'Uns wiegen lassen, wie / Auf schwankem Kahne der See' from 'Mnemoysne' and the girl in the punt in *Krapp's Last Tape* (*CDW* 223).
20. With thanks to John Pilling for the reference.
21. Beckett also owned two academic and critical books on Heine, both by the scholar S. S. Prawer: *Heine; The Tragic Satirist* (1961) and '*Heine's Jewish Comedy; A Study of his Portraits of Jews and Judaism*' (1983), presented by the author on Beckett's birthday in 1986.
22. Beckett's reading of Heine appears to have intensified in November 1977; on the 11th he told Charles Juliet that he had been 'immersed in Heine's last poetry' (162), and in a letter to Nick Rawson four days later he states that he is tackling Heine's 'Lamentations' – presumably the second book of the volume *Romanzero* (1851).

23. Cf. letters to Pamela Mitchell (undated [January 1955]), Barbara Bray (undated [postmark is 23 August 1967] and 27 May 1977).
24. André Bernold states that Beckett gave him his copy of Kleist's 'Marionettentheater' in late 1983 (103).
25. Interestingly, Beckett had already referred to an actor as being 'very Kleistian' during the production of *Krapp's Last Tape* in Berlin 1969 (letter to Barbara Bray, 2 September 1969; TCD MS10948/1/432).
26. 'And the advantage such a puppet would have over a living dancer? The advantage? First a negative gain, my excellent friend, specifically this: that such a figure would never be affected. For affectation appears, as you know, when the soul (*vis motrix*) locates itself at any point other than the center of gravity of the movement' (Kleist 1972, 24).
27. Beckett's library contains the novella *Lenz* by Georg Büchner in the first English translation (1969) by Michael Hamburger. Hamburger inscribed the book and sent it to Beckett in August 1970.
28. The first English translation was only published in 1967 by Penguin.
29. Beckett reread the book in Tanger in September 1974 (letters to Barbara Bray, 9 and 29 September 1974), and it was the topic of conversation with André Bernold on 11 February 1982 (42). Antoni Libera records that during their last meeting in May 1986, Beckett turned up with an old copy of *Effi Briest*, which he had been reading. Paraphrasing his own play *Krapp's Last Tape* ('Yes . . . a page a day, scalding the eyes out'), Beckett apparently stated that he used to dream of writing such a novel (Libera 2004, publishers' excerpt).
30. While in Berlin (2 February 1975; TCD MS10948/1/572), Beckett told Barbara Bray he was reading *Unwiederbringlich*, and quoted the closing lines of the last poem at the end of the book: 'Wer hasst, ist zu bedauern, / Und mehr noch fast, wer liebt' [Who hates, is to be pitied and almost more, one who loves] (Fontane 1958, 1051; 1964, 52 fn.1).
31. 'Do you think of vanished days, Marie, / As you stare in the fire at night? / Do you wish for those hours & days / To return when you laughed full of joy and happiness? // I do think of vanished days, John, / And always they fill me with happiness / But those which were dearest to me, / I do not wish them back again' (Fontane 1964, 293).
32. It is possible that Beckett had already read the novel earlier, in 1955, as the title of the book is invoked in a letter to Alan Schneider of 27 December 1955: 'Pozzo's sudden changes of tone, mood, behaviour etc., may I suppose be related to what is going on about him, but their source is in the dark of his own inner *upheavals and confusions*' (qtd. in Harmon, 6; our emphasis).
33. There is a telling moment in the Bray correspondence, as Beckett tells her that 'someone sent Rilke's Sonnets' before adding 'I can't', only to realize that it was indeed Bray who had sent them, so that he proceeds to thank her warmly (letters of 23 January and 1 February 1969; TCD MS10948/1/422 and 424).
34. Nelly Sachs inscribed the copy of *Späte Gedichte*: 'Für Sam Beckett / O du Drama schwarze Zeit – / Nelly / Stockholm d. 28.1.67'; cf. also Beckett's letter

to Barbara Bray of 25 May 1970: 'Nelly Sachs dead. Celan suicided' (TCD MS10948/1/471).
35. See letter to Barbara Bray of 22 January 1960: 'Reading more Benn. Often insufferable, often moving and convincing. A beautiful essay – one of the last – a lecture I think – on the aging artist' (TCD MS10948/1/66). The essay in question is 'Altern als Problem für Künstler' (1954). In the 1930s, Beckett had noted four lines from Benn's poem 'Hergelaufene Söhne' in the 'Whoroscope' Notebook (WN 67r).
36. These are: Max Brod: *Franz Kafka, souvenirs et documents* (1945); Marthe Robert: *Kafka* (1960) and Joachim Unseld: *Franz Kafka; Ein Schriftstellerleben* (1982). Beckett read the latter in August 1983, commenting on its impressive research (letter to Barbara Bray, 23 August 1982).

CHAPTER 5

1. On virtually every page, individual words or phrases are underlined. Several marginal notes indicate dates or the English translation of certain words. There is no obvious pattern to the numerous markings in both grey pencil and coloured pencils (blue, green, brown, purple), other than that they seem to indicate that Beckett read the book at different intervals. There are no markings after page 302, that is, after the chapter on Manzoni and Romanticism (the next chapter being on Leopardi and Pessimism).
2. Pages 56, 57 and 58 contain several underlined passages, such as 'l'amore appena nato, simile ancora a' primi fuggevoli sogni della giovanezza, che acquista la sua realtá presso alla tomba ed oltre la tomba' (1.58) and 'Intendere è per lui il principio del fare; e la forza che dá attivitá all'intelletto ed efficacia alla volontá è l'amore' (1.58).
3. 'Il poeta non s'intromette niente nella sua storia' (2.23).
4. The first underlined passage characterizes Guarini by contrasting him with Tasso: 'Giambattista Guarini fu poeta di occasione e cortigiano di natura, dove il Tasso fu tutto l'opposto: cortigiano per bisogno e per istinto poeta' (2.179); the following pages are also marked (180–5).
5. On 26 July 1936, Beckett wrote to MacGreevy that he was 'reading Guarini's Pastor Fido again', before he started reading Goethe's *Faust* (*LSB* 361).
6. 'Baci pur bocca curiosa e scaltra / o seno, o fronte, o mano: unqua non fia / che parte alcuna in bella donna baci, / che baciatrice sia, / se non la bocca, ove l'un'alma e l'altra / corre e si bacia anch'ella, e con vivaci / spiriti pellegrini / dà vita al bel tesoro / de' bacianti rubini' (2.184–5).
7. Next to the passage from *Il Pastor Fido*, Beckett wrote: '"Béatrice," Marcel Schwob: "Tandis que je baisais Agathon mon âme est venue sur mes lèvres – Elle voulait, l'infortunée, passer en lui"' (2.185).
8. On 8 October 1932, Beckett refers to Marcel Schwob in a letter to George Reavey (*LSB* 125).
9. Frost and Maxwell 2006, 133–6; Knowlson 1996, 224–5. See also Beckett's letter to MacGreevy, 29 January 1936: 'Ethna MacCarthy has got the job of doing his

[Rudmose-Brown's] Provençal lectures and I have been helping her out of the Tresor du Felibrige. Aubanel seems the best of them' (*LSB* 306).

10. On page 218 (vol. 2) Beckett marked the following passage in pencil: 'È il fondo della commedia italiana dal Boccaccio all' Aretino, salvo che gli altri vi si spassano, massime l'Aretino, ed egli se ne stacca e rimane al di sopra. Chiamasi "accedemico di nulla academia, detto il Fastidito". Nel tempo classico delle academie il suo titulo di Gloria è di non essere accademico.' The only other marked passage relating to Bruno is the quotation on page 225, starting as follows: 'Nella natura, variandosi in infinito e succedendo l'una a l'altra le forme, è sempre una materia medesma.'

11. The chapter shows pencil marks on pages 247, 249, 261, 264, 267, 274–7.

12. 'Perciò Galileo, Bacone, Cartesio sono i veri padri del mondo moderno, la coscienza della nuova scienza. Il metodo, che Galileo applicava alle scienze naturali, diviene nelle mani di Bacone il metodo universale e assoluto, la via della veritá in tutte le sue applicazioni' (274).

13. Postcard from Bianca Esposito ('B.E.') to Beckett, 10 April 1926: 'In fatti, mi sembio della Sua voce l'altro giorno che Si doveva sentire più male che non lo diceva. In ogni modo non si disperi per lo sforzato riposo. Lei troverà che la Sua mente ne avrà del bene. Non si affretti ad [alzarsi]' (UoR MS3481).

14. Beckett to Duthuit, 'Il [Dante] appelait la poésie "una bella menzogna"' (26 May 1949; *LSB II* 154).

15. Beckett to Duthuit, 1 June 1949: 'Bella menzogna = beau mensonge, tout bonnement, je crois que c'est dans le Convivio. La poésie était autre chose bien sûr, mais il fallait que la fausseté y fût, aussi bien fondée que possible' (*LSB II* 161).

16. The following passages in Cantos 3, 4 and 5 are underlined or marked:
    Canto 3: page 34: 'premier amour' and 'défiance', page 37: 'pureté', 'Ces esprits n'ont pas l'espoir de la mort, et leur destinée obscure est si avilie, qu'ils sont envieux même d'un sort plus terrible', 'dévoré', 'piqués';
    Canto 4: page 41: 'l'âme sans torment'; page 42: 'de choses qu'il est beau de taire en ce moment';
    Canto 5: page 43: 'chargé d'en connaître'; page 44: '*muette*', 'Soudan. Cette autre' (next to this line, the word 'Didon' is pencilled in the left margin).

17. Artaud de Montor's translation reads as follows: 'Par moi l'on va dans la cité des larmes; par moi l'on va dans l'abîme des douleurs; par moi l'on va parmi les races criminelles. La justice anima mon sublime créateur: je suis l'ouvrage de la divine puissance, de la haute sagesse et du premier amour; rien ne fut créé avant moi, que les substances éternelles, et moi je dure éternellement. O vous qui entrez, laissez toute espérance!' (34).

18. The book is very brittle. On page 110, in the sentence 'Quel honte pour un Alessio interminei da Lucca' there is a cross beside 'interminei', and the word 'Interminelli' is pencilled at the bottom of the page.

19. In the 'German Diaries', Beckett wrote on 18 January 1937: 'The pity that is an impertinence. All mere pity an impertinence. Proof: self-pity. Art can only

Notes to pages 108–120 241

proceed from hate/love, not from pity. Pity gives a luke art. There is no passion of compassion' (qtd. in Lüscher-Morata 2005, 198).
20. See Chapter 3; (*DN* 214).
21. Letter to MacGreevy, 20 December 1931 (*LSB* 100).
22. For instance 'bathos = deep!' (WN 51v), 'the geology of conscience' (WN 62r).
23. See Bray correspondence, TCD MS10948/1/580–588; 608; 627; 651.
24. 'leur supposant parfois un sens plus précis qu'elles n'ont, il eût désiré savoir ce qu'on voulait dire exactement par celles qu'il entendait le plus souvent employer: la beauté du diable, du sang bleu, une vie de bâton de chaise, le quart d'heure de Rabelais, être le prince des élégances, donner carte blanche, être réduit à quia, etc.' (1.289).
25. In the summer of 1971 Ruby Cohn sent some queries to Beckett regarding *More Pricks than Kicks* to which Beckett replied from St Margherita Ligure (6 July 1971, UoR MS5100; Pilling 2006a, 14).
26. The library in Beckett's apartment contains a few other books by and on Petrarch, dating from after the war: *Le Rime* (with a preface by Luigi Baldacci 1962) and Morris Bishop's *Petrarch and his World* (1964).
27. In: *The Sonnets, Triumphs, and Other Poems of Petrarch*, with a Life of the Poet by Thomas Campbell (London: Henry G. Bohn, 1859), 160.
28. Michel de Montaigne, *Essais I* (Paris: Gallimard Folio Classique, 1965), 60.
29. In the 3rd volume of Boccaccio's *Decamerone*, the following pages are marked: 5, 12, 20, 31, 38, 41–2, 46, 48, 51, 54, 59, 64, 72, 78, 84, 87, 91, 93, 101, 103, 110, 117, 129, 144, 147–8, 151, 155, 160, 164, 166, 169, 174, 177, 180, 188–93, 198, 204, 206, 211, 215, 217, 224, 230, 234, 237–8, 241, 247–8, 253, 259, 262, 266–7, 272, 285, 291–2, 295, 300, 303–4, 306, 308–10, 312, 314, 316, 318, 332.
30. Beckett's notes on Machiavelli and Ariosto are preserved at Trinity College, Dublin (TCD MS10962; see Frost and Maxwell 2006, 29–37).
31. Giacomo Leopardi, *I Canti* (1936); Giacomo Leopardi, *Prose, con uno studio di Pietro Giordani*, with a postcard sent from Norwich to 'S.B. Beckett' at 34 Gertrude Street, London, on '9/7/35'; Giuseppe Giacosa, *Diritti dell'Anima / Tristi Amori* (1923; corner of page 22 folded down). Giacosa's *Il Conte rosso* was on the list of prescribed books for the Michaelmas examination for junior freshmen.

CHAPTER 6

1. See Beckett's note to Joyce, 26 April 1929 (*LSB* 8), which contains Greek fragments and linguistic clarifications, and his response to a query regarding this note in a letter to Patricia Hutchins, 25 June 1954 (*LSB II* 485).
2. Lebaigue's *Dictionnaire latin-français* (1898) and K. E. Georges' *Lateinisch-deutsches Handwörterbuch* (1864).
3. Annotations are found on following pages: vol. 1 = f-piece, 85, 86, 91, 92, 93, 109, 117, 165, 192, 205, 214, 279, 283, 285, 298, 308, 343, 346, 348i, 356, 360, 362, 373, 378, 390, 391, 400, 427, 431, 457, 459, 497, inside back cover; vol. 2 = 45, 48, 69, 78, 79, 85, 86, 87, 97, 100, 102, 115, 133, 134, 138, 139, 152, 153, 154, 175, 208, 209, inside back cover; vol. 3 = 282, inside back cover.

4. Morris Sinclair told Knowlson that Beckett had a reproduction of this painting on the wall of his room at Cooldrinagh. It is conceivable that Beckett took the card with him to Germany, and then left it behind by mistake. Cissie Sinclair wrote on the card: 'Feb 16th Am sending the things you left here on today. I was waiting to know your permanent address but as that is not forthcoming apparently... Am disappointed not to hear from you and hope you are alright. Things as usual here, only more so.
Lebewohl
C.
[bottom left:] I hope you got the [sleevelinks] alright.
[bottom right:] Contents of packet
    1 Scarf
    1 silk handkerchief
    2 pair socks
    1 scissors (in socks)'
5. In 1962, Beckett also read Runciman's *Sicilian Vespers*; surprisingly, given his comments on German literary histories (see Chapter 4), he did not like the fact that it was 'All names & dates' (letter to Barbara Bray, 3 December 1962; TCD MS10948/1/211).
6. Other historical books in the library are Victor Duruy's *Petite Histoire générale extraite de l'abrégé d'histoire universelle* (1883 [1874]) and Nancy Mitford's *The Sun King; Louis XIV of Versailles* (1966). Beckett's interest in history is evident from the very first entries on Napoleon in the 'Dream' Notebook. There are also notes taken from Albert Sorel's *Europe et la révolution française* and George Peabody Gooch's *Germany and the French Revolution* (TCD MS10969).
7. Beckett's anonymous response to a negative review of the production of *Le Kid*, published in *TCD: A Miscellany* on 12 March 1931, was entitled 'The Possessed'.
8. Beckett also possessed a reprint of Henri Troyat's 1946 biography of Dostoevsky.
9. This is reflected in the book plate inserted at the back of the book, showing 'official representatives of British Culture, Archangel, 1942', one of them being Reavey.
10. Beckett's library also contains Gogol's *Les âmes mortes* (*Dead Souls*) in a translation by Arthur Adamov and illustrated by Avigdor Arikha (who inscribed the book for Beckett in 1956).
11. However, the following month (February 1959), he told the translator Patrick Bowles that he had not liked the book.
12. Beckett's library also contains a copy of Mandelstam's autobiography *Hope against Hope*, but again it is unclear whether Beckett read it.
13. Cf. letter to Barbara Bray, 9 June 1959; TCD MS10948/1/35.
14. Beckett told Reavey in a 7 March 1974 letter that he was happy for Reavey to refer to the original letter in which he made the suggestion, but went on to state that he could not remember the lecture he had attended in 1937.

15. In 1981 Beckett told Anne Atik that he did not think the translations of Chekhov's work were very good, but that they did manage to convey the particular atmosphere and mood of his work (Atik 2001, 105).
16. The library also contains a French translation of Strindberg's *Inferno* (published 1966).
17. Beckett's correspondence with Barbara Bray reveals that he was reading a book by or about Ibsen in December 1978.

CHAPTER 7

1. Beckett to Gabriel D'Aubarède (16 February 1961, qtd. in Graver and Federman 1979, 217).
2. See Fifield 2011, 77.
3. 'Alexandre, à Corinthe, lui ayant demandé s'il désirait quelque chose: 'Oui' répondit Diogène, 'que tu t'ôtes de mon soleil.' À la vue d'un enfant buvant à une fontaine dans le creux de sa main, 'Cet enfant m'apprend que je conserve encore du superflu', et il brisa son écuelle. (Voir tableaux de Poussin – Louvre, Salvator Rosa – Ermitage, Karel Dujardin – Dresde.)' (TCD MS10967, 68r).
4. '.. mouvement, nombre, espace .. / qui comprennent tout l'univers, selon ces paroles: Omnia in mensura, et numero et pondere, disposuisti (Sagesse: XI, 21) / Réflexions sur la Géométrie' (WN 71r).
5. For a discussion of Debricon's edition, see Feldman 2006a, esp. 47.
6. For instance: 'Quand la volonté affirme une idée claire, elle fait passer cette idée de la simple possibilité logique à la vérité objective' (30, pencil line in left margin).
7. For instance: 'le doute cartésien implique <u>une foi absolue en la raison</u>; il n'est qu'une étape vers la certitude' (24).
8. 'nous rendre comme maîtres et possesseurs de la nature' (95, pencil mark in right margin).
9. 'et, pour ce qu'il y a des hommes qui se méprennent en raisonnant ... je rejetai comme fausses toutes les raisons que j'avais prises auparavant pour démonstrations' (75).
10. For instance 'Nous sommes uni à un corps: Imperfection' (125) or 'C'est un signe de l'imperfection de notre esprit' next to the last paragraph on the subsequent page (regarding God's revelation of things 'qui surpassent la portée ordinaire de notre esprit').
11. Notes on WN 71r: cf. Brunschvicg 1923, 52, note 162. Notes on WN 71v: cf. Brunschvicg 1923, 22; 58, note 181; 61, note 205; 190; 339.
12. The dating of this letter by John Pilling (2006a, 41) and Chris Ackerley and Stan Gontarski (2004, 49) differs from the dating in *LSB* ('23 [April 1933]'; *LSB* 154).
13. Everett Frost and Jane Maxwell suggest that the major work on the philosophy notes was undertaken 'in the Summer of 1932 in London in the British Museum reading room – probably not with Alexander but with Windelband and Burnet' (Frost and Maxwell 2006, 71), but also indicate that he may have continued in 1933: 'whenever he continued, he would do so exclusively with

Windelband. Since he mentions reading Leibniz in a 1933 letter to MacGreevy (TCD MS10402/57; K[nowlson 1996], 174 [6 December 1933]), he has presumably finished Windelband (or maybe it is an indication that he had progressed that far in Windelband by then)' (Frost and Maxwell 2006, 73).

14. '[You will perhaps say that *matter*, though it be not perceived by us, *is* nevertheless *perceived by God*, to whom it is the occasion of exciting ideas in our minds.] For, say you, since we observe our sensations to be imprinted in an *orderly and constant manner*, it is but reasonable to suppose there are certain constant and regular occasions of their being produced' (Berkeley 1926, 148; LXX).

15. The following passages in the *Three Dialogues* are marked:

245:        [Second Dialogue; *Phil.*] When I conclude, not that they have no real existence, but that seeing they depend not on my thought, and have an existence distinct from being perceived by me, *there must be some other mind wherein they exist.*

245–6:   [Second Dialogue; *Phil.*] For philosophers, though they acknowledge all corporeal beings to be perceived by God, yet they attribute to them an absolute subsistence distinct from their being perceived by any mind whatever, which I do not.

248:        [Second Dialogue; *Phil.*] Nor is it less plain that these ideas, or things by me perceived, either themselves or their archetypes, exist independently of my mind, since I know myself not to be their author, it being out of my power to determine at pleasure, what particular ideas I shall be affected with upon opening my eyes or ears. They must therefore exist in some other mind, whose will it is they should be exhibited to me.

266:        [Third Dialogue; *Phil.*] When I deny sensible things an existence out of the mind, I do not mean my mind in particular, but all minds. Now it is plain they have an existence exterior to my mind, since I find them by experience to be independent of it.

274:        [Third Dialogue; *Phil.*] I deny therefore that there is any unthinking substratum of the objects of sense, ... philosophical quiddities, which some men are so fond of.

274–5:   [Third Dialogue: see quotation in main text]

282:        [Third Dialogue] *Phil.* You mistake me. I am not for changing things into ideas, but rather ideas into things; since those immediate objects of perception, which, according to you, are only appearances of things, I take to be the real things themselves.

282:        [Third Dialogue] *Phil.* What you call the empty forms and outside of things, seems to me the very things themselves.

16. 'Das Wort "*De nobis ipsis silemus*", das er aus Bacon entnimmt, um es der "Kritik der reinen Vernunft" als Motto voranzusetzen, tritt nun mehr und mehr in Kraft' (Cassirer in Kant 1921, XI.5).

17. As John Pilling notes, it is on Westminster Bridge that Arsene claims to have met Mr. Ash in *Watt* (Pilling 2005, 45).

18. 'Wie Goethe als siebenjähriger Knabe sich von dem 'ausserordentlichen Weltereignis' des Erdbebens von Lissabon ergriffen und zum erstenmal zu tieferer geistiger Betrachtung aufgeregt fühlte, wie der Streit zwischen Rousseau und Voltaire über die 'beste Welt' an diesem Ereignis sich entfachte: so sah sich auch Kant hier zur gedanklichen Rechenschaftsablegung aufgefordert.' (Cassirer 1921, XI.59–60).
19. 'Wenn alle vorhergehende Metaphysik mit dem 'Was' des Gegenstandes begonnen hatte, so beginnt Kant mit dem 'Wie' des Gegenstandsurteils.' (XI.140).
20. The excerpts on pages 64v–65r and 65r–65v correspond, respectively, to pages 574 and 576 in Heimsoeth's chapter.
21. The next Kantian excerpts in the 'Whoroscope' Notebook (134r, 133v in retrograde direction) correspond with the marked passages on pages 45–6 and 49 (the passage quoted above). The only note on the next page (in retrograde direction) is 'middling class' (133r); between this page and 87r, the notebook pages are blank.
22. 'Entweder das Prädikat B gehört zum Subject A als etwas, was in diesem Begriffe A (versteckter Weise) enthalten ist; oder B liegt ganz ausser dem Begriff A, ob es zwar mit demselben in Verknüpfung steht. Im ersten Fall nenne ich das Urteil analytisch, in dem andern synthetisch' (III.40).
23. For an analysis of Kant's influence on Beckett, see also Murphy 1994; 2011.
24. 'Ein Imperativ heisst hypothetisch, wenn er lediglich anzeigt, welches Mittel gebraucht oder gewollt werden muss, damit ein Anderes, das als Ziel vorausgesetzt wird, sich verwirkliche' (Cassirer 1921, 261).
25. Corresponding to the following passage: 'Reiz und Annehmlichkeit mag für ihn vieles haben, darum bekümmert sich niemand; wenn er aber etwas für schön ausgibt, so mutet er andern eben dasselbe Wohlgefallen zu: er urteilt nicht bloss für sich, sondern für jedermann und spricht alsdann von der Schönheit, als wäre sie eine Eigenschaft der Dinge' (Cassirer 1921, 339).
26. This first entry on page 35r is written in the same blue ink as the entries on the latter half of the previous page, next to which Beckett has written the date 'Germany, 2/10/36' (33v).
27. Marginalia 'Cf. Schopenhauer' in the right margin, next to: 'Er hebt das Schöne aus dem Bezirk der Kausalität heraus – denn auch die Freiheit ist nach Kant eine eigene Art der Kausalität – um es rein unter die Regel der inneren Gestaltung zu stellen' (Cassirer 1921, 333).
28. In his typed notes on the *Beiträge zu einer Kritik der Sprache*, Beckett excerpted Mauthner's assessment of the perspicuity of this 'thinker-poet' ('Denkdichter') and his most lively metaphorical representation of abstract concepts (TCD MS10971/5/4; Mauthner 1923, II.478).
29. 'Seit der Scholastik, ja eigentlich seit Platon und Aristoteles, ist nach Schopenhauer die Philosophie grossentheils ein fortgesetzter Missbrauch allgemeiner Begriffe. . . . Auch Spinoza's ganze Demonstrirmethode beruhe auf solchen ununtersuchten und zu weit gefassten Begriffen' (Frauenstädt 1923, I.11). On the next page, Frauenstädt denotes the philosophy of (notably) Hegel as 'Wortkram' (I.12).

30. With special reference to *Dichtung und Wahrheit*, Mauthner points out Goethe's 'überlegene Art, die Worte als blosse Worte zu gebrauchen' and the way he employs words ironically ('weil er die Worte in einer unnachahmlichen Weise gewissermassen ironisch gebraucht'; Mauthner 1923, 2.506–7).
31. Kapitel XXIII. 'Ueber Schriftstellerei und Stil' (536–586); Kapitel XXV. 'Ueber Sprache und Worte' (599–615); Kapitel XXIV. 'Ueber Lesen und Bücher' (587–98); Kapitel XXX. 'Ueber Lerm und Geräusch' (678–82)].
32. As an established author, he still appreciated Schopenhauer's essay on writing and style. On 27 May 1977 he wrote to Barbara Bray: 'Great things in Ueber Schriftstellerei' (TCD MS10948/1/615).
33. 'Er führt selbst Beispiele an, zu welchen Abwegen die Algebra mit blossen Begriffen, die keine Anschauung controlirt, führe' (Frauenstädt 1923, I.11).
34. In Ovid's *Metamorphoses* (1.15–16) the primal chaos is described as follows: 'utque erat et tellus illic et pontus et aer, / sic erat instabilis tellus, innabilis unda' [And where the earth was, there was sea and air too, / thus the earth was unstable, the waves unswimmable].
35. 'Nur durch die Kant'sche Unterscheidung zwischen empirischem und intelligiblem Charakter gelangen wir nach Schopenhauer zu der wahren Ansicht von der Freiheit' (Frauenstädt 1923, I.57–8).
36. Meyer had published not only a book on *Schopenhauer* (1871), but also a lecture against Schopenhauer's pessimism, 'Weltelend und Weltschmerz: Eine Rede gegen Schopenhauers und Hartmanns Pessimismus gehalten im wissenschaftl. Verein zu Berlin' (1872).
37. '"Diese seine Auffassung, nach der wir also einen fremden Schmerz nur deshalb mitfühlen, weil wir im Wesen der Dinge diesen Schmerz selber leiden, verwandelt das edle Mitleid in unedles Selbstgefühl"' (Meyer qtd. in Frauenstädt 1923, I.115).
38. '"Es kann hiermit so weit kommen, dass vielleicht Manchem, zumal in Augenblicken hypochondrischer Verstimmung, die Welt, von der ästhetischen Seite betrachtet, als ein Karikaturencabinet, von der intellektuellen, als ein Narrenhaus, und von der moralischen, als eine Gaunerherberge erscheint. Wird solche Verstimmung bleibend; so entsteht Misanthropie"' (Frauenstädt 1923, I.123).
39. 'Whoroscope' Notebook, just before the passage dated 'Germany 2/10/36' (WN 34r).
40. On 23 May 1977 Beckett thanked Bray for some books she sent and told her that he was 'Beginning the Schopenhauer' (TCD MS10948/1/614).
41. 'Sch[openhauer] zeichnet am Rande einen Stuhl.' (54); the drawing is also mentioned in the introduction: 'Neben Fichtes Lieblingssatz "Das Ich ist, weil es sich setzt" malt Schopenhauer einen Stuhl an den Seitenrand' (xvii).
42. Sandro Barbera has analysed the remarkable marginalia in Schopenhauer's library within the context of genetic criticism (Barbera 2001, 108).
43. 'wichtiger als das Lesen, war ihm doch das Selbstdenken. Das viele Lesen hielt er für nachtheilig, da das fortwährende Einströmen fremder Gedanken die eigenen hemme und ersticke, ja, auf die Länge die Denkkraft lähme' (I.175).

44. 'Nicht dem Vergnügen, sondern der Schmerzlosigkeit geht der Vernünftige nach' (I.177).
45. With many thanks to Mark Byron for his help with reference to the Addenda; see also Byron 2004, 13.
46. 'Hegel, diesen geistigen Kaliban' (II.xx); 'den Unsinn der Hegelei' (II.xxv) – both fragments are marked in pencil.
47. 'der Alleszermalmer' ('Fragmente der Geschichte der Philosophie' in *Parerga und Paralipomena I*, V.47).
48. Beckett had already made a pun on this concept in 'What a Misfortune' (*MPTK* 112), where it is turned into '*Beltschmerz*'.
49. The addition is in pencil, whereas the insertion mark is in black ink.
50. The opening sentence of the 1907 lecture 'Der Dichter und diese Zeit' mentions both the notions of the 'poetical element' and 'our time' explicitly: 'Man hat Ihnen angekündigt, daß ich zu Ihnen über den Dichter und diese Zeit sprechen will, über das Dasein des Dichters oder des dichterischen Elementes in dieser unserer Zeit, und manche Ankündigungen, höre ich, formulieren das Thema noch ernsthafter, indem sie von dem Problem des dichterischen Daseins in der Gegenwart sprechen' (Hugo von Hofmannsthal, *Gesammelte Werke in zehn Einzelbänden. Reden und Aufsätze* 1–3. Vol. 1, Frankfurt am Main: Fischer, 1979, 54–81; 54).
51. Klaus Albrecht notes that Axel Kaun had been hired by Rowohlt Verlag in February 1937, but he left the company in June of the same year (Albrecht 2005, 33).
52. The colophon reads: 'Dieser Auszug aus einem 1907 in Wien vom Dichter gehaltenen Vortrag wurde im Herbst 1937 von Axel Kaun in der Offizin Haag-Drugulin, Leipzig aus der Claudius-Fraktur gesetzt und in 20 Exemplaren handabgezogen.'
53. 'Alles, was in einer Sprache geschrieben wird, und, wagen wir das Wort, alles, was in ihr gedacht wird, deszendiert von den Produkten der wenigen, die jemals mit dieser Sprache schöpferisch geschaltet haben' (63).
54. For instance, the word 'self-consciousness' among the marginalia on the interleaf facing pages 125 in Plümacher's *Der Pessimismus* differs considerably from the same word as it is written in the 'Whoroscope' Notebook (WN 61v). The handwriting of some other notes in the 'Whoroscope' Notebook (such as the note 'Leibniz to Locke "Nihil est in intellectu..."' on page 62r, excerpted from Sartre's *L'Imagination*) comes much closer to the handwriting of the English translations and summaries in Plümacher. The pen is equally thick, the ink equally black, but some of the letters are consistently written differently. The 'z' at the end of the word 'Weltschmerz' in the Plümacher notes, for instance, differs from the 'z' at the end of 'Leibniz' with the short extra horizontal line in the middle (which is also the way it is written in Beckett's German excerpts from Mauthner).
55. For the purposes of this chapter, the survey is limited to the Kant-Mauthner notes. Each notebook page is characterized by means of just a few of the notes it contains, focusing on Beckett's reading of philosophical works.

56. 'C'est la grande œuvre de Kant, accomplie dans les cinquante pages de l'Esthétique transcendantale, d'avoir démontré que l'espace et le temps n'ont point, d'une part, une existence suprasensible, que, d'autre part, ils ne sont pas non plus des propriétés de l'objet; qu'au contraire ils appartiennent au sujet de la connaissance et qu'ils sont les formes de la sensibilité de ce sujet. (Jules de Gaulthier [sic])' (WN 60v).

57. The corners of the following pages are folded down: 110, 126, 131, 150, 237, 243, 261, 276, 298, 301, 332, 334, 338, 340, 341, 345, 351, 359, 361, 363.

58. Dhan Gopal Mukerdji, *Brahmane et paria. [Caste and outcast.]* Traduit de l'anglais par Sophie Godet. Collection Orient 2. Paris/Neuchâtel: Attinger, 1928.

59. 'Philosophy in 20th Century stresses process of cognition: "Ihre bedeutsamste Ausprägung hat diese erkenntniskritische u. wissenschaftstheoretisch gerichtete Philosophie gefunden in der Denkweise des "transzendentalen Idealismus", – vertreten in Deutschland vor allem durch die .. Richtungen u. Schulen des Neu-Kantianismus (vor allem die "Marburger Schule": H. Cohen, P. Natorp, E. Cassirer u. die "badische" oder "südwestdeutsche Schule": W. Windelband u. H. Rickert, E. La[sk], Br. Bauch) . . . (Heimsoeth)' (WN 64v).

60. The following pages show pencil lines in the margins (sometimes more than one per page): Volume 1:

xi, xiv, xv, xvi, 2, 13, 19, 31, 33, 35, 41, 42, 43, 48, 50, 51, 52, 53, 54, 55, 56, 59, 60, 61, 64, 65, 66, 67, 69, 70, 77, 83, 84, 85, 86, 87, 88, 89, 90, 93, 97, 98, 99, 100, 101, 102, 103, 104, 110, 119, 134, 135, 136, 137, 142, 144, 145, 146, 147, 148, 149, 151, 153, 154, 155, 156, 157, 159, 162, 164, 166, 167, 169, 170, 171, 172, 173, 176, 177, 181, 183, 185, 188, 193, 199, 200, 202, 203, 204, 209, 210, 213, 219, 225, 228, 229, 230, 243, 244, 245, 247, 250, 251, 257, 258, 259, 260, 261, 262, 263, 264, 266, 268, 269, 270, 271, 274, 275, 276, 278, 280, 288, 289, 290, 291, 293, 300, 303, 304, 306, 316, 317, 318, 321, 322, 323, 324, 325, 326, 327, 328, 329, 330, 331, 332, 333, 334, 335, 336, 337, 339, 340, 341, 342, 343, 344, 345, 346, 352, 353, 354, 355, 356, 358, 359, 360, 361, 363, 364, 365, 366, 367, 368, 369, 372, 373, 375, 376, 377, 379, 382, 391, 393, 396, 397, 399, 403, 405, 409, 410, 411, 413, 414, 415, 422, 424, 425, 427, 428, 429, 433, 436, 437, 438, 439, 446, 448, 449, 451, 452, 454, 455, 456, 457, 459, 460, 463, 466, 469, 470, 471, 473, 485, 489, 490, 491, 493, 494, 495, 506, 517, 520, 521, 522, 523, 531, 532, 533, 534, 535, 536, 537, 538, 540, 541, 543, 546, 547, 553, 554, 557, 558, 561, 564, 566, 568, 570, 571, 577, 578, 579, 580, 581, 582, 583, 584, 586, 587, 588, 589, 591, 592, 593, 594, 597, 598, 600, 601, 603, 604, 606, 607, 611, 612, 615, 617, 618, 632, 633, 634, 635, 636, 637, 638, 639, 641, 642, 643, 646, 647, 648, 650, 652, 654, 655, 656, 666, 667, 669, 670, 671, 676, 678, 680, 681, 682, 684, 686, 687, 688, 689, 690, 691, 693, 695, 696, 700, 701, 702, 703, 704, 705, 706, 707, 709, 712, 713, 715, 717, 719

Volume 2:

1, 3, 4, 10, 11, 13, 14, 15, 17, 20, 21, 23, 24, 25, 26, 28, 31, 39, 43, 45, 46, 47, 48, 55, 56, 58, 71, 83, 99, 100, 123, 132, 138, 140, 141, 144, 147, 149, 150, 151, 152, 153, 155,

158, 159, 160, 161, 162, 164, 170, 171, 172, 173, 174, 175, 176, 180, 181, 182, 183, 184, 187, 189, 192, 193, 194, 197, 200, 201, 203, 204, 205, 208, 214, 216, 219, 220, 222, 226, 227, 232, 245, 248, 267, 268, 269, 270, 272, 274, 276, 282, 283, 285, 289, 293, 295, 296, 299, 300, 301, 315, 316, 323, 325, 329, 330, 337, 348, 349, 354, 355, 356, 371, 384, 385, 409, 410, 411, 423, 426, 427, 428, 432, 433, 434, 437, 438, 444, 450, 454, 455, 456, 457, 460, 461, 474, 476, 477, 478, 479, 480, 483, 487, 489, 498, 507, 513, 514, 515, 525, 526, 550, 551, 552, 555, 556, 557, 558, 559, 562, 567, 570, 576, 579, 580, 581, 582, 583, 584, 585, 586, 587, 588, 589, 594, 595, 596, 597, 613, 614, 618, 629, 646, 649, 651, 652, 657, 659, 676, 683, 684, 685, 687, 689, 691, 695, 697, 699, 700, 701, 702, 703, 704, 705, 706, 707, 708, 710, 711, 712, 713, 714, 715, 716, 717, 718

Volume 3:

vii, x, xi, xvi, 2, 3, 10, 42, 43, 48, 56, 80, 81, 84, 101, 133, 137, 153, 154, 189, 197, 198, 207, 208, 214, 216, 217, 223, 224, 234, 235, 243, 244, 245, 246, 248, 249, 251, 253, 255, 256, 257, 258, 266, 267, 271, 286, 287, 290, 291, 292, 297, 309, 311, 321, 332, 347, 348, 349, 350, 351, 359, 362, 363, 366, 367, 368, 369, 370, 371, 373, 384, 393, 395, 396, 401, 402, 416, 420, 421, 422, 423, 431, 458, 459, 461, 462, 463, 468, 472, 473, 474, 475, 479, 483, 484, 485, 486, 487, 488, 492, 493, 495, 515, 519, 520, 521, 522, 523, 524, 525, 526, 529, 530, 532, 535, 536, 541, 542, 544, 547, 552, 553, 556, 564, 565, 567, 568, 569, 578, 579, 580, 585, 591, 592, 596, 597, 599, 602, 603, 604, 605, 612, 613, 614, 615, 616, 617, 618, 619, 621, 622, 626, 627, 628, 629, 631, 632, 634, 635, 636, 639, 640, 641

61. 'Und die indischen Weisen bilden dazu noch den Begriff einer Überstille aus.' (Mauthner 1923, I.83).
62. In *Finnegans Wake* notebook VI.B.41 (235–6; 269–74), Joyce's notes on Mauthner start with two references to pages 455 and 479, both of which feature a subheading 'Vico' (Van Hulle 2002). These characteristically short and paratactic notes span the first two volumes of Mauthner's *Beiträge*. The notes on the third volume can be found in notebook VI.B.46 (46–60; cf. Van Hulle 1999). Joyce's notes do not correspond any better with the marked passages in the Mauthner volumes in Beckett's library. Only 13 out of 99 Mauthner entries correspond with a passage that is marked in the copy of the *Beiträge* in Beckett's library.
63. When Linda Ben-Zvi wrote another letter to Beckett (one year later), asking him directly what the significance of Mauthner was with respect to his writing, Beckett replied (on 2 September 1979): 'I skimmed through Mauthner for Joyce in 1929 or 30' (Ben-Zvi 1984, 66). Beckett had to retrospectively reconstruct the situation forty years after the facts. The date he mentions conflicts with the dating of the Mauthner notes ('late spring and early summer of 1938', Pilling 2006b, 164).
64. See Beckett 1978, 69.
65. '"Nicht *wie* die Welt ist, ist das Mystische, sondern *dass* sie ist" (6.44). "Sinn", der aus einer Erklärung kommen müsste, ist nicht in der Welt' (12).

66. The following passages in Russell's introduction are marked in pencil:

'The essential business of language is to assert or deny facts'. (x)

'In order that a certain sentence should assert a certain fact there must, however the language may be constructed, be something in common between the structure of the sentence and the structure of the fact. This is perhaps the most fundamental thesis of Mr Wittgenstein's theory'. (x)

'Mr Wittgenstein maintains that everything properly philosophical belongs to what can only be shown, to what is in common between a fact and its logical picture'. (xii)

'In this way the naming of simples is shown to be what is logically first in logic'. (xiii)

'All the propositions of logic, he maintains, are tautologies, such, for example, as "*p* or not-*p*"'. (xiv)

'There cannot, in Wittgenstein's logic, be any such thing as a causal nexus. "The events of the future", he says, "*cannot* be inferred from those of the present. Superstition is the belief in the causal nexus"'. (xvi)

'This amounts to saying that "object" is a pseudo-concept. To say "*x* is an object" is to say nothing'. (xvii)

'Objects can only be mentioned in connexion with some definite property'. (xvii)

'We here touch one instance of Wittgenstein's fundamental thesis, that it is impossible to say anything about the world as a whole, and that whatever can be said has to be about bounded portions of the world'. (xvii)

'According to this view we could only say things about the world as a whole if we could get outside the world, if, that is to say, it ceased to be for us the whole world'. (xviii)

'This, he says, gives the key to Solipsism. What Solipsism intends is quite correct, but this cannot be said, it can only be shown. That the world is *my* world appears in the fact that the boundaries of language (the only language I understand) indicate the boundaries of my world. The metaphysical subject does not belong to the world but is a boundary of the world'. (xviii)

'This reduces ultimately to the question of the meaning of propositions, that is to say, the meaning of propositions is the only non-psychological portion of the problem involved in the analysis of belief'. (xx)

'Everything, therefore, which is involved in the very idea of the expressiveness of language must remain incapable of being expressed in language, and is, therefore, inexpressible in a perfectly precise sense'. (xxi)

'What causes hesitation is the fact that, after all, Mr Wittgenstein manages to say a good deal about what cannot be said, thus suggesting to the skeptical reader that possibly there may be some loophole through a hierarchy of languages, or by some other exit. The whole subject of ethics, for example, is placed by Mr Wittgenstein in the mystical, inexpressible region. Nevertheless he is capable of conveying his ethical opinions'. (xxi)

'These difficulties suggest to my mind some such possibility as this: that every language has, as Mr Wittgenstein says, a structure concerning which, *in the language*, nothing can be said, but that there may be another language dealing with the structure of the first language, and having itself a new structure, and that to this hierarchy of languages there may be no limit'. (xxii)

67. 'Die Sprache ist nur ein Scheinwert wie eine Spielregel, die auch umso zwingender wird, je mehr Mitspieler sich ihr unterwerfen, die aber die Wirklichkeitswelt weder ändern noch begreifen will' (Mauthner 1923, I.25).

68. A ticket (possibly a bookseller's ticket, mentioning 'DEC 10', but no year) is inserted between pages 90 and 91. The majority of pencil marks (on pages 6–7, 9, 17, 25, 27, 31, 40, 41, 146, 148) are marginal ticks (v). The longest marginalia (in the bottom margin of page 6) is in French: 'A rappeler, Traité de Psycho – [xx] – l'image / A rappeler, Mercier, les grands courants de la psycho. contemporaine / même [plan], de retrospection / historique [é] partant de la / psycho. de Descartes – mais traitement métaphysique, [xxiste]. / [Certaines] différences de vocabulaire, [de] quo, / entre lui et Sartre'.

69. In between, on page 27, the following passage is accompanied by a check in pencil and a marginal reference to one of the books on the history of philosophy from which Beckett took his philosophy notes (v. Burnet / Early Gk. Φ.'): 'Ce qu'on a pris longtemps pour un empirisme n'est donc qu'une métaphysique réaliste manqué'.

70. For a more detailed discussion of Beckett and Adorno, see the Adorno dossier in the *Journal of Beckett Studies* 19.2 (2010).

CHAPTER 8

1. 'Achevé d'imprimer le 10 janvier 1930.'
2. 'Triplex distinguitur **castitas**, scilicet **conjugalis**, **vidualis** et **virginalis**. Conjugalis, usum matrimonii juxta rationis dictamen moderatur; vidualis, in eo consistit ut pos matrimonii dissolutionem ab omnibus venereis abstineatur; virginalis, perfectae huic abstinentiae integritatem carnis jungit' (Bouvier 1852, 8). The words in Beckett's 'Dream' Notebook, derived from Bouvier, are marked in bold.
3. 'CAPUT PRIMUM: *De luxuria in genere* . . . Rectè definitur, **Appetitus inordinatus delectationis venereae**' (9).
4. 'Caput II. De speciebus luxuriae naturalis consummatae: Art. I. De simplici fornicatione (§1. De meretricio; §2. De concubinatu); Art. II. De stupro; Art. III. De raptu; Art. IV: De adulterio; Art. V. De incestu; Art. VI: De sacrilegio' (210).
5. Beckett's note 'caeteris paribus' derives from page 18 (in the section 'De simplici fornicatione, §1. De meretricio'): 'At *Sylvius, Billuart, Dens*, aliique theologi docent ut probablilius virum qui com meretrice fornicatur, hanc circumstantiam declarare non teneri, quia, **ceteris paribus**, talis fornicatio respectu ipsius gravior esse non videtur' (17; 'Dream' Notebook 432). The following notes derive from the sections 'De stupro' and 'De raptu': '**Stuprum** verò, quatenùs speciale est vitium, à multis definitur *violenta*, et meliùs ab aliis, ***illicita virginis***

defloratio' (24; *DN* 433). The first paragraph of the Articulus Tertius, *De raptu*, opens as follows: 'Raptus in genere est vis cuicumque personae aut parentibus ejus causâ explendae libidinis illata. Haec definitio **raptui violentiae** et **raptui seductionis** aequaliter competit' (28; *DN* 435).

6. '*ponitur in viâ meretricandi, à quâ retrahebatur ne **signaculum virginitatis** amitteret*; sunt verba S. Thomae' (25–6; *DN* 434).
7. 'ergo pollutio extra concubitum naturalem, est evidenter contra naturam; quod ipsi pagani agnoverunt, ut patet sequentibus Martialis versibus, *Epig*. 42: 'Ipsam, crede, tibi naturam dicere verum: / **Istud quod digitis, Pontice, perdis homo est.**" (58–9, '§I. *De pollutione voluntariâ in se*'; *DN* 436). The next note in the 'Dream' Notebook derives from Bouvier's claim that 'pollutio' is a mortal sin, starting with the tag 'Certum est 1.° ... Certum est 2.° ...' and closing with the formula: '**hoc patet**' (this suffices) (60, §II. *De pollutione voluntariâ in causâ*; *DN* 437). The last note on this verso page is based on Bouvier's definition of 'Distillatio': '**Distillatio** est fluxus **seminis** imperfecti vel alterius humoris **muscosi**, quasi **guttatim** et sine gravibus concupiscentiae motibus' (66, §III. *De pollutione nocturnâ*; *DN* 439).
8. '*Quaeritur* 1.° ad quid teneatur homo qui evigilans advertit se pollutionem experiri. R. Debet mentem ad Deum elevare, eum invocare, signo crucis se munire, nihil ad expellendum semen positive facere, delectation voluptatis renuntiare' (Bouvier 1852, 65). The next note in Beckett's 'Dream' Notebook derives from Bouvier's section §IV. '*De motibus inordinatis*': 'tutius est igitur Deum placidè invocare, **B. Virginem**, Angelum custodem, patronum aliosque Sanctos precari' (68; *DN* 448).
9. '4.ᵉ Q. *Quand l'accouchement est laborieux ou paraît impossible, faut-il baptiser l'enfant dans le sain de sa mère?* ... Si on n'aperçoit aucun membre à l'extérieur, et si cependant l'accouchement s'annonce comme très-difficile ou impossible, Benoît XIV est d'avis qu'on essaie de baptiser l'enfant dans le sein de sa mère. ... On introduit de l'eau tiède avec la main, une seringue ou un syphon, de manière qu'elle touche l'enfant ou au moins son enveloppe, n'importe en quel endroit, et on prononce en même temps les paroles de la forme.' (200–1)
10. Dublin Local Studies Collection, GA EX00 027790 8001. We owe a debt of gratitude to Martha Black for drawing our attention to this copy and for helping us access and consult the physical document.
11. We owe a debt of gratitude to Iain Bailey and Feargal Whelan for their kind help with this annotation.
12. 'And there were also two other, malefactors, led with him to be put to death. And when they were come to the place, which is called Calvary, there they crucified him, and the malefactors, one on the right hand, and the other on the left. Then said Jesus, Father, forgive them; for they know not what they do. And they parted his raiment, and cast lots' (Luke 23:32–4).
13. Isaiah remained an interest of Beckett's. For instance, on the last page of the manuscript of 'For to End Yet Again', near the phrase 'sky forsaken of its vultures', Beckett has written in the margin 'Isa. vii. 16' ('For before the child

shall know to refuse the evil, and choose the good, the land that thou abhorrest shall be forsaken of both her kings.')

14. John 2:8: 'And he saith unto them, Draw out now, and bear unto the governor of the feast'; John 3:8: 'The wind bloweth where it listeth, and thou hearest the sound thereof, but canst not tell whence it cometh, and whither it goeth: so is every one that is born of the Spirit.' Leviticus 9:2: 'And he said unto Aaron, Take thee a young calf for a sin offering, and a ram for a burnt offering, without blemish, and offer them before the LORD'; Lev. 9:12: 'And he slew the burnt offering; and Aaron's sons presented unto him the blood . . .'; Lev. 9:13: 'And they presented the burnt offering unto him . . .'; Lev. 9:24: 'And there came a fire out from before the LORD . . .'; Numbers 14:1–2: 'And all the congregation lifted up their voice, and cried; and the people wept that night. And all the children of Israel murmured against Moses and against Aaron: and the whole congregation said unto them, Would God that we had died in the land of Egypt! or would God that we had died in this wilderness!'; Numbers 14:9: 'Only rebel not ye against the LORD, neither fear ye the people of the land . . .'.
15. 'And the LORD gave unto Israel all the land which he sware to give unto their fathers; and they possessed it, and dwelt therein. And the LORD gave them rest round about, according to all that he sware unto their fathers: and there stood not a man of all their enemies before them; the LORD delivered all their enemies into their hand. There failed not ought of any good thing which the LORD had spoken unto the house of Israel; all came to pass.' (The marked words are underlined in pencil.)
16. A possible candidate is Beckett's aunt Cissie Sinclair. The handwriting resembles that on the postcard of Dürer's drawing of two praying hands (sent from Kassel to Paris on 16 February 1932) inserted in volume 2 of Victor Bérard's translation of the *Odyssée* (see Chapter 6; the difference in writing tools slightly complicates the comparison).
17. John 5:20: 'And we know that the Son of God is come, and hath given us an understanding . . .'.
18. The note is located on the verso side of page 63r, containing notes from an article by H. Spencer Jones, published in January 1939 (see Chapter 7).
19. The Martin translation reads: 'car Dieu est charité' (1 John 4:8).
20. The Segond translation reads: 'Ses compassions ne sont pas à leur terme; elles se renouvellent chaque matin'.
21. 'Quoniam tres sunt, qui testimonium dant in coelo: Pater, Verbum, et Spiritus Sanctus: et hi tres unum sunt' (Lalanne 1857, 176).
22. In the chapter on 'Supposition d'auteurs' under the subheading '1re épitre de saint Jean': 'Ce verset manque non seulement dans les manuscrits les plus anciens, mais aussi dans tous les manuscrits grecs, si l'on en excepte trois ou quatre qui ne sont pas antérieurs au seizième siècle' (Lalanne 1857, 176).
23. Voltaire, 'Troisième lettre du journal d'Amabed', in: *Œuvres Complètes de Voltaire avec des notes et une notice historique sur la vie de Voltaire*, vol. 8, Paris: Furne, 1836, 515.

24. Another edition (Garnier) mentions explicitly that the footnotes are Voltaire's. Each of the notes is marked as '*Note de Voltaire*' in the *Œuvres Complètes de Voltaire*, tome 21 (Paris: Garnier 1879), 455–8.
25. The context in Hosea is the following: 'So he went and took Gomer the daughter of Diblaim; which conceived, and bare him a son. ... And she conceived again, and bare a daughter. And [God] said unto him, Call her name Loruhamah: for I will no more have mercy upon the house of Israel; but I will utterly take them away' (King James Bible, Hosea 1:3; 1:6).
26. The 'Oholiba' of 'Hell Crane to Starling' is changed to 'Aholiba' in the HRC re-write ('To My Daughter'). With many thanks to John Pilling for this reference.
27. We owe a debt of gratitude to the late Seán Lawlor for pointing out the intertextual reference between 'Hell Crane to Starling' and Genesis 19.
28. Beckett probably found the notion of the 'petites perceptions' in Windelband, who defines them as follows: 'In the language of to-day the *petites perceptions* would be *unconscious mental states (Vorstellungen)*' (1958, 424).
29. The Veronica, most prominent as a motif in *Endgame*, but also present in 'Enueg II', 'What a Misfortune' and *Watt* (Ackerley and Gontarski 2004, 605), was apparently part of Beckett's vocabulary in everyday life as well. Deirdre Bair mentions an occasion in Sean O'Sullivan's studio, when some friends were praising the work of an Irish realist painter and Beckett suddenly disagreed, calling the painter a 'Veronicist who would wipe the face of Christ with a sanitary towel' (Bair 1978, 116).
30. 'Des écrivains un peu crédules ont raconté que saint Maclou ou Malo dit un jour la messe en pleine mer sur le dos d'une baleine qu'il prit pour une île' (73). The marginalia next to this passage note: 'Aussi Saint-Brendan'.
31. 'On est guéri du mal caduc en proférant ces paroles: *Dabit, habet, hebet*, ou en portant au doigt un anneau d'argent au dedans duquel il y aurait écrit: *Dabi, habi, haber, hebar* (chacun de ces mots précédés d'une croix), ou en portant sur soi les noms des trois rois mages, Gaspar, Melchior, Balthasar. Plusieurs rituels, entre autres celui de Chartres, de l'an 1500, témoignent du crédit qu'avait obtenu cette tradition:

   Gaspar fert myrrham, thus Melchior Belthasar aurum.
   Haec tria qui secum portabit nomina regum
   Solvitur a morbo, Christi pictate, *caduco*. (107)
32. 'Une des reliques les plus fameuses est la Véronique ou *Sainte Face* que quelques églises sont fières de posséder.

   Le nom de *Vera icon* était consacré aux images de Jésus-Christ; on l'appliqua plus tard par confusion à la sainte femme qui, suivant une tradition fort accréditée, reçut sur le voile dont elle essuyait la figure du Sauveur l'empreinte révérée appelée Sainte Face. Des savants avaient pensé que le nom de Véronique était une altération de Bérénice, nom [p. 58] que l'Évangile apocryphe de Nicodème donne à la femme que Jésus-Christ guérit d'un flux de sang. Il parait toutefois que le nom de Bérénice est une modification de celui de

Prounice, qu'une des sectes les plus importantes des Gnostiques, les Valentiens, donnaient à cette même hémorroïsse. . . .

On raconte que le suaire ayant été plié en trois par la sainte, l'image du Sauveur s'y était imprimée en trois endroits et que ces trois exemplaires étaient conservés à Rome, à Turin et à Irun en Espagne.

L'histoire de la Sainte Ampoule, conservée à Reims et apportée, dit-on, par un ange lors du couronnement de Clovis, a longtemps été célèbre. C'est Hincmar qui, dans son *Historia Francorum*, a le premier raconté ce miracle . . .' (57–8)

33. Rosemary Pountney pointed out that Beckett noted the instruction 'vaguen' to himself in the margin of a typescript of *Happy Days* (Pountney 1988, 149).
34. 'Un jésuite d'Annecy, nommé Jean Ferrand, composa un gros livre au sujet des reliques, dans lequel il n'hésita pas à dire que lorsqu'il se trouve dans diverses églises des têtes ou des corps du même saint, c'est la Providence qui a produit cette multiplication miraculeuse afin d'entretenir la dévotion des fidèles' (59).
35. The opening words of the relevant paragraph are underlined: 'L'excommunication des animaux durant le moyen âge est un fait étrange, mais il est attesté de la façon la plus irrécusable dans le recueil des consultations de Barthélemy de Chassanée, jurisconsulte célèbre dans la première moitié du seizième siècle; cette collection, imprimée à Lyon en 1531, in-folio, a obtenu plusieurs éditions. La première de ces consultations est intitulée: De excommunicatione animalium insectorum' (91).
36. 'Dans la cinquième partie, Chassanée définit l'anathème et la malédiction. Après quoi il établit que les animaux ne peuvent être excommuniés. Dix à douze pages sont employées à établir ce point . . . que les péchés des hommes ont excité la colère de Dieu, et qu'on ne saurait punir des animaux qui sont les instruments de ses vengeances. A ce propos, il fait une énumération des crimes que commettent les juges, les avocats, les notaires, les gens d'église, les femmes, les jeunes gens et les vieillards.' (94).
37. 'Mais voici le revers de la médaille. L'auteur, combattant lui-même les assertions qu'il a posées, développe de longs et nombreux argument pour établir que les animaux peuvent être excommuniés' (94).
38. The French version of *Watt* employs the word 'processionnaires' instead of the term 'chenille' in the source text: 'Autre exemple. Les **anguilles** abondaient jadis dans le lac de Genève, à tel point que les Génevois non-seulement les prirent en dégoût, mais en furent même tourmentés. Pour s'en défaire ils eurent recours à l'excommunication, à la suite de laquelle toutes les anguilles disparurent; depuis lors le lac n'en produit plus.

Après des faits pareils rapportés sur la foi d'autrui, Chassanée cite ce qu'il a vu lui-même; . . . il dit avoir vu plusieurs sentences d'excommunication prononcées par l'officialité d'Autun et par celles de **Lyon** et de **Mâcon**, tant contre les insectes dont il s'agit ici que contre d'autres animaux nuisible, tels que les **rats** et les **limaçons**. . . .

Ce n'est pas d'ailleurs dans la Bourgogne seulement [p. 97] que nous rencontrons des exemples de procéder par voie d'excommunication contre des animaux dévastateurs. Les habitants de Constance et de **Côme** dirigèrent des poursuites contre de gros vers qui ravageaient leurs campagnes. Voir ce que dit à ce sujet le jésuite Delrio (*Disquisitiones magicae*, liv. III, part. II, quest. 4, sect. 8). Cet auteur raconte aussi qu'un évêque de **Lausanne** excommuniait les **sangsues** qui infectaient de leur venin les poissons du lac . . .

Chorier, dans son *Histoire générale du Dauphiné*, t. II, p. 712, dit en parlant de l'année 1584: 'Elle fut remarquable par les pluies continuelles; il y eut un nombre infini de chenilles . . . Les murailles, les fenêtres et les chinées des maisons en étoient couvertes, même dans les villes; c'étoit une vive et hideuse représentation de la plaie d'Egypte par les sauterelles. Le grand-vicaire de **Valence** fit citer les **chenilles** devant lui; il leur donna un procureur pour les défendre; la cause fut plaidée solennement, et il les condamna à vider le diocèse' (95; 96–7).

39. 'Chassanée fait ressortir les graves inconvénients qu'il y aurait à vouloir, par des excommunications, empêcher les animaux de nuire aux hommes, et remplir ainsi leur destination céleste. Il y aurait évidemment conflit entre Dieu et son Église.' (94).
40. Chris Ackerley notes, with reference to the eels of Como, that 'Beckett's source, as Mary Bryden discovered (2008a, 78) is E. P. Evans, *The Criminal Prosecution and Capital Punishment of Animals* (1906)' (Ackerley 2005, 44). Based on the reading traces in Beckett's library, it seems safe to say that the source is most probably Beckett's copy of *Curiosités théologiques*.
41. 'L'auteur s'est proposé de se moquer de certaines opinions qui poussaient l'interprétation des dogmes jusqu'au ridicule' ([Brunet 1884], 179).

CHAPTER 9

1. Two pages have been 'desecrated' – there is a page (349–50) missing in volume XVIII (entries 'Giacomo Meyerbeer, 'Vsevolod Meyerhold', 'Alice Meynell' and 'Meyrifab' and the entry on the Dutch painter Jan Steen has been cut out.
2. Beckett also identified the edition in a letter to Ruby Cohn of 17 November 1986 (UoR MS5100).
3. See also Beckett's early mention of possessing a copy of Larousse's dictionary in a letter to MacGreevy of 1 January 1935.
4. Although he does go on to say, 'Get me a copy, will you, to bring back with you'.
5. As the editors of the letters note, this comment refers to the discussion of the pronunciation of these consonants on an unnumbered page under the heading 'Avvertenze'.
6. 'Vejamos como dois mestres da língua, Miguel Torga Aquilino Ribeiro, *aperfeiçoaram*, buscando uma *expressão de maior valor artístico*, o que haviam anteriormente redigido'.
7. Cf. Beckett's story 'A Wet Night' in *More Pricks than Kicks*, which mentions Bartlett (45).

8. Beckett also owned a copy of *La Vie des Animaux*, 2 vols (Larousse, 1952 [1950]), mentioned in a letter to Barbara Bray as having 'nice plates' (31 October 1961; TCD MS10948/1/165).

CHAPTER 10

1. As John Pilling notes, the bulk of *Dream* was written in Paris between February and July 1932 (Pilling 1999, xiv) and toward the end of June 1932, Beckett sent the manuscript to Chatto and Windus (Pilling 2006a, 37). On 5 July, Charles Prentice reacted positively to the new part ('THREE'), but on 19 July he turned down *Dream of Fair to Middling Women*, after which it was rejected by Jonathan Cape and the Hogarth Press (to whom Beckett had offered it on 29 July; Pilling 2006a, 38).
2. In *Samuel Beckett's 'More Pricks than Kicks'*, John Pilling suggests that the 'varieties' and 'species' distinction is 'probably also from Darwin' (2011, 198). Although the passage is not marked in Beckett's copy of *The Origin of Species*, the sentence occurs in the second edition (Darwin 1860, 49).
3. Cf. Chapter VIII. Hybridism, last part: '*Hybrids and Mongrels compared, independently of their fertility*', discussing the differences between the so-called hybrid offspring of species and the so-called mongrel offspring of varieties.
4. Beckett jotted down the same line almost half a century later, in the so-called 'Super Conquérant' Notebook (UoR MS2934, 9v; www.beckettarchive.org) when he was writing the third and last part of *Stirrings Still*. For a discussion of this line's occurrences in Beckett's work, see Van Hulle 2008, 149–56.
5. 'The wide difference of the fish on opposite sides of continuous mountain-ranges, which from an early period must have parted river-systems and completely prevented their inosculation, seems to lead to this same conclusion' (Darwin 1860, 383–4).
6. Published in *Discovery: A Monthly Popular Journal of Knowledge*, New Series, Vol. II, No. 10, January 1939, 36–47. Beckett's notes are on pages 62r–63r of the 'Whoroscope' Notebook.
7. 'La science expliquera tout; et nous n'en serons pas plus éclairés. Elle fera de nous des dieux ahuris' (Rostand 1967, 67).
8. For a digital facsimile, see the Beckett Digital Manuscript Project, www.beckettarchive.org
9. Discussing Bergson, Sartre concludes: 'il a eu recours, pour justifier ces deux opérations contradictoires, à un syncrétisme de la conscience et de la matière. Mais, pour avoir constamment confondu le noème et la noèse, il a été amené à doter cette réalité syncrétique qu'il nomme image, tantôt d'une valeur de noème, tantôt d'une valeur noétique, selon les besoins de sa construction. D'unification, point : mais une ambiguïté perpétuelle' (Sartre 1936, 51).
10. Beckett had been reading Sartre in the previous months. On 26 May 1938, he wrote to MacGreevy: 'I have read Sartre's Nausée & find it extraordinarily good. But you would not agree with me' (*LSB* 626).

CHAPTER 11

1. At the time of his death in 1989, Beckett also owned A. L. Bacharach's *Lives of the Great Composers* (1935) and Albert Lavignac's *La Musique et les musiciens* (1938).
2. Beckett also mentioned the 'schwer gefasste Entschluss' in a letter to A. J. Leventhal of 14 March 1934. Beckett used the reference to inevitability ('Muss es sein') throughout his correspondence, such as in a letter to Jocelyn Herbert of 3 January 1979 in anticipation of forthcoming TV work in Stuttgart.
3. Duthuit's letter subtly anticipates the future disagreements with Beckett that ultimately led to an irreparable break in their relationship. Beckett's last surviving letters to Duthuit date from 1954 and hint at some kind of dispute. Georges Duthuit's letters to Mary Hutchinson give further insight into the change of mood between the two close friends. On receipt of Beckett's *Fin de partie*, Duthuit wrote to Hutchinson in February 1957 as follows: 'À ce propos j'ai reçu la dernière pièce de Beckett, «Fin de Partie», que je trouve imbécile et dégoûtante, pas dans le sens où il espérait que cette pièce le soit. Je n'ai pas eu le courage d'aller jusqu'à son histoire, dont vous me parlez pour la [radio?]. En voilà un qui met trop de temps à mourir, et qui parle trop pour un silencieux. Il m'a envoyé une dédicace avec le mot 'ami', mais c'est à choisir: ou les sentiments communs sont [volables?], ou, comme il le considère, ils ne sont que farce macabre et honteuse absurdité, comme il le considère, tout à son avantage. J'en ai fini avec ces grosses ficelles irlandaises, trop bien ajustées, et je le lui ai fait savoir, en essayant de ne pas le blesser. Qu'il garde son public bourgeois. On finira par les jours à l'OTAN: c'est tout indiqué'. [In this respect, I received Beckett's latest piece, 'Endgame', which I find stupid and disgusting, not in the way he hoped the piece would be. I didn't have the courage to go to the story of which you speak for the radio. There's one who takes too much time to die, and who speaks too much for one who is quiet. He sent me a dedication with the word 'friend', but one is to choose: either the common sentiments are [stealable?], or, as he believes, they are merely a gruesome joke, a shameful absurdity, all to his advantage. I'm done with these all too well adjusted big Irish tricks, and I have told him so, trying not to hurt him. Let him keep his bourgeois public. We will end the days at NATO: all points to this]. In a further letter dated 30 August 1959, Duthuit confesses that he cannot write like Beckett, when one is feeling 'moribond'. Finally, in a letter dated 1 March 1962, Duthuit appears to berate Hutchinson for jumping on the critical bandwagon and applauding Beckett's 'great denunciation of life' and 'captivating Irish complaint', before going on to discuss the reception of the 'Three Dialogues'.
4. Beckett would continue to listen to and engage with Beethoven's work throughout his life, and the TV play 'Ghost Trio' is based on the piece 'Der Geist' (op. 70, #1).
5. Pilling notes that Beckett had told MacGreevy in a letter of 31 December 1935 that it was a shame that there was no recording of Elena Gerhardt singing 'An die Musik' (2011, 190).
6. See also Beckett's comment to John Beckett in 1975 that he was 'shivering through the grim journey again' (qtd. in Knowlson 1996, 626).

7. Anne Atik (2001, 114) notes that she played Beckett the recording of Elisabeth Schumann singing Schubert's 'Nacht und Träume' on 4 November 1981; a first version of Beckett's play was finished by June 1982.
8. Some of these catalogues were displayed in an exhibition at the Literaturhaus Berlin in 2006. They contain few marginal notes, mostly cross-references to paintings held in other galleries. See Dittrich et al. 2006.

Appendix: A Catalogue of Samuel Beckett's Library

Note: The books in this catalogue are located in Beckett's library in Paris except those marked with the following abbreviations:

AA   Anne Atik, Paris
BIF   Beckett International Foundation, The University of Reading
JEK   James and Elizabeth Knowlson Collection, The University of Reading, JEK A/1/4/3 [photocopies]
NA   Noga Arikha, New York

Abrahams, Gerald (1964[1960]), *The Chess Mind*, 2nd ed. (Harmondsworth: Penguin).
Adorno, Theodor W. (1958), *Noten zur Literatur* (Frankfurt a.M.: Suhrkamp).
Agnon, S. Y. (1960), *A Stray Dog*, illustr. by Avigdor Arikha (Jersusalem: Tarshish Books).
Alekhine, Alexander (1949[1939]), *My Best Games of Chess 1924–1937* (London: G. Bell and Sons).
Alexander C. H.O'D. (1972), *Fischer v. Spassky, Reykjavik, 1972* (Harmondsworth: Penguin).
Allem, Maurice, ed. (n.d.), *Anthologie poétique française du XVIe Siècle: Poèmes choisis, avec introduction, notices et notes*, Second Volume (Paris: Librairie Garnier Frères).
Anderson, B. and M. North, ed. (1968), *Beyond the Dictionary in German: a Handbook of Colloquial Usage* (London: Cassell).
Angely, A. and J. McLaughlin, ed. (n.d.), *Diccionario Inglés-Español / Español-Inglés* (Paris: Garnier).
Apollinaire, Guillaume (1927), *Le Poète assassiné* (Paris: Au Sans Pareil).
  (1967[1965]), *Œuvres poétiques* (Paris: Gallimard Pléiade).
  (1972), *Zone*, trans. by Samuel Beckett (Dublin: Dolmen Press).
  (1975), *Le flâneur des deux rives, suivi de contemporains pittoresques* (Paris: Gallimard, Collection Idées).
Arakawa (1971), *Mechanismus der Bedeutung (Werk im Entstehen: 1963–1971)* (Munich: Bruckmann).
Aretino, Pietro (1933), *L'Œuvre du Divin Arétin*, 2 vols, introd. et notes par Guillaume Apollinaire (Paris: Bibliothèque des Curieux).

Arikha, Avigdor (1970), *Samuel Beckett by Avigdor Arikha* [A Tribute to Samuel Beckett on his 70th Birthday] (London: Victoria & Albert Museum).
— (1971), *Dessins 1965–1970*, preface by Samuel Beckett, exhibition catalogue December 1970–January 1971 (Paris: Centre National d'Art Contemporain).
— (1973), *Ink Drawings 1965–1972*, preface by Samuel Beckett, exhibition catalogue, April–May 1973 (Fort Worth Art Center Museum).
— (1973), *Paintings 1957–1965 and 1968*, exhibition catalogue, March–April 1973 (The Tel-Aviv Museum).
— (1974), *Ink Drawings and Etchings*, exhibition catalogue, February–March 1974 (London: Marlborough London).
— (1974), *39 Gravures 1970–1973*, exhibition catalogue (Centre National d'Art Contemporain).
— (1975), *Paintings and Watercolours 1973–1975*, exhibition catalogue, October–November 1975 (New York: Marlborough).
— (1977), *Oelbilder, Aquarelle, Zeichnungen*, preface by Samuel Beckett, exhibition catalogue, April–May 1977 (Zurich: Marlborough).
— (1978), *Oil Paintings, Watercolours, Drawings*, exhibition catalogue (London: Marlborough).
— (1979), *Drawings, Watercolours and Paintings*, exhibition catalogue, February–March 1979 (Houston, TX: Janie C. Lee Gallery).
— (1979), *Twenty-two Paintings 1974–76*, exhibition catalogue June–August 1979 (Washington, DC: The Corcoran Gallery of Art).
— (1980), *Dessins et Gravures* (Paris: Berggruen).
— (1980), *Recent Work October–November 1980*, exhibition catalogue (New York: Marlborough).
— (1981), *Exposition au Musée des Beaux Arts de Dijon*, exhibition catalogue, March–June 1981.
— (1982), *Oil Paintings and Drawings*, exhibition catalogue, May–June 1982 (London: Marlborough).
— (1983), *Paintings, Drawings and Pastels*, exhibition catalogue, September–October 1983 (New York: Marlborough).
— (1983), *Nicolas Poussin: The Rape of the Sabines* (Houston, TX: Museum of Fine Arts).
— (1984), *New York Drawings*, exhibition catalogue, January–May 1984 (New York: Marlborough).
— (1985), *Avigdor Arikha*, texts by R. Chanin, Fermigier, R. Hughes, J. Livingstone, B. Rose and Samuel Beckett (Paris: Hermann).
— (1985), *Recent Paintings* May–June 1985 (New York: Marlborough). [two copies].
— (1986), *Oil Paintings, Pastels and Drawings*, exhibition catalogue, October 1986 (London: Marlborough).
— (1988), *Oils, Watercolours, Pastels, Inks and Drawings*, catalogue, April–May 1988 (London/Tokyo: Marlborough).
Arnaud, Claude (1988), *Chamfort: Biographie, suivie de soixante-six maximes, anecdotes, mots et dialogues inédits, ou jamais réédités* (Paris: Editions Rorbert Laffont).

Arrabal, Fernando (1980), *Chroniques de l'express: Les échecs féériques et libertaires* (Monaco: Editions du Rocher).
   (1983), *La Tour prends garde* (Paris: Bernard Grasset).
   (1983), 'Lettre à Fidel Castro: an "1984"' (Paris: Christian Bourgois Editeur).
   (1984), *Échecs et Mythe* (Paris: Payot).
   (1984), *Théâtre XV* (Paris: Christian Bourgois Editeur).
   (1986), *Théâtre XVI* (Paris: Christian Bourgois Editeur).
Artaud, Antonin (1958), *The Theatre and its Double*, trans. by Mary Caroline Richards (New York: Grove Press).
Atik, Anne (1974), *Words in Hock: Poems* (London: Enitharmon Press).
Attali, Jacques (1977), *Bruits: essai sur l'économie politique de la musique* (Paris: Presses universitaires de France).
Attwater, Donald (1966[1965]), *The Penguin Dictionary of Saints* (Harmondsworth: Penguin).
Augé, Paul (n.d.), *Petit dictionnaire français*, 116th ed. (Paris: Larousse).
Austen, Jane (1953), *Northanger Abbey and Persuasion*, introd. by R. Brimley Johnson (London and Glasgow: Collins).
   (1956[1955]), *Selected Letters 1796–1827*, ed. by R. W. Chapman (Oxford: Oxford University Press).
   (1959), *Sense and Sensibility*, introd. by Lord David Cecil, 'The World's Classics' (London: Oxford University Press).
   (1960), *Persuasion*, introd. by Forrest Reid, 'The World's Classics' (London: Oxford University Press).
   (1960), *Mansfield Park*, introd. by Mary Lascelles, 'The World's Classics' (London: Oxford University Press).
Auster, Paul (1976), *Wall Writing* (Berkeley: The Figures).
Aveline, Claude (1961), *Le Code des jeux*, 'Livre de Poche' (Paris: Hachette).
Bachelard, Gaston (n.d.), *L'Intuition de l'instant* (Paris: Gonthier).
Bacon, Francis (n.d.), *Essays and Apophthegms of Francis Lord Bacon* (London and Felling-on-Tyne: The Walter Scott Publishing Co.).
Bailly, René (1947), *Dictionnaire des synonymes* (Paris: Larousse).
Barker, J. W. (1968), *Teach Yourself Portuguese* (London: The English Universities Press).
Bataille, Georges (1979), *Madame Edwarda* (Paris: Pauvert).
Bate, Walter Jackson (1979), *Samuel Johnson* (New York: Harvest / Harcourt)
Batistini, Yves, ed. (1961[1955]), *Trois contemporains: Héraclite, Parménide, Empédocle*, 'Collection Les Essais LXXVIII (Paris: Gallimard NRF).
Baudelaire, Charles (1928[1926]), *Les Fleurs du mal*, introd. by Paul Valéry, 'Collection Prose et Vers' (Paris: Payot).
   (1951), *Œuvres complètes*, ed. by Y.-G. Le Dantec (Paris: N.R.F / Gallimard Pléiade).
   (1965), *Les Fleurs du mal*, ed. by Jean-Paul Sartre (Paris: Le Livre de Poche).
   (1976[1972]), *Le Spleen de Paris: petits poèmes en prose*, ed. by Yves Florenne (Paris: Le Livre de Poche).
Beaumarchais (1941), *Théâtre choisi*, introduction et notes de Alfred Péron (Angers: Éditions Jacques Petit).

Beethoven, Ludvig van (1959), *Beethoven im Gespräch* (Wiesbaden: Insel Verlag).
Bellow, Saul (1963), *Dangling Man* (Harmondsworth: Penguin).
Benstock, Bernard, ed. (1985), *Critical Essays on James Joyce* (Boston, MS: G.K. Hall & Co.).
Berenson, Mary (1983), *A Self-Portrait: From her Letters and Diaries*, ed. by Barbara Strachey and Jayne Samuels (New York and London: W.W. Norton and Co.).
Berkeley, George (Bishop) (1926[1910], *A New Theory of Vision and Other Select Philosophical Writings* (Everyman's Library No. 483), ed. by A. D. Lindsay (London: J.M. Dent; New York: E. P. Dutton).
(1930), *Berkeley's Commonplace Book*, ed. by G. A. Johnston (London: Faber).
(1953), 'Homage to George Berkeley: A Commemorative Issue', *Hermathena* vol. 82 (November).
Bertin, Léon (1952), *La Vie des Animaux*, 2 vols. (Paris: Larousse).
Bestermann, Theodore (1969), *Voltaire* (London and Harlow: Longmans, Green and Co.).
Betteridge, Harold T. and Karl Breul (1968), *Cassell's German–English / English–German Dictionary* (London: Cassell).
Die Bibel (1970), nach der Uebersetzung von Martin Luther (Stuttgart: Württembergische Bibelanstalt).
Holy Bible: The Comprehensive Teacher's Bible (London: S. Bagster and Sons).
Holy Bible: Authorized King James Version (Oxford: Oxford University Press).
La Sacra Bibbia (1924) (Roma: Società Biblica Britannica e Forestiera).
Sainte Bible (1874) (New York: Société Biblique Américaine).
Sainte Bible (1921), par Louis Segond (Paris).
Biely, Andrei (1974), *The Silver Dove*, trans. and with introd. by George Reavey (New York: Grove Press).
Billy, André (1956), *Apollinaire* (Paris: Seghers).
Bishop, Morris (1964), *Petrarch and His World* (London: Chatto & Windus).
Bishop, Tom (1989), *Le Passeur d'océan: Carnets d'un ami américain* (Paris: Payort).
Blakeney, E. H. (1923[1910]), *A Smaller Classical Dictionary*, 'Everyman' (London: J.M. Dent & Sons Ltd.).
Blanchot, Maurice (1969), *L'Entretien infini* (Paris: Gallimard NRF).
(1983), *Après coup* (Paris: Éditions de Minuit).
Blau, Herbert (1982), *Take Up the Bodies: Theater at the Vanishing Point* (Urbana, IL: University of Illinois Press).
(1987), *The Eye of Prey, Subversions of the Postmodern* (Bloomington, IN: Indiana University Press).
Boccacio, Giovanni (1812), *Decamerone*, volume 3 (Livorno: Presso Tommaso Masi, e Comp.).
Böll, Heinrich (1964), *Entfernung von der Truppe. Erzählung* (Köln und Berlin: Kiepenheuer und Witsch).
(1969), *Geschichten aus zwölf Jahren* (Frankfurt a.M.: Suhrkamp).
Bonnefoy, Yves and Niny Garavaglia, eds. (1978), *Tout œuvre peint de mantegna* (Paris: Flammarion).

Boswell, James (1887), *Life of Johnson, with Hebrides Journal and Johnson's Diary of Journey to North Wales*, ed. by George Birkbeck Hill, 6 vols. (Oxford: Clarendon Press).
  (1951[1950]), *Boswell's London Journal 1762–1763*, ed. by Frederick A. Pottle (London: William Heinemann Ltd.).
Botticelli (1896), *Zeichnungen von Sandro Botticelli zu Dantes Göttlicher Komödie*, ed. by F. Lippmann (Berlin: Grote).
Bouchard, Thierry, ed. (1986), *Théodore Balmoral*, 2/3 (éte) [journal].
Bouvier, J. B. (1852), *Dissertatio in Sextum Decalogi Praeceptum, et Supplementum ad Tractatum de Matrimonio* (Paris: Facultatis Theologiae Bibliopolas).
Boyle, Kay (1985), *This Is Not a Letter and Other Poems* (Los Angeles: Sun & Moon Press).
  (1988), *Life Being the Best and Other Stories*, ed. by Sandra Whipple Spanier (New York: New Directions).
  (1989[1936]), *Death of a Man*, introd. by Burton Hatlen (New York: New Directions Books).
Breul, Karl, ed. (1930[1909]), *A German and English Dictionary* (London: Cassell).
Breytenbach, Breyten (1987), *Métamortphase* (Paris: Grasset).
Brittain, Frederick (1962), *The Penguin Book of Latin Verse* (Harmondsworth: Penguin).
Brod, Max (1945), *Franz Kafka, souvenirs et documents*, trans. by Hélène Zylberberg (Paris: Gallimard NRF).
[Brunet, Pierre Gustave] (n.d.[1884]), *Curiosités théologiques par un bibliophile*, nouvelle edition (Paris: Garnier Frères).
Brunschvicg, Léon (1923), *Spinoza et ses contemporains* (Paris: Librarie Félix Alcan).
Budgen, Frank (1937[1934]), *James Joyce and the Making of Ulysses*, 2nd ed. (London: Grayson & Grayson).
Buechner, Georg (1969), *Lenz*, trans. by Michael Hamburger ([London]: Frontier Press).
[BIF] Bürgel, Bruno H. (1944[c.1920s]), *Les Mondes lointains*, trans. by Paule Montescourt, 'Savoir Collection' (Paris: Librairie Arthème Fayard).
[AA] Burton, Robert (1893), *The Anatomy of Melancholy*, 3 vols, ed. by A. R. Shilleto, with introduction by A. H. Bullen (London: George Bell & Sons).
Bushrui, Suhei Badi and Bernard Benstock (1982), *James Joyce: an International Perspective* (Gerrards Cross: Colin Smythe).
Butlin, Martin (1980), *Turner at the Tate* (London: The Tate Gallery).
Büttner, Gottfried (1968), *Absurdes Theater und Bewusstseinswandel* (Berlin-Wilmersdorf: Westliche Berliner Verlagsgesellschaft Heenemann).
Byrne, Patrick (1953), *The Wildes of Merrion Square: The Family of Oscar Wilde* (London and New York: Staples).
Byron, Lord Alfred (n.d.[1861?]), *Poetical Works, with the Life of Lord Byron by Alexander Leighton* (Edinburgh: William P. Nimmo).
Cafferty, Bernard (1972), *Spassky's 100 Best Games* (London: B.T. Batsford).
Carré, L. (1928), *Éléments de grammaire anglaise* (Paris, Librairie Vuibert).
Catalogue Beaux-Arts, Sciences Humaines (1989) (Paris: Hermannn).

Célice, Pierre (n.d.), *Célice le cancre: reproductions de ses travaux* (Paris: Les Editions de la Gamelle).
Céline, Louis-Ferdinand (1960), *Nord* (Paris: Gallimard).
  (1969[1957], *D'un château l'autre* (Paris: Gallimard).
  (1973[1969]), *Rigodon* (Paris: Gallimard).
Chaamba, Abdallah (1954), *Le vieillard et l'enfant* (Paris: Éditions de Minuit).
Chamfort (1950[1944]), *Maximes et anecdotes*, introd. et notes par Jean Mistler, 2nd ed. (Monaco: Editions du Rocher).
Chekhov, Anton (1963), *Tchekhov, l'essentiel* (Paris).
  (1959), *Plays*, trans. by Elisaveta Fen (Harmondsworth: Penguin) [library also contains 1980 reprint].
Chekhov, Anton, and Maxime Gorki (1972), *Correspondance d'Anton Tchékhov et Maxime Gorki* (Paris: Les éditeurs français réunis).
Cherbury, Edward Lord Herbert (1809), *The Life of Edward Lord Herbert of Cherbury, Written by Himself* (Edinburgh: John Ballantyne & Co. / London: John Murray).
Chernev, Irving (1965), *The Most Instructive Games of Chess ever played: 62 Masterpieces of Modern Chess Strategy* (London: Faber & Faber).
Chesterfield, Lord (1881), *Letters, Sentences & Maxims*, with a critical essay by Sainte-Beuve, 6th ed. (London: Sampson Low, Marston, Searle, and Rivington).
Christ, Yvan and G. Franceschi (1966), Les cryptes mérovingiennes de l'abbaye de Jouarre (Paris: Etditions d'histoire et d'art).
Chuquet, M. A. (1893), *J.-J. Rousseau* (Paris: Librairie Hachette).
Cioran, E. M. (1949), *Précis de décomposition*, Les Essais XXXV, 2nd ed. (Paris: Gallimard NRF).
  (1952), *Syllogismes de l'amertume*, Les Essais LII (Paris: Gallimard NRF).
  (1960), *Histoire et utopie*, Les Essais XCVI (Paris: Gallimard NRF).
  (1961), *La Tentation d'exister*, Les Essais LXXXII (Paris: Gallimard NRF).
  (1964), *La Chute dans le temps*, Les Essais CXIV (Paris: Gallimard NRF).
  (1969), *Le mauvais Démiurge*, Les Essais CXLVII (Paris: Gallimard NRF).
  (1970), *Valéry face à ses idoles* (Paris: L'Herne).
  (1973), *De l'Inconvénient d'être né*, Les Essais CLXXXVI (Paris: Gallimard NRF).
  (1979), *Écartèlement*, Les Essais CCVII (Paris: Gallimard NRF).
  (1986), *Des Larmes et des saints* (Paris: L'Herne).
  (1986), *Aveux et anathèmes* (Paris: Gallimard Arcades).
  (1986), *Exercices d'admiration: essais et portraits* (Paris: Gallimard Arcades).
Clarke, P. H. (1961), *Mikhail Tal's Best Games of Chess* (London: G. Bell and Sons Ltd.).
  (1964), *Petrosian's Best Games of Chess 1946–1963* (London: G. Bell and Sons Ltd.).
[AA] Claudius, Matthias (n.d.), *Sämtliche Werke des Wandsbecker Boten*, 3 vols. (Fischer Verlag).
  (1958), *Sämtliche Werke* (Berlin and Darmstadt: Tempel Verlag).
Clifford, James L. (1955), *Young Samuel Johnson* (London: Heinemann).

Coffey, Brian (1982), *Death of Hektor: a Poem* (London: The Menard Press).
(1986), *Advent* (London: The Menard Press).
Cohen, J. M. and M. J. Cohen, ed. (1972[1960]), *The Penguin Dictionary of Quotations* (Harmondsworth: Penguin).
Cohn, Ruby (1976), *Modern Shakespeare Offshoots* (Princeton: Princeton University Press).
Coleridge, Samuel Taylor (1958[1907]), *Biographia Literaria*, 2 vols., ed. by J. Shawcross, Oxford: Oxford University Press).
Collier, L. D. (1982), *Everyday Spanish*, 'Teach Yourself' (London: Hodder & Stoughton; New York: D. McKay Co).
The Compact Edition of the Oxford English Dictionary (1971), complete text reproduced micrographically, 2 vols. (Oxford: Clarendon Press).
The Concise Oxford Dictionary (1983) (Oxford: Clarendon Press).
Le Coran (1970) (Paris: Garnier-Flammarion).
[JEK] Corneille, Pierre (1913). *Le Menteur* (Paris: Librairie Hachette).
[BIF] (1920), *La Galerie du palais*, ed. by Thomas B. Rudmose-Brown (Manchester/London: Manchester University Press/Longmans, Green & Co.).
[JEK] (1921) *Nicomède* (Paris: Librairie Hachette).
Cousin, John W. (1925[1910]), *A Short Biographical Dictionary of English Literature*, 'Everyman', rev. ed. (London: J.M. Dent & Sons).
Cousse, Raymond (1986), *L'envers vaut l'endroit* (Paris: Édition Dilettante).
Crébillon, Fils (1963), *The Wayward Head and Heart*, trans. by Barbara Bray, introd. by Rayner Heppenstall (London: Oxford University Press).
Cunard, Nancy (1925), *Parallax* (London: Hogarth Press).
(1954), *Grand Man: Memories of Norman Douglas – with Extracts from his Letters, and Appreciations by his Friends* (London: Secker and Warburg).
Curtius, Ernst Robert (1952), *Marcel Proust* (Frankfurt a.M.: Suhrkamp).
Dante Alighieri (n.d.), *La divine Comédie*, trans. by Artaud de Montor (Paris: Collection des Grands Classiques Français et Etrangers).
(1869), *The Vision of Hell, Purgatory and Paradise*, trans. by Henry Cary (London: Bell and Daldy).
[NA] (1957) *La divina Commedia*, ed. by Natalino Sapegno (Milan: Riccardo Ricciardi Editore).
[BIF] (1960), *La divina Commedia*, ed. by C. T. Dragone (Alba: Edizione Paoline).
(1965), *A Concordance to the Divine Comedy of Dante Alighieri*, ed. by Ernest Hatch Wilkins and Thomas Goddard Bergin (Cambridge, MS: The Belknap Press of Harvard UP / London: Oxford University Press).
[BIF] (1967), *The Divine Comedy*, trans. by Henry Cary, ed. by Edmund Gardner, 'Everyman' (London: Dent).
Darwin, Charles (1902), *On the Origin of Species by Means of Natural Selection or the Preservation of Favoured Races in the Struggle for Life* (London: Grant Richards).
Dauphin, Henri (1869), *Vie du Dante: Analyse de la divine Comédie* (Paris: A. Durand & Pédone Lauriel / Amiens: Prevost-Allo).

Dauzat, Albert (1938), *Dictionnaire étymologique* (Paris: Larousse).
Defoe, Daniel (1968 [1902]), *The Life and Adventures of Robinson Crusoe*, 'The World's Classics' (London: Oxford University Press).
Démocrite (1928), *Doctrines philosophiques et réflexions morales*, trans. and introd. by Maurice Solovine (Paris: Alcan).
De Quincey, Thomas (n.d.[1895?]), *Selected Essays of De Quincey*, introd. by Sir George Douglas (London and Felling-on-Tyne: The Walter Scott Publishing Co.).
Derrida, Jacques (1987), *Ulysse gramophone: Deux mots pour Joyce* (Paris: Éditions Galilée).
Descartes, René (n.d.), *Choix de textes*, ed. by L. Debricon, 'Les grands philosophes français et étrangers' (Paris: Louis-Michaud Éditions).
Des Granges, C. H. M. (1920[1910]), *Histoire illustrée de la littérature française* (Paris: Librairie A. Hatier).
Deutsch, Otto Erich, ed. (1980[1964]), *Schubert: Die Dokumente seines Lebens* (Basel und Kassel: Bärenreiter Verlag).
Devlin, Denis (1989), *Collected Poems of Denis Devlin*, ed. by J. C. C. Mays (Dublin: The Dedalus Press).
Dictionnaire Français-Allemand / Deutsch-Französisch (1967) (London: Cassell).
Dictionnaire illustré des auteurs français (1961) (Paris: Seghers).
Donne, John (1958[1950], *A Selection of his Poetry*, ed. and introd. by John Hayward (Harmondsworth: Penguin).
Dostoievski, Fjodor (n.d.[1884]), *Le Crime et le châtiment*, trans. by Victor Derély (Paris: Librairie Plon).
— (n.d.[1923?]), *La Confession de Stavroguine*, trans. and commented by E. Halpérine-Kaminsky (Paris: Librairie Plon).
— (n.d.[1930?]), *Souvenirs de la maison des morts*, trans. by M. Neyroud (Paris: Librairie Plon).
Doumic, René (n.d.), *Lamartine*, 4th ed. (Paris: Librairie Hachette).
Doyle, Arthur Conan (1965), *The Hound of the Baskervilles* (London: John Murray).
Duff, Charles (1956), *A New Handbook on Hanging* (London: Panther Books).
Dufourcq, Norbert (1957), *Larousse de la musique*, 2 vols. (Paris: Larousse).
Dufy, Raoul (1983), *Raoul Dufy 1877–1953* (Arts Council London).
Dumont, Jean-Paul, ed. (1988), *Les Présocratiques*, trans. by Jean-Paul Dumont, Daniel Delattre and Jean-Louis Poirier, 'Bibliothèque de la Pléiade' (Paris: Gallimard).
Dunlap, Ian (1986), *The Companion Guide to the Country around Paris* (London: Collins).
Dupré, P. (1961[1959]), *Encyclopédie des citations* (Paris: Editions de Trévise).
Duras, Marguerite (1986), *The Sea Wall* (London: Faber).
Duruy, Victor (1883[1874]), *Petite Histoire générale extraite de l'abrégé d'histoire universelle* (Paris: Librairie Hachette).
Dutton, Brian, Leonard P. Harvey and Roger M. Walker (1969), *Cassell's Compact Spanish-English / English-Spanish Dictionary* (London: Pan Books).

Dux, Pierre (1981), *La Comédie française racontée par Pierre Dux* (Paris: Librairie Académique Perrin).
— (1984), *Vive le théâtre: Souvenirs pour Elodie* (Paris: Stock).
Eadie, John, ed. (1875), *A New Concordance to the Holy Scriptures* (London: Charles Griffin & Co.).
Edwards, G. B. (1981), *The Book of Ebenezer Le Page*, introd. by John Fowles (Harmondsworth: Penguin).
Egan, Desmond (1984), *Collected Poems* (Maine: The National Poetry Foundation / Newbridge: The Goldsmith Press).
— (1986), *Poems for Peace*, introd. by Sean MacBride (Dublin: AFRI [Action from Ireland]).
— (1989), *A Song for My Father* (Newbridge: Kavanagh Press / Calstock: Peterloo Poets).
Eich, Günther (1964), *Zu den Akten* (Frankfurt a.M.: Suhrkamp).
Ellmann, Richard (1949), *Yeats: The Man and the Masks* (London: Macmillan & Co. Ltd.).
— (1954), 'The Backgrounds of Ulysses', in: *Kenyon Review* XVI.3 (Summer) [offprint].
— (1955), 'The Limits of Joyce's Naturalism', in: *The Sewanee Review* (October) [offprint].
— (1956), 'A Portrait of the Artist as Friend', in: *Kenyon Review* (Winter) [offprint].
— (1965[1959]), *James Joyce* (Oxford: Oxford University Press).
— (1967), *Eminent Domain: Yeats among Wilde, Joyce, Pound, Eliot and Auden* (New York: Oxford University Press).
— (1972), *Ulysses on the Liffey* (London: Faber & Faber).
— (1982), *James Joyce*, new rev. ed. (Oxford: Oxford University Press).
— (1982), 'James Joyce's Hundredth Birthday: Side and Front Views: A lecture delivered at the Library of Congress on March 10, 1982' (Washington, DC: Library of Congress).
— (1983), 'The Uses of Decadence: Wilde, Yeats, Joyce' (originally delivered at Bennington College as Lecture Six in the Ben Belitt Lectureship Series, September 28, 1983) (Vermont: Bennington College).
— (1984), 'Oscar Wilde at Oxford: A lecture delivered at the Library of Congress on March 1, 1983' (Washington, DC: Library of Congress).
— (1985), 'Samuel Beckett: Nayman of Noland: A lecture delivered at the Library of Congress on April 16, 1985' (Washington, DC: Library of Congress).
— (1985), 'W. B. Yeats's Second Puberty: A lecture delivered at the Library of Congress on April 2, 1984' (Washington, DC: Library of Congress).
— (1987), *James Joyce*, trans. by André Coeuroy and Marie Tadié, 2 vols, rev. ed., (Paris: Gallimard).
— (1987), *Four Dubliners: Wilde, Joyce, Yeats and Beckett* (London: Hamish Hamilton).
— (1987), *Oscar Wilde* (London: Hamish Hamilton).
Éluard, Paul (1984), *Poèmes d'amour / Love Poems*, Illustrations by S. W. Hayter, versions by Brian Coffey (Wiltshire: 107 Workshop).

270 Appendix: A Catalogue of Samuel Beckett's Library

Encyclopaedia Britannica (1910), 11th edition (Cambridge: Cambridge University Press).
English Larousse (1968) (Paris: Larousse)
Erhardt, Hans Martin (1978), *Hans Martin Erhardt* (Stuttgart: Manus Presse).
Ernst, Max (1984), *Les collages: inventaire et contradictions*, ed. by Werner Spies (Paris: Gallimard).
Euwe, Max (1970), *Feldherrnkunst im Schach* (Berlin: Walter de Gruyter).
Evelyn, John (1965[1963]), *John Evelyn's Diary*, ed. by Philip Francis (London: The Folio Society).
Fahy, Catherine (1989), *W. B. Yeats and his Circle* (Dublin: National Library of Ireland).
Farazzi, Patricia (1988), *La Porte peinte* (Paris: L'Eclat).
Farinha, A. Dias (1968), *Une Inscription portugaise inédite à El-Jadida*, in: *Studia* 25 (December) [offprint].
Faucheux, Pierre, Bernard Gheerbrant et al. (1949) *James Joyce: sa vie, son œuvre, son rayonnement*, exhibition catalogue (Paris: La Hune).
Ferrers Howell, Alan George (1920), *Dante, his Life and Works*, rev. ed. (London and Edinburgh: T.C. & E.C. Jack / T. Nelson & Sons).
Figueiredo, José Nunes de, and António Gomes Ferreira (1968), *Compêndio de Gramàtica Portuguesa* (Lisbon: Sà da Costa).
Fine, Reuben (1946[1945]), *Chess Marches On: A Vivid Record of Chess Activities in the Leading Centres of the World* (London: Sir Isaac Pitman).
Fischer, Bobby (1972), *My 60 Memorable Games* (London: Faber & Faber).
Fitter, Richard and Maisie (1967), *The Penguin Dictionary of British Natural History* (Harmondsworth: Penguin).
Flannery, James W. (1976), *W. B. Yeats and the Idea of a Theatre* (New Haven, CT and London: Yale University Press).
Fluchère, Henri (1965), *Laurence Sterne from Tristram to Yorick: an interpretation of Tristram Shandy*, trans. by and abridged by Barbara Bray (London and New York: Oxford University Press).
Fonseca, Fernando V. Peixotoda, ed. (1968[1957]), *Dictionnaire Francais-Portugais / Português-Francês* (Paris: Larousse).
Fontaine, Jean de la (1826), *Œuvres complètes* (Paris: Ignotte).
 [JEK] (1921), *Fables* (Paris: Librairie Hachette)
Fontane, Theodor (n.d.[1958?]), *Werke*, 2 vols., ed. by Walter Keitel (Munich: Carl Hanser Verlag).
 (n.d.), *Effi Briest* (Leipzig: Insel-Verlag).
Fornaciari, Raffaello (1901), *Disegno storico della letteratura italiana* (Florence: G.C. Sansoni).
Forster, Leonard, ed. (1959[1957]), *The Penguin Book of German Verse* (London: Penguin).
Fowler, H. W. (1930[1926]), *Fowler's Dictionary of Modern English Usage* (Oxford: Clarendon Press).
Fowler, H. W. and F. G. Fowler (1962[1931]), *The King's English*, 3rd ed. (Oxford: Clarendon Press).

Fowler, H. W., and F. G. Fowler (1947), *The Pocket Oxford Dictionary* (Oxford: Clarendon Press).
Freud, Sigmund (1960), *Briefe 1873–1939* (Frankfurt a.M.: S. Fischer Verlag).
Freud, Sigmund, and C. G. Jung (1974), *The Freud – Jung Letters: The Correspondence between Sigmund Freud and C.G. Jung*, ed. by William McGuire, trans. by Ralph Manheim and R. F. C. Hull, 'Bollingen Series XCIV' (Princeton, NJ: Princeton University Press).
Fried, Erich (1987[1984]), *Befreiung von der Flucht: Gedichte und Gegengedichte* (Frankfurt a.M.: Fischer Verlag).
Frisch, Max (1955), *Die chinesische Mauer* (Frankfurt a.M.: Suhrkamp).
  (1967), *Biographie: ein Spiel* (Frankfurt a.M.: Suhrkamp).
Gailly, Christian (1987), *Dit-il* (Paris: Minuit).
Gaskell, Elizabeth Cleghorn (1960[1908]), *The Life of Charlotte Brontë*, 'Everyman's Library' (London: Dent & Sons).
Gay-Lussac, Bruno (1979), *L'Heure* (Paris: Gallimard).
Gelb, Arthur and Barbara Gelb (1962), *O'Neill* (London: Jonathan Cape).
Georges, K. E. (1864), *Lateinisch-Deutsches Handwörterbuch* (Leipzig: Hahn'sche Verlags-Buchhandlung).
Giacosa, Giuseppe (1923), *Diritti dell'anima / Tristi amori* (Milan: Fratelli Treves).
Gilcrist, J, and David Hooper (1963), *José Raoul Capablanca: Sämtliche (568) Turnier- und Wettkampfpartien des Weltmeisters*, 'Weltgeschichte des Schachs' 14 (Hamburg: Verlag Wildhagen).
Girard, Denis (1962), *Cassell's New French–English / English–French Dictionary* (London: Cassell).
[NA] Gizycki, Jerzy (1972), *History of Chess*, ed. by B. H. Wood (London: The Abbey Library).
Goethe, Johann Wolfgang von (n.d.), *Goethes Werke: Auswahl in sechzehn Bänden*, vols. I, III and IV (Berlin: Verlagsgesellschaft für Literatur und Kunst).
Gogol, Nikolai (1956), *Les Adventures de Tchitkov, ou Les âmes mortes*, trans. by Arthur Adamov, illustr. by Avigdor Arikha (Lausanne: La Guilde du Livre).
  (1957), *Dead Souls*, trans. by George Reavey, introd. by Sir Maurice Bowra (London: Oxford University Press).
Goichon, A. M. (1951), *La Philosophie d'Avicenne et son influence en Europe médiévale* (Paris: Adrien-Maisonneuve).
Goldsmith, Oliver (n.d.), *The Vicar of Wakefield* (New York and Chicago: Butler Brothers).
Gorky, Maxim (1964), *A Sky-Blue Life and Selected Stories*, trans. and with foreword by George Reavey (New York: The New American Library).
Gould, Glenn (1983), *Le Dernier puritain*, ed. by Bruno Monsaingeon (Paris: Fayard).
Goya (n.d.[1980?]), *120 dibujos del Mueseo del Prado*, ed. by Alfonso E. Pérez Sanchéz (Madrid: Ediciones Alfiz).
Graves, Robert (1962[1955]), *The Greek Myths*, 2 vols. (Harmondsworth: Penguin).
Gray, Thomas (1928[1912]), *The Poems of Thomas Gray, with a Selection of Letters and Essays*, 'Everyman' (London: Dent).

Gregory, Horace and Marya Zaturenska, eds. (1957), *The Mentor Book of Religious Verse* (New York: New American Library).
Green, John Richard (1920), *A Short History of the English People*, rev. ed. (London: Macmillan).
Greene, David H. and Edward M. Stephens (1959), *J. M. Synge 1871–1909* (New York: Macmillan).
Greg, W. W. (1962), *The Editorial Problem in Shakespeare: The Clarke Lectures* [Trinity College, Cambridge, Lent Term 1939], 3rd ed. (Oxford: Clarendon Press).
Grevisse, Maurice (1969), *Le bon Usage: grammaire française* (Paris: Duculot).
Grimal, Pierre (1960), *La Civilisation Romaine* (Paris: Arthaud).
Grimm, Jacob and Wilhelm Grimm (1918), *Die Märchen der Brüder Grimm*, 2 vols. (Leipzig: Insel Verlag).
Grimmelshausen, Hans Jakob Christoffel von (n.d.), *Der Abenteuerliche Simplicissimus* (Leipzig: Insel Verlag).
Guralnik, David Bernard (1974), *Webster's New World Dictionary of the American Language*, 2nd College Edition (New York: New American Library).
Hale, Jane (1984), 'Perspective in the Theater of Samuel Beckett', PhD Diss. (Stanford University).
Halliday, F. E., ed. (1964), *A Shakespeare Companion 1564–1964* (Harmondsworth: Penguin).
Harris, Frank (1930), *Oscar Wilde: His Life and Confessions* (Garden City, NY: Garden City Publishing Co.).
 (1963[1925]), *My Life and Loves*, ed. and introd. by John F. Gallagher (New York: Grove Press).
Hausenstein, Wilhelm (1980), *Die Masken des Komikers Karl Valentin* (Munich: Deutscher Taschenbuchverlag).
Hauser, Erich (1976), *Manfred De La Motte*, exhibition catalogue (Bonn: Galerie Hennemann).
Havel, Vaclav (1980), *Audience, vernissage, pétition*, preface by Milan Kundera, trans. by Marcel Aymonin and Stephan Meldegg (Paris: Gallimard NRF).
 (1980), *The Memorandum*, trans. by Vera Blackwell, introd. by Tom Stoppard (New York: Grove Press).
 (1986), 'Acceptance Speech written on the occasion of the award of the Erasmus Prize, 1986' (Amsterdam: Foundation Praemium Erasmianum).
Hayman, David (1956), *Joyce et Mallarmé*, 2 vols. (Paris: Lettres Modernes).
Hayward, John, ed. (1956), *The Penguin Book of English Verse* (London: Penguin).
Hedberg, Johannes (1986), *Pieces on Joyce* ([Lund]: The James Joyce Society of Sweden and Finland).
Heine, Heinrich (n.d.[c.1930]), *Buch der Lieder* (Leipzig: Insel Verlag).
Heinemann, Karl (n.d.[1930]), *Die deutsche Dichtung: Grundriss der deutschen Literaturgeschichte*, 8th ed. (Leipzig: Alfred Kröner Verlag).
Hemleben, Johannes, ed. (1972), *Johannes der Evangelist in Selbstzeugnissen und Bilddokumenten*, ed. by Johannes Hemleben (Reinbeck bei Hamburg: Rohwolt).

Hensel, Georg (1983), *Theaterskandale und andere Anlässe zum Vergnügen* (Stuttgart: Deutsche Verlag-Anstalt).
L'Herne no.50, 1985 [special issue on James Joyce] (Paris: L'Éditions de l'Herne).
Hibbert, Christopher (1971), *The Personal History of Samuel Johnson* (London: Longman).
Higgins, George V. (1985), *Three Complete Novels: The Friends of Eddie Coyle, Cogan's Trade, and The Rat on Fire* (London: Robinson Publishing).
Hillairet, Jacques (1951), *Évocation du vieux Paris* (Paris: Éditions de Minuit).
[BIF] Hölderlin, Friedrich (n.d.[1926?]), *Sämtliche Werke* (Leizpig: Insel Verlag).
   (1952), *Dichtungen und Briefe*, ed. by Hannsludwig Geiger (Munich: Winkler Verlag).
   (1970), *In Memoriam Friedrich Hölderlin 20 March 1770 – 7 June 1843* (London: Menard Press).
   (1977[1963]), *Werke, Briefe, Dokumente* (Munich: Winkler Verlag).
Hofmannsthal, Hugo von (1932), *Das dichterische Element in unserer Zeit* (Leipzig: printed for Axel Kaun).
Homer, *L'Odyssée* (1925), trans. by Victor Bérard, 3 vols. (Paris: Société d'édition "Les Belles Lettres").
Horizon, A Magazine of the Arts (1960), III.1 (September).
Hutchins, Patricia (1957), *James Joyce's World* (London: Methuen).
Ingres, J. A. D. (1981), *53 Dessins sur le vif du Musée Ingres et du Musée du Louvre*, ed. by Avigdor Arikha (Jerusalem: Musée d'Israel).
   (1986), *Fifty Life Drawings from the Musée Ingres at Montauban*, catalogue exhibition (Houston, TX: The Museum of Fine Arts).
Ionesco, Eugène (1973), *Le Solitaire* (Paris: Mercure de France).
Isherwood, Christopher (1954), *The Berlin Stories* ['The Last of Mr. Norris', 'Goodbye to Berlin'] (New York: New Directions).
James, Henry (1961), *The Turn of the Screw: The Aspen Papers and Other Stories*, introd. by Michael Swan (London: Collins).
Janvier, Ludovic (1964), *Une Parole exigeante: le nouveau roman* (Paris: Éditions de Minuit).
   (1966), *Pour Samuel Beckett* (Paris: Éditions de Minuit).
   (1968), *La Baigneuse* (Paris: Gallimard NRF).
   (1975), *Face: récit* (Paris: Gallimard NRF).
   (1984), *Naissance* (Paris: Gallimard NRF).
   (1987), *La Mer à boire: poèmes* (Paris: Gallimard, NRF).
   (1988), *Monstre, va* (Paris: Gallimard NRF).
Jaspers, Karl (1953), *Strindberg et Van Gogh: Hoelderlin et Swedenborg*, trans. by Hélène Naef, preface by Maurice Blanchot (Paris: Éditions de Minuit).
[NA] Johnson, Samuel (1785) *The Poetical Works of Samuel Johnson, LL.D.* (London: printed for W. Osborne).
   (1799), *A Dictionary of the English Language by Samuel Johnson*, 2 vols., 8th ed., corr. and rev. (London: printed for J. Johnson [etc]).
   (1957[1908]), *Johnson on Shakespeare: Essays and Notes Set Forth with an Introduction*, ed. by Walter Raleigh (Oxford: Oxford University Press).

(1958), *Diaries, Prayers, Annals*, ed. by E. L. McAdam Jr., 'The Yale Edition of the Works of Samuel Johnson, Volume 1' (New Haven, CT: Yale University Press).

(1966[1897]), *Johnsonian Miscellanies*, ed. by George Birkbeck Hill, 2 vols. (London: Constable and Co.).

(1971), *The Complete English Poems*, ed. by J. D. Fleeman (Harmondsworth: Penguin).

Jones, Ernest (1953), *Sigmund Freud: Life and Work*, 3 vols. (London: Hogarth Press).

Jonson, Ben (1984), *Epigrams and The Forest* (Manchester: Fyfield Books).

Joyce, James (1918), *Exiles: a play in 3 acts* (London: G. Richards).

(1927), *Pomes Penyeach* (Paris: Shakespeare & Co.).

(1939), *Finnegans Wake* (London: Faber & Faber).

(1949[1927]), *Chamber Music* (London: Jonathan Cape).

(1949), *A James Joyce Yearbook*, ed. by Maria Jolas (Paris: Transition Press).

(1952), *Exiles* (London: Jonathan Cape).

(1953), *Dublin: Novellen*, trans. by Georg Goyert (Frankfurt a.M.: Fischer Bücherei).

(1954), *Dubliners* (London: Jonathan Cape).

(1956), *Epiphanies*, introd. and with notes by O. A. Silverman (Buffalo: Lockwood Memorial Library, University of Buffalo).

(1957), *Letters of James Joyce*, ed. by Stuart Gilbert (London: Faber & Faber).

(1958), *The Voice of Shem, passages from Finnegans Wake: freely adapted for the theater by Mary Manning*, introd. by Denis Johnston (London: Faber & Faber).

(1960), *Ulysses* (London: Bodley Head).

(1961), *Lettres de Joyce*, ed. by Stuart Gilbert, trans. by Marie Tadié (Paris: Gallimard NRF).

(1961), *Musica da camera: poesie giovanili di James Joyce*, trans. by Aldo Camerino (Milan: All'insegna del pesce d'oro).

(1964), 'Daniel Defoe', ed. from Italian manuscripts and trans. by Joseph Prescott (New York: State University of New York at Buffalo).

(1966), *Letters, Volumes II and III*, ed. by Richard Ellmann (New York: The Viking Press).

(1968), *Giacomo Joyce*, ed. by Richard Ellmann (Franfurt a.M.: Suhrkamp).

(1968), *Verbannte*, trans. by Klaus Reichert (Frankfurt a.M.: Suhrkamp Verlag).

(1968), *Giacomo Joyce*, introd. and with notes by Richard Ellmann (New York: Viking Press).

(1970), *Exiles*, theatre programme, Mermaid Theatre, London.

(1974), *Dublinois: Les Morts, Contreparties = Dubliners: The Dead, Counterparts* (bilingual edition), trans. by Jean-Noël Vuarnet, introd. by Hélène Cixous (Paris: Aubier Flammarion).

(1986), *Lettres IV*, ed. by Richard Ellmann, trans. by Marie Tadié (Paris: Gallimard NRF).

(1986), *Dubliners*, with lithographs by Louis Le Brocquy (édition de luxe sous étui) (Dublin: The Dolmen Press).

Joyce, Stanislaus (1958), *My Brother's Keeper*, ed. by Richard Ellmann, pref. by T. S. Eliot (London: Faber & Faber).
   (1958), *My Brother's Keeper: James Joyce's Early Years* (New York: Viking Press).
   (1962), *The Dublin Diary of Stanislaus Joyce*, ed. by George Harris Healey (London: Faber & Faber).
Kafka, Franz (1963), *Er: Prosa*, ed. by Martin Walser (Frankfurt a.M.: Suhrkamp).
[AA] Kant, Immanuel (1921–22), *Immanuel Kants Werke*, 11 vols., ed. by Ernst Cassirer (Berlin: Bruno Cassirer).
Kavanagh, Patrick (1984), *The Complete Poems*, ed. by Peter Kavanagh (Newbridge: The Goldsmith Press).
Kavanagh, Peter (1988[1959]), *Irish Mythology: A Dictionary*, introd. by Patrick Kavanagh (Newbridge: The Goldsmith Press).
Kay, George, ed. (1958), *The Penguin Book of Italian Verse* (Harmondsworth: Penguin).
Keats, John (1954), *Selected Letters*, sel. by Frederick Page, 'The World's Classics' (Oxford: Oxford University Press).
   (1968), *Poèmes choisis / Selected Poems* [bilingual edition], trans. and ed. by Albert Laffay (Paris: Aubier Flammarion).
Kempf, Roger (1968), 'James Job Joyce', in: *Critique* (April) [offprint].
Kenner, Hugh (1955), *Dublin's Joyce* (London: Chatto & Windus).
   (1961), *Samuel Beckett: A Critical Study* (New York: Grove Press).
   (1962), *Flaubert, Joyce and Beckett*, illustr. by Guy Davenport (Boston: Beacon Press).
Kilvert, Francis (n.d.), *Kilvert's Diary*, ed. and introd. by William Plomer (London: Jonathan Cape).
Kirsch, Sarah (1989), *Schneewärme: Gedichte* (Stuttgart: Deutsche Verlags-Anstalt).
Kleist, Heinrich von (1968[1954]), *Über das Marionettentheater: Aufsätze und Anekdoten* (Leipzig: Insel-Verlag).
Kluge, Friedrich (1960), *Etymologisches Wörterbuch der Deutschen Sprache*, 17th ed. (Berlin: Walter de Gruyter & Co.).
Kober, Jacques (1984), *Un puits nommé plongeon*, with frontispiece and hors-texte by Geer Van Velde (Paris: Le pont de l'Epée).
Kolb, Annette (1968[1941]), *Franz Schubert: Sein Leben* (Zurich: Eugen Rentsch Verlag).
Kott, Jan (1975), *Manger les dieux: essais sur la tragédie grecque et la modernité* (Paris: Payot).
Labé, Louise (1958), *Élégies & sonnets* (Paris: Guy Lévis Mano).
Lafenestre, Georges (1909), *Molière* (Paris: Librairie Hachette).
Lalande, André (1932), *Vocabulaire technique et critique de la philosophie*, 3 vols. (Paris: Librairie Félix Alcan).
[BIF] Lalanne, Ludovic (1857), *Curiosités littéraires* (Paris: Adolphe Delahays).
Langenscheidt dizionario universale francese-italiano / italiano-francese (Berlin: Langenscheidt). [3 copies]
Larousse, Pierre (n.d.), *Grammaire supérieure*, 27th ed. (Paris: Larousse).
Larousse français–anglais / English–French (n.d.) (Paris: Larousse).

Larousse francese–italiano / italiano–francese (n.d.) (Paris: Larousse).
Larousse universel en 2 volumes (1922–23) (Paris: Larousse).
Lasserre, Pierre (1930?), *Un Conflit religieux au XIIème siècle: Abélard contre Saint Bernard* (Paris: L'Artisan du livre)
Lautréamont, Comte de (1968), *Œuvres complètes d'Isidore Ducasse*, texte établi par Maurice Saillet (Paris: Le Livre de poche).
Lavignac, Albert (1938), *La Musique et les musiciens* (Paris: Librairie Delagrave).
Lawrence, D. H. (1976), *Poèmes [bilingual edition]*, ed. by J.-J. Mayoux (Paris: Aubier Flammarion).
Lebaigue, Ch. (1898), *Dictionnaire latin-français* (Paris: Belin Frères).
Le Breton, Auguste (1960), *Langue verte et noirs desseins* (Paris: Presses de la Cité).
Le Brocquy, Louis (1976), *À la recherche de W.B. Yeats: cent portraits imaginaires*, exhibition catalogue, 15 October–28 November 1976 (Paris: Musée d'art moderne de la ville de Paris).
  (1979), *Images de Yeats, Joyce, Beckett, Lorca, Strindbert, Bacon* (Paris: Galerie Jeanne Bucher).
  (1981), *Eight Irish Writers* [édition de luxe sous coffret: feuillets séparés sur Vélin] (Dublin: s.n.).
  (1981), *Le Brocquy and the Celtic Head Image*, exhibition catalogue, September-November 1981 (New York: New York State Museum).
  (1982), *Louis Le Brocquy*, exhibition catalogue of Palais des Beaux-Arts Charleroi, October–November 1982.
  (1982), *Studies towards an Image of William Shakespeare*, ed. by Bernard Noel, L'Atelier Mental (Paris: Galerie Jeanne Bucher).
  (1988), *Images 1975–1987*, exhibition catalogue (South Brisbane: Museum of Contemporary Art) [2 copies].
Legouis, Émile, and Louis Cazamian (1929), *Histoire de la littérature anglaise* (Paris: Hachette).
Le Lionnais, François and Ernst Maget (1967), *Dictionnaire des échecs* (Paris: Presses universitaires de France). [2 copies]
Lemon, Don, ed. (1890), *Everybody's Scrapbook of Curious Facts: a book for odd moments* (London: Saxon & Co.).
Lemprière, John (1831), *Lemprière's Classical Dictionary* (London: printed for T. Allman).
Leopardi, Giacomo (1936), *I Canti*, ed. by Ettore Fabietti (Milan: Casa per Edizioni Popolari).
  (n.d.), *Prose, con uno studio di Pietro Giordani* (Milan: Istituto Editoriale Italiano).
Leslie, C. R. (1980[1951]), *Memoirs of the Life of John Constable* (Oxford: Phaidon).
Leventhal, A. J. (1950), 'George Darley 1795–1846' [memorial lecture delivered at Trinity College Dublin] (Dublin: The Dublin University Press).
  (1972), 'Samuel Beckett, about him and about' [lecture on the occasion of the exhibition of Samuel Beckett's works and Mss at Trinity College], in: *Hermathena* CXIV [offprint].
Leyda, Jay (1969), *Sidney Myers: Vision is my dwelling place* (Jay Leyda).

Liddy, James (1962), 'Esau My Kingdom for a Drink: Homage to James Joyce on his LXXX Birthday' [a memorial address delivered at King's Inns, Dublin, February 1962] (Dublin: Dolmen Press).
Lillo, George (1952), *The London Merchant or the History of George Barnwell*, introd. by Bonamy Dobrée (New York: Grove Press).
Lindon, Jérôme (1978), *La FNAC et les livres* (Paris: Éditions de Minuit).
Linhart, Robert (1978), *L'Etabli* (Paris: Éditions de Minuit).
Littré, Emil (1959), *Littré, Dictionnaire de la langue française*, 7 vols. (Paris: Gallimard/Hachette).
Logue, Christopher (1959), *Songs* (London: Hutchinson and Co.).
Lorenz, Konrad Z. (1965), *King Solomon's Ring: New Light on Animal Ways*, introd. by W. H. Thorpe, 'University Paperbacks' (London: Methuen).
Lowry, Malcolm (1963[1962]), *Under the Volcano* (Harmondsworth: Penguin Modern Classics in association with Jonathan Cape).
Lynch, Brian (1989), *Voices from the Nettle-Way* (Dublin: Raven Arts Press).
Lynd, Robert (1946), *Dr Johnson and Company* (Harmondsworth: Penguin).
MacGreevy, Thomas (1931), *T.S. Eliot, a study*, Dolphin Series (London: Chatto & Windus).
— (1931), *Richard Aldington, an Englishman*, Dolphin Series (London: Chatto & Windus).
— (1934), *Poems* (London: William Heinemann Ltd.).
— (1945), *Pictures in the Irish National Gallery* (Cork: The Mercier Press).
— (1960), *Nicolas Poussin* (Dublin: The Dolmen Press).
— (1971), *Collected Poems*, foreword by Samuel Beckett ['Humanistic Quietism'], ed. by Thomas Dillon Redshaw (Dublin: New Writers' Press).
Machatscheck, Heinz (1956), *111 Sowjetische Meisterpartien* (Berlin: Sportverlag).
Machiavelli, Niccolò (1888), *Le Istorie fiorentine* (Florence: Successori Le Monnier).
— (1947), *Le Prince* (Paris: Fernand Hazan).
Madden, Anne (1983), Peintures et papiers récents, *Février-Mars* 1983 (Saint-Paul: Fondation Maeght).
— (1985), Peintures et dessins récents, *exhibition catalogue, July-August* 1985 (Cannes: Galerie Joachim Becker).
— (1985), *Pintures*, exhibition catalogue (Barcelona: Galeria Maeght).
[BIF] Maeterlinck, Maurice (n.d.[1939]), *Théâtre*, volume 1 [*La Princesse Maleine, L'Intruse, Les Aveugles*] (Paris: Charpentier).
Magalaner, Marvin, and Richard M. Kain (1957), *Joyce: the Man, the Work, the Reputation* (London: John Calder).
Maguinness, William Stuart (1958), 'Bimillennial Reflections on Ovid', in: *Greece & Rome*, V.1 (March) (Oxford: Clarendon Press) [offprint].
— (1961), 'Virgil and Milton', in: *Romanistas* III.3&4 [offprint].
— (1963), 'Bentley as Man and Scholar', in: *Proceedings of the Leeds Philosophical Society* X.3 (February) [offprint].
— (1963), 'Petit Plaidoyer pour la poésie trochaique', in: *Rivista di cultura classica e medioevale* V.2 (Rome: Edizioni dell'Ateneo) [offprint].

278   *Appendix: A Catalogue of Samuel Beckett's Library*

(1965), 'The Language of Lucretius', in: *Lucretius*, ed. by D. R. Dudley (London: Routledge & Kegan Paul) [offprint].
Malcolm, Norman (1967[1962]), *Wittgenstein: A Memoir* (Oxford: Oxford University Press).
Mallarmé, Stéphane (1961[1945]), *Œuvres complètes* (Paris: Gallimard Pléiade).
Mandelstam, Nadezhda (1971), *Hope against Hope: A Memoir*, trans. by Max Hayward, introd. by Clarence Brown (London: Collins & Harvill Press).
Mannoni, Octave (1968), *Freud*, 'Écrivains de Toujours' (Paris: Éditions du Seuil).
Mansion, J. E. (1967), *Harrap's Shorter French and English Dictionary* (Paris: Bordas; London: Harrap).
Marc Aurèle (1964), *Pensées pour moi-même, suivi de Manuel d'Épictète*, ed. and trans. by Mario Meunier (Paris: Garnier Flammarion).
Marlowe, Christopher (1963[1955]), *Plays and Poems*, 'Everyman' (London: Dent & Sons).
Maspero, François (1984), *Le Sourire du chat* (Paris: Éditions du Seuil).
Matthews, Honor (1968), *The Hard Journey: The Myth of Man's Rebirth* (London: Chatto & Windus).
Maulnier, Thierry (1939), *Introduction à la poésie française* (Paris: Gallimard NRF).
Mauriac, François (1928), *La Vie de Jean Racine* (Paris: Plon).
Mauthner, Fritz (1923), *Beiträge zu einer Kritik der Sprache*, 3 vols., 3rd ed. (Leipzig: F. Meiner).
Mayoux, Jean-Jacques (1958), *Melville par lui-même*, 'Collection Écrivains de Toujours' (Paris: Éditions du Seuil).
   (1960), *Vivants Piliers: le roman anglo-saxon et les symboles* [Coleridge, De Quincey, Hawthorne, Melville, Henry James, Conrad, Joyce, Woolf, Faulkner, Beckett] (Paris: Julliard).
   (1962), 'Laurence Sterne parmi nous', in: *Critique* 177 (February) [offprint].
   (1965), *Joyce*, 'La Bibliotheque idéale' (Paris: Gallimard NRF).
   (1966), *Shakespeare* (Paris: Seghers).
   (1981), *Sous de vastes portiques: études de littérature et d'art anglais* (Paris: Les Lettres Nouvelles / M. Nadeau et Papyrus).
   (1982), *Shakespeare* (Paris: Aubier-Montaigne).
McDowell, C. H. (1957), *A Short Dictionary of Mathematics* (New York: The Philosophical Library).
McHugh, Roger, ed. (1971), *Jack B. Yeats: A Centenary Gathering* (Dublin: The Dolmen Press).
Melander, Ingrid (1987), *The Transcendent Flame: Thematic/Structural Complexity in Francis Warner's Experimental Sonnets* (Stockholm: Umea).
Melville, Herman (1925[1907]), *Moby-Dick, or the White Whale*, 'Everyman' (London: Dent).
Melzi, G. B. (n.d.), *Melzi's Italian–English / English–Italian Dictionary* (London: Hirschfeld Brothers).
Ménétrier, Jacques (1972), *Origines de l'Occident: nomades et sédentaires* (Paris: Wéber).
Michaut, Gustave (1921), *Sainte-Beuve* (Paris: Librairie Hachette).

Michaux, Henri (1961), *Connaissance par les gouffres* (Paris: Gallimard).
Milton, John (1713), *Paradise Regain'd: a poem in four books. To which is added Samson Agonistes, etc.*, 5th ed. (London: printed for J. Tonson).
  (1904[1898]), *Paradise Lost: a poem in twelve books*, 'The Temple Classics', 5th ed. (London: J.M. Dent & Co.).
  (1969), *Poetical Works*, ed. by Douglas Bush (London: Oxford University Press).
Mitchell, Joan (1984), La Grande valée / *Yves Michaud:* Colour (Paris: Galerie J. Fournier).
Molière (n.d.), *Théâtre complet*, 5 vols. [missing volume 3] (Paris: Bibliothèque Hachette).
Montague, John (1984), *The Dead Kingdom* (Portlaoise: Dolmen Press, in association with Winston-Salem: Wake Forest University Press).
  (1989), *The Figure in the Cave and Other Essays* (Dublin: The Lilliput Press).
Montaigne, Michel de (1958[1950]), *Essais* (Paris: Gallimard Pléiade).
Moore, George (1888), *Confessions of a Young Man* (London: Swan Sonnenschein, Lowrey and Co.).
  [AA] (1926[1921]), *Héloïse and Abélard* (London: William Heinemann Ltd.)
  (1927), *Celibate Lives* (Leipzig: Tauchnitz Edition).
  [AA] (1928), *A Storyteller's Holiday*, vol. 1 (New York: Horace Liveright).
  [AA] (1932), *The Lake* (London: William Heinemann Ltd.).
  (1947), *Hail and Farewell: Ave: Salve: Vale*, 3 vols., 'The Works of George Moore' (London: Heinemann).
Moore, Gerald (1975), *The Schubert Song Cycle and Thoughts on Performance* (London: Hamish Hamilton).
More, Thomas (1913[1879]), *Utopia* (Cambridge: Cambridge University Press).
Morrisroe, Patrick (Most Rev.) (1926), *A Little Manual of Liturgy* (Dublin: M.H. Gill and Son, Ltd.).
Morten, Honnor (1895), *The Nurse's Dictionary of Medical Terms and Nursing Treatment*, 3rd rev ed. (London: The Scientific Press).
Murray, K. M. Elizabeth (1979), *Caught in the Web of Words: James Murray and the Oxford English Dictionary* (Oxford: Oxford University Press).
Nadeau, Maurice (1963), *Le roman français depuis la guerre* (Paris: Gallimard NRF).
  (1969), *Gustave Flaubert écrivain*, 'Dossiers des Lettres Nouvelles' (Paris: Denoël).
Neizvestny, Ernst (1987), *Dante's Inferno* (New York: Nakhamkin Fine Arts).
Nerval, Gérard de (1953), *Sylvie: Aurelia* (Éditions de la Bibliothèque mondiale).
Nietzsche, Friedrich (1966[1950]), *Le gai savoir*, trans. by Alexandre Vialette (Paris: Gallimard NRF).
Nobel Foundation Directory 1983–1984 (Stockholm).
Noël, Lucie (1950), *James Joyce and Paul L. Léon: The Story of a Friendship* (New York: Gotham Book Mart).
Nuevo pequeño Larousse illustrad, diccionario enciclopédico (1954) (Paris: Larousse).
O'Brien, Eoin, ed. (1984), *A. J. Leventhal, Dublin Scholar, Wit and Man of Letters 1896–1979* (Dublin: The Con Leventhal Scholarship Committee).

O'Brien, Eoin and Anne Crookshank, with Sir Gordon Wolstenholme (1984), *A Portrait of Irish Medicine: An Illustrated History of Medicine in Ireland* (Swords, Country Dublin: Ward River Press).
O'Brien, Eoin et al., eds. (1988), *A Closing Memoir: The Richmond Whitworth and Hardwicke Hospitals* (Dublin: Anniversary Press).
O'Casey, Sean (1928), *The Silver Tassie* (London: Macmillan).
O'Connor, Conleth (1987), *A Corpse Auditions its Mourners – New and Selected Poems* (Dublin: Raven Arts Press).
Oster, Pierre (1970), *Nouveau dictionnaire de citations françaises* (Paris: Hachette/ Tschou).
O'Sullivan, Seumas and Estella F. Solomons (1973) *The Work of O'Sullivan 1879–1958 and Solomons 1882–1968: A Retrospect*, ed. by Liam Miller (Dublin: Dolmen Press).
Otto, Emil (1930), *German Conversation-Grammar: Method Gaspey-Otto-Sauer for the Study of Modern Languages* (Heidelberg: Julius Groos).
Oulton, Thérèse (1988), 'Lachrimae', exhibition catalogue, January–February 1988 (London: Marlborough).
[NA] Pachman, Ludek (1975), *Complete Chess Strategy: First Principles of the Middle Game*, trans. by John Littlewood (Garden City, NY: Doubleday & Company Inc.).
Palgrave, Francis, ed. (1862), *The Golden Treasury of the Best Songs & Lyrical Poems in the English Language* (London: Macmillan & Co.).
Pascal, Blaise (n.d.), *Pensées* (Paris: Flammarion).
Passerini, G. L., ed. (1917), *Le Vite di Dante, scritte da Giovanni e Filippo Villani, da Giovanni Boccaccio, Leonardo Aretino e Giannozzo Manetti* (Florence: G. C. Sansoni).
Pasternak, Boris (1959), *The Poetry of Boris Pasternak*, ed. and trans. by George Reavey (New York: G.P. Putnam's Sons).
Pears Cyclopedia (n.d.), 57th edition (Isleworth: Pears).
Penguin Companion Dictionary English-Spanish / Spanish-English (1982) (Harmondsworth: Penguin).
Pepys, Samuel (1920[1906]), *The Diary of Samuel Pepys*, 2 vols. (London: J.M. Dent & Sons Ltd.).
— (1987), *The Shorter Pepys: Selection from the diary of Samuel Pepys*, ed. by Robert Latham and William Matthews (Harmondsworth: Penguin).
Petit Larousse illustré (1974) (Paris: Larousse).
[AA] Petrarch, Francesco (1824), *Le Rime del Petrarca*, 2 vols. (Milan: Nicolò Bettoni).
— (1962), *Le Rime*, pref. by Luigi Baldacci (Bologna: Zanichelli).
Pia, Pascal (1971), *Romanciers, poètes, essayistes du XIXème siècle* (Paris: Denoël - Les Lettres Nouvelles).
Picasso, Pablo (1986), *Pastelle, Zeichnungen, Aquarelle*, ed. by Werner Spies, exhibition catalogue, Kunsthalle Tübingen (Stuttgart: Gert Hatje).
Pickvance, Ronald, ed. (1986), *Van Gogh in Saint-Remy and Auvers*, exhibition catalogue (New York: Metropolitan Museum of Art).

Pinget, Robert (1953), *Le Renard et la boussole* (Paris: Gallimard NRF).
  (1965), *Autour de mortin* (Paris: Éditions de Minuit).
  (1965), *Quelqu'un* (Paris: Éditions de Minuit).
  (1980), *L'Apocryphe* (Paris: Éditions de Minuit).
  (1984), *Le Harnais* (Paris: Éditions de Minuit).
  (1985), *Charrue* (Paris: Éditions de Minuit).
  (1986), *Un Testament bizarre* (Paris: Éditions de Minuit).
  (1987), *L'Ennemi* (Paris: Éditions de Minuit).
Pinter, Harold (1960), *The Birthday Party and Other Plays* (London: Methuen).
  (1968), *Mac* ([London]: Pendragon Press).
  (1968), *Poems*, sel. by Alan Clodd (London: Enitharmon Press).
  (1969), *Landscape and Silence* (London: Methuen).
  (1971), *Poems*, 2nd ed. (London: Enitharmon Press).
  (1977), *The Proust Screenplay: À la recherche du temps perdu*, in collaboration with Joseph Losey and Barbara Bray (New York: Grove Press).
  (1980), *The Hothouse* (London: Methuen).
  (1981), *Arthur Wellard 1902–1980* (London: Villiers Publications).
  (1982), *Other Places: Three Plays* (London: Methuen).
  (1985[1984]), *One for the Road* (London: Methuen).
  (1988?), *Mountain Language* [typescript].
  (1989), *The Trial: a Screenplay* [typescript].
Pinter, Harold, Geoffrey Godbert and Anthony Astbury (1986), *100 Poems by 100 Poets: an anthology* (London: Methuen/Greville Press).
The Pinter Review (1987), 1.1 (University of Tampa).
Plautus, *Plautus in Four Volumes* (1916), volume 1, trans. by Paul Nixon (London: Heinemann).
Plessner, Helmuth, Alwin Diemer and Ivo Frenzel (1960[1958]), *Philosophie, das Fischer Lexikon* (Frankfurt a.M.: Fischer Bücherei).
Plümacher, O. von (1888), *Der Pessimismus in Vergangenheit und Gegenwart: Geschichtliches und Kritisches*, 2nd ed. (Heidelberg: Georg Weiss Verlag).
Pole, David (1958), *The Later Philosophy of Wittgenstein* (London: The Athlone Press).
Pope, Alexander (n.d.[1881?]), *The Poetical Works of Alexander Pope, with Life* (Edinburgh: Gall and Inglis).
  (1909), *Essay on Criticism*, ed. by John Sargeaunt (Oxford: Clarendon Press).
[AA] Poussin, Nicolas (1964), *Lettres et propos sur l'art*, ed. by Anthony Blunt, 'Miroirs de l'art' (Paris: Hermann).
Prawer, S. S. (1961), *Heine: The Tragic Satirist* (Cambridge: Cambridge University Press).
  (1983), *Heine's Jewish Comedy: A Study of his Portraits of Jews and Judaism* (Oxford: Clarendon Press).
The Prayer Book as proposed in 1928 (n.d.), [The Book of Common Prayer] (London: Cambridge University Press).
Pierre-Quint, Léon (1928), *Marcel Proust, sa vie, son oeuvre, suivi de: Le comique et le mystère chez Proust*, rev. ed. (Paris: Simon Kra).
Preminger, Alex (1965), *Encyclopedia of Poetry and Poetics* (Princeton, NJ: Princeton University Press).

282   *Appendix: A Catalogue of Samuel Beckett's Library*

Prior, Larry (1979), *Et tournent les chevaux de feu* (Paris: Gallimard NRF).
[BIF] Proust, Marcel (1919–1927), *À la Recherche du temps perdu*, 15 vols. [of 16] (Paris: Gallimard).
   (1954), Contre Sainte-Beuve, *suivi de* Nouveaux mélanges (Paris: Gallimard NRF).
Pyle, Hilary (1970), *Jack B. Yeats: A Biography* (London: Routledge & Kegan Paul).
Rabelais, François (1968), *La vie très honorifique du grand Gargantua* (Paris: Garnier-Flammarion).
[BIF] Racine, Jean (n.d.[1863]), *Théâtre complet, avec des remarques littéraires et un choix de notes classiques par M. Félix Lemaistre; précédé d'une notice sur la vie et le théâtre de Racine par L.-S. Auger* (Paris: Garnier Frères).
[BIF] Rand, E. K., E. H. Wilkins and A. C. White (1912), *Dantis Alagherii Operum Latinorum Concordantiae* (Oxford: Clarendon Press).
Rat, Maurice (1957), *Dictionnaire des locutions françaises* (Paris: Librairie Larousse).
Reavey, George (1946), *Soviet Literature Today* (London: Lindsay Drummond).
   (1955), *The Colours of Memory* (New York: Grove Press).
Recklinghausen, Daniel von (1968), *James Joyce – Chronik von Leben und Werk* (Frankfurt a.M.: Suhrkamp).
Rehberg, Walter und Paula (1947), *Franz Schubert, sein Leben und Werk*, 2nd ed. (Zürich: Artemis Verlag).
Renard, Jules (n.d.[1901?]), *Le Vigneron dans sa vigne* (Paris: Editions Nilsson).
   (1927), *Le Journal de Jules Renard 1887–1910*, 4 vols. (Paris: François Bernouard).
   (1928), *Correspondance de Jules Renard 1864–1910* (Paris: François Bernouard).
Reynolds, Mary T. (1970), 'Two Essays on James Joyce', in: *The Sewanee Review* of Winter 1964 and Summer 1968 (CT: New Haven) [offprints].
Rhees, Rush, ed. (1984), *Recollections of Wittgenstein* (Oxford: Oxford University Press).
Rhys, Jean (1978), *Voyage in the Dark* (Harmondsworth: Penguin).
Rilke, Rainer Maria, *Die Weise von Liebe und Tod des Cornets Christoph Rilke* [Hebrew translation].
Rimbaud, Arthur (1929), *Œuvres de Arthur Rimbaud: vers et prose*, pref. by Paul Claudel (Paris: Mercure de France).
Rinck, Henri (1909), *150 fins de partie* (Leipzig: Verlag von Veit and Comp.).
Robbe-Grillet, Alain (1984), *Le miroir qui revient* (Paris: Éditions de Minuit).
Robert, Louis (1967), *Le Petit Robert* (Paris: Société du Nouveau Littré).
   (1972), *Le Petit Robert* (Paris: Société du Nouveau Littré).
Robert, Marthe (1960), *Kafka*, 'La Bibliothèque Idéale' (Paris: Gallimard NRF).
Roget, Peter Mark (1972), *Roget's Thesaurus* (London: Pan Reference Books).
Rostand, Jean (1967), *Inquiétudes d'un biologiste* (Paris: Stock).
Rousseau, Pierre (1939), *Explorations du ciel*, 'Collection le Roman de la Science' (Paris: Hachette).
Roycroft, A. J. (1981), *The Chess Endgame Study: A Comprehensive Introduction*, rev. ed. (New York: Dover).
Ryan, John, ed. (1970), *A Bash in the Tunnel: James Joyce by the Irish* (Brighton: Clifton Books).

Ryck, François (1977), *Nos intentions sont pacifiques* (Paris: Gallimard).
Sachs, Nelly (1965), *Späte Gedichte* (Frankfurt a.M.: Suhrkamp).
Sade, Marquis de (1909), *L'Œuvre du Marquis de Sade*, introd., essai bibliographique et notes par Guillaume Apollinaire (Paris: Bibliothèque des Curieux).
Sanctis, Francesco de (1925), *Storia della letteratura italiana*, 2 vols., new ed. (Benedetto Croce, Bari: Gius. Laterza & Figli).
Sandry, Géo and Marcel Carrère, eds. (1953), *Dictionnaire de l'argot moderne* (Paris: Éditions du Dauphin).
Sartre, Jean-Paul (1936), *L'Imagination* (Paris: Alcan).
— (1965[1964]), *Les Mots* (Paris: Gallimard NRF).
Sasse, Hans Christopher, Joseph Horne and Charlotte Dixon (1966), *Cassell's Compact German–English / English–German Dictionary* (London: Cassell).
[AA] Scève, Maurice (1916), *Delie: Object de plus haulte vertu*, ed. by Eugène Parturier (Paris: Hachette).
Schaffenburg, Carlos A. (1989), *Genesis: a poem* (MD, Bethesda).
Schiff, Daniel (1982), *La Ligne de sceaux* (Paris: Éditions de Minuit).
Schiff, Michael (1982), *L'Intelligence gaspillée: inégalité sociale, injustice scolaire* (Paris: Éditions de Seuil).
Schmidt, Leopold (1924), *Beethoven, Werke und Leben* (Berlin: Völkerverband der Bücherfreunde, Wegweiser-Verlag).
Schneider, Alan (1986), *Entrances: an American Director's Journey*, preface by Edward Albee (New York: Viking).
Schneider, Alexander (1988), *Sasha: A Musician's Life* (New York: Folio Graphics Co.).
Schneider, Pierre (1956), *Jules Renard par lui-même*, 'Écrivains de Toujours' (Paris: Éditions du Seuil).
Schopenhauer, Arthur (1923), *Sämmtliche Werke*, 6 vols., 2nd ed., ed. by Julius Frauenstädt (Leipzig: F.A. Brockhaus).
— (1968), Der Handschriftliche Nachlass, *Volume 5: 'Randschriften zu Büchern'*, ed. by Arthur Hübscher (Frankfurt a.M.: Waldemar Kramer).
Scholes, Percy A. (1944[1938]), *The Oxford Companion to Music* (Oxford: Oxford University Press).
Seghers, Hercules (1967), *Grafiek* (Amsterdam: Rijksprentenkabinet).
Sévigné, Mme de (1863), *Lettres de Mme de Sévigné*, ed. by M. Suard (Paris: Librarie de Firmin Didot Frères).
Sewell, Brocard, ed. (1987), *Frances Horovitz Poet: A Symposium* (Wirral: The Aylesford Press).
Shakespeare, William (n.d.), *The Works of William Shakespeare* (London: Frederick Warne & Co.).
— (1957[1954]), *The Complete Works of Shakespeare*, with illustrations from modern stage productions (Oxford: Oxford University Press).
— (1960), *Le Roi Lear, Mesure pour mesure*, trans. by (Paris: A. Colin).
— (1976[1956]), *Comme il vous plaira*, trans. by Jean-Jacques Mayoux (Paris: Aubier-Montaigne).
— (1986), *The Sonnets and The Lovers' Complaint*, ed. by John Carrogan (Harmondsworth: Penguin).

The Sonnets (1988), ed. by M. R. Ridley, 'Everyman' (London: J.M. Dent & Sons).
Sharp, R. Farquharson (1933), *Biographical Dictionary of Foreign Literature*, 'Everyman' (London: J.M. Dent & Sons).
The Shorter Oxford English Dictionary (1972), 2 vols. (Oxford: Clarendon Press).
Sidur, Vadim (1978), *Skulpturen, Graphik* (Konstanz: Universitätsverlag).
   (1980), *Skulpturen, Graphiken*, exhibition catalogue, September 1980, Schloss Charlottenburg.
Siebzehner-Vivanti, Giorgio (1965[1954]), *Dizionario della Divina commedia* (Milan: Feltrinelli).
Sima (1981), *Présence de Sima 1891–1971*, texte liminaire de Ludovic Kozovoi, exhibition catalogue, May–July 1981 (Paris: Le point Cardinal).
Simond, Charles (n.d.[1907]), *Schiller 1759–1805* (Paris: Bibliothèque Larousse).
Smith, William (1868), *A Smaller History of Rome* (London: James Walton / John Murray).
Smollett, Tobias (n.d.), *The Expedition of Humphrey Clinker* (London: Hutchinson).
Solinas, Franco, and Barbara Bray (1980), *Operation Shakespeare: A Screenplay* [typescript].
Somervell, David (1918[1917]), *A Companion to Palgrave's Golden Treasury* (London: Grant Richards Ltd.).
Sophocles (1955), *König Oedipus*, trans. by Wolfgang Schadewaldt (Berlin und Frankfurt a.M.: Suhrkamp).
Spinoza, Baruch (n.d.), *Ethics, and 'De Intellectus Emendatione'* (London: J.M. Dent & Sons).
Spoon, Harriman (1981), *Scatastrophes* (Limited Edition Ltd.).
Der Sprach-Brockhaus (1958), 7th ed. (Wiesbaden: F.A. Brockhaus).
Steiner, George, ed. (1966), *The Penguin Book of Modern Verse Translation* (Harmondsworth: Penguin).
[BIF] Stendhal [Henri Beyle] (1925), *Le Rouge et le noir* (Paris: Garnier).
Stern, Richard (1989), *Noble Rot: Stories 1949–1988* (New York: Grove Press).
Sterne, Laurence (1780), *The Works of Laurence Sterne*, volume 4 (Dublin: printed for D. Chamberlaine, J. Potts and W. Colles) [contains *A Sentimental Journey through France and Italy*, *Letters from Yorick to Eliza* and *Sterne's Letters to his Friends*].
   (1910[1903]), *The Life and Opinions of Tristram Shandy*, from *The Works of Laurence Sterne*, [volume 1], 'The World's Classics' (London: Oxford University Press).
   (1959[1903]), *The Life and Opinions of Tristram Shandy*, 'The World's Classics' (London: Oxford University Press).
Stobart, J. C. (1961), *The Grandeur That Was Rome*, 4th ed., ed. and rev. by W. S. Maguiness and H. H. Scullard (London: Sidwick and Jackson).
Stopp, Frederick J., (1969[1960]), *A Manual of Modern German*, 2nd ed. (London: University Tutorial Press).
Strindberg, August (1958–62), *Théâtre*, 8 vols. (Paris: L'Arche).
   (1966), *Inferno*, introd. by Torsten Eklund (Paris: Mercure de France).

Stuckenschmidt, H. H. (1959), *Arnold Schoenberg*, trans. by Edith Temple Roberts and Humphrey Searle (London: Calder).
Swift, Jonathan (1922), *The Drapier's Letters*, ed. by Temple Scott, volume 6, 'The Prose Works of Jonathan Swift' (London: G. Bell & Sons).
  (1963), *Gulliver's Travels*, ed. by John Hayward, 'The World's Classics' (London: Oxford University Press).
Synge, J. M. (1971), My Wallet of Photographs: *The photographs of J. M. Synge arranged and introduced by Lilo Stephens* (Dublin: Dolmen Press).
Tasso, Torquato (1923), *Gerusalemme Liberata*, 6th ed. (Milan: Ulrico Hoepli).
Tejera, Nivaria (1987), *Fuir la spirale*, trans. by Jean-Marie Saint-Lu (Paris: Actes Sud).
Thomas, Edward (1981), *Selected Poems and Prose*, ed. by David Wright (Harmondsworth: Penguin).
Thompson, A. Hamilton (1914), *A History of English Literature, and of the Chief English Writers*, rev. ed. (London: John Murray).
Thrale, Hester Lynch (1984), *Dr Johnson by Mrs Thrale: 'The Anecdotes' of Mrs. Piozzi in their Original Form*, ed. by Richard Ingrams (London: Chatto & Windus).
Tindall, William York (1960), *The Joyce Country* (Pennsylvania: Pennsylvania State University Press).
Toussaint, Jean-Philippe (1985), *La Salle de bain* (Paris: Éditions de Minuit).
  (1986), *Monsieur* (Paris: Éditions de Minuit).
Turner, J. M. W. (1975[1974]), *Turner 1775–1851*, exhibition catalogue (London: Tate Gallery).
Uberquoi, Marie-Claire (1982), *Memorialia: ceremonia de la confusion ibicenca* (Barcelona: Fandos).
Unseld, Joachim (1982), *Franz Kafka: Ein Schriftstellerleben* (Munich: Carl Hanser Verlag).
Unseld, Siegfried (1978), *Der Autor und sein Verleger: Vorlesungen in Mainz und Austin* (Frankfurt a.M.: Suhrkamp).
Ussher, Arland (1967), *Sages & Schoolmen* (Dublin: Dolmen Press).
Vaissière, Robert de la, ed. (1923), *Anthologie poétique du XXème siècle*, Volume 1 (Paris: Les Editions G. Crès et Cie.).
Velde, Bram van (1974), *Repères*, 'Cahiers d'art contemporain', preface by Yves Perey (Paris: Maeght).
  (1989), *Bram Van Velde 1895–1981*, exhibition catalogue, Bonnefantenmuseum Maastricht (Bern: Benteli Verlag).
  (1989), *Bram Van Velde*, exhibition catalogue, Centre Georges Pompidou (Paris: Centre Georges Pompidou.
Verlaine, Paul (1968 [1962]), *Œuvres poétiques complètes* (Paris: Gallimard Pléiade).
Vigny, Alfred de (1935), *Poésies choisies*, ed. by Henri Maugis (Paris: Librairie Larousse).
Villon, François (1931), *Œuvres poétiques* (Paris: René Hilsum).
Vladislav, Jan, ed. (1986), *Vaclav Havel or Living in Truth* (London: Faber & Faber).
Vogelweide, Walter von der (n.d.[c.1926]), *Walter von der Vogelweide* – altdeutsch und übertragen von Walther Bulst (Berlin und Leipzig: Tempel Verlag).

Vulliamy, C. E. (1936), *Mrs Thrale of Streatham: Her Place in the Life of Dr Samuel Johnson etc.* (London: Jonathan Cape).

Wade, Robert G., and Kevin J. O'Connell (1972), *The Games of Robert J. Fischer* (London: B.T. Batsford).

Walton, Isaak (n.d.), *The Lives of Donne, Wotton, Hooker, Herbert, Sanderson* (London: printed for the Society for Promoting Christian Knowledge).

Warner, Francis (1988), Healing Nature. The Athens of Pericles *(a play)*, 'Oxford Theater Texts 9' (Gerrards Cross: Colin Smythe).

Webster's New International Dictionary of the English Language, unabridged (1961), 3rd ed. (Springfield, Mass.: G. & C. Merriam Co.).

Weekley, Ernest (1924), *A Concise Etymological Dictionary of Modern English* (London: John Murray).

Weiss, Peter (1961), *Abschied von den Eltern* (Frankfurt a.M.: Suhrkamp).

Wenman, P. (1946), *Thirty-Two Movers* (London: The Mitre Press).

Wilde, Oscar (1987), *More Letters of Oscar Wilde*, ed. by Rupert Hart-Davis (Oxford: Oxford University Press).

(1987[1986]), *The Importance of Being Ernest, and Other Plays* (Harmondsworth: Penguin).

(1987[1985)], *The Picture of Dorian Gray*, ed. by Peter Ackroyd (Harmondsworth: Penguin).

Wilson, Harriette (1985), *Harriette Wilson's Memoirs* (London: Century Publishing).

Wilson, P. G. (1966 [1950]), *Teach Yourself German Grammar* (London: The English Universities Press).

Windelband, W. and H. Heimsoeth (1935), *Lehrbuch der Geschichte der Philosophie* (Tübingen: J.C.B. Mohr [Paul Siebeck]).

Witte, Bernd (1988), *Walter Benjamin: une biographie*, trans. by André Bernold (Paris: Cerf).

Wittgenstein, Ludwig (1960), *Schriften*, 2 vols. (Frankfurt a.M.: Suhrkamp).

(1960), *Schriften: Beiheft* [mit Beiträgen von Ingeborg Bachmann, Maurice Cranston, Jose Ferrater Mora, Paul Feyerabend, Erich Heller, Bertrand Russell, George H. von Wright] (Frankfurt a.M.: Suhrkamp).

(1961), *The Tractatus Logico-Philosophicus*, trans. by D. F. Pars and B. F. McGuinness, introd. by Bertrand Russell (London: Routledge and Kegan Paul).

(1963), *Tractatus Logico-Philosophicus: Logisch-philosophische Abhandlung* (Frankfurt a.M.: Suhrkamp).

(1966), *Lectures and Conversations on Aesthetics, Psychology and Religious Beliefs*, ed. by Cyril Barrett (Oxford: Basil Blackwell).

(1967), *Letters from Ludwig Wittgenstein, with a Memoir*, ed. by Paul Engelmann (Oxford: Basil Blackwell).

(1968), *Über Ludwig Wittgenstein* (Frankfurt a.M.: Suhrkamp).

Wolff, Kurt (n.d.), *Autoren, Bücher, Abenteuer: Betrachtungen und Erinnerungen eines Verlegers* (Berlin: Wagenbach).

Wolfskehl, Karl and Friedrich von der Leyen, eds. and trans. (1932[1909]), *Älteste deutsche Dichtung* (Urtext und Übertragung) (Leipzig: Insel Verlag).
Woodforde, James (1967), *The Diary of a Country Parson 1758–1802*, ed. by John Beresford, 'The World's Classics' (London: Oxford University Press).
Worth, Katharine (1983), *Oscar Wilde* (London and Basingstoke: MacMillan).
Wurm, Franz (1989), *In diesem Fall* (Zürich: Pendo-Verlag).
Wyatt, A. J. and W. H. Low (1920), *Intermediate Text Book of English Literature*, 2 vols. (London: W.B. Clive, University Tutorial Press Ltd.).
Yeats, Jack Butler (1938), *The Charmed Life* (London: Routledge & Sons).
  (1947), *The Careless Flower* (London: The Pilot Press).
  (1964), *In Sand and The Green Wave* (Dublin: The Dolmen Press).
Yeats, William Butler (1943), *The Wind among the Reeds*, 4th ed. (London: Elkin Mathews).
  (1955), *The Collected Poems*, 2nd ed. (London: Macmillan & Co Ltd.).
  (1960), *The Collected Plays*, 2nd ed. (London: Macmillan & Co Ltd.).
  (1961), *The Senate Speeches of W. B. Yeats*, ed. by Donald R. Pearce (London: Faber & Faber).
  (1975), *Choix de poèmes*, ed. and trans. by Réne Fréchet, 'Collection Bilingue' (Paris: Aubier-Montaigne).
  (1984), *La Taille d'une Agathe et autres Essais*, ed. by Pierre Chabert (Paris: Klincksieck).
  ([1985?]), *The Lake Isle of Innisfree* (New York: Grenfell Press)
  (1987), *Where there is nothing*, by W. B. Yeats / *The unicorn from the stars*, by W.B. Yeats and Lady Gregory (1908), with an introd. by Katharine Worth (Washington, DC: The Catholic University of America Press, and Gerrards Cross: Colin Smythe).
  (1989), *Quarante-cinq poèmes de Yeats suivis de* La Résurrection, ed. by Yves Bonnefoy (Paris: Hermann).
Yeats, W. B., ed. (1937[1936]), *The Oxford Book of Modern Verse 1892–1935* (Oxford: Clarendon Press).
Yung, Kai Kin, ed. (1984), *Samuel Johnson 1709–84* (London: The Herbert Press).
Zeltner-Neukomm, Gerda (1960): *Das Wagnis des französischen Gegenwartromans: Die neue Welterfahrung in der Literatur* (Reinbeck bei Hamburg: Rohwolt).
Zingarelli, Nicola ed. (1954), *Vocabolario della lingua italiana* (Bologna: Nicola Zanichelli).

Bibliography

SAMUEL BECKETT – PUBLICATIONS

Beckett, Samuel, *Company / Ill Seen Ill Said / Worstward Ho / Stirrings Still*, ed. by Dirk Van Hulle (London: Faber & Faber, 2009).
The Complete Dramatic Works (London: Faber & Faber, 1990).
Dream of Fair to Middling Women (Dublin: Black Cat Press, 1992).
Disjecta: Miscellaneous Writings and a Dramatic Fragment, ed. by Ruby Cohn (London: John Calder, 1983).
The Expelled / The Calmative / The End & First Love, ed. by Christopher Ricks (London: Faber & Faber, 2009).
Fin de partie (Paris: Les Éditions de Minuit, 1957).
How It Is, ed. by Magessa O'Reilly (London: Faber & Faber, 2009).
L'Innommable (Paris: Les Éditions de Minuit, 1953).
Krapp's Last Tape, vol. 3 of The Theatrical Notebooks of Samuel Beckett, ed. by James Knowlson (London: Faber & Faber, 1992).
The Letters of Samuel Beckett, 1929–1940, ed. by Martha Dow Fehsenfeld, Lois More Overbeck, George Craig and Dan Gunn (Cambridge: Cambridge University Press, 2009).
The Letters of Samuel Beckett, 1941–1956, ed. by George Craig, Martha Dow Fehsenfeld, Dan Gunn and Lois More Overbeck (Cambridge: Cambridge University Press, 2011).
Malone Dies, ed. by Peter Boxall (London: Faber & Faber, 2010).
Mercier and Camier, ed. by Seán Kennedy (London: Faber & Faber, 2010).
Mercier et Camier (Paris: Les Éditions de Minuit, 1970).
Molloy, ed. by Shane Weller (London: Faber & Faber, 2009).
Molloy (Paris: Les Éditions de Minuit, 1996).
More Pricks than Kicks, ed. by Cassandra Nelson (London: Faber & Faber, 2010).
Murphy, ed. by J. C. C. Mays (London: Faber & Faber, 2009).
Oh les beaux jours (Paris: Minuit, 2001).
Proust and *Three Dialogues with Georges Duthuit* (London: John Calder, 1965).
Selected Poems, 1930–1989, ed. by David Wheatley (London: Faber & Faber, 2009).

Texts for Nothing and Other Shorter Prose 1950–1976, ed. by Mark Nixon (London: Faber & Faber, 2010).
The Unnamable, ed. by Steven Connor (London: Faber & Faber, 2010).
Watt (Paris: Les Éditions de Minuit, 2001).
Watt, ed. by Chris Ackerley (London: Faber & Faber, 2009).

SAMUEL BECKETT – ARCHIVAL MATERIAL

All unpublished archival material © The Estate of Samuel Beckett, c/o Rosica Colin, London.

Beckett Samuel, 'Clare Street' Notebook, Beckett International Foundation, The University of Reading, MS5003.
  'Echo's Bones' [typescript], Baker Library, Dartmouth College. Photocopy at Harry Ransom Humanities Research Center, The University of Texas at Austin, Leventhal Collection.
  He, Joe [annotated copy], Beckett International Foundation, The University of Reading, MS3626.
  Faust notebooks, Beckett International Foundation, The University of Reading, MS5004 and MS5005.
  Film [original manuscript notebook], Beckett International Foundation, The University of Reading, MS1227/7/6/1.
  'German Diaries' [6 Notebooks], Beckett International Foundation, The University of Reading.
  German Vocabulary notebooks, Beckett International Foundation, The University of Reading, MS5002 and MS5006.
  Human Wishes [3 Notebooks], Beckett International Foundation, The University of Reading, MS3461/1–3.
  Imagination Dead Imagine [manuscript notebook], Trinity College Library Dublin, MS11223.
  Notes from Samuel Beckett's lectures, Trinity College Library Dublin, taken by Rachel Dobbin [Burrows], Trinity College Library Dublin, MIC60.
  Notes on Italian Literature, Trinity College Library Dublin, MS10965 and MS10965a.
  Notes on Philosophy, Trinity College Library Dublin, MS10967.
  Notes on English Literary History, Trinity College Library Dublin, MS10970.
  Notes on German Literature, Trinity College Library Dublin, MS10971/1.
  Notes on the 'Trueborn Jackeen' and 'Cow', Trinity College Library Dublin, MS10971/2.
  Notes on the 'University Wits', Trinity College Library Dublin, MS10971/3.
  Notes on Psychology, Trinity College Library Dublin, MS10971/7–8.
  Notes on Fritz Mauthner, Trinity College Library Dublin, MS10971/5.
  Notes on Geulincx, Trinity College Library Dublin, MS10971/6.
  'Sam Francis' Notebook, Beckett International Foundation, The University of Reading, MS2926.

Samuel Beckett Questionnaire, University of Reading, Special Collections, James and Elizabeth Knowlson Archive, JEK A/1/2/4.
'Sottisier' Notebook, Beckett International Foundation, The University of Reading, MS2901.
Stirrings Still / Soubresauts and Comment dire / what is the word: an electronic genetic edition (Series 'The Beckett Digital Manuscript Project', module 1), ed. by Dirk Van Hulle and Vincent Neyt. Brussels: University Press Antwerp (ASP/UPA), 2011, <http://www.beckettarchive.org>
Stirrings Still [manuscript], Beckett International Foundation, The University of Reading MS2935/1/1.
Stirrings Still [manuscripts], IMEC, Fonds Calder, Dossiers Beckett N° 3 in CAL2 C51 B2 [1–4].
'Super Conquérant' Notebook, Beckett International Foundation, The University of Reading, MS2934.
That Time [production notebook, Berlin 1976], Beckett International Foundation, The University of Reading, MS1976.
'Whoroscope' Notebook, Beckett International Foundation, The University of Reading, MS3000.

SAMUEL BECKETT – CORRESPONDENCE

All unpublished letters © The Estate of Samuel Beckett, c/o Rosica Colin, London.
Letters to Barbara Bray, Trinity College Library Dublin, MS10948/1.
Letters to Ruby Cohn, Beckett International Foundation, The University of Reading, MS5100.
Letters to Nancy Cunard, Harry Ransom Humanities Research Center, The University of Texas at Austin.
Letters to Jocelyn Herbert, Beckett International Foundation, University of Reading, MS5200.
Letters to Aidan Higgins, Harry Ransom Humanities Research Center, The University of Texas at Austin.
Letters to Mary Hutchinson, Harry Ransom Humanities Research Center, The University of Texas at Austin.
Letters to James Knowlson, University of Reading, Special Collections, James and Elizabeth Knowlson Archive, JEK B/1.
Letters to John Kobler, Harry Ransom Humanities Research Center, The University of Texas at Austin.
Letters to A. J. Leventhal, Harry Ransom Humanities Research Center, The University of Texas at Austin.
Letters to Thomas MacGreevy, Trinity College Library Dublin, MS10402.
Letters to Stuart Maguinness, Beckett International Foundation, The University of Reading, MS4199/1.
Letters to Mary Manning Howe, Harry Ransom Humanities Research Center, The University of Texas at Austin.

Letters to Pamela Mitchell, Beckett International Foundation, The University of Reading, MS5060.
Letters to Mania Péron, Harry Ransom Humanities Research Center, The University of Texas at Austin.
Letters to Harold Pinter, British Library London, Add MS 88880/7/2.
Letters to Nick Rawson, Trinity College Library Dublin, MS10513.
Letters to George Reavey, Harry Ransom Humanities Research Center, The University of Texas at Austin.
Letters to Jake Schwartz, Harry Ransom Humanities Research Center, The University of Texas at Austin.
Letters to Herbert Martyn Oliver [Ho] White, Trinity College Library Dublin, MS3771/12–25.

WORKS CITED

Ackerley, C. J. (1996), '"Do Not Despair": Samuel Beckett and Robert Greene', in: *Journal of Beckett Studies*, n.s., 6.1: 119–24.
  (1999), 'Samuel Beckett and the Bible: A Guide', in: *Journal of Beckett Studies* 9.1: 53–126.
  (2005), *Obscure Locks, Simple Keys: The Annotated Watt* (Tallahassee: Journal of Beckett Studies Books).
Ackerley, C. J. and S. E. Gontarski (2004), *The Grove Companion to Samuel Beckett* (New York: Grove Press).
Adorno, Theodor W. (1982), 'Trying to Understand Endgame', trans. by Michael T. Jones, in: *New German Critique 26: Critical Theory and Modernity* (Spring-Summer), 119–50.
Albrecht, Klaus (2005), 'Günter Albrecht – Samuel Beckett – Axel Kaun', in: *Beckett the European*, ed. by Dirk Van Hulle (Tallahassee: Journal of Beckett Studies Books), 24–38.
Atik, Anne (1999), 'Beckett as Reader', in: *American Poetry Review* 28 (September-October), 33–9.
  (2001), *How It Was: A Memoir of Samuel Beckett* (London: Faber & Faber).
Bailey, Iain (2009), 'Beckett, Drama, and the Writing on the Wall', in: *The Tragic Comedy of Samuel Beckett*, ed. by Daniela Guardamagna and Rossana M. Sebellin (Rome: Laterza), 143–55.
  (2010), *Samuel Beckett, Intertextuality and the Bible* (Manchester: thesis submitted to the University of Manchester for the degree of Doctor of Philosophy in the Faculty of Humanities).
Bair, Deirdre (1978), *Samuel Beckett: A Biography* (New York: Harcourt).
  (1990), *Samuel Beckett: A Biography* (London: Vintage).
Baker, Phil (1997), *Beckett and the Mythology of Psychoanalysis* (Basingstoke: Macmillan).
Ball, Robert S. (1892), *The Story of the Heavens* (London, Paris, Melbourne: Cassell).

Barbera, Sandro (2001), 'La bibliothèque d'Arthur Schopenhauer', in: *Bibliothèques d'écrivains*, ed. by Paolo D'Iorio and Daniel Ferrer (Paris: CNRS editions), 101–20.
Barge, Laura (1988), *God, the Quest, the Hero: Thematic Structures in Beckett's Fiction* (Chapel Hill: U.N.C. Dept. of Romance Languages).
Barry, Elizabeth (2000), '"Faith Cometh by Hearing, and Hearing by the Word of God": The Status of Beckett's Religious Language', in: *Samuel Beckett Today/ Aujourd'hui* 9: 173–83.
Barthes, Roland (1984), 'Sur la lecture', in: *Le bruissement de la langue: Essais critiques IV* (Paris: Éditions du Seuil), 37–48.
  (1993), *S/Z*, transl. by Richard Miller (New York: Hill and Wang/The Noonday Press).
Beal, Timothy K. and David M. Gunn (1997), *Reading Bibles, Writing Bodies: Identity and the Book* (London: Routledge).
Begam, Richard (1996), *Samuel Beckett and the End of Modernity* (Stanford: Stanford University Press).
  (2007), 'How to Do Nothing with Words, or Waiting for Godot as Performativity', in: *Modern Drama* 50.2 (Summer), 138–67.
Beja, Morris, S. E Gontarski and Pierre Astier, eds. (1983), *Samuel Beckett: Humanistic Perspectives* (Columbus: Ohio State University Press).
Ben-Zvi, Linda (1980), 'Samuel Beckett, Fritz Mauthner, and the Limits of Language', in: *PMLA* 95: 183–200.
  (1984), 'Fritz Mauthner for Company', in: *Journal of Beckett Studies* 9: 65–88.
  (1988), *Samuel Beckett* (Boston: Twayne).
  (2004), 'Biographical, Textual and Historical Origins', in: *Palgrave Advances in Samuel Beckett Studies*, ed. by Lois Oppenheim (Basingstoke: Palgrave), 133–53.
Berensmeyer, Ingo, '"Twofold Vibration": Samuel Beckett's Laws of Form', in: *Poetics Today* 25.3: 465–95.
Bernold, André (1992), *L'Amitié de Beckett 1979–1989* (Paris: Hermann).
Bowles, Patrick (1994), 'How to Fail: Notes on Talks with Samuel Beckett', in: *PN Review* 96, 20.4 (March–April), 24–38.
Brater, Enoch (1994), *The Drama in the Text: Beckett's Late Fiction* (Oxford: Oxford University Press).
Bredeck, Elizabeth (1992), *Metaphors of Knowledge: Language and Thought in Mauthner's Critique* (Detroit: Wayne State University Press).
Brienza, Susan D. (1987), *Samuel Beckett's New Worlds: Style in Metafiction* (Norman: Oklahoma University Press).
Brun, Bernard (1984), 'Sur le Proust de Beckett', in: *Beckett avant Beckett: Essais sur les premières œuvres*, ed. by Jean-Michel Rabaté (Paris: P.E.N.S.), 79–91.
Bryden, Mary (1993), *Women in Samuel Beckett's Prose and Drama: Her Own Other* (Houndmills: Macmillan).
  (1998a), *Samuel Beckett and the Idea of God* (Basingstoke: Macmillan).
  ed. (1998b), *Samuel Beckett and Music* (Oxford: Clarendon Press).

Butler, Lance St. John (1992), '"A mythology with which I am perfectly familiar": Samuel Beckett and the Absence of God', in: *Irish Writers and Religion*, ed. by Robert Welch (Gerrards Cross: Colin Smythe).
— (1994), 'Two darks: A Solution to the Problem of Beckett's Bilingualism', in: *Samuel Beckett Today/Aujourd'hui* 3: 115–35.
Byron, Mark (2004), 'Beckett's Tenth Rate Xenium', in: *Literature and the Writer*, ed. by Michael J. Meyer (Amsterdam and Atlanta: Rodopi), 1–18.
Calder, John (2001), *The Philosophy of Samuel Beckett* (London: John Calder).
Casanova, Pascale (1997), *Beckett l'abstracteur: Anatomie d'une révolution littéraire* (Paris: Éditions du Seuil).
Caselli, Daniela (2000), '"God that old favourite": Issues of Authority in *How It Is*', in: *Samuel Beckett Today/Aujourd'hui* 9: 159–72.
— (2005), *Beckett's Dantes: Intertextuality in the fiction and criticism* (Manchester: Manchester University Press).
— (2006), 'The Promise of Dante in the Beckett Manuscripts', in: *Samuel Beckett Today/Aujourd'hui* 16: 237–57.
— ed. (2010), *Beckett and Nothing: Trying to Understand Beckett* (Manchester: Manchester University Press).
Chartier, Roger (2003), 'Du livre au lire', in: *Pratiques de la lecture*, ed. by Roger Chartier (Paris: Éditions Payot & Rivages), 81–117.
Cioran, E. M. (1995), *Exercices d'admiration*, in: *Œuvres* (Paris: Gallimard).
Cohn, Ruby (2001), *A Beckett Canon* (Ann Arbor: University of Michigan Press).
Connor, Steven (1988), *Samuel Beckett: Repetition, Theory and Text* (Oxford: Blackwell).
— (1989), '"Traduttore, traditore": Samuel Beckett's Translation of *Mercier et Camier*', in: *Journal of Beckett Studies* 11: 27–46.
Cronin, Anthony (1996), *Beckett: The Last Modernist* (London: HarperCollins).
Dante (1995), *The Divine Comedy*, in: *The Portable Dante*, trans. by Mark Musa (London: Penguin).
Dittrich, Lutz, Carola Veit and Ernest Wichner, eds. (2006), *Obergeschoss still closed – Samuel Beckett in Berlin*. Texte aus dem Literaturhaus Berlin, Band 16 (Berlin: Verlag Matthes & Seitz).
Dowd, Garin (2008), 'Prolegomena to a Critique of Excavatory Reason: Reply to Matthew Feldman', in: *Samuel Beckett Today/Aujourd'hui* 20: 375–88.
Duthuit, Georges, unpublished letters to Mary Hutchinson, Mary Hutchinson Collection, Harry Ransom Humanities Research Center, The University of Texas at Austin.
Ellmann, Richard (1983), *James Joyce*. Revised Edition (Oxford: Oxford University Press).
Engelberts, Matthijs (2001), *Défis du récit scénique: Formes et enjeux du mode narratif dans le théâtre de Beckett et de Duras* (Geneva: Droz).
Engelmann, Paul (1967), *Letters from Ludwig Wittgenstein: The Man and His Philosophy*. (New York: Dell).
Fadiman, Anne (1999), *Ex Libris: Confessions of a Common Reader* (London: Allen Lane, The Penguin Press).

Feldman, Matthew (2006a), *Beckett's Books: A Cultural History of Samuel Beckett's 'Interwar Notes'* (New York and London: Continuum).
  (2006b), 'Beckett and Popper, or, "What Stink of Artifice": Some Notes on Methodology, Falsifiability, and Criticism in Beckett Studies', in: *Samuel Beckett Today/Aujourd'hui* 16 (2006), 373–91.
  (2006c), Returning to Beckett Returning to the Presocratics, or "All their balls about being and existing"', in: *Genetic Joyce Studies* 6, at: www.geneticjoyce studies.org
  (2008), 'In Defence of Empirical Knowledge: Rejoinder to "A Critique of Excavatory Reason"', in: *Samuel Beckett Today/Aujourd'hui* 20: 389–99.
Ferrer, Daniel (2004a), 'Towards a Marginalist Economy of Textual Genesis', in: *Reading Notes*, ed. by Dirk Van Hulle and Wim Van Mierlo (Amsterdam: Rodopi), 7–18.
  (2004b), '"The conversation began some minutes before anything was said . . .": Textual Genesis as Dialogue and Confrontation (Woolf vs Joyce and Co)', in: *Études britanniques contemporaines, Numéro hors series*, ed. by Chrisine Reynier (Fall), 47–68.
Ferrini, Jean-Pierre (2003), *Dante et Beckett* (Paris: Hermann).
  (2006), 'Dante, Pétrarque, Leopardi, Beckett', in: *Samuel Beckett Today/ Aujourd'hui* 17: 53–66.
Fifield, Peter (2010), '"Accursed Progenitor!": *Fin de partie* and Georges Bataille', in: *Samuel Beckett Today/Aujourd'hui* 22: 107–21.
  (2011), '"Of being – or remaining": Beckett and Early Greek Philosophy', in: *Sofia Philosophical Review* 5.1. Special Issue Beckett/Philosophy, ed. by Matthew Feldman and Karim Mamdani, 70–93.
Fitch, Brian (1988), *Beckett and Babel: An Investigation into the Status of the Bilingual Work* (Toronto: University of Toronto Press).
Fletcher, John (1964), *The Novels of Samuel Beckett* (New York: Barnes & Noble).
Fontane, Theodor (1958), *Werke in zwei Bänden* (Munich: Hanser).
  (1964), *Beyond Recall*, trans. by Douglas Parmée (Oxford: Oxford University Press).
Fontenelle, Bernard de (1826), *Entretiens sur la pluralité des mondes* (Paris: Janet et Cotelle).
Fowler, Harold N. (1902), *A History of Ancient Greek Literature* (New York: D. Appleton and Company).
Frost, Everett and Jane Maxwell (2006), 'Catalogue of "Notes Diverse[s] Holo[graph]"', in: *Samuel Beckett Today/Aujourd'hui* 16: 15–182.
Garforth, Julian (2005), 'Samuel Beckett, Fritz Mauthner, and the *Whoroscope Notebook:* Becketts Beiträge zu einer Kritik der Sprache', in: *Beckett the European*, ed. by Dirk Van Hulle (Tallahassee: Journal of Beckett Studies Books), 49–68.
Gellhaus, Axel (2004), 'Marginalia: Paul Celan as Reader', in: *Reading Notes*, ed. by Dirk Van Hulle and Wim Van Mierlo (Amsterdam: Rodopi), 207–19.
Germoni, Karine (2009), *Écarts, jeux et enjeux de la punctuation dans l'œuvre bilingue de Samuel Beckett* (Doctorat Aix-Marseille Université; Aix-en-Provence).

Gide, André (1932), *Œuvres Complètes d'André Gide*, 2 vols. (Paris: NRF).
Gontarski, S. E. (1985), *The Intent of Undoing in Samuel Beckett's Dramatic Texts* (Bloomington: Indiana University Press).
  ed. (2010), *A Companion to Samuel Beckett* (Oxford: Wiley-Blackwell).
Graver, Lawrence and Raymond Federman, eds. (1979), *Samuel Beckett: The Critical Heritage* (London: Routledge and Kegan Paul).
Greetham, David C., ed. (1997), *The Margins of the Text* (Ann Arbor: University of Michigan Press).
Grimsley, Ronald (1971), 'Two Philosophical Views of the Literary Imagination: Sartre and Bachelard', in: *Comparative Literature Studies* 8: 42–57.
Grindley, Carl James (2001), 'Reading Piers Plowman C-Text Annotations: Notes toward the Classification of Printed and Written Marginalia in Texts from the British Isles 1300–1641', in: *The Medieval Professional Reader at Work: Evidence from Manuscripts of Chaucer, Langland, Kempe, and Gower*, ed. by Kathryn Kerby-Fulton and Maidie Hilmo (Victoria, B.C.: English Literary Studies), 77–91.
Grossman, Évelyne (2006), 'Qu-est-ce qu'une archive? (Beckett, Foucault)', in: *Samuel Beckett Today/Aujourd'hui* 17: 46–81.
Gulette, David (1972), 'Mon Jour chez Sam: A Visit with Beckett', in: *Ploughshares* 1.2 (Summer), 65–9.
Harmon, Maurice, ed. (1998), *No Author Better Served: The Correspondence of Samuel Beckett and Alan Schneider* (Cambridge, Massachusetts: Harvard University Press).
Hatch, David A. (2003), "'I Am Mistaken': Surface and Subtext in Samuel Beckett's *Three Dialogues*', in: *Samuel Beckett Today/Aujourd'hui* 13: 57–71.
Hesla, David (1971), *The Shape of Chaos* (Minneapolis: University of Minnesota Press).
Hisgen, Ruud and Adriaan van der Weel (1998), *The Silencing of the Sphinx* (Leiden, private edition).
Hoefer, Jacqueline (1950), 'Watt', in: *Perspective* 11: 166–82.
Hölderlin, Friedrich (1965), *Hyperion*, trans. by Willard R. Trask (London: Signet).
  (1967), *Poems and Fragments*, trans. by Michael Hamburger (Ann Arbor: University of Michigan Press).
  (1990), *Hyperion and Selected Poems*, ed. by Eric L. Santner (London: Continuum).
Hunkeler, Thomas (2008), 'Dante à Lyon: des "rime petrose" aux "durs épigrammes"', in: *Italique* XI, 9–27.
Hutcheon, Linda (1989), *The Politics of Postmodernism* (New York: Routledge).
Izenberg, Gerald N. (2000), *Mann, Wedekind, Kandinsky through World War I* (Chicago: University of Chicago Press).
Jackson, Heather J. (2001), *Marginalia : Readers Writing in Books* (New Haven and London: Yale University Press).
Janvier, Ludovic (1969), *Samuel Beckett: par lui-même* (Paris: Éditions du Seuil).
Joyce, James (1992), *A Portrait of the Artist as a Young Man* (Harmondsworth: Penguin).

Juliet, Charles (1986), *Rencontre avec Samuel Beckett* (Paris: Fata Morgana).
    (1995), *Conversations with Samuel Beckett and Bram van Velde*, trans. by Janey Tucker (Leiden: Academic Press Leiden).
Katz, Daniel (1999), *Saying I No More: Subjectivity and Consciousness in the Prose of Samuel Beckett* (Illinois: Northwestern University Press).
Kennedy, Seán (2004), '"The artist who stakes his being is from nowhere": Beckett and Thomas MacGreevy on the Art of Jack B. Yeats', in: *Samuel Beckett Today/Aujourd'hui* 14: 61–74.
    (2005), 'Introduction to "Historicising Beckett"', in: *Samuel Beckett Today/Aujourd'hui* 15: 21–7.
Kennedy, Seán, and Katherine Weiss, eds. (2009), *Samuel Beckett: History, Memory, Archive* (Basingstoke: Palgrave).
Kieser, Rolf (1990), *Olga Plümacher-Hünerwadel. Eine gelehrte Frau des 19. Jahrhunderts* (Lenzburg: Lenzburger Druck).
Kleist, Heinrich von (1972), 'On the Marionette Theatre', trans. by Thomas G. Neumiller, in: *The Drama Review* 16.3 (September), 22–6.
Knowlson, James (1980), *Samuel Beckett's 'Krapp's Last Tape': A Theatre Workbook* (London: Brutus Books).
    (1996), *Damned to Fame: The Life of Samuel Beckett* (London: Bloomsbury).
Knowlson, James and Elizabeth (2006), *Beckett Remembering / Remembering Beckett: A Centenary Celebration* (New York: Arcade Publishing).
Knowlson, James and John Pilling (1979), *Frescoes of the Skull* (London: John Calder).
Krance, Charles (1993), 'Traces of Transtextual Confluence and Bilingual Genesis: *A Piece of Monologue* and *Solo* for Openers', *Samuel Beckett Today/Aujourd'hui* 2: 133–8.
Lake, Carlton, ed. (1984), *No symbols where none intended: a catalogue of books, manuscripts and other material relating to Samuel Beckett in the collections of the Humanities Research Center* (Austin: Humanities Research Center).
Laubach-Kiani, Philip (2004), *Becketts Welten im 'Off': Eine textgenetisch orientierte Analyse der Raumsemantik in den Dramen Samuel Becketts*, PhD dissertation, Ludwig-Maximilians-Universität München.
Lawley, Paul (2001), '"The Grim Journey": Beckett Listens to Schubert', in: *Samuel Beckett Today/ Aujourd'hui* 11: 255–66.
Le Juez, Brigitte (2007), *Beckett avant la lettre* (Paris: Grasset).
Lernout, Geert (1994), 'James Joyce and Fritz Mauthner and Samuel Beckett', in: *In Principle Beckett Is Joyce*, ed. by Friedhelm Rathjen (Edinburgh: Split Pea Press), 21–7.
Libera, Antoni (2004), *Błogosławien'stwo Becketta i inne wyznania literackie* [*Beckett's Blessing and Other Literary Confessions*] (Warsaw: Sic! Publishers).
Locatelli, Carla (1990), *Unwording the World: Samuel Beckett's Prose Works after the Nobel Prize* (Philadelphia: University of Pennsylvania Press).
    (2001), 'Theo-less-ology: God Talk and God Unwording in Beckett', in: *Samuel Beckett Today/Aujourd'hui* 11: 341–50.
Long, Joseph (1996), 'The Reading of Company', in: *Forum for Modern Language Studies* 33.4: 314–28.

(2000), 'Divine Intertextuality: Samuel Beckett, *Company, Le Dépeupleur*', in: *Samuel Beckett Today/Aujourd'hui* 9: 145–57.
Louar, Nadia (2004), 'Le bilinguisme dans l'œuvre de Samuel Beckett: pas d'après', in: *Samuel Beckett Today/Aujourd'hui* 14: 564–78.
Lüscher-Morata, Diane (2005), *La Souffrance portée au langage dans le prose de Samuel Beckett* (Amsterdam: Rodopi).
Maiorini, Giancarlo (2008), *Pages: A Poetics of Titles* (Pennsylvania: Pennsylvania University Press).
McQueeny, Terence (1977), *Samuel Beckett as Critic of Proust and Joyce* (unpublished PhD thesis, Chapel Hill: The University of North Carolina).
Mégevand, Martin (2010), 'Pinget Seen by Beckett, Beckett According to Pinget: The Unpublishable', in: *Journal of Beckett Studies* 19.1: 3–14.
Mercier, Vivian (1978), 'Samuel Beckett, Bible Reader', in: *Commonweal* 105 (28 April), 266–8.
(1989), '"All That Fall": Samuel Beckett and the Bible', in: *Omnium Gatherum: Essays for Richard Ellmann*, ed. by Susan Dick et. al. (Gerrards Cross: Colin Smythe), 360–73.
(1990), *Beckett/Beckett* (London: Souvenir Press).
Moliterno, Gino (1993), 'The Candlebearer at the *Wake*: Bruno's *Candelaio* in Joyce's Book of the Dark', in: *Comparative Literature Studies* 30.3: 269–94.
Mooney, Sinéad (2000), '"Integrity in a Surplice": Beckett's (Post-) Protestant Poetics", in: *Samuel Beckett Today/Aujourd'hui* 9: 223–37.
Moorjani, Angela (2010), 'Beckett's Parisian Ghosts (Continued): The Case of the Missing Jules Renard', in: *Limit(e) Beckett* 1 (Autumn 2010), http://limite beckett.paris-sorbonne.fr/one/moorjani.html
Mori, Naoya (2008), '"No Body is at Rest": The Legacy of Leibniz's *Force* in Beckett's Oeuvre', in: *Beckett at 100: Revolving It All*, ed. by Linda Ben-Zvi and Angela Moorjani (Oxford: Oxford University Press), 107–22.
Morrison, Kristin (1983), 'Neglected Biblical Allusions in Beckett's Plays: "Mother Pegg" Once More', in: *Samuel Beckett: Humanistic Perspectives*, ed. by Morris Beja et. al. (Columbus: Ohio State University Press), 91–8.
Murphy, P. J. (2011), 'Beckett's Critique of Kant', in: *Sofia Philosophical Review* 5.1. Special Issue Beckett/Philosophy, ed. by Matthew Feldman and Karim Mamdani, 202–18.
Murphy, P. J., Werner Huber, Rolf Breuer and Konrad Scholl, eds. (1994), *Critique of Beckett Criticism: A Guide to Research in English, French and German* (Columbia: Camden House).
Nixon, Mark (2006), '"Scraps of German": Beckett reading German Literature', in: *Samuel Beckett Today/Aujourd'hui* 16: 259–82.
(2007a), 'Beckett and Romanticism in the 1930s', in: *Samuel Beckett Today/Aujourd'hui* 18: 61–76.
(2007b), '"the remains of trace": intra- and intertextual transferences in Beckett's *Mirlitonnades* manuscripts', in: 'Transnational Beckett', ed. by S. E. Gontarski, William J. Cloonan, Alec Hargreaves and Dustin Anderson, *Journal of Beckett Studies* 16.1&2 (Fall 2006/Spring), 110–22.

(2009), 'Samuel Beckett's "Film Vidéo-Cassete projet"', in: *Journal of Beckett Studies* 18.1&2: 32–43.
(2010), 'Beckett – Frisch – Dürrenmatt', in: *Samuel Beckett Today/Aujourd'hui* 22: 315–27.
(2011), *Samuel Beckett's German Diaries 1936–1937* (London: Continuum).
O'Hara, J. D. (1988), 'Beckett's Schopenhauerian Reading of Proust: The Will as Whirled in Representation', in: *Schopenhauer: New Essays in honor of His 200th Birthday*, ed. by Eric von der Luft (Lewinston: The Edwin Mellen Press), 273–92.
Parrott, Jeremy (2002), 'The Gnostic Gospel of Sam: *Watt* as Modernist Apocryphon', in: *Samuel Beckett Today/Aujourd'hui* 11: 425–33.
(2003), '"Nothing neatly named": The Beckettian Aesthetic and Negative Theology', in: *Samuel Beckett Today/Aujourd'hui* 13: 91–101.
Pattie, David (2000), *The Complete Critical Guide to Samuel Beckett* (Abingdon: Routledge).
Perloff, Marjorie (1981), *The Poetics of Indeterminacy: Rimbaud to Cage* (Princeton, New Jersey: Princeton University Press).
Pilling, John (1976a), *Samuel Beckett* (London: Routledge and Kegan Paul).
(1976b), 'Beckett's Proust', in: *Journal of Beckett Studies* 1 (Winter), 8–29.
(1992), 'From a (W)horoscope to Murphy', in: *The Ideal Core of the Onion*, ed. by John Pilling and Mary Bryden (Reading: Beckett International Foundation), 1–20.
(1995), 'Losing One's Classics: Beckett's Small Latin, and Less Greek', in: *Journal of Beckett Studies* 4.2: 5–14.
(1996), 'Beckett's Stendhal: "Nimrod of Novelists"', in: *French Studies* 50.3 (July), 311–17.
(1997), *Beckett before Godot* (Cambridge: Cambridge University Press).
(2000), 'Beckett and "The Itch to Make": The Early Poems in English', in: *Samuel Beckett Today/Aujourd'hui* 8: 15–25.
(2004), *Companion to* Dream of Fair to Middling Women (Tallahassee: Journal of Beckett Studies Books).
(2005), 'Dates and Difficulties in Beckett's *Whoroscope* Notebook', in: *Beckett the European*, ed. by Dirk Van Hulle (Tallahassee: Journal of Beckett Studies Books), 39–48.
(2006a), *A Samuel Beckett Chronology* (London: Palgrave Macmillan).
(2006b), 'Beckett and Mauthner Revisited', in: *Beckett after Beckett*, ed. by S. E. Gontarski and Anthony Uhlmann (Gainesville: University Press of Florida), 158–66.
(2006c), '"For Interpolation": Beckett and English Literature', in: *Samuel Beckett Today/Aujourd'hui* 16: 203–36.
(2009), 'Beckett and Italian Literature (after Dante)', *The Tragic Comedy of Samuel Beckett*, ed. by Daniela Guardamagna and Rossana M. Sebellin (Rome: Laterza), 5–19.

(2010), 'A Critique of Aesthetic Judgment: Beckett's "Dissonance of Ends and Means"', in: *A Companion to Samuel Beckett*, ed. by S. E. Gontarski (Oxford: Blackwell), 63–72.

(2011a), *Samuel Beckett's More Pricks Than Kicks* (London: Continuum).

ed. (2011b), 'Dossier: Samuel Beckett Translating Georges Duthuit', in: *Journal of Beckett Studies* 20.2: 197–212.

Poe, Edgar Allan (1965), *Marginalia*, in: *The Complete Works of Edgar Allan Poe*, vol. XVI, ed. by James A. Harrison (New York: AMS Press).

Pothast, Ulrich (2008), *The Metaphysical Vision: Arthur Schopenhauer's Philosophy of Art and Life and Samuel Beckett's Own Way to Make Use of It* (New York: Peter Lang).

Pountney, Rosemary (1988), *Theatre of Shadows: Samuel Beckett's Drama 1956–76* (Gerrards Cross/Totowa, NJ: Colin Smythe/Barnes and Noble Books).

Proust, Marcel (1993), *La Prisonnière*, suivi de *Albertine disparue*, ed. by Nathalie Mauriac (Paris: Le Livre de poche/Librairie générale française).

(2008), *Days of Reading*, trans. by John Sturrock. Great Ideas 53 (London: Penguin).

Quadflieg, Roswitha (2006), *Beckett was here; Hamburg im Tagebuch Samuel Becketts von 1936* (Hamburg: Hoffmann und Campe).

Rabinovitz, Rubin (1985), 'Samuel Beckett's Figurative Language', in: *Contemporary Literature* 26.3 (Autumn), 317–30.

Robertson, J. G. (1935), *A History of German Literature* (Edinburgh: Blackwood & Sons).

Robinson, Michael (1969), *The Long Sonata of the Dead* (London: Hart-Davis).

Rosen, Steven J. (1976), *Samuel Beckett and the Pessimistic Tradition* (New Brunswick, NJ: Rutgers University Press).

Sherman, William H. (2008), *Used Books: Marking Readers in Renaissance England* (Philadelphia: University of Pennsylvania Press).

Shields, Paul (2001), 'Beckett's Labours Lost: *Company* and the Paradox of Creation', in: *Samuel Beckett Today/Aujourd'hui* 11: 475–85.

Silverman, Michael (2010), Bookseller Catalogue (August).

Skerl, Jennie (1974), 'Fritz Mauthner's Critique of Language in Samuel Beckett's Watt', in: *Contemporary Literature* 15.4 (Autumn), 474–87.

(1980), 'Beckett and Mauthner's Influence: To the Editor', in: *PMLA* 95.5 (October): 877–8.

Slights, William W. E. (1997), 'The Cosmopolitics of Reading: Navigating the Margins of John Dee's General and Rare Memorials', in: *The Margins of the Text*, ed. by David C. Greetham (Ann Arbor: University of Michigan Press), 199–228.

Slocum, John J., and Herbert Cahoon (1953), *A Bibliography of James Joyce* (New Haven, CT: Yale University Press).

Smith, Frederik N. (2002), *Beckett's Eighteenth Century* (Basingstoke and New York: Palgrave).

Taylor, Juliette (2005), '"Pidgin Bullskrit": The Performance of French in Beckett's Trilogy', in: *Samuel Beckett Today/Aujourd'hui* 15: 211–23.

Tiedemann, Rolf (1994), '"Gegen den Trug der Frage nach dem Sinn": Eine Dokumentation zu Adornos Beckett-Lektüre', in: *Frankfurter Adorno Blätter III*, ed. by Theodor W. Adorno Archiv (Munich: edition text + kritik), 18–77.
Tonning, Eric (2007), *Samuel Beckett's Abstract Drama: Works for Stage and Screen 1962–1985*, Stage and Screen Studies 10 (Oxford: Peter Lang).
Tophoven, Elmar (1984), 'Becketts Company im Computer', in: *Samuel Beckett*, ed. by Hartmut Engelhardt (Frankfurt a.M.: Suhrkamp), 280–93.
Uhlmann, Anthony (2007), *Samuel Beckett and the Philosophical Image* (Cambridge: Cambridge University Press).
Van Hulle, Dirk (1999), 'Beckett – Mauthner – Zimmer – Joyce', in: *Joyce Studies Annual* 10 (Summer), 143–83.
    (2002), '"Out of Metaphor": Mauthner, Richards and the Development of Wakese', in: *James Joyce: The Study of Languages*, ed. by Dirk Van Hulle (Brussels: Peter Lang), 91–118.
    (2004a), 'Note on Next to Nothing: Ellipses in Samuel Beckett's Reading Notes', in: *Variants: The Journal of the European Society for Textual Scholarship* 2/3: 327–34.
    (2004b), *Joyce and Beckett Discovering Dante* (Dublin: National Library of Ireland / Joyce Studies).
    (2006), 'Samuel Beckett's *Faust* Notes', in: *Samuel Beckett Today/Aujourd'hui* 16: 283–97.
    (2007), '"Accursed Creator": Beckett, Romanticism and "the Modern Prometheus"', in *Samuel Beckett Today/Aujourd'hui* 18: 15–29.
    (2008), *Manuscript Genetics. Joyce's Know-How, Beckett's Nohow* (Gainesville: University Press of Florida).
    (2011), *The Making of Samuel Beckett's 'Stirrings Still' / 'Soubresauts' and 'comment dire' / 'what is the word'* (Brussels: University Press Antwerp ASP/UPA).
Van Hulle, Dirk and Mark Nixon (2009), 'Beckett's Library – From Marginalia to Notebooks', in: *The Tragic Comedy of Samuel Beckett*, ed. by Daniela Guardamagna and Rossana Sebellin (Rome: Laterza), 57–71.
Vogelweide, Walther von der (1938), *'I saw the world'; sixty poems from Walther von der Vogelweide*, trans. by Ian G. Colvin (London: Edward Arnold & Co.).
Völker, Klaus (1986), *Beckett in Berlin* (Berlin: Hentrich).
Weiler, Gershon (1958), 'On Fritz Mauthner's Critique of Language', in: *Mind*. New Series, 67.265 (January), 80–7.
    (1970), *Mauthner's Critique of Language* (Cambridge: Cambridge University Press).
Weller, Shane (2005), *A Taste for the Negative: Beckett and Nihilism* (London: Legenda).
    (2006), *Beckett, Literature and the Ethics of Alterity* (Basingstoke: Palgrave Macmillan).
    (2007) 'Beckett/Blanchot: Debts, Legacies, Affinities', in: *Beckett's Literary Legacies*, ed. by Matthew Feldman and Mark Nixon (Newcastle: Cambridge Scholars Press), 22–39.

Wimsatt, W. K. (1968), 'Genesis: A Fallacy Revisited', in: *The Disciplines of Criticism*, ed. by Peter Demetz et. al. (New Haven: Yale University Press), 193–225.

Wimsatt, William, and Monroe C. Beardsley (1954), 'The Intentional Fallacy', in: *The Verbal Icon: Studies in the Meaning of Poetry* (Lexington: University of Kentucky Press), 3–18.

Windelband, Wilhelm (1958), *A History of Philosophy*, 2 vols., reprinted from the revised edition of 1901, trans. by James H. Tufts (New York: Harper & Row).

Wolf, Maryanne (2008), *Proust and the Squid: The Story and Science of the Reading Brain* (Cambridge: Icon Books).

Woolf, Virginia (1972), 'How Should One Read a Book?', in: *Collected Essays*, vol. 2 (London: The Hogarth Press), 1–11.

Zeifman, Hersh (1974), 'Religious Imagery in the Plays of Samuel Beckett', in: *Samuel Beckett: A Collection of Criticism*, ed. by Ruby Cohn (New York: Macgraw Hill), 85–94.

Index

Note: References to Beckett's texts in French or German translation are given after the English title.

Abélard, 129–30, 155
Ackerley, Chris, 185, 256n.40
Adorno, Theodor W., xvi, 168–9, 177, 214, 251n.70
Aist, Dietmar von, 84
Albrecht, Günter, 98
Aldington, Richard, 40, 69
Alekhine, Alexander, 225n.3
Alexander, Archibald, 129
Allard, Roger, 76
Allem, Maurice, 44
Apollinaire, Guillaume, xv, 56–7, 76–7, 115
Aragon, Louis, 78
Arcos, René, 76
Aretino, Pietro, 56–7, 106, 115
Arikha, Avigdor, xiv, 27, 45, 86, 87, 90, 100, 113, 137–8, 194, 218, 219, 226n.11, 236n.7, 237n.16, 242n.10
Aristotle, 118, 141, 147
Arnoux, Paul-Alexander, 76
Ariosto, Ludovico, 20, 103, 104, 115, 223
Arnaud, Claude, 56
Arrabal, Fernando, 81, 127
Artaud, Antonin, 81
Atik, Anne, xiv, 27, 38, 44, 45, 76, 77, 86, 87, 89, 90, 96, 113, 117, 119, 137–8, 163, 172, 174, 193, 194, 218, 219, 221, 226n.11, 234n.80, 236n.7, 237n.16, 243n.15, 259n.7
Attwater, Donald, 199
Aubanel, Théodore, 104, 240n.9
Aubarède, Gabriel d', 128
Auden, W. H., xiii, 194
Austen, Jane, 12, 30
Auster, Paul, 42
Avicenna, 129

Bacharach, A. L., 258n.1
Bachelard, Gaston, 167

Bachmann, Ingeborg, 164, 166
Bacon, Francis, 104, 130, 138, 155
Bailey, Iain, 173, 252n.11
Bailly, René, 196
Bair, Deirdre, 13, 65, 68, 98, 254n.29
Baker, Phil, 213
Ball, Robert S., 208
Balzac, Honoré de, 48, 58, 59, 74
Barker, J. W., 198
Barthes, Roland, 14, 16, 52
Bartlett's Familiar Quotations, 198
Bataille, Georges, 80
Bate, Walter Jackson, 34
Batistini, Yves, 128
Baudelaire, Charles, 60, 72, 177
Beardsley, Monroe, 10
Beaufret, Jean, 131–2, 143, 153
Beaumarchais, 54–5
Beckett, Edward, xiv, 6
Beckett, John, 258n.6
Beckett, Samuel Barclay
  and chess, 225n.3
  directing his plays, 7, 13, 86, 93, 97, 99, 121, 164, 165, 169
  and extensive reading, 4–6, 23, 36, 103, 180, 183, 185, 223
  gives away books, xiv
  and intensive reading, 4–6, 68, 91, 112, 152, 173, 177, 180, 183
  library in Ussy, xiv, 192, 193
  student reading, xv, 20–1, 25, 29, 30, 32, 38, 43, 45, 48, 52, 107, 123, 179, 195, 196
  working in libraries, xiv, 22, 104, 114
Beckett, Samuel Barclay – Works
  Manuscript Material
    'Clare Street' Notebook, 32, 144

303

304 Index

Beckett, Samuel Barclay – Works (cont.)
  'Dream' Notebook, 11, 21, 33, 35, 53, 58, 64, 89, 91, 95, 119, 120, 123, 138, 141, 142, 157, 170–1, 174, 177–8, 180, 184, 207, 215, 225n.1, 229n.22, 231n.49, 242n.6
  'Ernest et Alice', 186
  'Film Vidéo-Cassette projet', 44
  'German Diaries', xvi, 6, 35, 65, 82, 88, 133, 148, 219, 236n.4, 240n.19
  'Gloaming, The', 226n.7
  'Magee Monologue', 13
  Notes on Italian Literature (TCD MS10965 and MS10965a), 116
  Notes on Philosophy (TCD MS10967), 128, 129, 132, 135, 142
  Notes on Rabelais (TCD MS10969), 44
  Notes on English Literary History (TCD MS10970), 22, 29
  Notes on German Literature (TCD MS10971/1), 83, 84, 87, 88, 89, 91
  Notes on the 'Trueborn Jackeen' (TCD MS10971/2), 192
  Notes on the 'University Wits' (TCD MS10971/3), 22
  Notes on Fritz Mauthner (TCD MS10971/5), 6, 158–63
  Notes on Psychology (TCD MS10971/7–8), 213
  'Sam Francis' Notebook, 113, 216
  'Sottisier' Notebook, 14, 27, 30, 63, 90, 95, 96, 113, 149, 150, 151, 193
  'Super Conquérant' Notebook, 27, 34, 45, 114, 257n.4
  'Trueborn Jackeen', 31, 192
  'Whoroscope' Notebook, 6–7, 22, 24, 25, 30, 45, 59, 78–9, 84, 87, 88, 99, 108–9, 117, 118–20, 121, 127, 129, 130, 133, 138–43, 147, 150, 153, 155–7, 161, 168, 179, 184–5, 203–7, 210, 211, 218, 225n.1, 226n.8, 227n.17, 239n.35, 247n.54
Other Works
  An Anthology of Mexican Poetry, 127, 197
  'An Imaginative Work!' (review of Jack B. Yeats's *The Amaranthers*), 103
  'Denis Devlin's *Intercessions*', 92, 184, 233n.76
  'Les Deux Besoins', 58, 59
  'Ex Cathezra' (review of Ezra Pound's *Make it New*), 64, 76
  Film, 95
  'Hommage a Jack B. Yeats', 220
  'Humanistic Quietism' (review of Thomas MacGreevy's *Poems*), 41, 236n.2
  'MacGreevy on Yeats', 220
  'Papini's Dante', 106
  'Peinture des van Velde ou le monde et le pantalon, La', 51, 87
  'Poems by Rainer Maria Rilke' (review), 100
  Proust, 13, 17, 35, 49, 68–74, 103, 111, 116, 123
  'Proust in Pieces' (review of Albert Feuillerat's *Comment Proust a composé son roman*), 233n.70
  'Recent Irish Poetry', 36, 85, 102
  'Schwabenstreich' (review of Eduard Mörike's *Mozart on the Way to Prague*), 73
  Three Dialogues with Georges Duthuit, 212, 258n.3
  Zone (translation of Apollinaire's poem 'Zone'), 77
Plays
  All That Fall, 14, 86, 98
  Breath, 55
  . . .but the clouds. . ., 37, 209, 211
  Come and Go, 49
  Eh Joe, 89, 179, 237n.16
  Endgame / Fin de partie / Endspiel, 55, 60, 66, 80, 121, 164, 169, 173, 177, 186, 206, 254n.29, 258n.3
  productions, 99, 121, 164, 169
  Footfalls, 194
  Ghost Trio, 97, 258n.4
  Happy Days / Oh les beaux jours, xvii, 50, 61, 97, 117, 230n.43, 255n.33
  productions, 97
  Human Wishes, 32–4
  Krapp's Last Tape, 7, 10, 13, 86, 98–9, 193, 237n.19, 238n.25, 238n.29
  productions, 7, 13, 238n.25
  Nacht und Träume, 186, 218, 259n.7
  Not I / Pas moi, 127, 179
  A Piece of Monologue / Solo, 61
  Play / Spiel, 99
  'Rough for Radio II', 111
  'Rough for Theatre I', 26, 226n.7
  That Time / Damals, 93
  productions, 93
  Waiting for Godot / En attendant Godot, 9, 12, 40, 53, 66, 113, 126, 175, 179–80, 223
  What Where / Was Wo, 62, 218, 237n.16
Poetry
  'Alba', 84, 171
  'Cascando', 121
  'Casket of Pralinen for a Daughter of a Dissipated Mandarin', 225n.2
  'Dieppe', 92
  Echo's Bones and Other Precipitates, 84
  'Enueg II', 185, 254n.29
  'Hell Crane to Starling', 183, 254n.26
  'joues rouges, les', 77, 138

Long after Chamfort, 55
'Malacoda', 215
Mirlitonnades, 14
'Sanies II', 123
'Serena I', 121
'Text', 182
'What Is the Word' / 'Comment dire', 64, 169
Prose
  All Strange Away, 26, 35
  'Calmative, The', 85
  'Closed place' / 'Se voir', 166
  Company, 14, 96
  'Dante and the Lobster', 105, 107, 112, 182, 185
  'Draff', 53, 96, 105, 202
  Dream of Fair to middling Women, xvii, 11, 21, 26, 44, 52, 53, 57–8, 60, 62, 63, 64, 70, 89, 91, 94, 96, 107, 115, 116, 119, 120, 121, 123, 174, 201, 215, 225n.1, 257n.1
  'Echo's Bones', 8, 53, 64, 96, 108, 171, 202
  'End, The' / 'La Fin', 232n.58
  'Fingal', 54, 57
  'First Love' / 'Premier amour', 65, 88–9, 106
  Fizzles, 166, 195
  For to End Yet Again, 252n.13
  From an Abandoned Work, 199
  How It Is / Comment c'est, 34, 63, 227n.26
  Ill Seen Ill Said / Mal vu mal dit, 9, 14, 27, 207
  'Imagination Dead Imagine' / 'Imagination morte imaginez', 25–6
  Lessness / Sans, 169
  Malone Dies / Malone meurt, 59, 236n.11
  Mercier and Camier / Mercier et Camier, 59, 108, 109, 223
  Molloy, xvii, 79, 80, 116, 140, 146, 229n.22
  More Pricks Than Kicks, 29, 96, 112, 119, 121, 241n.25
  Murphy, 8, 21, 22–3, 25, 29, 30, 59, 67, 100, 105, 119, 150, 170, 202, 205
  'Smeraldina's Billet-Doux, The', 236n.8
  Stirrings Still / Soubresauts, 27, 64, 85, 93–4, 207, 210, 257n.4
  Texts for Nothing / Textes pour rien, 80, 109, 111, 121, 218
  Unnamable, The / L'Innommable, 60, 102, 108, 110, 138, 209–10, 211
  'Walking Out', 112, 218
  Watt, 8, 9, 14, 25, 30, 93, 102, 118, 139, 150, 162, 163, 166, 171, 172, 185–91, 202, 209, 211, 244n.17, 254n.29, 255n.38
  'Wet Night, A', 256n.7
  'What a Misfortune', 171, 174, 185, 201, 215, 247n.48, 254n.29
  Worstward Ho, 14, 27, 64
  'Yellow', 57

Beckett Digital Manuscript Project, xvii, 257n.8
Beckett International Foundation (Reading University), xiii, 105, 226n.15
Beethoven, Ludwig van, 142, 214–16, 258n.4
Begam, Richard, 166
Bellow, Saul, 42
Belmont, Georges (Pelorson), 33, 47
Benjamin, Walter, xvi
Benn, Gottfried, 100, 239n.35
Benoit, Pierre, 76
Ben-Zvi, Linda, 162, 249n.63
Bérard, Victor, 120
Bergson, Henri, 167, 257n.9
Berkeley, George, xvi, 5–6, 128, 132, 133–7
Berlin, Isaiah, 125
Bernard, Jean-Marc, 76
Bernold, André, 62, 121, 163, 232n.61, 237n.19, 238n.24, 238n.29
Bestermann, Theodore, 53
Bianchi, Enrico, 107
bibles, xvi, 4, 9, 53, 57, 60, 107, 146, 172–85
Biely, Andrei, 125–6
Billy, André, 59, 234n.79
Bizet, René, 76
Blakeney, E. H., 117
Blanchot, Maurice, xvi, 79
Blin, Roger, 120
Boccaccio, Giovanni, 114
Böll, Heinrich, 100
Bookman, The (journal), 106
Borges, Jorge Luis, xiii, xvii, 143
Boswell, James, 33–4
Botticelli, Sandro, 219
Bouvier, Jean-Baptiste, 170–2
Bowles, Patrick, 90, 242n.11
Boyle, Kay, 41, 77, 112, 233n.78
Bray, Barbara, xiv, 15, 27, 28, 33, 34, 38, 42, 53, 55, 59, 60, 63, 65, 67, 68, 77, 79, 81, 86, 90, 92, 97, 99, 100, 106, 107, 109, 110, 121, 122, 125, 126, 127, 131, 148, 164, 165, 167, 169, 193, 194, 195, 197, 198, 206, 212, 217, 219, 225n.1, 226n.9, 230n.35, 230n.39, 236n.98, 238n.30, 238n.33, 239n.34, 239n.35, 241n.23, 243n.17, 246n.32, 246n.40, 257n.8
Brinsley, John, 1
British Library (London), xiii, 236n.2
British Museum (London), 22
Brocquy, Louis le, 219
Brod, Max, 239n.36
Brunet, Pierre Gustave, 185, 189–91
Bruno, Giordano, 104
Brunschvicg, Léon, 133, 153
Bryden, Mary, 187–8, 256n.40
buddhism, 146, 154, 172

Budgen, Frank, 40
Büchner, Georg, 238n.27
Bürgel, Bruno H., 207
Burrows, Rachel, 48, 54, 57, 58, 59, 124, 233n.66
Büttner, Gottfried, 81
Burnet, John, 6, 129
Burton, Robert, 119–20
Byron, Lord Alfred, 35

Calder, John, 39, 219
Camo, Pierre, 76
Camus, Albert, 77–8
Carducci, Giosuè, 116
Carré, L., 195
Caselli, Daniela, 107
Cassirer, Ernst, 137–43, 155, 212, 213
Cazamian, Louis, 22–5, 29
Celan, Paul, 39, 223, 239n.34
Céline, Louis-Ferdinand, 78–9, 155–6, 212
Chamfort, Nicolas, 55–6, 131
Chartier, Roger, 4, 173, 177, 183, 223
Chatto & Windus (publishers), 40, 69, 123, 257n.1
Chaucer, Geoffrey, 20, 21
Chekhov, Anton, 126
Cherbury, Lord Edward Herbert, 35
Chesterfield, Lord, 20, 32, 33, 67, 130, 223
Christie, Agatha, 197
Chuquet, M. A., 53–4
Cioran, E. M., xvi, 169
Claudel, Paul, 62, 76
Claudius, Matthias, 10, 86–7, 88, 95, 217
Clifford, James, 34
Clodd, Alan, 220
Cluchey, Rick, 89, 179
Coffey, Brian, xvi, 41, 77, 132, 153
Cohn, Ruby, 25, 33, 34, 39, 55, 101, 112, 162, 186, 226n.13, 227n.24, 234n.91, 236n.10, 241n.25, 256n.2
Coleridge, Samuel Taylor, 15, 35
Comte, Auguste, 167
Corbière, Tristan, 61
Corneille, Pierre, 46–8, 49, 51, 52
Costello, Nuala, 226n.10
Cousin, John W., 23
Cousin, Victor, 129
Cousineau, Thomas, 169
Cros, Guy-Charles, 76
Cunard, Nancy, 36, 41
Curtius, Ernst Robert, 68

Dahlberg, Kajsa, 2
Dahlström, Mats, 2
Daiken, Leslie, 48, 56

D'Annunzio, Gabriele, 116
Dante Alighieri, xiv, xvi, 45, 63, 67, 73, 95, 103–13, 116, 117, 146, 155, 204, 221, 222, 223
  Convivio, 105, 117
  La Divina Commedia, 73, 95, 104–5, 107–13, 116, 155, 204
  La Vita Nuova, 104–5
Dantec, Y.-G. Le, 60
Darley, George, 226n.4
Darwin, Charles, 7, 8, 112, 200–6
Dauphin, Henri, 106, 222
Dauzat, Albert, 195
Debricon, L., 131
Defoe, Daniel, 30, 31
Delaquys, Georges, 76
Democritus, 128
De Quincey, Thomas, 35
Derély, Victor, 126
Derême, Tristan, 76
Derennes, Charles, 76
Derrida, Jacques, xvi, 40
Descartes, René, 15, 104, 128, 130, 131–2, 134–5, 142, 149, 153, 167–8
Deschevaux-Dumesnil, Suzanne (Suzanne Beckett), 79, 80, 95, 163, 169
Des Granges, C. H. M., 43, 56
Deutsch, Otto Erich, 218
Devine, George, 37
Devlin, Denis, 41
Dickens, Charles, 21
dictionaries, xvi, 117, 192–9
Diderot, Denis, 53
Dionisio, João, 227n.25
Donne, John, 28–9
Dostoevsky, Fjodor, 123–4, 126
Doumic, René, 57
Dowden, Hester, 88
Dryden, John, 20
Dubech, Lucien, 76
Dürer, Albrecht, 121
Duhamel, Georges, 76
Dupré, P., 198
Duras, Marguerite, 80
Durtain, Luc, 76
Duthuit, Georges, 63, 79, 102, 105, 111, 216, 233n.66, 234n.84, 258n.3
Dyssord, Jacques, 76

Eadie, John, 172
Earle, John, 25
Eco, Umberto, xiii
École Normale Supérieure (Paris), 143
Egam, Desmond, 41
Eich, Günther, 100
Eliot, T. S., 40, 41, 120, 194

Ellmann, Richard, 36, 37, 39–40
Éluard, Paul, 77, 215
Encyclopaedia Britannica, 7, 13, 118, 192–3
Engelmann, Paul, 166
Enzensberger, Hans Magnus, 100
Eon, Francis, 76
Esposito, Bianca, 104
Esslin, Martin, 81, 236n.98
etymologies, 195
European Caravan, The, 182, 183
Evans, E. P., 188
Evelyn, John, 35

Fadiman, Anne, 4–5
Fargue, Léon-Paul, 76
Farquhar, George, 25
Feldman, Matthew, 185, 213, 243n.5
Ferguson, Samuel, 86
Fermat, Pierre de, 1–2
Ferrer, Daniel, 3–4, 15
Ferrers Howell, Alan George, 106
Fichte, Johann Gottlieb, 147–8
Fielding, Henry, 24, 30, 85
Fifield, Peter, 80
Fischart, Johann, 223
Fischer-Dieskau, Dietrich, 218
Fitter, Richard and Maisie, 199, 206
Flaubert, Gustave, 59–60, 78, 98
Fletcher, John, 31, 92, 163
Fletcher, John (author), 23
Fontaine, Jean de la, 52–3
Fontane, Theodor, 97–9
Fontenelle, Bernard de, 52–3
Ford, John, 22
Fornaciari, Raffaello, 103
Fowler, Harold N., 118
Fowler, H. W. and F. G., 195
Frauenstädt, Julius, 144–9
Freud, Sigmund, 142, 212–13
Fried, Erich, 100
Fries-Dieckmann, Marion, 89
Frisch, Max, 100, 225n.3

Garnier, Pierre, 170–1
Gaultier, Jules de, 155, 157
Gazanion, Edouard, 76
Gellhaus, Axel, 8, 202
Genette, Raymonde Debray, 183
Georges, K. E., 241n.2
Geulincx, Arnold, 6, 117, 130, 132, 134–6, 146, 203, 223
Giacosa, Giuseppe, 116
Gilbert, Stuart, 39
Gide, André, 43, 49, 57, 59, 62, 124, 143

Goethe, Johann Wolfgang von, 20, 84, 87–90, 91, 93, 94, 102, 108, 115, 140, 142, 148, 149, 217, 221, 223, 236n.8, 239n.5
Gogol, Nikolai, 124
Goichon, A. M., 129
Goldoni, Carlo, 104
Goldsmith, Oliver, 29
Gooch, George Peabody, 242n.6
Gorky, Maxim, 124
Gozzi, Alberto, 104
Gray, Thomas, 29
Greg, W. W., 226n.6
Green, John Richard, 122
Green, Julien, 78
Greene, David H., 38
Greene, Robert, 22, 24
Greene & Co. (bookshop, Dublin), 29, 32, 118, 195, 226n.14
Grevisse, Maurice, 196
Grillparzer, Franz, 97, 236n.11
Grimal, Pierre, 122
Grimm, Jacob and Wilhelm, 96
Grimmelshausen, Hans Jakob Christoffel von, 85
Grimsley, Ronald, 168
Grindea, Miron, 216
Grindley, Carl James, 4
Guarini, Giovanni Battista, 103, 104, 222
Gulette, David, 100

Haerdter, Michael, 99
Hamburger, Michael, 238n.27
Handke, Renate, 164–5
Hartmann, Eduard von, 151, 152
Harvey, Lawrence, 198
Hatch, David A., 213
Hayden, Henri, 219
Hayman, David, 63, 116
Hebbel, Friedrich, 97
Hegel, Georg Wilhelm Friedrich, 149, 151
Heimsoeth, Heinrich, 140, 155, 157
Heine, Heinrich, 94–6, 217, 218
Heine, Maurice, 79
Heinemann, Karl, 83
Heraclitus, 142
Herbert, Jocelyn, xiv, 258n.2
Hibbert, Christopher, 34
Higgins, Aidan, xvii, 39, 41
Hodeir, André, 219
Hoefer, Jacqueline, 166
Hölderlin, Friedrich, xiii, 90–4
Hofmannsthal, Hugo von, 99–100, 153
Homer, 63, 117, 120–1
Hone, Joseph Maunsel, 24, 36, 133
Horace, 121, 157
Howe, Mary Manning, 34, 40, 102, 144

Hugo, Victor, 59
Hunkeler, Thomas, 45, 228n.2
Husserl, Edmund, 168, 210
Hutcheon, Linda, 47
Hutchinson, Mary, 35, 112, 165, 216, 258n.3

Ibsen, Henrik, 127
Ionesco, Eugène, 37, 81, 236n.98
Izenberg, Gerald, 151

Jackson, Heather J., 2–3, 6, 15
James, Henry, 41
Janvier, Ludovic, 80
Jaspers, Karl, 79
Johnson, Samuel, xiii, xiv, 32–4, 142, 193–4
Jolas, Eugene, 101
Jones, Ernest, 212
Jones, H. Spencer, 133, 156, 157, 205, 207, 210
Jonson, Ben, 22
Joyce, James, xiii, xvi, 11–12, 15, 21, 36, 38–40, 61, 63, 66, 74, 104, 116, 117, 120, 140, 145, 146, 148, 159, 161–3, 168, 177, 187, 192, 194, 201–2, 204, 207, 209, 223, 241n.1
  Finnegans Wake, 12, 38, 40, 104, 111, 117, 159, 163, 249n.62
  Portrait of the Artist as a Young Man, 192
  Ulysses, 15, 39, 120, 207
Joyce, Lucia, 40
Joyce, Stanislaus, 39

Kafka, Franz, 101, 221–2
Kahane, Jack, 56
Kant, Immanuel, 137–43, 145, 146, 147, 148, 149, 151, 154, 155, 156, 157, 211–13
Kaun, Axel, 83, 89, 90, 100, 144–5, 153, 214, 215
Keats, John, 35
Kenner, Hugh, 40, 59
Kilvert, Francis, 35
Kleist, Heinrich von, 97
Klossowski, Pierre, 79
Kluge, Friedrich, 195
Knowlson, James, xiii, xiv, 10, 31, 37, 47, 50, 60, 98, 104, 107, 121, 122, 126, 127, 176, 192, 242n.4
Kobler, John, 27, 55, 195
Kolb, Annette, 218
Koran, the, 172

Labé, Louise, 44
Lafenestre, Georges, 51–2
Lalanne, Ludovic, 52, 180, 221
Lamartine, Alphonse de, 57
Lasserre, Pierre, 129–30, 155, 170
Lautréamont, Comte de, 60
Lavignac, Albert, 258n.1

Lawlor, Seán, 254n.27
Lawrence, D. H., 41, 143, 194
Le Brocquy, Louis, 219
Legouis, Émile, 22–5, 29
Legré, Ludovic, 104
Leibniz, Gottfried Wilhelm, 130, 133, 135, 149, 156, 168, 185
Le Juez, Brigitte, 48
Lemaire, Jean, 45
Lemon, Don, 199
Lemprière, John, 117–18
Leopardi, Giacomo, 116, 239n.1
Leslie, C. R., 219
Lessing, Gotthold Ephraim, 87
Leventhal, A. J., 31, 33, 39, 41, 84, 99, 102, 110, 114, 116, 133, 212, 226n.4, 258n.2
Lindon, Jérôme, 79
Lodge, Thomas, 22
Lorenz, Konrad Z., 206
Losey, Joseph, 68
Lourenço, M. S., 227n.25
Low, W. H., 20
Lowry, Malcolm, 42
Luther, Martin, 83, 172, 178, 179
Lyly, John, 22, 23
Lynd, Robert, 34

MacCarthy, Ethna, 98, 104
MacGreevy, Thomas, xvi, 11, 12, 13, 17, 18, 24, 29, 30, 31, 35, 36, 37, 40–1, 42, 44, 54, 56, 57, 58, 59, 62, 63, 65, 67, 69, 71, 73, 77, 90, 95, 102, 106, 108, 114, 115, 120, 121, 122, 132, 133, 136, 137, 140, 142, 143, 145, 148, 171, 197, 200, 201, 205, 214, 215, 218, 222, 223, 226n.3, 226n.5, 226n.10, 226n.12, 228n.1, 230n.34, 230n.42, 232n.53, 232n.54, 232n.56, 232n.62, 234n.84, 236n.2, 239n.5, 239n.9, 241n.21, 244n.13, 256n.3, 257n.10, 258n.5
Machiavelli, Niccolò, 104, 114–15
Madden, Anne, 219
Maeterlinck, Maurice, 64
Maguinness, William Stuart, 122
Mahler, Gustav, 214
Mahon, Derek, 40
Malcolm, Norman, 165
Mallarmé, Stéphane, 60, 63–4, 116
Malraux, André, 77–8
Malthus, Thomas, 201
Mandelstam, Osip, 242n.12
manichaeism, 7, 13, 193
Mann, Thomas, 143
Mannheim, Ralph, 233n.66
Mannoni, Octave, 212

Index

Marlowe, Christopher, 21, 22, 23, 25
Marston, John, 22, 23, 25, 226n.5
Martin, David, 178–9
Maugham, W. S., 23
Maulnier, Thierry, 75
Maupassant, Guy de, 59
Mauriac, François, 48–50
Mauriac, Nathalie, 73
Mauthner, Fritz, 6–7, 78, 108, 118, 128, 138–40, 144–5, 153, 155–6, 158–63, 165–6, 168, 203, 222, 245n.28, 246n.30
Mayoux, Jean-Jacques, 226n.6
McDowell, C. H., 199
McHugh, Roger, 219
McKinley, Grace, 48
Mégevand, Martin, 81
Melville, Herman, 42
Mercier, Vivian, 50
Michaut, Gustave, 67, 222
Michaux, Henri, 80
Middleton, Thomas, 23
Milton, John, 20, 21, 29, 221
Minchin, George, 206
Mirbeau, Octave, 59
Mistral, Frédéric, 104
Mitchell, Pamela, 42, 59, 60, 68, 78, 177, 196, 225n.3, 238n.23
Mitford, Nancy, 242n.6
Molière, xv, 51–2
Montague, John, 41
Montaigne, Michel de, 44–5, 113–14, 130
Montgomery, Niall, 40
Montor, Artaud de, 106
Moore, George, 36
Moore, Gerald, 218
Morrisroe, Patrick, 172
Morungen, Heinrich von, 84
Murphy, P. J., 141, 143
Murray, James, 194
Musil, Robert, 143

Nadeau, Maurice, 59, 77
Nashe, Thomas, 22, 24
National Library of Ireland (Dublin), 104
Naumann, Hans, 101, 163, 221–2
Nerval, Gérard de, 60
Nietzsche, Friedrich, 128, 157

O'Casey, Sean, 36
O'Grady, Standish, 86
O'Malley, Ernest, 78
Oster, Pierre, 60, 198
Ostervald, Jean-Frédéric, 185
O'Sullivan, Sean, 254n.29
Otto, Emil, 82

Ovid, 121–2, 145
Oxford English Dictionary, 194–5

Palgrave, Francis, 21
Pascal, Blaise, 49, 55, 130–1, 168
Passerini, G. L., 106, 130, 222
Pasternak, Boris, 124–5
Peele, George, 22
Pepys, Samuel, 35
Perloff, Marjorie, 166
Péron, Alfred, 54, 143
Péron, Mania, 24, 33, 62, 120, 194, 230n.38, 231n.46
Pessoa, Fernando, 127, 197
Petrarch, Francesco, 45, 112–14, 223
Pia, Pascal, 60
Pierhal, Armand, 68
Pierre-Quint, Léon, 68
Pilling, John, 6, 22, 31, 35, 58, 64, 78, 112, 114, 117, 138, 139, 155, 163, 174, 204, 205, 210, 212, 225n.1, 226n.2, 232n.61, 233n.66, 234n.80, 235n.97, 237n.20, 244n.17, 254n.26, 257n.1, 257n.2, 258n.5
Pinget, Roger, 80–1, 218
Pinter, Harold, xvi, 39, 42, 68, 81, 236n.98
Plato, 141, 147
Plautus, 122–3
Plümacher, Olga, 4–5, 78, 100, 128, 151–6, 161, 172
Plutarch, 122
Poe, Edgar Allan, 3, 15
Poincaré, Henri, 206
Pole, David, 164–5
Pope, Alexander, 20, 21, 30–1, 39, 223
Pothast, Ulrich, 143–4
Pound, Ezra, xiii, 41, 64, 76, 120
Pountney, Rosemary, 95
Poussin, Nicolas, 129, 219
Prawer, S. S., 237n.21
Praz, Mario, 94
Prentice, Charles, 123, 124, 257n.1
Proust, Marcel, xiii, 13, 15–19, 21, 68–75, 110, 111, 116, 123, 143, 178, 222, 223
Pyle, Hilary, 220

Queneau, Raymond, 60, 77

Rabelais, François, 43–4, 85
Racine, Jean, 20, 43, 47, 48–52, 56, 60, 63, 222, 223
Raimbourg, Claude, xvii
Rat, Maurice, 196
Rawson, Nick, 28, 237n.22
Reavey, George, 14, 55, 56, 78, 124–6, 142, 229n.29, 239n.8
Rehberg, Walter and Paula, 86, 88, 89, 95, 217–18
Renard, Jules, 11, 59, 64–7, 78, 108, 142, 184

Ribeiro, Aquilina, 197
Richardson, Samuel, 24
Rilke, Rainer Maria, 100, 143
Rimbaud, Arthur, 43, 60, 62–3, 231n.46, 232n.56
Riverside Studios (London), 121
Robbe-Grillet, Alain, 77, 80
Robertson, J. G., 82–7, 91, 93, 94, 99
Rolland, Romain, 215–16
Rosset, Barney, 98
Rossetti, D. G., 193
Rostand, Jean, 206
Rouse, W. H. D., 117
Rousseau, Jean-Jacques, 53–4
Rousseau, Pierre, 207–9
Rudmose-Brown, Thomas, 44, 47, 104, 240n.9
Ruskin, John, 15, 17, 19
Russell, Bertrand, 164–5
Rutherford, W. Gunion, 117

Sachs, Nelly, 100
Sade, Marquis de, 43, 56–7, 79, 115, 187
Sainte-Beuve, Charles Augustin, 67–8, 222
Salinger, J. D., 42
Sanctis, Francesco de, 73, 103–5, 222
Sand, George, 72
Sartre, Jean-Paul, 77–8, 128, 155–6, 167–8, 210–11, 247n.54
Scève, Maurice, 44, 45–6, 47, 114
Scherer, Wilhelm, 83
Schiller-Theater (Berlin), 7, 13, 93, 99, 164, 169
Schmidt, Leopold, 216
Schneider, Alan, 126, 127, 238n.32
Schneider, Pierre, 67
Schönberg, Arnold, 169
Scholes, Percy A., 214
Schopenhauer, Arthur, xvi, 13, 14, 21, 67, 68, 69, 92, 107, 128, 143–54, 161, 214
Schubert, Franz, 10, 86, 87, 90, 95, 155, 165, 214, 216–18
Schultz, Eva-Katharina, 97
Schumann, Robert, 95–6, 218
Schwartz, Jake, 13, 33, 38, 192
Schwob, Marcel, 103, 222
Seghers, Hercules, 219
Seneca, 45, 114
Shakespeare, William, 9, 14, 20, 21, 23, 24, 25–8, 50, 67, 122, 162, 177, 221
 King Lear, 9, 26–7
Sharp, R. Farquharson, 199
Sherman, William H., 1, 15
Sidney, Philip, 20, 23
Sidur, Vadim, 219
Siebzehner-Vivanti, Giorgio, 106
Simond, Charles, 90
Sinclair, Cissie, 121, 242n.4, 253n.16

Sinclair, Morris, 82, 96, 101, 106, 215, 216, 242n.4
Sinclair, Peggy, 69, 98
Skerl, Jennie, 163
Slights, William W. E., 2
Smith, Frederik N., 29
Smith, William, 122
Smollett, Tobias, 29
Socrates, 141
Somervell, David, 21
Sophocles, 123
Sorel, Albert, 242n.6
Spenser, Edmund, 20, 23
Spinoza, Baruch, xvi, 128, 130, 132–3, 147, 149
Starkie, Walter, 104
Stein, Gertrude, 145
Stendhal (Henri Beyle), 57–9, 108–9, 124
Stephens, Edward M., 38
Stepun, Fyodor, 125
Stern, James, 39, 227n.22
Sterne, Laurence, 24, 29, 31
Stieve, Friedrich, 83
Stobart, J. C., 122
Stravinsky, Igor, 169
Strindberg, August, 127
Stuckenschmidt, H. H., 219
Swift, Jonathan, 21, 24, 29, 31–2, 36
Synge, J. M., 38

Tasso, Torquato, 104, 115
This Quarter (journal), 77, 112, 231n.48
Thomas, Edward, 36
Thompson, A. Hamilton, xv, 20, 21, 23
Titus, Edward W., 112, 231n.48
Tophoven, Elmar, 89, 96
Torga, Miguel, 197
Toussaint, Jean-Philippe, 80
transition / Transition (journal), 77, 92, 101, 184
Trinity College Dublin, xv, 6, 20, 21, 22, 25, 26, 29, 32, 35, 36, 43, 45, 48, 52, 104, 114, 117, 121, 123, 124, 179, 180, 196

Ueberweg, Friedrich, 129
Uhlmann, Anthony, 9, 66
Unseld, Siegfried, 177
Ussher, Arland, 41, 84, 94, 138, 144, 156, 175

Vaissière, Robert de la, xv, 76
Valéry, Paul, 60
Vasari, Giorgio, 219
Velde, Bram van, 120, 219, 225n.3
Velde, Geer van, 219
Velde, Jacoba van, 13, 98, 193
Verlaine, Paul, 60–2
Vigny, Alfred de, 57, 173–4
Villon, François, 43

Index

Virgil, 108, 109, 121
Vogelweide, Walther von der, 84–5, 147, 221, 223
Voltaire, 53, 65, 181–3
Vonnegut, Kurt, 42
Vulliamy, C. E., 32

Wall, Thomas, 68, 232n.62
Wallace, Edgar, 23
Walton, Izaak, 30
Warner, Francis, 40
Wedekind, Frank, 83, 151–2
Weekley, Ernest, 195
Weiler, Gershon, 163
Weiss, Peter, 100
Weller, Shane, 79
Welter, Nikolaus, 104
Whitaker, Elaine, 4
White, Herbert Martyn Oliver, 227n.19
Wilamowitz-Moellendorff, Ulrich von, 117
Wilde, Oscar, xiii, 37

Windelband, Wilhelm, 6, 118, 128–30, 132, 134–5, 138, 140, 145, 157
Wittgenstein, Ludwig, xvi, 128, 163–7, 222
Wodehouse, P. G., 23
Wolf, Marianne, 16–17, 19
Wolfskehl, Karl, 85
Woodforde, James, 35
Woolf, Virginia, xiii, 2–3, 15–16, 74, 194
Wordsworth, William, 111
Worth, Katharine, 37, 227n.18
Wurm, Franz, 100
Wyatt, A. J., 20

Yeats, Jack B., 24, 103, 219–20
Yeats, W. B., xvii, 37, 38, 39, 194, 221

Zeltner-Neukomm, Gerda, 77
Zimmer, Heinrich, 146, 162
Zingarelli, Nicola, 196
Zola, Émile, 59, 98